National Economic Planning

UNIVERSITIES-NATIONAL BUREAU CONFERENCE SERIES

National
Economic Planning

A CONFERENCE OF THE

UNIVERSITIES-NATIONAL BUREAU COMMITTEE

FOR ECONOMIC RESEARCH

MAX F. MILLIKAN, *Editor*

MASSACHUSETTS INSTITUTE OF TECHNOLOGY

NATIONAL BUREAU OF ECONOMIC RESEARCH

NEW YORK   1967

Distributed by COLUMBIA UNIVERSITY PRESS

NEW YORK AND LONDON

RELATION OF NATIONAL BUREAU DIRECTORS TO PUBLICATIONS REPORTING CONFERENCE PROCEEDINGS

Since the present volume is a record of conference proceedings, it has been exempted from the rules governing submission of manuscripts to, and critical review by, the Board of Directors of the National Bureau. It has, however, been reviewed and accepted for publication by the Director of Research.

(Resolution adopted July 6, 1948, as revised November 21, 1949)

Contents

National Economic Planning

Introduction

MAX F. MILLIKAN

MASSACHUSETTS INSTITUTE OF TECHNOLOGY

Fashions among economists are almost as fickle as among dress designers. It would have been inconceivable for a conference volume with this title to have appeared thirty-five years ago. Twenty-five years ago it would have been assumed that it was a volume about economic policy in the Soviet Union, which was the only country then regarded as having a "planned economy." Fifteen years ago the assumption would have been that it was a book about the planned development of the so-called underdeveloped countries, where the idea of national economic planning was beginning to gain wide popularity as a necessary and even sometimes sufficient condition for economic growth. Within the last ten years the term has become so popular and has been applied to so many different kinds of activities that it could now refer to almost any kind of economic analysis or policy thinking in almost any country in the world. Whereas before World War II the term economic planning frequently carried, for many people in both professional and popular discourse, unfavorable connotations of centralization and autocratic control, it is now widely regarded as a good thing which should be practiced in one form or another by all governments.

The reasons for this change in both the content and value overtones of the term are complex. They are to be found partly in changes in the nature of the policy problems with which applied economists have been forced to concern themselves and partly in changes in the analytic tools which the profession has been engaged in fashioning over the past couple of decades. The focus of attention of the economics profession—even of those of its members most disdainful of applied work—has always been profoundly influenced by the dominant policy issues of the day. During the great depression of the 1930's, Ph.D. theses in economics reflected the concerns of both the students and their faculty advisers in their titles, the majority of which related to the theoretical and

applied problems of the business cycle, the full employment of resources, and the control of short-term fluctuations in economic activity.

World War II brought shifts in both problems and methods. With the
rise in defense spending, the generation of effective demand took care
of itself and inflation was handled in considerable part by direct price
control. Attention shifted to resource allocation. Even those who believed that in peacetime this could be left largely to the market were
forced to concede that in wartime at least some important allocative
decisions had to be made by government and that new tools would
have to be developed for this purpose. The most important of these at
the aggregate level was national income and product accounting, which
was given a big push forward by wartime requirements. It was recognized that interindustry analysis of the input-output sort was highly
relevant to wartime allocative problems, but inadequacies of data and
computational difficulties prevented it from being extensively used. After
the war, the problems of postwar European recovery posed the issue
of what would now be called planning in a clear-cut fashion. Governments involved in the Marshall Plan negotiations had to make projections of gross national product, domestic savings, investment requirements, and foreign exchange needs over a five-year period. While little
use was made of the now popular planning models in these exercises,
what is now the flourishing planning activity of many European governments had its embryonic development in the Marshall Plan era. This
was notably true in France, for instance, under the influence of Jean
Monnet.

Meanwhile, in the underdeveloped world, country after country was
achieving independence from former colonial masters, often after many
years of concentration on the goal of political freedom, and its leaders
were turning their attention from the all-consuming struggle for independence to the problems of industrialization and economic growth.
They turned naturally to economic planning as a tool, in some cases
because of the socialist background of the leadership, but increasingly
because the emerging theories of economic development being spawned
by economists suggested that only through conscious and determined
governmental policy could these countries escape from the low-income
trap in which they found themselves. The developed countries, and particularly the United States, came increasingly to feel that they had an
interest both in enlarging their understanding of how countries might
achieve self-sustaining economic growth and in helping to promote that
process through such instruments as foreign aid. The economics profession responded to this new set of policy problems with alacrity and

a swelling volume of literature appeared focusing on the problems of development and on the kinds of economic planning necessary to bring it about.

Another and initially unrelated strand of economic thinking was meanwhile taking shape, sparked by a quite different set of policy concerns. Soviet acquisition of atomic weapons followed by the shock of Sputnik led a concerned western world to wonder how an economy which had started so far behind in terms of the conventional indexes could be so threatening. The detailed work launched just after the war in a number of centers concentrating on Soviet studies had begun to document what appeared to be fairly long-term growth rates in the Soviet economy well above what the western countries were then experiencing. The game became popular of extrapolating growth curves for East and West and predicting when they would cross. Western economists, reassured by postwar history that they had mastered at least in broad outline both the diagnostic and prescriptive problems of short-term fluctuations and full employment, turned back once again to the classic preoccupation with the analysis of economic growth. As Soviet growth slowed down somewhat and the Western European economies rather unexpectedly accelerated during the 1950's, the East-West comparison became less engrossing than the transatlantic one, but the concern with the determinants of growth in the developed economies persisted. It came to be increasingly accepted in the developed countries, as it had been earlier in much of the underdeveloped world, that the secular growth rate of the economy was a parameter manipulable by public policy and an appropriate dimension for a social welfare function even in capitalist states. The process of selecting a growth rate and a set of policies appropriate to implement it came to constitute an important part of what was included under the heading of economic planning.

One final substantive change is worthy of comment. World War II left in its wake public sectors representing a much larger fraction of the gross products of the countries of the western world than that in the prewar period. This was partly a consequence of the high levels of defense expenditure associated with the East-West conflict, but equally importantly resulted from the growing demand in the West for public goods of a sort not readily allocable through the market, like education, road transport, public health, and urban renewal. Along with these growing demands for public goods came an increasing awareness of the many complementarities and interdependencies between investment in the private sector and these public investments in infrastructure. Economic projections of the sort required for aggregate economic planning were increasingly needed as a basis for fundamental decisions about both the revenue and the expenditure sides of national governmental budgets. In all of these problem areas the economics profession saw an opportunity to bring its analytic techniques to bear.

During the twenty years following World War II, these techniques themselves underwent a transformation that made many kinds of economic planning much more feasible. The essence of this transformation was the emerging possibility, enormously facilitated by the appearance of the high-speed computer, of dealing quantitatively with much more complex systems of interdependent variables than had ever been possible before. The groundwork for these systems was substantially laid before the computer came to maturity in the early work of input-output analysis, linear programing, and the econometric estimation of statistical parameters. But the proliferation of testable models of real-life situations using these analytic techniques became economical only with the advent of the computer. Until then, the limits on model complexity were frequently set by what was computationally feasible. Now they are set much more largely by the capacity of the human mind to understand the results once produced. The extent of the revolution is indicated by the fact that in our graduate schools the economics students are no longer identified by the books in their briefcases or the diagrams on their blackboards, but rather by their decks of punch cards and the stacks of computer printouts.

These changes in the applied problems with which economists have been called upon to deal and the associated changes in the analytic techniques at their disposal have led to an enormous broadening of the concept of economic planning. Virtually all countries now have government policies of one sort or another for both the secular growth of the economy and the broad pattern of resource allocation which is to be utilized to achieve these and other goals. This is now broadly true whatever the stage of development of the economy or the degree of central control over resource allocation exercised by its government. While it is perhaps less true of the United States than of almost any other economy in the world, even the United States requires countries that hope to be recipients of U.S. economic aid to engage in planning, and the U.S. government does in fact a good deal of what in other countries would be called planning while still avoiding the term.

About three years ago the Universities-National Bureau Committee concluded that the time was ripe to hold a conference on national economic planning. There was no lack of conferences and symposia with titles similar to this. But planning has many dimensions and there had not been a symposium focusing on the common elements in the analytic tools which the economics profession was bringing to bear on the planning process in countries at different stages of growth and with different degrees of centralization of decision-making. As with all conferences, the papers prepared for this one and included in the present volume reflect partly the views of the committee responsible for planning the conference and partly the particular current interests of the individual economists requested to contribute papers and comments on them. I would like to describe briefly what the conference planning committee had in mind in laying out the conference program and leave it to the reader to decide how far these intentions were realized in the final product. The Committee consisted of Abram Bergson, Everett Hagen, and Edward Mason in addition to myself.

We thought there should be two sorts of papers. First, we felt there were a number of functional problems common to planning everywhere which had been inadequately treated in the literature and which should be dealt with in the first half of the conference. Second, we thought it would be useful to have a series of country papers looking at the techniques of planning used in a selected group of countries at different stages of growth and with different political philosophies, and making some appraisal of the impact of planning on performance in this wide range of situations.

The functional papers raised a very serious problem of selection. There was time for only about five such papers in our schedule and the possible topics to be dealt with were legion. We could have had papers on planning for each of the major sectors of an economy such as agriculture, fuel and power, transport, industry, services, and housing and construction. Or we could have had papers on the main areas of economic policy affected by planning such as price policy, monetary policy, fiscal policy, regulatory policy, and educational policy. Or we could have filled the time with a detailed examination of a number of the principal analytic tools employed in planning exercises such as national income projections, input-output analysis, linear and nonlinear programing, statistical estimation of econometric parameters, and computer simulation. We ended up by being selective and eclectic, using as our principal criterion topics which we felt were both important and relatively neglected in the literature.

We decided to start with an over-all review of the methodology of planning models. Richard Stone at Cambridge University was, we knew, engaged in a systematic survey of the characteristics of planning models being used by economists all over the world. The first paper in the volume is a report by him and his colleague Colin Leicester on the results of this survey. Second, we felt that a problem of great practical importance which had received less attention than it deserved in the analytic literature was that of locational choices for investment projects. One of the most common simplifications of reality in the macroeconomic analysis of national aggregates is to neglect the spatial aspects of the problem. We asked Thomas Vietorisz of the International Business Machines Corporation to address himself to this range of issues. Third, we felt that while a great deal of attention had been paid by operating agencies to the economic appraisal of particular projects, the links between this kind of work and aggregate and national planning were in a quite underdeveloped state. The third paper, by Arnold Harberger of the University of Chicago, is concerned with some of these issues.

Fourth, we were impressed with the fact that while no planner can neglect the foreign trade of the economy with which he is dealing, many national plans and the models on which they are based treat foreign trade either as an exogenous factor or as determined by unrealistically simple and arbitrary relationships. The paper by Don Humphrey of the Fletcher School treats this topic. Finally, in virtually all countries a very substantial fraction of the resources over which the planners have some influence is devoted to activities which are not subject to the usual type of cost benefit calculation, either because costs do not give the signals they should, as in the case of public utilities, or because benefits cannot be measured in the usual way, as with public services, education, and health. Arthur Lewis addresses himself to the rationale underlying the public expenditure portions of a plan in the fifth essay in this volume.

The problem of country selection for case studies was not much easier. Ideally we would have liked to pick countries representing all the permutations and combinations of at least three stages of development and three degrees of centralization of decision-making. This would have required nine papers and we had room for only four. It was clear that a symposium on national economic planning had to have an appraisal of the Soviet experience. Alexander Erlich of Columbia University produced this for us. Of the Western noncentralized and reasonably developed economies, most of whom cut their planning teeth on postwar rehabilitation requirements, the country most associated with new directions in planning was France. We asked Charles Kindleberger of M.I.T. to write about the French planning experience. At the underdeveloped end of the spectrum, there is an abundance of paper plans, but real planning experience with at least a decade of history is confined to a few countries of which the biggest and most important is India. Richard Eckaus of M.I.T. reviews the techniques used in Indian planning and describes a model developed in collaboration with a group of M.I.T. colleagues designed to illuminate some of the problems of capital allocation. Finally, one of the most interesting cases with many unique features of its own is that of Yugoslavia which is in an intermediate position, both in its stage of development and in the degree of centralization of decision-making. Jaroslav Vanek of Cornell University reviewed the Yugoslav case in the final paper.

No clear consensus emerges from this symposium, either as to the influence planning has had on the actual course of events in the countries where it has been tried, or as to the utility for practical planning problems of the newer techniques of analysis of allocative efficiency being evolved by the economics profession. On the first point, there is not much disposition to question that in the relatively centralized Soviet system the planners, interpreting that term broadly, have called the tune. Erlich and Bergson focus on whether Soviet planning has been as efficient as it might have been in furthering the presumed goals of the leadership. In the other three cases the effect of the planning process is more deeply in doubt. Eckaus and Vanek credit it with more influence in India and Yugoslavia than Mason and Montias are prepared to concede. In the case of France, Kindleberger and Wellisz agree that in effect there is simply no way of telling how influential it has been.

On the second question of whether the art of fashioning more formal planning models has yet advanced to the stage at which these models can be genuinely useful to decision-makers, the debate is joined in scattered places through the symposium, perhaps most explicitly in the colloquy between Mason and Eckaus, but can hardly be said to be resolved. The case that these models are still too primitive to be of much practical help rests on a number of major criticisms. In the first place, in spite of all the effort which the model builders have put into lessening the restrictiveness of the assumptions they must make to confine the complexities of the real world to manageable proportions, the critics still feel that some of the most important phenomena of growth are excluded by the use of linear relations, by the assumed constancy of coefficients known to be variable, and by the arbitrary weighting systems which must be used to bring a nearly infinite range of variables within the grasp of even the enormously expanded capability of the modern computer (and perhaps even more importantly within the grasp of the human mind that can understand what it computes when it processes the information supplied to it). The dialogues in this volume highlight

the second question of whether, even in those cases in which the ingenuity of the model builder has been able to cope with complexities
in real-world relationships, we can in fact find the statistical information necessary to estimate values for the parameters assumed to be at
work which will permit solutions. The charge here is that the data are
much too rough and uncertain to warrant the relatively sophisticated
manipulation applied to them in these models. Thirdly, many of the
planning models now available are optimizing models designed to produce solutions which maximize an objective function. The critics complain that what is being maximized in these models reflects only a very
restricted portion of the goals that motivate planners in the design of
their national plans. Customarily the focus of the models is on maximizing the growth rate of aggregates, such as national income, product, or
consumption, and no allowance is made even for such other quantifiable
goals as employment and income distribution, let alone intangibles like
political cohesion and national prestige. Finally, so the critics argue,
even if the models improve the rationality and the efficiency of the
paper plans, there is seldom any effective machinery for implementing
the plan once drawn up and any correspondence between what happens
and what was planned is very largely accidental.

To each of these criticisms, the proponents of model building have a
rebuttal. As far as restrictive assumptions are concerned, these are implicit in any orderly thinking about a complex problem. The models
focus attention on their unreality by forcing the analyst to define very
explicitly and precisely the assumptions he is making instead of permitting him to gloss over and bury them in imprecise literary formulations. No one has found a good way to deal analytically, for instance,
with external economies or with the determinants of technological progress, and an explicit formulation that calls attention to their omission
from a model underlines a warning about the limits of the analysis which
is too often overlooked in more descriptive studies. It serves the further
function of stimulating model builders to try to find precise ways of
dealing with these phenomena which might be otherwise left to a vague
verbal qualification. The models undoubtedly have a long way to go in
the direction of realism, but progress is being made more rapidly than
if there were no attempt at precision.

As far as the inadequacy of data is concerned, sensitivity analysis of
the models with the aid of computers can tell us how important errors
in different kinds of data are to our conclusions and thus direct the
limited resources available to governments for improving data to the
most urgent tasks. Models will frequently focus attention on the im-

portance of collecting kinds of information that would not otherwise be gathered. Input-output analysis, for example, has stimulated the collection of information about interindustry flows, which is important for a wide variety of purposes. As to the multiplicity of goals, conflicts of objectives are not easy to deal with formally in the present state of the art, but models frequently make it possible to estimate the magnitude of the loss of one value being maximized required by the adoption of a policy intended to pursue some different value. If, for instance, employment and growth are in conflict, a well-designed model can tell the policymaker how much growth he has to give up in order to get how much additional employment. Finally, the fact that many plans are not implemented is not to say that they have no influence. The role of the planner is not to run the country for which he is planning but to improve the insights of those who do. The test of his success is not the correspondence of his plans with *ex post* performance but the extent to which that performance would have been worse had the planning process never been undertaken.

Wherever one comes out in this debate on the present usefulness of some of the newer planning techniques—and it is very much a matter of judgment—there can be very little question but that in the years to come there will be more planning rather than less and that the techniques will become more complex and sophisticated. This volume suggests some of the directions this evolution is currently taking.

The conference was held at Princeton, New Jersey, on November 27–28, 1964. The volume was edited by Ester Moskowitz and the charts were drawn by H. Irving Forman.

PART I

Functional Issues

The Methodology of Planning Models

RICHARD STONE AND COLIN LEICESTER

UNIVERSITY OF CAMBRIDGE

Introduction

When a group of us at the Department of Applied Economics started work some four years ago on a computable model of the British economy, we had only vague ideas about the extent to which large econometric models were being built in other parts of the world. From time to time we felt that we ought to try to improve our knowledge, but for one reason or another nothing got done. The stimulus for the present survey came from the invitation to prepare a paper on the methodology of planning models for the 1964 Universities–National Bureau Conference on National Economic Planning.

What follows is an empiricist's reply to this request. It consists simply of a preliminary report on a number of models whose directors were kind enough to complete a questionnaire on their work. At the end of this paper we reproduce a copy of the questionnaire, a list of the directors of the projects reported on, and a selected bibliography. So far we have received reports on thirty-one models, and, from this sample, we have attempted to generalize on a number of methodological questions. We have been promised a number of further replies and intend to produce a final report on the subject in our series *A Programme for Growth.*

The Survey

We should make it clear at the outset that the subject we set out to cover is the methodology of planning models. Accordingly, we did not attempt to examine the vast range of published material on specific economic relationships, demand functions, input-output, production functions and so on, nor did we attempt to cover practical planning methodology which, in many cases, does not involve a model of the economy at all.

Our interest has centered on models directed to forecasting and planning: it is complete models rather than isolated ingredients or practical purposes that are considered here.

Our procedure was to draw up .a questionnaire and to send it to research centers which we knew or believed to be engaged in applied economic model building. We enclosed a list of the centers to which our questionnaire had been sent and invited further suggestions. These we received in considerable number, and it is partly for this reason that our survey is not yet completed.

It follows from this that our sample is not representative. If anyone is engaged in purely theoretical large-scale model building, he may well not have been approached. Our personal contacts with model builders were heavily weighted in the direction of work in developed countries. Our invitation to correspondents to suggest further correspondents proved extremely useful but meant that our original intentions were mediated to some extent through our correspondents' interpretation of them. In fact, this does not seem to have led to any distortion.

A few internationally famous model builders found it impossible to reply to our questionnaire and, as a result, their work is not reported here. We sympathize with their difficulties and regret these gaps in our survey. To most readers, however, their models are probably well known.

Our result to date is: a fairly good coverage of Western Europe; a limited coverage of the United States; the socialist countries represented by Czechoslovakia, Hungary, Yugoslavia, and Poland; other areas represented by Argentina, India, Israel, Japan, New Zealand, and models intended for application in Egypt and Turkey; and several models established by international organizations. We expect to increase this coverage in our final report.

The form of our questionnaire was largely based on our own experience and for this reason must have given difficulties to many of our correspondents. Nevertheless the response rate was high, and a warm interest in what we were trying to do was an encouraging feature of many of the replies we received. We should like to take this opportunity of thanking all who have contributed for their cooperation. They have helped to draw a picture of world econometric model building which is perhaps not generally appreciated. The broad outlines of this picture are described in the following sections.

General Characteristics

Questions 4, 5, 6, and 13 in our questionnaire deal with general characteristics and can conveniently be considered together:

Correspondents were invited to say whether their model was theoretical or numerical and, in the latter case, whether it had yet been applied. All the models in our sample are numerical, and about two-thirds of them have already been applied. In general, this application is not a once-and-for-all affair, as has so often been the case with econometric models in the past, but is part of a continuous process of use, checking, refinement, and reuse. The fact that a substantial number of models have come to stay is a comparatively new feature on the economic scene and the best guarantee we could have for solid improvement in the future.

On the question of geographical coverage, most models were national models. Of these very few had, or planned to have, any regional subdivision. Naturally enough the position was different with models constructed by international organizations; here the area covered was the European Economic Community in one case and the whole world divided into three regions in another.

Correspondents were invited to say whether the main purpose of their model was for description, forecasting, or planning. The great majority indicated planning as a use, though in a number of cases this should perhaps be interpreted as economic decision-making in a wide sense. Most model builders indicated a second use, and some indicated all three.

The models in our sample differed widely in their planning horizon—from under one year to infinity. They fell broadly into two groups: one with a horizon of around two years, another with a horizon of around ten years. Twenty-eight models could be classified in this way; of these, eleven were short term (or short to medium term), and seventeen were medium to long term (or long term).

At this point it is convenient to deal with question 13, which asked if the model was static or dynamic. This question was not, perhaps, ideally formulated. Our intention was to find out whether the models involved differences or differentials and so could work out a future path from a given initial state, or whether they depended on data or assumptions to provide a basis for a consistent picture of the future. We did not intend by this question to inquire whether relationships contained residual time trends or whether past estimates of parameters were modified before application to future conditions. Interpreted as we intended, the answers indicate that rather more than half the short-term models and about one-third of the long-term models should be classified as dynamic.

This result is not surprising. The kind of short-term model that aims at projecting a set of variables from a given initial state until the estimates may be expected to be swamped by the accumulation of residual errors, must, of necessity, be dynamic. At the other extreme, the kind of model that tries to draw up a series of consistent pictures of the future based on a few basic assumptions that can be varied will usually be formulated in static terms.

The Accounting Framework

Given our special interest in the accounting aspect of economic models, we sought information on various issues of this kind in question 7:

Part a. Most of our correspondents stated that their models were contained within a social accounting framework. Without exception, correspondents in the socialist countries replied "no" to this question or left it unanswered; they were not alone in this respect.

Part b. The different classes of accounts employed in the various models were not, on the whole, very well specified, and it was impossible in many cases to form a clear picture of the accounting structure underlying the models. The clearest picture emerged for input-output accounts and indicated a tendency toward medium-sized tables distinguishing some twenty to fifty branches of production.

Part c. In only five models was a distinction made between industries and commodities. In one case as many as 2,500 commodities were mentioned.

Part d. As regards capital expenditures, we asked whether gross investment had been subdivided between (i) depreciation and net investment and (ii) replacements and extensions. We received seven positive replies to (i) and (ii); a further seven positive replies to (i) only; and a further five positive replies to (ii) only.

Part e. We asked if a separate set of capital accounts had been established for consumer durables other than housing. In almost every case the answer was "no."

Part f. A distinction between complementary and competitive imports was used in about half the models. Other distinctions were also mentioned, "tropical agriculture" versus "mining products" and "finished" versus "unfinished" being two examples.

Part g. We asked whether a separate subsistence sector appeared in the accounting system. Since most of the models in our sample relate to economically developed countries, most of the answers were "no." The few positive answers probably reflect the fact that imputations are made for a few important nonmarket transactions rather than the existence of a separate subsistence sector.

Part h. We asked our correspondents whether existing national accounts statistics proved adequate for their model-building purposes. About one-third said "yes." Of the two-thirds who said "no," comments ranged from "not entirely" to "of course not!" This somewhat negative state of affairs may explain the small number of detailed accounting frameworks reported and indicates that the importance of close working relationships between economic statisticians and model builders, which already exist in some countries, should be more widely recognized.

Assumptions

The role of assumptions in model building formed the subject of question 8: Assumptions about variables of the kind specified in this question formed an important element in the majority of models, though there were some clear-cut exceptions to this general statement.

Broadly speaking, there were two main reasons for the introduction of assumptions. First, assumptions were made about the dependent variables of potential relationships which had not yet been specified. This category would include assumptions about the rate of growth of the population or of the labor force and about the rate of technical progress. Second, assumptions were made about variables which reflect economic aims. This category would include assumptions about the rate of growth of consumption or of GNP or about the level of the balance of payments in a future year.

Relationships

The extent to which various economic relationships were employed in the model formed the subject of question 9:

Part a. Demand functions for private consumption appear in almost all the models. Similar functions for public consumption were mentioned in a few cases but, as might be expected, reliance is mainly placed on policy projections or known plans. Demand functions for imports appear in about half the models; for exports, in about one-third.

Part b. In most models use was made of current input-output relationships relating either to domestic intermediate production alone or
to this plus competitive imports. In a number of cases complementary
imports into the branches of production were also determined by similar
coefficients.

Part c. Surprisingly little use seems to be made of production functions. Of the few positive replies, two or three mentioned each of the
following: Cobb-Douglas, Cobb-Douglas with time trend for productivity growth, and vintage forms. Connections between labor and output
and between capital and output by means of coefficients were frequently
mentioned.

Part d. We also asked about the use of capital input-output relationships. About three-fifths of the replies were positive; but this should
be interpreted to mean that more or less aggregated capital coefficients
are much used, not that most models have a matrix of such coefficients
classified by using industry and type of equipment.

Part e. About three-fifths of our correspondents indicated that they
used price-formation relationships, but it is not clear how this statement
should be interpreted. In many cases it would seem to indicate that
product prices are calculated from the cost of primary inputs per unit
of output by means of a matrix multiplier.

Part f. About a third of our correspondents indicated that they made
use of foreign trading relationships. These were usually the same people who had already stated that they used demand functions for both
imports and exports. We had intended to isolate by this question models
in which imports and exports were sensitive in detail to relative prices
and exchange rates; but we have only ourselves to blame for uncertainties of interpretation.

Part g. About a third of our correspondents mentioned the use of
explicit saving functions.

Estimation

A number of questions relating to sources and methods of estimation
formed the subject of questions 10 and 11: About half the sample mentioned both tabulations of census data and special sample surveys as
bases used in estimating parameters. In a few cases only one of these
sources was used. About two-thirds of the sample mentioned the use of
impressions of outside experts in industry, government, etc. This seems
to suggest much more contact with the outside world than used to be

the case in economic model building. If this conclusion is justified it is clearly a good sign.

In almost all cases econometric analysis was mentioned. It is perhaps surprising that there were any exceptions. Almost everyone made use of time series and about half the sample mentioned the use of cross-section data as well. Over two-thirds of the sample used least squares methods of estimation; nearly a quarter mentioned the use of simultaneous equation methods as well. The positive answers to the second question show considerable geographical diversity, and it is perhaps of interest that they are so numerous.

Almost half the sample mentioned that attempts were made to measure changes over time in input-output coefficients; a much smaller proportion said the same thing in respect of coefficients relating to consumers' tastes or preferences.

Over half the sample indicated that the results of their calculations were modified subjectively before use.

Computation

The methods used in carrying out the calculations formed the subject of question 12: About four-fifths of the sample indicated that they used electronic methods. A wide range of equipment was reported. The name of IBM was mentioned in many cases, and the name of Elliott occurred a few times. In about one-quarter of the sample the program was written in stages, the maximum number mentioned being eleven. In about one-quarter of the sample iteration was said to play an important part.

Size and Scope

Plans for increasing the size and scope of the models formed the subject of questions 14 and 15:

Almost all our correspondents had plans for increasing the size of their models. Interestingly enough, only a small proportion, under one-quarter, proposed to do this simply by increasing the size of the model, keeping the form the same. A little over one-third said that they proposed to develop submodels. About one-third planned to adopt both methods.

About half the sample had plans for extending the scope of their models in various directions. All who had such plans mentioned their intention to explore the demand for labor skills. About one-third also intended to examine the role of education and training in satisfying these demands. About one-fifth intended to work on the role of research and development.

Organization

The size and composition of the staff employed and the nature of sponsorship and support formed the subject of questions 16 and 17:

In most cases our correspondents informed us about the size of the staff they employed. Although there are exceptions to this generalization, professional staffs tended to lie in the range six to twelve, clerical staffs in the range three to six. In making this statement we took account as far as possible of indications about part-time work. What we could not allow for was the range of activities undertaken by the model-building team: How far, that is to say, they could call on government departments or others for assistance.

In all cases where a classification of professionals was given, economists formed a substantial element but frequently not the majority of the professional group. Statisticians, mathematicians, and programers were all represented in most cases. Sociologists and other professionals were mentioned in a few cases.

In the great majority of cases a government or other public body was connected in one way or another with the model. In about one-fifth of the sample the work was undertaken at a university; in a rather larger proportion, by an independent research institute. In a few cases these two types of organization combined. The majority of models were built by government or international organizations. Other institutions were mentioned mainly in connection with finance.

Conclusions

This completes our preliminary survey, and it seems to us that the picture that emerges is distinctly encouraging.

In the first place, there is ample evidence of a large amount of model-building activity all over the world. As far as our results go to date, this is largely concentrated, as one would expect, in the economically advanced countries. The models are all intended for application and in most cases have been applied. In general they are not of the single-shot variety but are being maintained and improved. As time goes on they will provide a great deal of experience, the most needed ingredient in building better models.

In the second place, the models show considerable variety in terms of form and aim. They range from short-term forecasting models, which measure the future in quarters and try to look at the economic scene up to one or two years ahead, to long-term planning models, which measure the future in quinquennia and try to draw up balanced pictures of the economy from five to twenty-five years ahead.

In the third place, the survey shows the considerable strides that have been taken in recent years in systematic data processing and in the application of theory and statistical methods to economic phenomena. No one engaged in these processes can feel that he has reached the end of the road, but there are indications of a number of developments that may be expected to bring him perceptibly nearer. One is the increasing professionalization of business managements and the recognition that this often fosters the potentialities of model building. As a consequence, econometricians who seek practical help from industry receive, on the whole, a much more positive response than they did in the past. This widening of the range of communication is almost a *sine qua non* of successful model building. A second interesting development is that even when governments do not build models themselves, they are usually associated in one way or another with the model-building activity of others. Third, we can detect an increasing concern with social as opposed to purely economic phenomena; and particularly with questions of labor skills and the system of education and training in which they are learned. There is no need to believe that education exists simply to supply economically useful skills in order to welcome this development.

Finally, we see that all models in our survey are computable models generally making use of large, high-speed computers. It can fairly be said that without the development of the computer they could not exist. Yet, in spite of the immense number of calculations now required in solving the equation system of a large model, it is probably the general view of model builders that computing capacity does not and in the future will not provide any restriction on their activities. One great difficulty of the past has been overcome. We are now free to concentrate on our particular responsibilities as economists and statisticians: accurate model building, data processing, and closer contacts with the practical world whose help and approval are alike needed if today's efforts are to bear fruit.

Appendix 1

UNIVERSITY OF CAMBRIDGE
DEPARTMENT OF APPLIED ECONOMICS

AN INTERNATIONAL SURVEY
OF
THE METHODOLOGY OF PLANNING MODELS

Questionnaire

1. Name and address of Director of project

2. Full title of project

3. Short name, if any, of project and/or model

4. Is the model
   a. Purely theoretical
   b. Numerical and intended for application
      If so,
      (i) Has it yet been applied
      (ii) To what country or region has it been or will it be applied
      (iii) Does it contain or will it contain a regional subdivision

5. Is the model intended primarily for
   a. Description
   b. Forecasting
   c. Decision-making (planning or programing)

6. What is the planning or forecasting horizon of the model

7. Has the model a social accounting framework
   If so,
   a. How many classes of accounts do you distinguish in it
   b. What is the name of, and number of accounts in, each class
   c. Do you make a distinction between industries and commodities
      If so,
      (i) Are there more commodities than industries
      (ii) What classification do you adopt for each category
   d. Do you divide gross investment into
      (i) Depreciation and net investment
      (ii) Replacements and extensions
   e. Do you divide imports into
      (i) Complementary and competitive

(ii) Other categories (please specify)
f. Do you treat consumers' durables as capital goods
   If so, please give categories
g. Do you cover a subsistence sector in addition to the monetized economy
h. Do you find the national accounts of your country or region adequate

8. If basic assumptions form part of the model, do these relate to
   a. The rate of growth of the gross national product or similar total (please specify)
   b. The rate of growth of consumption
   c. The rate of growth of the population
   d. The rate of growth of the labor force
   e. The rate of technical progress
   f. The supply of domestic saving
   g. The balance of payments (surplus or deficit)
   h. Other variables (please specify)

9. Does the model include
   a. Demand functions for
      (i) Private consumption
      (ii) Government consumption
      (iii) Exports
      (iv) Imports
   b. Current input-output relationships for
      (i) Domestic intermediate product
      (ii) As above *plus* competitive imports
      (iii) Complementary imports
   c. Production functions of type
      (i) Cobb-Douglas
      (ii) As above with residual time trends for productivity growth
      (iii) Vintage
      (iv) Other (please specify)
   d. Capital input-output relationships
   e. Price-formation relationships
   f. Financial relationships relating to
      (i) Saving functions
      (ii) Preferred portfolio patterns
      (iii) Other (please specify)
   g. Foreign trading relationships
   h. Other relationships (please specify)

10. If estimates of parameters have been made, are they based on
    a. Tabulation of census data

b. Special sample surveys
c. Impressions of outside experts in industry, government, etc.
d. Econometric analysis
e. Other sources (please specify)

11. If estimates are based on econometric analysis
    a. Is the information derived from
       (i) Time-series
       (ii) Cross-section data
    b. Is use made of
       (i) Least squares methods
       (ii) Simultaneous equations methods
       (iii) Other methods (please specify)
    c. Is an attempt made to measure changes over time in
       (i) Input-output coefficients
       (ii) Preference coefficients
       (iii) Other coefficients (please specify)
    d. Are the results of the calculations modified subjectively before use

12. Are the calculations carried out by
    a. Electronic methods
       If so,
       (i) Is the program written in stages
       (ii) How many stages does it contain
       (iii) Does iteration play an important part
       (iv) What type or make of equipment do you use
    b. Other methods (please specify)

13. Is the model
    a. Mainly static, alternative solutions depending on initial assumptions
    b. Mainly dynamic

14. If you are planning to increase the size of the model, do you intend to
    a. Simply increase the number of variables, without altering the form
       of the model
    b. Develop submodels for different branches of production or sectors
       of the economy, such as transport, power, education, etc.
    c. Combine both methods

15. If you are planning to extend the scope of the model, do you intend to
    explore
    a. The demand for labor skills now and in the foreseeable future
    b. The role of education and training in satisfying this demand
    c. The role of research and development

   d. Human adaptability

   e. Other socio-economic phenomena (please specify)

16. How large is the staff you employ in terms of
   a. Economists
   b. Statisticians
   c. Mathematicians
   d. Programers
   e. Sociologists
   f. Other professionals
   g. Clerical and computing staff

17. Is the project sponsored and supported by
   a. A university
   b. An independent research institute
   c. Government or some other public body
   d. Some other institution (please specify)

18. Do you publish your results in
   a. A special series (please give bibliographical details)
   b. Other publications (please give bibliographical details)

Remarks

Appendix 2. A List of Correspondents

Area of Application	Director of Project	Title of Project
1. Argentina	Dr. Oscar Varsavsky, Instituto de Calculo, Peru 272, Buenos Aires	A Simulation Model for the Argentine Economy
2. Belgium	Monsieur Jean Wael- broeck, 49 rue du Chatelain, Bruxelles 5	Modele de croissance de l'économie belge
3. Britain	Professor Richard Stone, Department of Applied Economics, Sidgwick Avenue, Cambridge	Cambridge Growth Project

Area of Application	Director of Project	Title of Project
4. Czechoslovakia	inž. Jiři Skolka, Econometric Laboratory, Economic Institute, Czechoslovak Academy of Sciences, Politických vězňů 7, Praha 1	Long-term optimal plan
5. France	Professeur A. Nataf, Directeur du CERMAP, 19 rue de Passy, Paris 16^e	Essai de variante formalisée pour l'élaboration du Ve Plan
6. Germany, West	Dr. G. Gehrig, Ifo-Institut für Wirtschaftsforschung, 8 München 27, Poschingerstrasse 5	Forschungsvorhaben "Langfristige Projektion" des "IFO-Instituts"
7.	Professor Dr. Wilhelm Krelle, Direktor des Institutes für Gesellschafts- und Wirtschaftswissen-schaften der Universität Bonn, Bonn, Liebfrauenweg 5	Prognosemodell für die Bundesrepublik Deutschland
8.	Professor Dr. H. Langelütke Ifo-Institut für Wirtschaftsforschung, 8 München 27, Poschingerstrasse 5	Disaggregated growth model to be constructed by means of input-output analysis and regression analysis
9.	Professor Günter Menges, Institute for European Statistics, Saar University, Saarbrücken 15	Econometric Analysis for Short-term Forecasting

Area of Application	*Director of Project*	*Title of Project*
10. Germany, West	Professor Dr. Alfred E. Ott, Institut für Angewandte Wirtschaftsforschung, Tübingen, Biesingerstr. 25	Quarterly Model of the Federal Republic of Germany
11. Hungary	Dr. J. Kornai, Computing Center of the Hungarian Academy of Sciences, Budapest, V, Nádor u. 7	Macroeconomic programing, 1966–70
12.	Dr. T. Morva, National Planning Board, Budapest, V, Nádor u. 11	
13. India	Dr. S. Chakravarty, Presidency College, Calcutta	Research Project on Development Planning Methods
14. Ireland	Dr. R. C. Geary, The Economic Research Institute, 73 Lower Baggot Street, Dublin 2	An Input-Output Decision Model for Ireland
15. Israel	Dr. Michael Bruno, Research Department, Bank of Israel, Jerusalem	Linear Programing Model for Israel
16. Italy	Professor Vera Cao-Pinna, "Centro di studi e piani economici," Roma, Via Piemonte, 26	Econometric Model of Growth and Geographical Distribution of Resources in Italy
17.	Dr. Siro Lombardini, Ires via Bogino 18, Torino	A Model for National Economic Planning with Three Regions

Area of Application	*Director of Project*	*Title of Project*
18. Japan	Dr. Tsunehiko Watanabe, Economic Research Institute, Economic Planning Agency, Government of Japan, Chiyoda-ku Kasumigaseki, Tokyo	Methodology of Long-term and Medium-term Planning
19. Yugoslavia	Dr. Branko Horvat, Jogoslavenski Institut za Ekonomska, Istrazivanja, Beograd, Savska broj 35	A Simple Model for the Preparatory Stage of a Medium-term Economic Plan
20. New Zealand	Dr. C. A. Blyth, N. Z. Institute of Economic Research, 26 Kelburn Parade, Wellington	Long-term target making for the New Zealand economy
21. Norway	Dr. Odd Aukrust, Central Bureau of Statistics, Dronningensgth 16, Oslo	1) Modis I 2) Modis II
22. Poland	Dr. Józef Pajestka, Zaklad Badań Ekonomicznych Komisji Planowania, Warszawa, Plac Trzech Krzyzy 5	Structural Analysis for 1970
23. Portugal	Dr. Joao Salgueiro, Presidencia do Consello, Secretariado Tecnico, 51 Rua Alexandre Hermlano, Lisbon	Global Programing Project for III Plan of Portugal

Area of Application	*Director of Project*	*Title of Project*
24. Sweden	Professor Ingvar Svennilson, Stockholms Universitets Nationalekonomiska Institution, Oddengatan 61, Stockholm	The Royal Commission for Long-term Planning
25. United Arab Republic, Turkey	Professor Jan Tinbergen, Haviklaan 31, The Hague, Holland	Formulating the Optimum Method of Development Planning for Developing Countries
26. United States	Mr. Jack Alterman, Division of Economic Growth, Bureau of Labor Statistics, U.S. Department of Labor, Washington 25, D.C.	Interagency Growth Study Project
27.	Professor Lawrence Klein, Department of Economics, Wharton School of Finance and Commerce, University of Pennsylvania, Philadelphia 4, Pa.	Econometric Model Project U.S.A.

INTERNATIONAL ORGANIZATIONS

28. European Economic Community (member countries)	Dr. J. Paelinck, Secretary's office: EEC, rue d'Arlon, Bruxelles 4	Economic Development Prospects in the EEC from 1960 to 1970

Area of Application	Director of Project	Title of Project
29. International Monetary Fund (39 countries)	Dr. Jacques J. Polak, Director, Department of Research and Statistics, International Monetary Fund, 19th and H Streets, N.W., Washington 25, D.C.	Monetary Analysis of Income and Imports
30. I.M.F (Canada)	Dr. Rudolf R. Rhomberg, Chief, Special Studies Division, International Monetary Fund, 19th and H Streets, N.W., Washington 25, D.C.	Model of the Canadian Economy with Special Emphasis on the Balance of Payments
31. I.M.F (three world regions)	Dr. Jacques J. Polak and Dr. Rudolf R. Rhomberg, Department of Research and Statistics, International Monetary Fund, 19th and H Streets, N.W., Washington 25, D.C.	World Trade Model

Appendix 3. A Selected Bibliography

(Items concluding with a reference number are
associated with a project listed in Appendix 2)

Alterman, Jack, *First Stage—Demand, Production, Employment, Capital Projections,* U.S. Bureau of Labor Statistics, 1963. Project 26.

———, *Research Program of Economic Growth Studies,* U.S. Bureau of Labor Statistics, 1962. Project 26.

———, *Research Projects to be Used in Growth Studies Programme,* U.S. Bureau of Labor Statistics, 1964. Project 26.

Atkinson, L. Jay, "Long-term Influences Affecting the Volume of New Housing Units," *Survey of Current Business,* November 1963. Project 26.

Beld, C. A. Van der, and P. de Wolff, *Exercise in Medium-term Macro-forecasting for the Netherlands Economy,* Centre International d'Etude des Problemes Humains, Monaco, 1964.

Benard, Jean, "Reseau des échanges internationaux et planification ouverte," *Economie Appliquée,* 1963, pp. 249–76.

Benard, Jean, and D. L. Phan, "Elements d'une projection du commerce exterieur Francais en 1970," mimeo., CEPREL (Centre d'Étude de la Prospection Économique à Moyen et Long Termes), Paris, 1964. To be published in vol. 3 of ASEPELT, Amsterdam.

Blyth, C. A., and G. A. Crothall, *Alternative Policies for Economic Development: A Pilot Policy Model and Its Sensitivity Analysis,* New Zealand Institute of Economic Research, Wellington, 1962. Project 20.

———, "A pilot programming model of New Zealand economic development," *Econometrica,* January 1965. Project 20.

———, "A programmed model of the New Zealand economy." Paper presented at fifth annual conference of New Zealand Association of Economists, Wellington, February 1963. Project 20.

Brady, Dorothy, and F. Gerard Adams, *The Diffusion of New Products and Their Impact on Consumer Expenditures,* Philadelphia, 1962. Project 26.

Bruno, M., *Interdependence, Resource Use, and Structural Change in Israel,* Jerusalem, Israel, 1962. Project 15.

———, "Some Applications of Input-Output Techniques to the Analysis of the Structure and Development of Israel's Economy," *Structural Interdependence and Economic Development,* London, 1963. Project 15.

———, "The Use of a National Accounting Framework for Economic Policy and Development Forecasting: A Survey of Israel's Research Experience 1958–61," *Income and Wealth,* Series X, London, 1964. Project 15.

Cambridge University, Department of Applied Economics, *A Programme for Growth,* London, Project 3: No. 1, *A Computable Model of Economic Growth,* 1962; No. 2, *A Social Accounting Matrix for 1960,* 1962; No. 3, *Input-Output Relationships, 1954–1966,* 1963; No. 4, *Capital, Output, and Employment, 1948–1960,* 1964; No. 5, *The Model in Its Environment: A Progress Report,* 1964; No. 6, *Exploring 1970: Some Numerical Results,* 1965.

CERMAP, *"Un Modele d'étude de Variantes d'un Plan,"* mimeo., Paris, 1962. Project 5.

Chakravarty, S., and R. S. Eckaus, "An Appraisal of Alternative Planning Models," mimeo. Project 13.

———, "An Approach to a Multisectoral Intertemporal Planning Model," mimeo. Project 13.

———, "Choice Elements in Intertemporal Planning," mimeo. Project 13.

Chenery, H. B., and M. Bruno, "Development of Alternatives in an Open Economy: The Case of Israel," *Economic Journal,* March 1962. Project 15.

de Leeuw, Frank, "Financial Markets in Business Cycles: Simulation of an Aggregate Model." Paper presented at meeting of the Econometric Society, Boston, 1963. Project 27.

Duesenberry, James S., Gary Fromm, Lawrence R. Klein, and Edwin Kuh, *The Brookings Quarterly Econometric Model of the United States,* Chicago, 1965.

Eisner, Robert, "Forecasting investment spending," *Proceedings of the Eleventh Annual Conference on the Economic Outlook,* Ann Arbor, Mich., 1963. Project 27.

———, "Investment plans and realizations," *American Economic Review,* May 1962, pp. 190–203. Project 27.

———, "Overall View of the Model." Paper presented at meeting of the American Statistical Association, Cleveland, 1963. Project 27.

———, "Realizations of Investment Anticipations in a Quarterly Econometric Model of the United States Economy." Paper presented to CIRET conference, Vienna, 1963. To be published in *IFO-Studien.* Project 27.

European Economic Commission, *Economic Development Prospects in the EEC from 1960 to 1970,* Brussels, 1962. Project 28.

Ferber, Robert, and Harold W. Guthrie, *Factors Influencing Consumer Saving Behavior,* 1964.

Fisher, Franklin M., "Dynamic Structure and Estimation in Economy-wide Econometric Models," mimeo., 1963. Project 27.

Friedman, Charles, "Stocks of Passenger Cars: Postwar Growth and Distribution," *Survey of Current Business,* September 1963. Project 26.

Fromm, Gary, "Forecasting, Structural Analysis and Policy Evaluations: the Brookings-SSRC Model of the U.S. Economy." Paper presented at international meeting of Institute for Management Sciences, New York, 1963. Project 27.

Geary, R. C. (ed.), *Europe's Future in Figures,* North-Holland for ASEPELT, Amsterdam, 1962.

Geary, R. C., "Towards an Input-Output Decision Model for Ireland," *Journal of the Statistical and Social Inquiry Society of Ireland,* Dublin, 1964. Project 14.

Gehrig, Gerhard, "Eine ökonometrische analyse des Konsums von 1925 bis 1938 und 1950 bis 1957," *Schrifteneihe des IFO-Instituts,* 1952. Project 6.

———, "Ein makroökonomisches Modell für die Bundesrepublik Deutschland," *ibid.,* 1956. Project 6.

———, "Forschungsplan für die Erstellung eines disaggregierten Wachstumsmodells mit Hilfe von Input-Output und Regressions Analyse," *IFO-Studien,* 1962. Project 8.

———, "Gross National Product and Private Consumption in the Federal Republic of Germany in 1960 and 1970," in Jan Sandee (ed.), below. Project 6.

Horvat, Branko, "A Restatement of a Simple Planning Model with Some Examples from the Yugoslav Economy," *Sankhya,* 1960. Project 19.

———, "Methodological Problems in Long-term Economic Development Programming," *Industrialization and Productivity,* 1962. Project 19.

———, *Primjena Medusektorske Analize U Planskom Bilanciranju Privrede,* Jugoslavenski Institut za Ekonomska Istrazivanja, Belgrade, 1963. Project 19.

Houthakker, Hendrick, and Lester D. Taylor, *Projecting Personal Consumption Expenditures in 1970,* Parts 1, 2, 3 and 4, U.S. Bureau of Labor Statistics, 1963–64. Project 26.

———, "Recent Empirical Experience with Dynamic Demand Functions." Paper presented at meetings of the Econometric Society, Boston, 1963. Project 26.

Hungarian Academy of Sciences, *Input-Output Tables: Their Compilation and Use,* Budapest, 1962. Project 12.

———, *Commonwealth Program, 1966–70,* Budapest, 1964, Project 11.

IFO-Institut, *Bezug von Input-Output Tabellen für die Bundesrepublik mit vorläufigen Ergebnissen für 1961,* Berlin-Munchen, 1964. Project 8.

IRES-ITALCONSULT-SEMA, *Struttura e Prospettive Economici di Uno Regione,* Milan, 1962. Project 17.

Ivanović, Branislav, *Primena metode I—odstupanja u problemima Odredivanja stepena ekonomiske razvijenosti.* Project 19.

Jorgenson, Dale W., "Capital Theory and Investment Behavior," *American Economic Review,* May 1963, pp. 247–59. Project 27.

———, "The SSRC Econometric Model Project of the United States Economy." Paper presented at meetings of the Econometric Society, Copenhagen, 1963. Project 27.

Klein, Lawrence R., "A Postwar Quarterly Model: Description and Applications," mimeo., NBER, 1963. Project 27.

Kornai, J., and Th. Liptak, "Two-level planning," *Econometrica,* January 1965.

Krelle, Wilhelm, "Angewandte Wachstums- und Konjunkturtheorie: Ein Modell zur Wachstums- und Konjunkturprognose," mimeo. Project 7.

———, "Das Prognosemodell: I, II and III," mimeo., 1962. Project 7.

Lefeber, Louis, "*A Simple Optimizing Planning Model,*" mimeo. Project 13.

Leser, C. E. V., *A Further Analysis of Irish Household Budget Data 1951–52,* Dublin, 1964. Project 14.

———, *Demand Relationships for Ireland,* Dublin, 1962. Project 14.

———, "The Pattern of Personal Expenditure in Ireland," *Journal of the Statistical and Social Inquiry Society of Ireland,* 1963–64. Project 14.

Maisel, Sherman J., "Fluctuations in Residential Construction Starts," *American Economic Review,* June 1963, pp. 359–83. Project 27.

———, "The SSRC Econometric Model Project: Examples of Relationships." Paper presented at meetings of the Econometric Society, Copenhagen, 1963. Project 27.

Marimont, Martin L., "GNP by Major Industries," *Survey of Current Business,* October 1962. Project 26.

Marris, R. L., "The Development of Global Planning in Portugal," *Planeamento e Integracão Economica,* Lisbon, January 1964. Project 23.

Massé, Pierre, "Les principes de la planification francaise," *Weltwirtschaftliches Archiv,* 1964.

————, "The French Plan and Economic Theory." Paper read to meeting of the Econometric Society, Boston, 1963.

Moore, Frederick T., "Models for economic development." Paper presented at a NATO conference, 1963.

Morva, T., "The Role of the Balance of Social Product in the Price Changes of the Plan 1959 and Further Possibilities of Its Use," *Közgazdasági Szemle,* Budapest, 1960. Project 12.

Moustacchi, A., "The Interpretation of Shadow Prices in a Parametric Linear Economic Programme," *Econometric Analysis for National Economic Planning,* London, 1964.

Nataf, A., "Essais de formalisation de la planification," *Economie Appliquée,* 1963, pp. 277–97. Project 5.

Nerlove, Marc, *A Survey of Macro-Econometric Time-Series Models,* Netherlands School of Economics, 1963.

Netherlands Central Planning Bureau, *Central Economic Plan, 1961,* The Hague, 1961.

Norway, Central Bureau of Statistics, *Input-Output Analysis of Norwegian Industries, 1954,* Oslo, 1960. Project 21.

Paelinck, J., and J. Waelbroeck, "Étude empirique sur l'évolution de coefficients input-output," *Économie Appliquée,* 1963, pp. 81–111. Project 2.

Polak, J. J., "Monetary Analysis of Income Formation and Payments Problems," *IMF Staff Papers,* 1957–58, pp. 1–50. Project 29.

Polak, J. J., and L. Boissonneault, "Monetary Analysis of Imports and Its Statistical Application," *IMF Staff Papers,* April 1960, pp. 349–415. Project 29.

Polak, J. J., and R. R. Rhomberg, "Economic Instability in an International Setting," *American Economic Review,* May 1962. Project 31.

Portugal, Presidencia do Conselho, *Projecto de Plano Intercalar de Fomento para 1965–1967,* Lisbon, 1964. Project 23.

Pyatt, Graham, "A production functional model," *Econometric Analysis for National Planning,* London, 1964.

Rhomberg, Rudolf R., "A Model of the Canadian Economy Under Fixed and Fluctuating Exchange Rates," *Journal of Political Economy,* 1964. Project 30.

————, "Canada's Foreign Exchange Market: A Quarterly Model," *IMF Staff Papers,* April 1960. Project 30.

Rhomberg, Rudolf R., "The Foreign Sector." Paper presented at meeting of the Econometric Society, Pittsburgh, 1962. Project 27.

Rhomberg, R. R., and L. Boissonneault, "Effects of Income and Price Changes on the U.S. Balance of Payments," *IMF Staff Papers,* March 1964, pp. 59–124. Project 31.

Roma, Centro di Studi e Piani Economici, "Modello econometrico di sviluppo e di ripartizione territoriale nell' economia italiana," *Modelli Econometrici per la Programmazione,* Project 16, Florence, 1965.

Ryan, W. J. L., "The Methodology of the Second Programme for Economic Expansion," *Journal of the Statistical and Social Inquiry Society of Ireland,* 1964. Project 14.

Sandee, Jan, "An Experimental Phase Sector Model for the Netherlands," *Modelli Econometrici per la Programmazione,* Florence, 1965.

———— (ed.), *Europe's Future Consumption,* North-Holland for ASEPELT, Amsterdam, 1964.

Sevaldson, Per, "An Interindustry Model of Production and Consumption for Economic Planning in Norway," *Income and Wealth,* Series X, London, 1964. Project 21.

Stone, Richard, "A Framework for Economic Decisions," *Moorgate and Wall Street,* London and New York, 1964, pp. 5–24. Project 3.

————, "British Economic Balances in 1970: A Trial Run on Rocket." *Econometric Analysis for National Planning,* London, 1964.

————, "Private Saving in Britain, Past, Present and Future," *Manchester School,* 1964, pp. 79–112. Project 3.

Stone, Richard, Alan Brown, and D. A. Rowe, "Demand Analysis and Projections for Britain: 1900–1970," in J. Sandee (ed.), above. Project 3.

Stone, Richard, *et al., Economic Growth and Manpower,* Report of Spring Conference of British Association for Commercial and Industrial Education, London, 1963. Project 3.

Suits, Daniel B., "Forecasting and Analysis with an Econometric Model," *American Economic Review,* 1962.

Tübingen, Institut für Angewande Wirtschaftsforschung, "Arbeitsbericht über die Versuche zu einem ökonometrischen Modell für die Bundesrepublik Deutschland 1950 bis 1960," mimeo., 1962. Project 10.

U.S. National Planning Association, *Long Range Projections for Economic Growth: The American Economy in 1970,* Washington, D.C., 1959.

U.S. Department of Labor, "Economic Growth Studies," *Manpower Report of the President,* March 1963. Project 26.

Varsavsky, Oscar, "Modèle financier et physico-financier," CERMAP, mimeo., 1964. Project 1.

Verdoorn, P. J., and C. J. van Eyk, *Experimental Short-term Forecasting Models,* The Hague, 1958.

Verdoorn, P. J., and J. J. Post, "Capacity and Short-term Multipliers." *Econometric Analysis for National Economic Planning,* London, 1964.

COMMENT

Hollis B. Chenery, *Agency for International Development*

This survey of planning models should be very useful when it is completed. The preliminary results given here are so sketchy, however, that they only serve to whet the appetite. Although we are given a few generalizations from thirty-one answers to the authors' questionnaire, it is impossible to determine how representative they may be of planning models actually in use. From the studies on this list with which I am familiar, I would guess that the sample consists mainly of models being tested for methodological purposes rather than those used for decision-making.

The authors' summary of the responses gives little indication of the relations among the various characteristics which they tabulated. For example, the typical model is apparently built around some type of input-output framework. This in itself accounts for such features as reliance on cross-section rather than time series data, the form of production functions used, and the absence of price relationships. In their final report, perhaps Stone and Leicester may be able to give us a typology of models with typical features for each rather than separate generalizations for individual characteristics.

The most useful feature of this survey is its bibliography. The evidence which it gives of diversified activity on a broad scale is quite impressive. Whatever the deficiencies of the present sample of planning models, it provides a starting point from which it should be possible to build up a more representative inventory of the state of the art.

Locational Choices in Planning

THOMAS VIETORISZ

NEW SCHOOL FOR SOCIAL RESEARCH

Introduction

OBJECTIVE AND PROSPECT

This paper deals with the application of mathematical programing resource allocation models to the problems of economic development planning by geographical locations: local areas or regions within a country or countries within a partially integrated supranational economic community. Planning decisions in this field are politically highly sensitive, and the quantitative information that can now be provided to policymakers as a background for these decisions is far from satisfactory.

The models mentioned are among the most up-to-date tools for the quantitative study of planning problems. Such models can be formulated to represent the major developmental choices of economic systems; at the same time, they also furnish a frame of reference for the evaluation of individual projects and branches of economic activity, thus pointing the way toward the eventual consolidation of policy choices at different levels of detail into a unified decision system of balances and priorities. While the application of these models is subject to limitations —mathematical problems in dealing with economies of scale and other nonconvexities, time lags, probability distributions—their potential contributions to the conceptual understanding and empirical definition of planning problems, especially in regard to locational choices, are far from being fully exploited.

The bulk of the paper is dedicated to the formulation and analysis of multiperiod locational models, both in aggregated and disaggregated form. Since economic development is such a thoroughly dynamic phenomenon, the results of a purely static analysis are inherently to be distrusted; for this reason, it has been regarded as indispensable to deal with multiperiod models even if this places a considerable formal burden on the analysis. Since multiperiod models with locational and interindustry detail have not been thoroughly studied before, it was thought worthwhile to present and interpret in terms of such a comprehensive model a number of results derivable from partial models of different kinds, i.e., models without either locational, multiperiod, or interindustry detail.

A key question of planning in regard to locational choices is the extent to which development should be geographically balanced or unbalanced. While it has been far from possible to clarify this matter conclusively, the extent to which planning models formulated in different ways tend to lead to a greater or lesser degree of geographical concentration of economic activities has been a persistent concern throughout the paper.

The argument in favor of *unbalanced* growth asserts that the concentration of resources into limited areas will permit these areas to grow sufficiently fast to acquire a certain momentum of growth that will eventually be transmitted to the lagging areas, while a dispersal of the former resources over all areas would deny the possibility of a successful "take-off" to any area. The argument in favor of *balanced* growth points out that a development process limited to some points will lead to excessively narrow markets in many lines of production, thus leading to a failure to achieve adequate economies of scale, and that it will deprive the system as a whole of the potential contribution of savings, skills, and other resources that would be forthcoming from the lagging areas if their economic development and cultural transformation were not held back by the draining off of resources to other areas.

There seems to exist a widespread notion at present that mathematical programing models can be expected to yield optimal growth for a system of regions as a whole when growth is unevenly distributed among the regions. Thus it is often postulated that the maximization of national income without constraints on the regional distribution of this income will lead to socially and politically unacceptable results. Therefore, such constraints have to be introduced in explicit recognition that they will lead to a certain sacrifice of national income. This sacrifice, the reasoning goes, is the price that has to be paid for the social or political benefits to be won.

The foregoing notion is based on qualitative considerations rather than on solid empirical evidence or a careful analysis of the structure and behavior of regional allocation models. In point of fact, there is only one highly aggregated analytical model that explicitly arrives at a conclusion concerning the benefit of concentrated investments within a multiregional system, and the limitations of the approach that has been used are even in this case clearly recognized by the authors (Rahman, 1963, and comment by Dorfman). The origins of the notion are therefore to be sought in the great difficulty, well known to any person with practical planning experience, of finding economic activities in regard to which backward regions have a clear-cut advantage under customary criteria of project evaluation. In practice backward regions often come out poorly in regard to almost all conceivable activities, the classical theory of comparative advantage notwithstanding.

The argument in favor of balanced regional growth hinges on the presence of economies of scale—a consideration that has never been brought adequately within the purview of economic theory or practical criteria of project evaluation. It also hinges in part on qualitative and extraeconomic factors having to do with psychological motivations and cultural change. It is thus possible to hold an opinion in favor of the long-term optimality of balanced regional growth on the basis of such general considerations and still to subscribe to the notion that mathematical programing models will yield optimal growth data, under conditions of regional concentration of investments. The considerations regarding balanced regional growth can then be regarded as "background information" that is to be relied upon to "modify" the results of the incomplete mathematical analysis for purposes of policy decisions.

It will be shown that the over-all picture that emerges from the analysis of regional resource allocation models depends to a significant degree on the assumptions that are built into these models. It will also be shown that possibilities of reformulating these models exist which suggest that institutional arrangements involving planning can probably be created under which conflicts between over-all system growth and the geographical dispersion of this growth are reduced and perhaps eliminated.

The discussion is introduced by a survey of the principal areas in which locational choices arise in planning and the main analytical difficulties that are still unresolved, and is followed by an appraisal of methods for reconciliation of multiple objectives. Thereafter, a general locational model is formulated and its features—particularly the connections between optimal solutions of the model and standard social accounting concepts such as national or regional income and the relationship between production possibilities and preferences—are explored. Next, simplified versions of the general model, including aggregated and one-commodity formulations, are analyzed both by individual periods and by long-run behavior features, followed by a sketch of generalization possibilities to multicommodity models. Finally the relationship among preferences at different policy levels, incentives, and autonomous growth trends is discussed, and certain ways of reformulating the model are explored. The latter are illustrated by some simple numerical examples at a highly aggregated level.

SURVEY OF LOCATIONAL PROBLEMS IN ECONOMIC PLANNING

Problems involving locational choice occur at several levels in economic planning. National development plans are generally formulated without a spatial dimension in the first instance: Such plans, whether they are in global or interindustry terms, have to be *broken down* by major regions of the country in order to check their implications for regional growth; the general objectives set out in national-level plans, furthermore, have to be translated into specific development projects involving in each case the choice of particular locations. Conversely, in a given country a variety of regional or municipal development and promotion programs based on different assumptions and using widely varying planning methods may initially be formulated in relative independence: Such plans have to be *integrated* into a consistent national plan, or, if a national plan has been formulated independently, the inconsistencies between the set of area plans and the national plan have to be resolved. This problem, which arises in the context of planning for a single country, has a supranational counterpart involving the coordination of development plans of independent countries within the framework of common markets or industrial development communities.

The geographical breakdown of a single plan versus the integration of separate area plans are clearly complementary and call for an interplay between two or more planning levels which are organized, at least partially, in a hierarchical fashion, with geographical location acting as the organizing principle.

The problem of breakdown versus integration of plans arises also in a different context, namely, in the relation between central and sectoral (or industrial) planning. While the central plan itself may set out industrial targets in considerable detail, it is practically always found expedient to relegate detailed feasibility studies, project planning, and the execution of *sectoral plans* to lower-level planning organs. Locational analyses are often carried out at this level in connection with the feasibility and project studies. Their results subsequently are incorporated in sectoral development programs which, suitably summarized and abstracted, are communicated to the upper-level planning center. The choice of location thus also enters the decision-making process through a second hierarchical system whose organizing principle is the subdivision of the economy by sectors or industries rather than by geographical areas.

Finally, locational choices arise in connection with *city planning* and its extensions. The focus here has historically been on rational land use, the efficient layout of transportation arteries and terminals, and social problems arising in connection with urban life; in recent years, however, there has been an increasing extension of emphasis from physical to economic planning problems.

The first requirement to be met by any plan is that it should be free from major contradictions and should, in regard to secondary detail, also be as free as possible from inconsistencies. Locational choice does not offer a marked increase of analytical difficulties in comparison with other planning problems as long as this limited objective is at the center of planning efforts; there is, however, a heavy expansion of statistical requirements. Locational detail in data is not easy to come by when relying on traditional statistics the same way as, for example, industrial-process detail is hard to find. When the criterion of efficiency is introduced into locational planning several sources of analytical difficulty have to be faced, difficulties that are not peculiar to locational choices alone but are particularly troublesome in this field. They include, first of all, the setting of development goals, which will be one of the concerns of the present paper. Secondly, economies of scale and other sources of nonconvexity acquire a key importance since they are essential in the delineation of market areas and thus in the interaction between regions; the implications of nonconvexity with regard to the existence of multiple equilibriums and the breakdown of the price system in achieving an over-all optimum are of great practical consequence. Next, the problems of efficient allocation of resources in a double hierarchical planning system, organized both by sector and by geographical area, are far from being adequately understood even in the absence of nonconvexities and a fortiori in their presence. Finally, any adaptive system—whether of a free-market variety or involving organized planning decisions—when operating in the field of locational forces is subject to the effects of long-term lags in adjustments, due to the long lifetime of plant and equipment and of transport arteries and terminals. During the lifetimes of such investments they can be largely regarded as fixed parts of the economic environment, and a great variety of secondary adaptations will take place on the basis of their existing locations. These adaptations are generally of the kind which reinforce the original choice of location of the long-term investment; thus socially undesirable locational patterns, once established, acquire a life and momentum of their own which become exceedingly hard and costly to modify. For this reason locational choices have to be undertaken with a time perspective that is disproportionately long in comparison with the accustomed planning periods: It is often reasonable to consider a time span of fifty years or even more.

No attempt is being made in this paper to present a comprehensive study of current planning practices in relation to locational choices or a complete analysis of the theoretical and practical issues involved. A number of studies on regional planning in different countries have recently appeared, and a compilation and analysis of this material and other pertinent information is at present underway elsewhere. An encyclopedic summary of research in regional and locational problems in Western countries is available, together with a survey article of recent data covering the field of regional economies. References to this material are in the Bibliographical Note at the end of this paper.

The Setting of Development Goals

THE WELFARE IMPLICATIONS OF LOCATIONAL CHOICES

The problem of efficient choice between available alternatives involves the consideration of objectives in relation to instruments. The selection of proper objectives is, however, not obvious in regard to the locational choices that arise in planning, since there is generally more than one entity whose welfare has to be taken into account and which may participate in a more or less autonomous fashion in the process of goal setting. Thus in a country with several regions the question arises of the proper objective of development: Is it the advance of the country as a whole without regard to the regional distribution of this advance, or are the interests of the individual regions to be incorporated in the definition of a national goal and, if so, in what form?

There are very few explicit locational choices in which this dilemma does not enter in one way or another. Perhaps a plant location problem involving only a marginal part of the economy and considered against a background of a satisfactory regional balance might be thought of as being devoid of this multiplicity of goal units, in that a choice which contributes most to the system as a whole and does not disturb the balance of its parts could be regarded as advancing equally the welfare of all parts. Such a formulation, while apparently in accord with common sense, presupposes an understanding of what constitutes a "satisfactory" balance, and offers no clue as to how such a balance is to be established from a starting position that is unbalanced. Moreover, it offers no help in regard to the many important locational decisions in planning that are far from being marginal in their effects upon the economy. None the less, the formulation has some merit in a negative way, since it throws light upon investment decisions in planning that are *not regarded as having a locational dimension,* even though any investment obviously has to be located physically at some point in space. For example, when the question arises whether a store should be located at a given street corner or three blocks further away, the interests of groups of persons associated with either location may be influenced to some extent by the decision. Yet it is not customary for planners to think about such a decision as involving a principle of locational welfare balancing. While the example mentioned is trivial, the same lack of concern for locational welfare balancing often extends to much more important decisions involving more extended geographical areas. It would appear that efficiency decisions taken without overt concern for locational welfare balancing are based on some implicit assumption about an underlying "satisfactory" balance.

This problem is, of course, not peculiar to locational choice, since it arises in goal setting for any collection of individuals. It has been discussed extensively in the economic literature under such headings as interpersonal welfare comparisons and the derivation of community indifference maps or community welfare functions. In locational choices involving the regions of a country, however, the problem assumes particular political importance because political pressures, under many kinds of existing institutional arrangements, are relatively easy to organize on a geographical basis. A situation which is in many ways analogous to the political balance of regions within a country is the balance of sovereign nations within a common market or an economic development community. In both cases the different geographical units have common as well as contrary interests. Institutional rationalizations, however, tend to stress the common interests in the case of regions within a country, at the same time blunting the demands for an immediate and equal geographical sharing of over-all benefits, while the same rationalizations tend to stress the vigorous defense of "fair" shares in the supranational case, with a more reserved admission of common benefits. For this reason, the flexibility of supranational planning is greatly reduced, as witnessed by the problems of several contemporary attempts at common market formation. These difficulties are accentuated by an emphasis on joint investment decisions as against a more conservative approach largely restricted to trade liberalization and labor exchange.

The analytical approach to the problem of locational choices will differ according to whether (1) a single decision-making center can be assumed to exist which, if necessary, reconciles conflicts between the welfare objectives of the different units of the system (and, by implication, between any unit and the system as a whole); or whether (2) an interplay exists between several partially independent decision-making units. For the former case, a maximizing model can be constructed whose solutions are studied in conjunction with function of the welfare objectives adopted for different regions or locations. These solutions have a normative value, provided that the underlying welfare objectives are accepted. In the second case, the interplay between the different units has the nature of a strategic game whose outcome depends on the elements of strength possessed and the strategies followed by each participant.

Throughout the discussion that follows, attention will be centered on the first alternative. In particular, the question will be posed: "To what extent do necessary conflicts exist between the welfare objectives of individual geographical units within a larger system? To the extent that current formulations of allocation models overstate these conflicts, the interests of the separate subunits will be recognized as being more complementary than conflicting, and cooperation and the delegation of powers to a common decision-making center may often become the best strategy for these independent units. If the common interests do not dominate the divergent interests quite to the same extent, the analysis of alternative strategies cannot be avoided; the latter situation, however, will no be studied further in the present paper.

MULTIPLE OBJECTIVES AND PROGRAMING MODELS

The problem of efficient choices in planning can be analyzed by means of linear programing models and their nonlinear extensions. In such models an objective, defined in terms of activity scales, can (without loss of generality) be assumed to be maximized, subject to constraints imposed by technological possibilities and institutional limitations.[1] When there are several objectives which are to be observed simultaneously, as in the case of the development of a system of regions where

---

[1] A minimization problem can be converted into a maximization problem and a minimal constraint can be converted into a maximal constraint by a change of signs. For standard discussions of linear programing, see Dantzig (1963), Gass (1958), Hadley (1961), and Simonnard (1962).

the advance of each region is desirable for its own sake, these multiple goals must be reduced to a single objective by one of the following two techniques:

1. Maximization of a weighted sum of the several objectives
2. Maximization of a single objective while the remaining objectives are treated as constraints, in the sense that admissible solutions to the problem are required to attain or exceed prescribed levels of the latter objectives

For example, in an interregional development model where the maximization of the net products of two individual regions constitutes independent welfare objectives, the first technique assigns a weight to the net product of each region and maximizes the weighted sum of the net regional products, while the second technique maximizes the net regional product of one region subject to the subsidiary constraint that the net product of the other region has to exceed a certain minimum.

In national development models of the linear programing type the measure used for quantifying the national welfare objective is generally additive between geographical regions. Thus the objective may be to maximize national product or total consumption. If the regional distribution of development is to be treated as an independent welfare objective in such models, it is natural to incorporate it by means of the second technique discussed above, i.e., in the form of additional constraints imposed on the model that specify the absolute or relative levels of development to be attained in the individual regions. For example, if the over-all objective is the maximization of national product, the percentage of the total product to be generated in each individual region may also be prescribed. In this formulation the additivity of the measure of development between regions is preserved, i.e., the development of each region is given equal weight. In accordance with the previous discussion, however, there is an alternative formulation, corresponding to the first technique mentioned. In the objective function of the latter, the product (or other criterion of development) of each region is summed with *unequal* weights, so as to channel into selected regions more development than would result from a maximization undertaken with equal weights in the absence of prescribed levels of regional development. In this formulation the optimal value of the objective function no longer represents net national product (or other additive national measure), although the latter can of course be derived easily by means of a side calculation.

In these models, constraints on the interregional distribution of national product are generally imposed at the cost of a decrease in national product for the system as a whole. At best the constraints will leave the latter unchanged if they are either not binding in the optimal solution or if they are just on the margin of having become binding. While this inescapable fact is often interpreted to mean that some national income has to be sacrificed for the sake of attaining a greater equality between regions, it should be noted that the only conclusion that logically follows from what has been said above is that *any prescribed deviation* from the previous optimal solution, be it in the direction of greater equality or greater inequality between regions, will generally imply a sacrifice in national income. It is therefore essential to understand the behavior of models without built-in regional distribution constraints, because such models, if not adequately formulated, can easily point to incorrect policy conclusions.

The two ways of reducing multiple objectives to a single objective that have been cited earlier correspond to the use of price-type and quantity-type control instruments in planning. In general a separate control instrument is needed for setting the value of each separate policy objective.[2] In optimizing models the prescribed search for an optimum replaces one control instrument; with this understanding, the reduction of the multiplicity of regional-locational welfare objectives to a single objective reveals itself as a special case of the application of this principle. When using the first of the two techniques for effecting the reduction, the $n - 1$ relative weights assigned to the regional welfare goals of n regions act as price-type control instruments; with the second technique, the prescribed levels of welfare objectives in $n - 1$ regions act as quantity-type control instruments. Mixed formulations are also possible, i.e., maximizing the weighted sum of one group of regional objectives while the remaining ones are imposed as constraints.

The following important question arises in connection with the two alternative formulations of a problem in terms of price-type or quantity-type control instruments: Given one of the two formulations, is it possible to switch to the other formulation by appropriately choosing the weighting or constraint parameters of the latter in such a way that the optimal solutions will coincide? If it is possible to guarantee this in a given set of circumstances then the two formulations can be said to be equivalent.

Price- and quantity-type control instruments lead to equivalent re-

[2] On the use of control instruments in planning, see Tinbergen (1956), Sec. 3.3. On price-type versus quantity-type control instruments, see Chenery (1958).

sults in this sense only when the optimal solutions of the models are unique; in the case of multiple optimums there is only a limited correspondence. Unique solutions can be guaranteed when the models are *strictly convex* from a mathematical point of view; unfortunately, linear models are convex only in a weaker sense, and they will generally lead to multiple optimums in the course of the above reformulation. These multiple optimums are not of the kind familiar from the use of graphic techniques in economic analysis that result when two curves intersect at several points. They have the appearance of a mountaintop plateau rather than the unique tip of a sugarloaf-shaped mountain. When such multiple optimums occur only one thing can be guaranteed: By an appropriate choice of parameters the problem can be reformulated so that the two alternative formulations by the two techniques cited above will have *at least one optimal solution in common.* A more detailed inspection of this limited correspondence shows, moreover, that apart from the optimal solution that is shared between the two formulations many optimal solutions can exist under one formulation that are nonoptimal or even infeasible under the other formulation. When the model is not convex, i.e., when it embodies economies of scale or indivisibilities, it is no longer possible to make even the above limited assertion of correspondence.

These issues are discussed in more detail in Appendix 1.

Formulation of Resource Allocation Models for Locational Choices

A GENERAL MODEL: PRINCIPAL FEATURES

In order to offer a concrete basis for the subsequent discussion concerning the structure of allocation models as customarily formulated, a linear programing model with a threefold breakdown of detailed information (time periods, locations, industries) is presented in Table 1. While the empirical realization of such a model would overstrain the statistical resources of all but the most advanced economies and would seldom be useful unless a great emphasis was given to central planning decisions, it has the advantage of allowing the discussion of all the relevant factors in a unified way. In practice, unwanted detail can be eliminated by aggregation: thus, the model can be made static (single-period); it can be left dynamic and can instead by aggregated by regions while maintaining the interindustry detail; or it can be aggregated by

TABLE 1 An Illustrative Locational Model

Column group headers (top, reading across the periods):

- **PERIOD 1**: Production (XX_1^1, XX_2^1), Transport (XX_3^1, XZ_1^1, XZ_2^1), Stock-Holding (XH_1^1, XH_2^1)
- **PERIOD 2**: Production (XX_1^2, XX_2^2, XX_3^2), Transport (XZ_1^2, XZ_2^2), Stock-Holding (XH_1^2, XH_2^2)
- **PERIOD 3**: Production (XX_1^3, XX_2^3, XX_3^3), Transport (XZ_1^3, XZ_2^3), Stock-Holding (XH_1^3, XH_2^3)
- **Exogenous** ($= 1$): X_*^0
- **PERIOD 4** Terminal Stocks: $S0 = MAX!$; $*Y0$

Dual variables (right margin): Commodity Stocks ($*YR_1^1$, $*YR_2^1$ ...), Primary Factor Flows ($*YW_1^1$, $*YW_2^1$ ...), Commodity Flows ($*YP_1^1$, $*YP_2^1$ ...); Shadow Prices; ← Profits.

Primal variables / Activity Levels (left margin, Resource Surpluses):

PERIOD 1
- $*SB_1^1$, $*SB_2^1$
- $*SF_1^1$, $*SF_2^1$
- SA_1^1, SA_2^1

PERIOD 2
- SB_1^2, SB_2^2
- SF_1^2, SF_2^2
- SA_1^2, SA_2^2

PERIOD 3
- SB_1^3, SB_2^3
- SF_1^3, SF_2^3
- SA_1^3, SA_2^3

Exogenous column entries:
- H_1^0, H_2^0
- q_1^1, q_2^1
- $(H_1^0 - C_1^1)$, $(H_2^0 - C_2^1)$
- q_1^2, q_2^2
- $-C_1^2$, $-C_2^2$
- q_1^3, q_2^3
- $-C_1^3$, $-C_2^3$

Matrix coefficients (PERIOD 1 Production / Transport / Stock-Holding):
- $-B_{11}^1$, $-B_{12}^1$, $-B_{13}^1$, $-L_{11}^1$, $-L_{12}^1$
- $-B_{21}^1$, $-B_{22}^1$, $-B_{23}^1$, $-L_{21}^1$, $-L_{22}^1$
- $-F_{11}^1$, $-F_{12}^1$, $-F_{13}^1$, $-M_{11}^1$, $-M_{12}^1$
- $-F_{21}^1$, $-F_{22}^1$, $-F_{23}^1$, $-M_{21}^1$, $-M_{22}^1$
- A_{11}^1, A_{12}^1, A_{13}^1, $(T_1^1 - N_{11}^1)$, $-N_{12}^1$
- A_{21}^1, A_{22}^1, A_{23}^1, $-N_{21}^1$, $(T_2^1 - N_{22}^1)$
- Stock-Holding: -1, -1 ; 1, 1

PERIOD 2 coefficients:
- $-B_{11}^2$, $-B_{12}^2$, $-B_{13}^2$, $-L_{11}^2$, $-L_{12}^2$
- $-B_{21}^2$, $-B_{22}^2$, $-B_{23}^2$, $-L_{21}^2$, $-L_{22}^2$
- $-F_{11}^2$, $-F_{12}^2$, $-F_{13}^2$, $-M_{11}^2$, $-M_{12}^2$
- $-F_{21}^2$, $-F_{22}^2$, $-F_{23}^2$, $-M_{21}^2$, $-M_{22}^2$
- A_{11}^2, A_{12}^2, A_{13}^2, $(T_1^2 - N_{11}^2)$, $-N_{12}^2$
- A_{21}^2, A_{22}^2, A_{23}^2, $-N_{21}^2$, $(T_2^2 - N_{22}^2)$
- Stock-Holding: 1, 1 ; -1, -1

PERIOD 3 coefficients:
- $-B_{11}^3$, $-B_{12}^3$, $-B_{13}^3$, $-L_{11}^3$, $-L_{12}^3$
- $-B_{21}^3$, $-B_{22}^3$, $-B_{23}^3$, $-L_{21}^3$, $-L_{22}^3$
- $-F_{11}^3$, $-F_{12}^3$, $-F_{13}^3$, $-M_{11}^3$, $-M_{12}^3$
- $-F_{21}^3$, $-F_{22}^3$, $-F_{23}^3$, $-M_{21}^3$, $-M_{22}^3$
- A_{11}^3, A_{12}^3, A_{13}^3, $(T_1^3 - N_{11}^3)$, $-N_{12}^3$
- A_{21}^3, A_{22}^3, A_{23}^3, $-N_{21}^3$, $(T_2^3 - N_{22}^3)$
- Stock-Holding: 1, 1 ; -1

Terminal Stocks / Exogenous row:
- $(P_1^4 + R_1^4)(P_2^4 + R_2^4)$
- $-DH_1^1$, $-DH_2^1$, $-DH_1^2$, $-DH_2^2$, $-DH_1^3$, $-DH_2^3$

Bottom (Period 4, $S0 = MAX!$):
$$-D0 = MIN!$$
$-DX_1^1, -DX_2^1, -DX_3^1, -DZ_1^1, -DZ_2^1, -DH_1^1, -DH_2^1, -DX_1^2, -DX_2^2, -DX_3^2, -DZ_1^2, -DZ_2^2, -DH_1^2, -DX_1^3, -DX_2^3, -DX_3^3, -DZ_1^3, -DZ_2^3$

DUAL VARIABLES

industries while maintaining the interregional structure. Examples of each of these alternative aggregated formulations are available.[3]

The dynamic features of the model in Table 1 are set out in the simplest possible form in order to concentrate attention on the locational-interregional structure. Thus, consumptions of all commodities and supplies of primary resources are treated as exogenously given parameters while terminal stocks, with a prescribed weighting, are treated as the maximand. The presentation of the model follows Tucker's condensed linear programing format (Graves and Wolfe, 1963); the details of notation and formal interpretation will be found in Appendix 2.

The principal characteristics of the model are the following. The unused surpluses of all resources are expressed as linear combinations of the activity levels; the coefficients of the balances involving these resources appear as rows. There are three kinds of resources: commodity stocks, primary factors, and commodity flows. Each of these resources is distinguished by time periods and by locations. (The terms "location" and "region" will be used interchangeably.) The time periods appear in Table 1 in explicit form while the locations are left implicit by the use of matrix notation; in this notation the model appears very much as though only a single location existed. The model shows two commodities and two primary factors.

There are three kinds of activities: production, transport, and stock holding. These activities appear as columns of coefficients. The coefficients denote resource requirements or demands if negative, and outputs or supplies if positive. The levels of the activities are variable and appear as algebraic unknowns heading each column. *Production* activities have commodity outputs (A; if a given A is negative, it denotes an intermediate input); they also have stock requirements ($-B$) and primary factor requirements ($-F$); their unknown level is designated by the compound symbol XX. Production activities, like resources, are distinguished by time period and by location; the latter distinction is implicit in the matrix notation used. Three production activities are given. *Transport* activities show net regional imports of commodities (T), while transport costs are broken down by detailed stock requirements (L), factor inputs (M), and commodity inputs (N). The model includes a separate transport activity for each origin-destination pair, as can be seen in the detailed interpretation of the matrices in Appendix 2. The unknown levels of these activities are denoted by the compound

[3] See Bibliographical Note.

symbol *XZ*. *Stock-holding* activities transfer stocks from one time period to the next; they can be interpreted as the purchase of a unit of stock at the end of period *t*, its rental for productive purposes in period $(t + 1)$, and its resale at the end of period $(t + 1)$. The coefficients *I* refer to a unit of a commodity or stock in a given time period and at a given location. The unknown levels of these activities are denoted by *XH*. In addition to the foregoing activities, there is also a dummy activity of *exogenous supplies and demands* whose level (XO) is fixed at unity; it specifies the initial level of stocks (H); the time profile of the consumption of all goods (C) and the supply of all primary factors (Q) in all regions.[4]

Resource balances follow the format:

$$\begin{pmatrix} \text{surplus} \\ \text{of a} \\ \text{resource} \end{pmatrix} = \begin{pmatrix} \text{all} \\ \text{supplies or} \\ \text{outputs} \end{pmatrix} - \begin{pmatrix} \text{all} \\ \text{demands or} \\ \text{requirements} \end{pmatrix}.$$

Surpluses are treated as algebraic unknowns, in the same way as activity levels; in the model they are denoted by compound symbols whose first letter is *S*.

For example, the balance of the flow of the first commodity in the first time period is interpreted as follows:

$$SA_1^1 \quad = \quad H_1^0 \quad - \quad C_1^1 \quad +$$

surplus of first commodity in first time period   initial stock inherited from zero time period   consumption in first time period

$$(A_{11}^1 \cdot XX_1^1 + A_{12}^1 \cdot X_2^1 + A_{13}^1 \cdot XX_3^1) +$$

net output by the three production activities in the first time period, after deduction of intermediate inputs

$$T_1^1 \cdot XZ_1^1 - (N_{11}^1 \cdot XZ_1^1 + N_{12}^1 \cdot XZ_2^1) - I \cdot XH_1^1$$

net import into given region in first period   amount used directly in all transport activities in first time period   amount held as stock in first time period

As can be seen, the initial stock and the consumption are exogenously given constants, while the other quantities are derived as the products of the respective coefficients by the proper activity levels indicated in the

---

[4] Migration can be handled by adjusting the exogenous labor supplies for the periods in question.

column headings. Since this entire balance is in matrix notation, it is valid simultaneously for each separate region. In particular, in this notation multiplication by I corresponds to multiplication by 1 in ordinary algebra; thus the quantity

$$I \cdot XH_1^1 - H_1^0$$

is the increase in stocks between period zero and period 1, i.e., the investment in stocks of commodity 1 in each region.

Likewise, stock balances can be interpreted as follows: Surpluses of stocks in period t equal the amounts required for production and transport one period later (there is one-period time lag between investment and its utilization) minus the amount actually held in period t. The interpretation of primary factor balances is analogous but involves no time lag.

In this formulation the maximand is an ordinary resource surplus defined like any other. In the model, terminal stocks (in the fourth period) with a prescribed weighting are chosen as the maximand. The problem consists in programing the unknown activity levels and resource surpluses in such a way that terminal stocks (the last surplus) be a maximum, while no other resource surplus is negative (i.e., there are no overdrawn resources) and no activity level is negative (i.e., no activity runs in reverse).

The maximization of terminal stocks is a proper objective since it is equivalent to maximizing the growth potential of the system after the necessarily limited planning period. The composition of these terminal stocks by commodity and by region is determined as part of the solution of the problem; it will, however, depend strongly on the weighting that is exogenously assigned to the terminal stocks. The weights chosen summarize the assumptions on the nature of the growth process beyond the planning horizon of the model. Rather than assigning weights to the terminal stocks, the planning horizon can also be taken into account by assuming constant proportional growth for the system as a whole or prescribed rates of growth for individual parts of the system beyond the horizon. The advantage of the maximand presented in Table 1 is, however, that it is not only particularly simple, but also convenient for the analysis of problems of locational choice, since it is additive between regions.

Every resource allocation problem formulated by means of mathematical programing explicitly contains (or, in the case of linear models, implies) a resource valuation problem. For the present model the unknowns of this valuation problem are listed in the right-hand and bottom margins of Table 1 and are designated by compound symbols whose first letter is Y or D. The Y-type symbols are interpreted as forming a "shadow" price system based on a unit valuation of terminal stocks (which thus play the role of the *numeraire*). YR, YW, and YP designate stock rents of commodities, flow prices of primary factors (i.e., wages, etc.), and flow prices of commodities, respectively. The product of each input coefficient for a given activity by the corresponding shadow price of the right-hand margin represents a revenue (if positive) or a cost (if negative). The algebraic sum of these terms for a given activity represents profits (negative losses) computed at shadow prices. These shadow profits, which are algebraic unknowns, appear in the bottom margin. For example, the shadow profit on the first productive activity in period 1 is obtained as follows:

$(-B_{11}{}^1 \cdot YR_{11}{}^1 - B_{21}{}^1 \cdot YR_2{}^1)$ $(-)$ rental cost on stocks of commodities 1 and 2 used in the production activity

$+ (-F_{11}{}^1 \cdot YW_{11}{}^1 - F_{21}{}^1 \cdot YW_{21}{}^1)$ $(-)$ wage cost and other primary factor payments on primary factors used in the production activity

$+ (A_{11}{}^1 \cdot YP_{11}{}^1 + A_{21}{}^1 \cdot YP_{21}{}^1)$ $(+)$ net revenue on commodity output after deduction of payments for intermediate-input commodities

---

$= -DX_1{}^1$ (equals) profit on activity performed at unit level, where DX is a shadow loss, $-DX$ is a shadow profit

Due to mathematical reasons the optimal solution to the allocation problem simultaneously yields the shadow prices and shadow losses of the valuation problem. The latter are always nonnegative; i.e., shadow prices are positive or zero, and no activity ever shows profits at these prices but at best breaks even. At the same time the system of shadow prices is such that it minimizes profits on the exogenous supply-demand activity; in fact, this minimum is numerically equal to the maximum of the allocation problem.[5] Due to this equality the correspondence of

[5] Provided both the maximum of the allocation problem and the minimum of the valuation problem exist, Max $(SO) = $ Min $(-DO)$.

the allocation problem and the valuation problem in Table 1 can be stated in the following form: The optimal value of terminal stocks is imputed by the model to the scarce exogenous supplies minus exogenous demands. In particular, if factor supplies and commodity demands are zero at all time periods, the model imputes the entire value of terminal stocks to the initial stocks; moreover, it can be shown that the imputed value of stocks for intermediate time periods is also held constant (see Appendix 3). With given nonzero consumption profiles the model imputes to initial stocks as well as to stocks in all other periods a value that is larger than the value of terminal stocks by an amount exactly sufficient to finance consumption in periods subsequent to the period in question. If, in addition, nonzero factor supplies are also included in the model, their effect on the time profile of imputed stock values is the opposite of the effect of consumption.

The shadow prices utilized in the definition of aggregate social accounting concepts above, it should be noted, are *not* current prices for each period. This is clear from the fact that the revenues and costs of stock-holding activities are summed over two successive time periods; concepts based on current prices could not be summed in this way without appropriate discounting operations. The shadow prices are therefore seen to form a price system which has the properties of a set of current prices to which discounting operations have already been applied. It is, in fact, readily possible to define a set of current prices together with an appropriate discount rate once the shadow price system is given. The system of current prices is then anchored in one of the time periods by assuming that in this period current and shadow prices coincide; it is further assumed that an arbitrarily given commodity serves as the value standard between the base time period and another time period, in the sense that its current price remains constant between the two periods. The interest rate for discounting purposes on these assumptions turns out to be the current rent of the stock of the value-standard commodity; the current rents of the stocks of other commodities have to be adjusted for value changes of the stock between periods in order to arrive at the same interest rate (see Appendix 3). Instead of a single commodity, a weighted average can serve equally well as the value standard; the latter can, moreover, change between time periods.

The system of relative shadow prices is thus a more fundamental property of the model than the period-to-period interest rate associated with the choice of an arbitrary value standard. The arbitrariness of the latter can be reduced in practice by tying it to the structure of consumption from period to period or by some similar means, but in any event the shadow prices contain all the information necessary for defining any given system of current prices and the corresponding period-to-period interest rates.

The model lends itself readily to interpretation by means of standard social accounting concepts. The value aggregates embodying these concepts are built up from "accounting values" corresponding to each coefficient in the optimal solution of the model. These accounting values are obtained by multiplying each coefficient both by the corresponding activity level of the optimal solution (giving total physical resource amount) and by the proper shadow price (giving the value of the former). Accounting values have the mathematical property of summing to zero both by rows and by columns, since (by rows) any resource that may have a nonzero surplus will be a free good with a zero shadow price, yielding a zero *value* for the surplus, while (by columns) any activity that may have a nonzero loss will not be used in the optimal solution, yielding a zero *total* loss. This property is highly convenient for accounting purposes since it permits the definition of aggregate concepts based exclusively on activity scales and shadow prices, without reference to resource surpluses and losses on activities.

National income and product (jointly for all regions) can be derived for any time period from the accounting values of rows having the index of the given time period. Accounting values are first summed by rows to zero; then these equalities are themselves summed; finally, the terms corresponding to production and transport activities are canceled, since these sum to zero vertically for the given time period (see Appendix 3). In this way the following relation is obtained, for example, for the first period:

$$(H_1^0 \cdot YR_1^1 + H_2^0 \cdot YR_2^1) + (Q_1^1 \cdot YW_1^1 + Q_2^1 \cdot YW_2^1) =$$
$$(C_1^1 \cdot YP_1^1 + C_2^1 \cdot YP_2^1) +$$
$$[(XH_1^1 - H_1^0) \cdot YP_1^1 + (XH_2^1 - H_2^0) \cdot YP_2^1]$$

or in a more condensed notation:

$$H^0 \cdot YR^1 \quad + \quad Q^1 \cdot YW^1 \quad = \quad C^1 \cdot YP^1 \quad + (XH^1 - H^0) \cdot YP^1$$

stock rental income	wage and other primary factor income	consumption	investment

This is the well-known identity between national income at factor cost and national product, with all aggregates defined at shadow prices.

If this expression is transformed into current prices, stock rental income is replaced by the *difference* between interest income and the net increase in stock valuations (see Appendix 3). Alternately, national income and investment could both be redefined by adding to each side of the identity the net increase in stock valuations. Then national income becomes the sum of wage and interest incomes while investment is obtained as the difference of the current stock values in the two periods. Note, however, that these now become dependent on the choice of the value-standard commodity stock.

Corresponding expressions for regional income and product can also be derived from the subset of rows for one individual region in a given time period (see Appendix 3). When the operations are performed as indicated above for the national concepts, it is found that the expression for regional income at factor cost now equals the sum of consumption, investment, net regional exports having the nature of pure transfers (without regard to transport costs), plus all cost-type commodity and factor inputs of the region into transport activities. In other words, the model treats commodity and factor inputs into transport as part of the final product of each region, a somewhat surprising result in view of the fact that transport is thought of as an intermediate commodity. Since, however, intermediate commodity and factor inputs into *exports* are customarily treated as part of final product, it is clear that the model makes no distinction between commodities and factors leaving the region that actually arrive at other regions, and commodities and factors leaving the region that are utilized for running the transport activities themselves. Thus, it is convenient to redefine net regional exports to include all transport-cost-type commodity and factor inputs. Since in the derivation of national product for the system as a whole net exports so defined cancel out (see the definition of national product, above), it can be concluded that commodity and factor inputs into transport activities show up in national product in the form of consumption and investment totals *at the required locations*.

In sum, the model is characterized by the following key features:

1. It maximizes for the economy as a whole an over-all development criterion (value of terminal stocks) that is additive between regions. There are no constraints on the regional distribution of this criterion; i.e., the accumulation of terminal stocks may be realized by means of any technically feasible regional distribution of productive activities.

2. Consumption demands and factor supplies are prescribed in physical terms for all commodities and factors in all regions and all time periods. This feature of the model has several implications:

a. The structure of production exhibits a far-going independence from the structure of consumption; as an extreme, it could happen that a given region does not develop its productive structures at all while participating in consumption in the prescribed manner by means of a steady stream of interregional transfers.

b. All decisions with regard to time preference between present and future consumption and effort are prejudged in the formulation of the model. Thus, in particular, no *ex ante* relationship is prescribed for the division of national and regional product between consumption and saving, even though, of course, the respective ratios can be readily calculated *ex post* once the optimal solution to the model has been obtained.

c. All relations with regard to the price elasticities of commodity demands and factor supplies are likewise prejudged in the formulation of the model: Since the latter are given in physical quantities that are constant regardless of the corresponding shadow prices in the optimal solution of the model, all price elasticities are in fact taken to be equal to zero.

3. The treatment of dynamic features is the simplest possible in a multiperiod model. In particular:

a. All stocks are treated as completely liquid at the end of each accounting period. Thus, no distinction is made between fixed capital and inventories, and no limits are placed on the reduction of the levels of stocks between time periods.

b. The transfer of stocks from one time period to the next is treated as costless; no storage charges of any kind are included in the model, and thus no joint storage activities occur.

c. There are no time lags in the model, apart from the one-period lag between investment and the availability of stock capacity for production. In particular, the inputs and outputs of all production and transport activities are restricted to one given time period.

4. The treatment of transport is also kept comparatively simple. In particular:

a. There is only one transport activity connecting each pair of locations. Thus alternative regional inputs for running a given transport activity are excluded, and problems such as the carriage of shipments in the bottoms of one or the other region with corresponding income generation for one or the other region are prejudged. Likewise, the optimal means of transport, i.e., water or overland carriage, is also prejudged.

b. Joint carriage of different commodities by a single transport activity is excluded.

c. Joint service by a single transport activity to and from different locations, like for example a cargo ship touching a series of ports, is excluded.

5. All fixed costs and other elements of nonconvexity in production and transport are ignored. This feature of the model places a sharp restriction on its degree of realism, but it cannot be avoided without opening up a host of major analytical problems that fall outside the limits of the present paper.

6. The optimal solution to the model traces out, on the primal side, the time path of production activities and investments in all regions, as well as the evolution of interregional transport flows. On the dual side, it yields the time profile of commodity shadow prices, shadow wages for primary factors, and shadow rents of scarce stock capacities in all regions. Shadow prices, wages, and rents are expressed in units of terminal wealth (stock valuation) which acts as the numeraire resource of the shadow price system.

TECHNOLOGICAL CHOICES VS. PREFERENCES

This particular form of the model was chosen as the point of departure because it is a summary of technological choices open to the system of regions as a whole embracing alternatives in regard to production, transport, and stock holding, while the representation of preference functions is excluded. Thus the prescribed magnitudes of the parameters of the model and the optimal solution values of the variables satisfy purely technological relationships in the most efficient way possible, but the same constellation of parameters and optimal values of variables need not, and generally will not, be preferred to other possible constellations that can be obtained by prescribing different parameter values. In short, the optimal solutions to the model are Pareto-optimal for any prescribed set of parameters; by varying the parameters systematically, all trade-offs between parameters, i.e., the entire hypersurface of production possibilities, can be traced out.[6]

[6] It may be objected that the maximization of terminal wealth with prescribed weighting amounts to the inclusion of a preference function in the model. This, however, need be true only in a purely formal sense. The weights if desired can be regarded as completely arbitrary, having the sole purpose of defining a tangent that will allow the construction, one portion at a time, of the Pareto-optimal production-possibility surface. A genuine commodity- and time-preference function as envisaged by neoclassical economics could rarely be regarded as linear over extended ranges of the variables. A preference function with the required curvature, technically a concave function, if empirically derivable at all, could be satisfactorily approximated within a linear model in a piecewise linear fashion, in the

From the point of view of practical planning applications, some form of this general strategy is often attractive since, given the production possibility surface, the policymakers can apply to the latter an implicit set of preferences in the process of selecting a particular constellation as the most preferred from among the ones available. This strategy avoids the great difficulties of constructing a reliable explicit representation of the structure of preferences. At the same time, the effort required for tracing out the complete production-possibility hypersurface is overwhelming in almost any practical task, since the number of point solutions required for characterizing with any accuracy a function in a large number of dimensions is enormous. It is thus highly advantageous to be able to add to the model sufficient information with regard to the structure of preferences to permit the approximate identification of a "relevant range" for decision-making; the detailed description of production possibilities can then be restricted to this range.

This additional information regarding preferences can be included in the model in two forms:

1. The choice of the magnitudes of particular parameters in the numerical formulation of the model can be based on the approximate anticipation of the optimal solution; thus the parameter values chosen are such as are believed to result in a "reasonable" solution from the point of view of preferences. To the extent that this attempt is successful the first parameter-solution constellation falls within the "relevant range" for decision-making, and the exploration of production possibilities can thereafter be restricted to small parameter changes around the initial values. For example, with regard to regional growth preferences, i.e., the balancing of growth rates in individual regions against the growth of the system as a whole (in so far as a conflict exists), the initial parameter choice can well consist in an equal weighting of terminal stocks in different regions.

2. Certain parameters can be unlocked and made explicitly variable same way that production functions are approximated. The linear pieces would then obey relationships of the type:

$$x_1/g_{i,1} + x_2/g_{i,2} + \cdots + x_n/g_{i,n} \geqq V; j = 1, \ldots, m,$$

where the $g_{i,j}$ are the parameters of the ith linear piece and V is a new variable used as an index of the preference level that is being maximized.

Unless the weighting of terminal stocks is therefore explicitly interpreted as one local portion of the piecewise linearized concave preference function, it is entirely justified to regard the model as being restricted to the parametric representation of technological choices open to the planner.

within the formulation of the model, and specific relationships can be prescribed between this new variable and the other variables.

The most obvious candidate for such treatment is the set of consumption parameters included in the model, since the effect of time preferences connecting present and future consumptions can be reasonably approximated by prescribing savings in relation to final product. This can be done either for the system as a whole or for individual regions, on the assumption that savings equal investments. Preferences with regard to the interregional distribution of consumption can be added independently of production, since net production can be redistributed by means of uncompensated transfers; thus, for example, it can be prescribed that per capita consumption of all commodities be equalized in all regions. When the above relationships are prescribed in aggregate terms, it is generally also necessary to approximate the structure of preferences between different consumption goods in the same time period by means of constraints that specify ratios or other simple relationships between the physical consumptions of individual commodities; otherwise the process of optimization might tend to channel all consumption into one or a few goods.

The formal introduction of such constraints into the model of Table 1 is straightforward so long as the weights used in defining aggregate concepts are *constant*. In fact, if aggregate concepts are defined in terms of historical prices and their simple projections into future time periods, the condition of constancy for the weighting parameters will be fulfilled; however, this procedure is analytically questionable for two reasons: (1) Future prices depend on the structural changes introduced into the economy planning, and cannot be taken as simple projections of past prices. (2) The purpose of formulating mathematical programing models is to get away from the irrationalities of past prices observed in imperfect markets or under administrative control procedures; it is thus a flaw of the analysis to bring these back into the model by way of the definition of aggregate concepts.

While these drawbacks are undeniable it is recalled that the purpose of the relationships referred to in the foregoing paragraphs is *not* to arrive at the exact most-preferred solution, but only to identify the relevant decision range for further detailed exploration; the accuracy requirements in regard to preferences are therefore substantially relaxed. The pocedure is nevertheless inelegant. Then could not past and projected prices be replaced by the shadow prices themselves in the formulation of the aggregate concepts?

In considering the latter possibility, the first problem to be faced is that the prices to be used as weights in the aggregate constraints become unknowns; in other words, the aggregate constraints have terms that contain the product of a primal variable (activity scale) and a dual variable (shadow price). Such a model is no longer linear, as its "primal" side becomes inseparably fused with its "dual" side; the analytical problems it raises are largely unexplored, even though a clear resemblance to ordinary nonlinear programing problems is evident that can in all probability be exploited to obtain efficient solution algorithms. One intuitively obvious strategy, which may or may not be computationally efficient, consists in starting with a set of trial values of the shadow prices, solving the linear model formulated in terms of these, checking the trial values against the results, and iterating with revised trial values. In this manner, the circularity of formulating a model in terms of its own solution is broken, while the linearity of each trial model is preserved.

The use of aggregate concepts defined in terms of shadow prices is aesthetically appealing but raises the further problem that the aggregate magnitudes might be highly sensitive to the optimal values of the shadow prices. In so far as these are quite different from historical prices, the historical relationship between aggregate magnitudes will no longer furnish a reliable guide for approximating the structure of preferences. Thus the historical savings rate applied to the shadow-priced savings and income concepts may well be inappropriate for representing time preferences, and recourse to a savings rate expressed in stable prices may become the better choice after all in the absence of empirical observations on savings rates at near-equilibrium prices.

Behavior of Resource Allocation Models Involving Locational Choices

SIMPLIFIED VERSIONS OF THE GENERAL MODEL

Having formulated a general resource allocation model the question may now be posed: What does this model reveal about the problem of locational choices, in particular the choice between geographically balanced or unbalanced growth? In order to answer this question it is necessary to analyze the behavior of the model under different assumptions. Due to the complexity of the model it will, however, be convenient to analyze primarily the behavior of simplified versions and to generalize this analysis qualitatively by reference to the fully detailed model.

An aggregated multiperiod interregional growth model has been described in a recent article by M. A. Rahman (1963); the same model has been presented in a slightly different form and some of the results have been derived in a simpler way in a comment on the foregoing article by Robert Dorfman. This work, to be referred to as the Rahman-Dorfman model, will be used in the following discussion unless specifically noted to the contrary; it will become apparent that it constitutes a special case of the general model of Table 1. The discussion of the properties of this model is thus a convenient take-off point for subsequent generalization.

The Rahman-Dorfman model is formulated in terms of the aggregate capital stocks $K_{i,t}$ in each region i and each time period t.[7] Aggregate investment in a region is the difference between capital stock in the region in two subsequent time periods. Reinvestible surplus in each region is related to capital stock by means of constant reinvestment coefficients s_i that represent the ratio between the ordinary savings rate σ_i and the marginal capital-output ratio k_i:

$$s_i = \sigma_i / k_i$$

The Rahman-Dorfman model, like the general model of Table 1, maximizes terminal wealth, i.e., the valuation of terminal stocks at prescribed weighting parameters:

$$\text{Max!} \ \Sigma K_{iT} c_{iT}$$

where the c_{iT} coefficients correspond to the $(P^4 + R^4)$ parameters in the model of Table 1, except for the fact that the c_{iT} coefficients are aggregated by commodities. T is the time index of the last planning period. The maximization is subject to the constraint that total reinvestible

---

[7] While Rahman formulates an interregional model Dorfman's model is interpreted in terms of sectors rather than regions; the formal analogy between the two models is, however, very close; and Rahman makes explicit use of some of Dorfman's results in an interregional context. Thus where Dorfman refers to sector i I shall refer to region i in the subsequent exposition. Moreover, where Rahman explicitly uses aggregate concepts, such as income, consumption, investment and savings, Dorfman circumvents this by postulating that the capital stock in each of his sectors can be meaningfully measured in physical units chosen so as to make the price of a physical unit equal unity; on this assumption, he sums the capital stocks for different sectors. I shall drop this disguise and treat capital as a frankly aggregate concept. If this is done, Dorfman's s_i coefficient, the amount of reinvestible surplus generated per unit of physical capital in sector i, becomes identified with the ratio of the savings rate to the ordinary capital-output ratio in aggregate terms, as indicated in the text below.

surplus summed for all regions must be sufficient to cover all investments in each individual time period t:

$$\sum_i (K_{i,\,t+1} - K_{i,\,t}) \leqq \sum_i s_i\, K_{it}$$

The solution to this problem hinges on working backward in the determination of investments period by period. If there are no further constraints, the solution is trivial: Shift *all* existing capital in the last period
to the region where it has the highest valuation $\bar{c}_{iT}$, since this will maximize terminal wealth; in previous time periods, maintain *all* capital in
the region where it has the highest reinvestment ratio s_i, since this will
lead to the fastest buildup of the capital stock. The solution becomes
more interesting when decumulation constraints are added on the capital stock invested in each region: Since it is now no longer possible to
shift existing capital stock at will, but only to redirect further investment
from one region to another, there are opposed attractions for investment; on the one hand, toward regions where the terminal stock valuation is high, and on the other, toward regions where the reinvestment
ratio is favorable. In general, the effect of a high reinvestment ratio
which cumulates at compound interest will outweigh the effect of an
adverse terminal valuation if the planning period is chosen long enough.
In any event, if in a given period *some* investment goes to a given region,
all investment has to go there.

The reinvestment ratio, it is recalled, is high in a region to the extent
that the savings rate is high and the capital-output ratio is low. If stocks
are equally valued in all regions at the end of the planning period, the
former criterion will channel all investment into the region with highest
reinvestible surplus; this can be counteracted only by slanting terminal
stock valuations in favor of the low-reinvestment regions. Since in
underdeveloped regions the savings rate is low, the criterion under equal
weighting will not channel investment into these regions unless they
have an unusually favorable marginal capital-output ratio. As social
overhead investments in underdeveloped regions are likely to be deficient, favorable capital-output ratios cannot occur in these regions
unless the productivity of capital in directly productive activities is unusually high. The latter productivity depends, however, on several
elements: the inherent technological relationships, the supply of labor,
and the supply of other potentially scarce factors, primarily land and
natural resources. Since capital-output ratios and savings are measured
in aggregate terms at market prices that are known to be disequilibrium

prices—at least as far as labor is concerned, but very probably also in many or most other respects—the aggregate ratios cover up a tangle of diverse elements and leave the application of the suggested regional investment criterion on very shaky grounds. The tangle is further compounded if an attempt is made to value terminal stocks at projected market prices within each region.[8]

The analysis is largely unchanged when the maximization of terminal national product replaces the maximization of terminal wealth. The usual additive definition of system product (national product for all regions) implies equal weighting; the terminal consideration is now however no longer the reinvestment rate but just the capital-output ratio, since it is immaterial, from the point of view of the terminal national product, to what use—investment or consumption—that product is put. Thus productivity alone takes on the role of terminal weights, while savings and productivity both play a role, in the form of the reinvestment ratio, in all earlier periods.

The net policy conclusions of this analysis are highly prejudicial to underdeveloped regions unless the latter exhibit unrealistically favorable marginal capital-output ratios. These conclusions will, however, be greatly modified by a more detailed analysis of aggregation problems and the relaxation of the constancy of certain parameters.

In terms of the comprehensive linear programing model of Table 1, the Rahman-Dorfman model can be represented as a special case corresponding to the following assumptions:

1. A single commodity
2. Zero transport costs

A single-commodity, two-regional model with no transport costs is presented in Table 2. The nomenclature follows that of Table 1 except that in the present case all symbols refer to single scalars rather than to vectors or matrices as was the case in Table 1.[9] It can be seen that

[8] It should be clearly understood that the Rahman-Dorfman model has never been put forward by its authors as anything but a suggestive exercise in the consideration of certain resource allocation problems; in particular, the extreme solutions it gives by channeling all investment into a single activity in each period are explicitly regarded as wholly unrealistic. It is recalled that Dorfman in his reformulation of Rahman's model entirely abandoned the regional interpretation of the analytical structure of the model in favor of a sectoral interpretation within which the aggregation problems can to some extent be skirted by means of the measurement of the capital stock of a sector in terms of engineering units.

[9] Correspondingly, the stock, factor, and product coefficients B, F, and A, are carried in the present table in lower case. In order to simplify the subscripting of these coefficients, they have been subscripted 1 . . . 4, rather than being identified with regard to region (A or B), or activity (1 or 2).

TABLE 2

PRIMAL VARIABLES		Exogenous (=1)	PERIOD 1 Production Stocks					
Activity Levels →		X0	XX^1_{A1}	XX^1_{A2}	XX^1_{B1}	XX^1_{B2}	XH^1_A	XH^1_B
Resource Surpluses ↓		*	*	*	*	*	*	*
PERIOD 1	$SB^1 =$	H^0	$-b_1$	$-b_2$	$-b_3$	$-b_4$		
	$SF^1_A =$	Q^1_A	$-f_1$	$-f_2$				
	$SF^1_B =$	Q^1_B			$-f_3$	$-f_4$		
	$SA^1 =$	$(H^0 - C^1)$	a_1	a_2	a_3	a_4	-1	-1
PERIOD 2	$SB^2 =$						1	1
	$SF^2_A =$	Q^2_A						
	$SF^2_B =$	Q^2_B						
	$SA^2 =$	$-C^2$					1	1
PERIOD 3	$SB^3 =$							
	$SF^3_A =$	Q^3_A						
	$SF^3_B =$	Q^3_B						
	$SA^3 =$	$-C^3$						
PERIOD 4	MAX! $S0 =$							
		$=$	$=$	$=$	$=$	$=$	$=$	$=$
		$-D0$	$-DX^1_{A1}$	$-DX^1_{A2}$	$-DX^1_{B1}$	$-DX^1_{B2}$	$-DH^1_A$	$-DH^1_B$
		MIN!						

Simplified One-Commodity Model

	XX²_A1	XX²_A2	XX²_B1	XX²_B2	XH²_A	XH²_B	XX³_A1	XX³_A2	XX³_B1	XX³_B2	XH³_A	XH³_B	DUAL VARIABLES
	*	*	*	*	*	*	*	*	*	*	*	*	
													* YR^1 — Stock (Rent)
													* YW^1_A ⎫ Factors (Wages)
													* YW^1_B ⎬ in Reg. A, B
													* YP^1 — Flow (Price)
		$-b_2$	$-b_3$	$-b_4$									* YR^2 — Stock (Rent)
		$-f_2$											* YW^2_A ⎫ Factors (Wages)
			$-f_3$	$-f_4$									* YW^2_B ⎬ in Reg. A, B
		a_2	a_3	a_4	-1	-1							* YP^2 — Flow (Price)
					1	1	$-b_1$	$-b_2$	$-b_3$	$-b_4$			* YR^3 — Stock (Rent)
							$-f_1$	$-f_2$					* YW^3_A ⎫ Factors (Wages)
									$-f_3$	$-f_4$			* YW^3_B ⎬ in Reg. A, B
					1	1	a_1	a_2	a_3	a_4	-1	-1	* YP^3 — Flow (Price)
							$(P^4_A+R^4_A)$		$(P^4_B+R^4_B)$				* $Y0$ (=1) — Term. Stock Value
	=	=	=	=	=	=	=	=	=	=	=	=	Shadow Prices ↑
	$-DX^2_{A1}$	$-DX^2_{A2}$	$-DX^2_{B1}$	$-DX^2_{B2}$	$-DH^2_A$	$-DH^2_B$	$-DX^3_{A1}$	$-DX^3_{A2}$	$-DX^3_{B1}$	$-DX^3_{B2}$	$-DH^3_A$	$-DH^3_B$	← Profits

PERIOD 2 — Production Stocks
PERIOD 3 — Production Stocks

while primary factor flows are distinguished between regions A and B, the single commodity is balanced jointly rather than separately for the two regions. This procedure is justified by the fact that transport costs on this commodity between the two regions are assumed to be zero. Thus the two separate regional balances of the commodity can be merged, and transport activities can be dropped entirely.

Stock levels are identified as separate activities, but in the present model they are not balanced separately for each of the two regions, since all stocks are liquidated at the end of each period and thus can be transferred from one region to another at will. Since the model always works with the sums of stock levels in the two regions in any period, these two activities could have been merged into a single one. The present form has been retained to call attention to the possibility of imposing stock decumulation limits in each region, in a manner analogous to the Rahman-Dorfman model.

The primary factors in the two regions need not be the same ones; in fact, the structure of the model indicates that any interregional comparison of the absolute levels of factor inputs that are immobile between regions is meaningless: For example, there is no operational significance to the comparison of land-area inputs into analogous activities in the two regions, since the qualities of land (soil, climate, topography, etc.) are inherently different and thus a pure area measure means nothing; a weighting by means of prices simply begs the question; and no referral to a common standard is possible since land is immobile. Thus the only meaningful question is the scarcity of any immobile factor relative to its own total supply. An interregional comparison and weighting emerges only *after* an optimal solution and its corresponding shadow prices are obtained.

The virtue of the model in its present form is that it yields an over-all optimum whenever period-to-period transitions are optimized. The reason for this is that there is only a single connecting link—the combined level of stocks in region A and B, without distinction as to its regional structure—between successive time periods. When more than one link is introduced—for example, when more than one commodity is included, or when the unitary nature of the single commodity between the two regions is destroyed by introducing nonzero transport costs—then period-to-period optimization can no longer automatically achieve an over-all optimum, and substitutions between activities involving separate time periods have to be considered in addition to the substitutions between contemporaneous activities that suffice for solving the simpler problem (see below).

The model of Table 2 lends itself to two kinds of analysis: An investigation of investment decisions in each time period, and a study of the growth properties of the chain of one-period solutions. It should be noted that the main points of difference between this model and the Rahman-Dorfman model consist in the following:

1. The explicit inclusion of regional factor constraints in the present model;

2. The omission, for the time being, of capital decumulation constraints in the individual regions. It is recalled that in the Rahman-Dorfman model in the absence of regional capital decumulation constraints the effect of terminal stock-weighting coefficients upon the optimal solution is restricted to the last time period, instead of spreading into preceding time periods. Thus the advantage given to regions with high reinvestment coefficients is exaggerated when capital decumulation constraints are absent. Consequently any conclusion tending to soften the strong polarization of regional investment decisions that is reached in the absence of decumulation constraints will necessarily be strengthened when the latter are reimposed.

3. The exogenous treatment of consumption. This feature of the model will be subject to alteration later.

ALLOCATIONS IN A SINGLE TIME PERIOD

A convenient way of analyzing the nature of regional investment decisions in a single period is to maximize the generation of reinvestible surplus at the end of the period, on the assumption that reinvestible surplus inherited from the preceding period is fixed at a succession of constant levels that show a systematic increase. A single-period optimizing model is shown in Table 3-A. For simplicity, only one activity per region is shown. Let this be the one with the better capital productivity, i.e., a higher ratio a_i/b_i for each region. We also assume that region A is the one with a better capital productivity, i.e., the most productive activity in region A has a higher a_i/b_i ratio than the most productive activity in B. The period shown in Table 3-A is the first period, but it could be any period t: The level of stock inherited from the previous period $t - 1$ is always regarded as constant. The maximand, $X\Pi^t$, is total final product defined as

$$X\Pi^t = SA^t + XH_A{}^t + XH_B{}^t - H_A{}^{t-1} - H_B{}^{t-1} + C^1 =$$
$$a_1 XX_{A1}{}^t + a_3 XX_{B1}{}^t$$

In other words, the variable surplus of the commodity in the flow balance of period t, SA^t which in any case has to be reduced to zero in an optimal multiperiod solution, is merged with the variable total stock formation, $XH_A{}^t + XH_B{}^t$, and with some constant terms that do not affect the optimal level of the variables. The constants include the inherited stock levels in the two regions (in Table 3-A, the sum of these for the zero period is simply denoted by H^0) and the level of consumption.

Table 3 summarizes what happens as the amount of capital (stock of the commodity) inherited from the previous period is increased from a very low level to progressively higher levels. In each small linear programing problem this amount of capital is treated as a parameter. In Table 3-A we find the indicated solution (which is identical with the original formulation of the problem and specifies that production in both regions is zero: The "nonbasic" variables which are being set to zero appear in the top margin following the unit-level exogenous vector), to be primal-feasible, i.e., the entries in the first column are nonnegative, but dual-infeasible, since the a_1 and a_3 entries in the last row indicate forbidden positive profits. The entire stock H^0 is now in surplus since there is no production; stock rent is zero; and both productive activities are shown to be profitable. Since we assume the capital stock to be very scarce, we will increase the level of production of that activity which gives the largest production a_i per unit of capital stock used, b_i, at the same time, we reduce the slack of capital to zero. This can be accomplished by choosing the coefficient indicated by an asterisk ($*$) as the pivot and doing a Gaussian elimination (see Appendix 2, Transformation Rules); this leads to Table 3-B.

This table can immediately be seen to be dual-feasible, since the last two entries in the bottom row are negative, as required; it is also primal-feasible as long as the relative scarcity of capital is such that the primary factor in region A is in surplus; i.e., H^0 does not exceed the amount of stock required for the full utilization of available factor supply in A, $b_1 Q_A{}^1 / f_1$. Under these assumptions, this is an optimal solution: The value of total final product is $H^0 a_1 / b_1$; the activity in region A is used at a level H^0 / b_1 and the production activity in the other region not at all; stock rent equals a_1 / b_1; and factor wages in both regions are zero.

If the amount of capital inherited from the previous period is increased the available factor supply in region A will eventually be exceeded. Under these conditions Table 3-B becomes primal-infeasible: $Q_A{}^1 - (f_1 H^0 / b_1)$ becomes negative, indicating that the factor in region A is a bottleneck resource and the indicated level of final product, $H^0 a_1 / b_1$, cannot be attained. At this point the scale of the productive activity in region A is limited by the factor supply in region A. If another production activity existed in region A it would now be necessary to test which of two alternative choices to follow: To economize on the scarce factor of region A by beginning to use a second activity in region A that is less factor-intensive and more capital-intensive, or to turn to the production activity in region B that does not use the scarce factor of region A at all. Since we have limited ourselves to one activity per region in the present model this choice does not arise: The only available alternative is to start using the production activity in region B. After pivoting on the element designated by an asterisk we arrive at Table 3-C which is again found to be dual-feasible; it is also primal-feasible provided that H^0 is above the lower limit $b_1Q_A^1/f_1$ which corresponds to the capital requirement for full utilization of factor A, but below the upper limit $(b_1Q_A^1/f_1) + (b_3Q_B^1/f_3)$ which corresponds to the capital requirement for the full utilization of both regional factors. If H^0 expands even further the primal feasibility is again violated and has to be restored by making factor B a scarce factor and making capital stock free; after the required pivot-step we get Table 3-D.

By comparison of Tables B, C, and D, each of which may be optimal depending on the relative magnitudes of the parameters, it can be seen that the optimal value of final product is always obtained in the form

$$\text{opt. } (X\Pi^1) = H^0 \cdot YR^1 + Q_A^1 \cdot YW_A^1 + Q_B^1 \cdot YW_B^1$$

with rents and wages taking the values shown in the table below.

Table	Rent	Wage A	Wage B
3-B	a_1/b_1	free	free
3-C	a_3/b_3	$\dfrac{b_3a_1 - a_3b_1}{f_1b_3}$	free
3-D	free	a_1/f_1	a_3/f_3

With the introduction of additional activities in each region the number of possible optimal configurations increases and the formulas become more involved, but the optimal value of final product continues as a linear expression in terms of inherited stock and factor supplies.

We can now relate these results to the Rahman-Dorfman model. To begin with, we can relax the assumption of prescribed constant consumption and define the latter as a constant fraction of final product. Formally, this amounts to redefining the maximand as the final product net of consumption:

$$\overline{X\Pi}^t \equiv a_1 \cdot XX_{A1}^t + a_3 \cdot XX_{B1}^t + C^t = a_1 \cdot XX_{A1}^t \cdot (1 - c) + a_3 \cdot$$
$$XX_{B1}^t \cdot (1 - c) = (a_1\sigma) \cdot XX_{A1}^t + (a_3\sigma) \cdot XX_{B1}^t$$

TABLE 3

SINGLE-PERIOD SOLUTIONS

TABLE 3-A

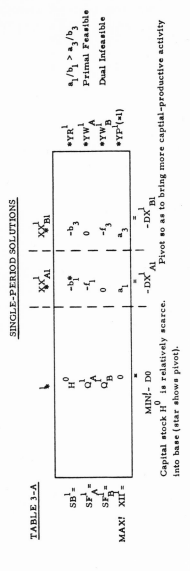

Capital stock H^0 is relatively scarce. Pivot so as to bring more capital-productive activity into base (star shows pivot).

$a_1/b_1 > a_3/b_3$
Primal Feasible
Dual Infeasible

TABLE 3-B

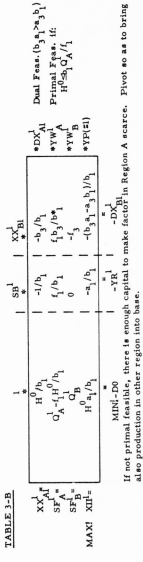

If not primal feasible, there is enough capital to make factor in Region A scarce. Pivot so as to bring also production in other region into base.

Dual Feas. $(b_3 a_1 > a_3 b_1)$
Primal Feas. if:
$H^0 \leq b_1 Q_A^1/f_1$

TABLE 3-C

	$1*$	SB^1*	SF^1_A*	
$XX^1_{A1} =$	Q^1_A/f_1	0	$-1/f_1$	$*DX^1_{A1}$
$XX^1_{B1} =$	$H^0/b_3-(b_1/b)(Q^1_A/f_1)$	$-1/b_3$	$b_1/f_1 b_3$	$*DX^1_{B1}$
$SF^1_B =$	$Q^1_B - f_3(H^0/b_3) - \dfrac{b_1}{b_3}\dfrac{Q^1_A}{f_1}$	f_3/b^*_3	$-f_3 b_1/f_1 b_3$	$*YW^1_B$
$MAX!\ XII^1 =$	$H^0 a_3/b_3 + Q^1_A \dfrac{b_3 a_1 - a_3 b_1}{f_1 b_3}$	$-a_3/b_3$	$\dfrac{-b_3 a_1 - a_3 b_1}{f_1 b_3}$	$*YP^1(=1)$
$MIN!-D0$		$= -YR^1$	$= -YW^1_A$	

Dual Feas. (as above)

Primal Feas. if:
$$b_1 Q^1_A/f_1 \le H^0 \le (b_1 Q^1_A/f_1 + b_3 Q^1_B/f_3)$$

If not primal feasible, there is enough capital to make factors of both regions scarce. Capital becomes free resource when pivoting on respective slacks.

TABLE 3-D

	$1*$	SF^1_B*	SF^1_A*	
$XX^1_A =$	Q^1_A/f_1	0	$-1/f_1$	$*DX^1_{A1}$
$XX^1_B =$	Q^1_B/f_3	$-1/f_3$	0	$*DX^1_{B1}$
$SB^1 =$	$H^0 - b_1 Q^1_A/f_1 - b_3 Q^1_B/f_3$	b_3/f_3	b_1/f_1	$*YR^1$
$MAX\ XII^1 =$	$Q^1_A a_1/f_1 + Q^1_B a_3/f_3$	$-a_3/f_3$	$-a_1/f_1$	$*YP^1(=1)$
$MIN!-D0$		$= -YW^1_B$	$= -YW^1_A$	

Dual Feas. (as above)

Primal Feas. if:
$$b_1 Q^1_A/f_1 + b_3 Q^1_B/f_3 \le H^0$$

where $\overline{X\Pi}^1$ is the redefined maximand, while c and σ are the consumption and savings ratios, respectively. It is clear that this change has no effect other than replacing the constant output coefficient of each activity by another constant obtained as a product of the former by the savings ratio; thus the entire analysis is formally unchanged; except for replacing a_i by $a_i' \equiv \sigma_i a_i$.

Next let us examine the conclusion based on the Rahman-Dorfman model that investment should be channeled (in the absence of decumulation constraints) to the region with the highest reinvestment ratio in all but the terminal period. The reinvestment ratio in each region is $\sigma_i(b_i/a_i) = \sigma_i a_i/b_i \equiv a_i'/b_i$. By reference to Table 3 the conclusion is correct as long as there is a surplus of primary factor in region A (and of course also in region B). We then have the situation corresponding to Table 3-B in which production takes place entirely in region A, yielding a stock rent of a_1'/b_1; thus all of the capital stock inherited from the previous time period has to be invested in region A. If investment were channeled instead into region B, stock rent would fall to a_3'/b_3, and activity 1 would show a positive profit, indicating that the solution was not dual-feasible. [These results follow from Table 3-B by symmetry between activities 1 and 3; the only difference is that an interchange of subscripts 1 and 3 will render $-(b_3 a_1 - a_3 b_1)$ positive.]

If, however, the parameters of the problem are such that the situation of Table 3-C is obtained, i.e., the primary factor in region A is in scarce supply, then investment can no longer be polarized into region A without incurring an inefficiency. Optimality requires a splitting of production (and investment) between A and B; if we insist on investing only in A, then the inherited capital cannot be fully utilized due to the shortage of factor A. Thus the criterion of polarizing investment into the region with highest reinvestible surplus breaks down. This is even more so for the case of Table 3-D, but the situation of a stock surplus has to be excluded in practice as unrealistic. In other words, regions with a less favorable reinvestment ratio obtain a share of total investment to the extent that the regions with more favorable reinvestment ratios run out of local primary factors.

This conclusion is further strengthened when we include additional activities in each region. When region A has a second activity with a less favorable capital productivity than the first, the polarization of investment toward region A would require that when the limit of factor-A supply is reached, the second activity should gradually begin replacing the first activity, in order to substitute the use of stock for the use of factor A. A detailed study of this case indicates that for the latter course to be optimal, it is required not only that the reinvestible surplus of the second activity a_2'/b_2 be higher than that of activity 3 in region B, but the more stringent condition

$$f_1(a_2'b_3 - a_3'b_2) \geqq f_2(a_1'b_3 - a_3'b_1)$$

also has to be satisfied.[10] When it is not, the application of the reinvestible-surplus criterion will result in a misallocation of resources even when the criterion is applied to the marginal investment decisions rather than to the entire investment.

INTERRELATIONS BETWEEN TIME PERIODS

What happens when the regional capital decumulation constraints of the Rahman-Dorfman model are reintroduced? In the former model these constraints have the effect of progressively reallocating investment, as the terminal period is approached, from regions with high reinvestment ratios to regions with high terminal stock valuation. These constraints, if included in the model of Table 2, will destroy the independence of period-by-period optimization from longer-term considerations, since they introduce additional links between time periods. Thus while in the case of a single link the Pareto-optimal frontier for each time period coincides with a single point (the optimal total stock carried forward into the next period), with decumulation constraints added there is a possibility of trading off terminal valuation benefits in a region against a lesser short-term capital generation. Finding an optimal time path then becomes a matter of solving the problem in the large.

The Rahman-Dorfman solution hinges on the application of elementary principles of dynamic programing to the above problem. Dorfman's solution is particularly simple: It consists in a recursive evaluation of the effects of investment in each time period upon the objective function. He determines investment in the last period by selecting the

---

[10] Lack of space prevents a detailed analysis of the more complete model. The criterion of choice in the text is closely related to the column selection criterion of the dual simplex algorithm. In a slightly modified form,

$$\frac{f_1}{b_3 \dfrac{a_1'}{a_3'} - b_1} \geqq \frac{f_2}{b_3 \dfrac{a_2'}{a_3'} - b_2},$$

it can be interpreted as follows. The denominators represent the amount of capital saved by activities 1 and 2, respectively, relative to activity 3. We prefer activity 2 over activity 3 when, per unit of the former saving, activity 2 is less factor-A intensive than activity 1.

region with the highest terminal stock valuation. Any investment in the previous period will have two effects: (1) It will contribute *directly* to the objective function by means of its own terminal valuation, which cannot be changed once it is committed since investment cannot be transferred to another region; and (2) it will also contribute *indirectly* to the objective function by generating reinvestible surplus that can be freely disposed of in the last period, at a payoff that has already been determined. Thus the summing of the known direct and indirect effects for each region will yield a linear expression of terminal payoff in terms of current investment variables; from among these, the best one can be selected. This, in turn, creates a known payoff for the indirect effects of investment one period further back, and so forth. In this fashion, the recursion runs all the way to the original time period and yields an optimal investment profile.

The feature of the Rahman-Dorfman model that allows the application of such a simple recursion is the fact that no matter how little or how much reinvestible surplus is carried forward from one time period into the next, the allocation decisions remain unaffected in all subsequent time periods. As long as this feature is preserved, the regional polarization of investment inherent in the structure of the model is not essential to the result. Thus if it were possible to guarantee in advance that factor A would be scarce and factor B would be in oversupply in all time periods (or even if it were possible to specify in advance any alternating sequence of patterns chosen from among those of Tables 3-B, 3-C, and 3-D, so that a given pattern could be guaranteed for a given time period in advance of the solution) the simple recursion could still be applied. If, however, the size of the reinvestible surplus carried forward affects the choice of an optimal allocation pattern—as is the general case with the model of Table 2 when decumulation constraints are imposed—the simplicity of the Dorfman solution is lost, and a systematic method of keeping track of the available alternatives is required. In any event the key feature of the Rahman-Dorfman solution is preserved: The effects of terminal valuation are carried backward into previous planning periods but become progressively weaker as the time span between a given period and the terminal period lengthens.

Returning now to the model of Table 2 with decumulation constraints excluded the next question concerns the dynamic behavior of this model over the planning period. This turns out to be a simple generalization of growth at compound interest once the rent and wages for each period have been determined by means of single-period optimizations.

Denoting the previously derived constant values of rent and wages in time period t by r^t, $W_A{}^t$, $W_B{}^t$, we obtain: [11]

$$XH^t = XH^0(1 + r^1) \cdots (1 + r^t) + (Q_A{}^1 \cdot W_A{}^1 + Q_B{}^1 \cdot W_B{}^1 -$$
$$C^1)(1 + r^2) \cdots (1 + r^t) + \cdots + (Q_A{}^{t-1} \cdot W_A{}^{t-1} + Q_B{}^{t-1} \cdot$$
$$W_B{}^{t-1} - C^{t-1})(1 + r^t) + (Q_A{}^t \cdot W_A{}^t + Q_B{}^t \cdot W_B{}^t - C^t)$$

On the dual side the flow price of the commodity is the numeraire for the price system in each period; interrelations between periods are created by the stock-holding activities which allow the referral of all prices to the numeraire of the model as a whole, associated with the terminal stock valuation row. If terminal stock valuations at time T in both regions are equal to unity, YP^{T-1} will equal unity, and the commodity flow prices will be:

$$YP^1 = (1 + r^2) \cdots (1 + r^{T-1}); YP^t = (1 + r^{t+1}) \cdots$$
$$(1 + r^{T-1})$$

For nonunitary terminal stock valuations, YP^{T-1} will be equal to the highest terminal stock valuation and all prices will be multiplied by this factor.

For the definition of an interest rate in current prices the value-standard good is the single commodity; if its current price is held constant for all periods, the interest rate in each period will coincide with the shadow rent of stock for that period. Growth of the initial stock at compound interest is then a special case that can arise when the a, b, and f

---

[11] The derivation is as follows:

$$XH_A{}^1 + XH_B{}^1 = XH^1 = XH^0 - C^1 + XH^0 \cdot r^1 + Q_A{}^1 \cdot W_A{}^1 + Q_B{}^1 \cdot W_B{}^1 =$$
$$XH^0(1 + r^1) + Q_A{}^1 \cdot W_A{}^1 + Q_B{}^1 \cdot W_B{}^1 - C^1$$

Likewise,

$$XH^2 = XH^1(1 + r^2) + Q_A{}^2 \cdot W^2 + Q_B{}^2 \cdot W_B{}^2 - C^2$$
$$= [XH^0(1 + r^1) + Q_A{}^1 \cdot W_A{}^1 + Q_B{}^1 \cdot W_B{}^1 - C^1](1 + r^2) + Q_A{}^2 \cdot W_A{}^2 +$$
$$Q_B{}^2 \cdot W_B{}^2 - C^2$$
$$= XH^0(1 + r^1)(1 + r^2) + (Q_A{}^1 \cdot W_A{}^1 + Q_B{}^1 \cdot W_B{}^1 - C^1)(1 + r^2) +$$
$$(Q_A{}^2 \cdot W_A{}^2 + Q_B{}^2 \cdot W_B{}^2 - C^2)$$

The generalization is immediate.

parameters are constant from period to period and consumption is exactly equal to the shadow wage bill in each period.[12]

In the general case, stock accumulation, i.e., system growth, depends both on the initial stock and on the time profile of consumption demands and factor supplies. In particular, factor supplies make a positive contribution to system growth. None the less, growth is faster when factor supplies are ample enough to leave a surplus and, accordingly, when wages are zero. The apparent contradiction between this statement and the structure of the accumulation formula can be reconciled by a detailed consideration of the transition between situations of unlimited and limited factor supply. By reference to Tables 3-B and 3-C, for example, consider what happens when $H^0 = b_1 Q_A^1 / f^1$, i.e., when the initial capital is exactly at the margin of exhausting the supply of factor A in period 1. Final product (the maximand) from Table 3-B is $H^0 a_1 / b_1$; the same expression can also be obtained from Table 3-C by substituting the value of Q_A^1 at the margin into the formula for the value of the maximand. This identical final product is, however, distributed between the factors of production in a different manner in the two cases. In Table 3-B it is imputed entirely to stock rent; in Table 3-C it is divided between rent and wages. If now, beginning at the marginal position which has been indicated above, we *reduce* the supply of factor A while leaving H^0 unchanged, final product will be reduced but unit rent and wages will remain constant. In sum, when a factor constraint becomes binding, the wage bill of the factor is taken out of total product, thereby reducing the unit rent and the rent bill; moreover, in all situations except at the margin, the total product itself also falls. Thus a factor shortage cuts into total rent in two ways: (1) It reduces the percentage share of total product imputed to rent, and (2) it reduces the size of total product. A corollary is that the share of final product imputed to a regional factor in any period may at times be increased by restricting the supply of this factor, but only at the expense of a drop in system product that is larger (except at the margin) than the increase in total imputation to the factor.

[12] This simple special case can be interpreted, if desired, as the outcome of an idealized perfectly competitive institutional situation with no savings out of wages and no consumption out of rents. It is recalled, however, that the term "wages" refers to the shadow flow prices of all primary factors that are not themselves produced by any activity, i.e., these factors include natural resources, land, etc., in regard to which the above institutional assumption becomes weak. It will be shown later that the interpretation can break down when more than one link between successive time periods (e.g., more than one commodity stock) is introduced.

An interesting property of the model is that it leaves the accumulation rate of the system as a whole unchanged at the margin while the interest rate undergoes a large discontinuous change. The reason for this is that savings are assumed to be independent of income distribution (at shadow prices) between rent and wages; this assumption holds regardless of whether consumption levels are prescribed exogenously or are determined as fixed proportions of final product in each region. Such an assumption can be realistic when savings decisions are arrived at by political methods and personal consumption is made independent of the shadow incomes imputed to factors, as can be done by the rationing of consumption or by the establishment of transfer payments that are superimposed on the shadow price system. Moreover, when the means of production are under community ownership, shadow rents are not directly related to the consumption or savings of any single group of individuals. The question of who controls the means of production of a given region as a whole can, however, remain open even under these conditions. Thus the issue of the regional distribution of income remains to be clarified.

MULTICOMMODITY GENERALIZATION POSSIBILITIES

Before proceeding to the above task it will be attempted to sketch out the generalization of these results from single-link models that can be optimized period by period to multiple-link models where such a procedure will not necessarily assure long-run optimality. If more than one commodity is present, then during each period a *weighted* combination of stocks, i.e., the capital wealth of this period evaluated at shadow flow prices, must be maximized. Given only the terminal stock weights, the proper shadow prices to be used for the maximization in a given period are not known in advance, thus proving *ex post* that a period-by-period optimization in fact attained within the over-all optimum solution is not the same thing as being able to produce the latter solution by means of a period-to-period optimization.[13] None

---

[13] On the relation between period-to-period optimums and efficient paths of capital accumulation over the long run, see Dorfman, Samuelson, and Solow (1958), Chap. 12. For the multicommodity case it remains true that with constant *a, b,* and *f* coefficients the system will grow at a compound rate of interest equal to the stock rent (in current prices) of the value-standard commodity whenever the total value of consumption equals the total wage bill. This case, however, can no longer always be interpreted as the outcome of perfect competition with no savings out of wages and no consumption out of rents. While it is true that in a multicommodity system perfect competition will assure that an efficient path of capital accumulation will be followed over any three successive periods and thus

the less, the properties of the single-period optimums can be analyzed on the assumption that constant weights exist for stocks at the end of each period; in addition, the long-term properties of the optimal solution can be studied by reference to von Neumann-type models, in search of regional "turnpike"-like theorems. The present discussion will be restricted entirely to the first type of analysis.

When transport costs are introduced into the single-commodity model of Table 2 with exogenously given consumption levels, they work against the concentration of production into a few regions, since a more dispersed production will reduce transport costs between sites of production and consumption. When consumptions are endogenously given as fractions of regional income including rent remissions, the same result will obtain. Moreover, in the presence of regional stock decumulation constraints transport costs will in all periods work in favor of regions with larger terminal stock weights over regions with a higher capital productivity, since the surplus of the latter will eventually have to be transferred at least in part to the former regions, at the expense of incurring transport costs.

When the number of commodities in the model is increased from one to several, the analysis indicates further tendencies toward the geographical dispersal of production:

1. Between different regions, the a and b coefficients and thus relative capital productivities can differ in different lines of production, with one region having a productivity advantage in one line, another region in another line. Under these conditions each region will tend to specialize in a given line of production. Thus for example, advanced countries differ in their specializations in regard to the products of high-level technology, thereby creating a basis for commodity interchange.

2. Between advanced and backward regions, however, the relations between a and b coefficients will tend to run parallel in most industries, as backward regions will tend to have generally poorer technology, i.e., poorer capital stock and intermediate-input coefficients. This will create an absolute disadvantage for backward regions in regard to these in-

over the entire long run—see the dynamic "invisible hand theorem," *ibid.*, p. 319— the perfect competitors are assumed to be aware, in addition to stocks inherited from the previous period and current prices, only of prices in the next period but not beyond. Thus when *terminal* stock valuations are prescribed, as in the models under discussion, the perfectly competitive mechanism assumed is not capable of selecting the required efficient path from among the many efficient paths that lead to different relative stock accumulations in the terminal period. On the other hand, if relative stock valuations are given either for the initial or for the following period, this will enable a perfectly competitive system to lock onto one efficient path and to trace it all the way through to its terminal implication.

puts: The disadvantage can be said to be "absolute," since the possibility of transporting commodities between regions allows a direct comparison of flow and stock inputs. An optimal program will therefore tend to channel investment into the regions that have better productivities with regard to stocks and intermediate-flow inputs, i.e., into the advanced regions.

Productive activities, however, also have inputs of immobile primary factors that are in limited supply in each region; these factor supplies in the more productive regions can be exhausted before all investment resources are fully utilized. At this point, as already indicated in the single-commodity case, two choices exist:

1. The scarce factors in the advanced region can be economized by means of substitution by commodity-stock or intermediate-flow inputs in the same region; i.e., there can be a progressive shift to activities in the same region that use less of the scarce primary factors and more of the stock and intermediate-commodity inputs.

2. The scarce factors in the advanced region can be economized by a shift to the activities of the backward regions that do not use the scarce primary factors of the advanced region at all. To be more precise, if labor is regarded as an immobile primary factor, both the activities in the advanced and the backward regions will use labor, but the backward regions will not use the labor of the advanced region.

A comparison of the two substitution possibilities above leads to the conclusion that the advanced regions will tend to shift to the backward regions those of their activities that are intensive users of the scarce primary factors in the advanced regions yet are not burdened with an excessive absolute disadvantage in the backward regions. This shift and with it the geographical dispersal of production and investment will be more pronounced to the extent that the pool of investible resources for the system as a whole is large in relation to the primary factor supplies of the advanced regions. Thus a larger over-all savings ratio will tend to disperse investments regionally even when the backward regions have an absolute disadvantage in all lines of production.

Preferences, Incentive Effects, and Autonomous Growth Trends

ALTERNATIVE PREFERENCE SYSTEMS

In the foregoing sections consumption was at times treated as exogenously given and at times tied to regional or over-all product by means of a constant savings ratio. The fact has, moreover, been pointed out that consumption and investment can under certain conditions be tied directly to factor shadow incomes by suitable institutional assumptions. The present section will be dedicated to a more systematic discussion of the underlying issues and to the sketching out of certain reformulations of the model that are possible once the customary assumptions are modified.

It is recalled from the section Interrelations Between Time Periods, above, that the general locational model can be regarded as a representation of the technological possibilities open to a society, with preference functions excluded from the model. If so interpreted the model can be used to trace out parametrically the Pareto-optimal production possibility hypersurface. Approximate representations of preference functions can then be adjoined to the former model, e.g., in the form of savings or commodity-by-commodity consumption ratios, in order to locate the relevant decision range. Once this range has been located in an approximate fashion the savings ratios or other approximate preference indicators can be dropped and the relevant range of the Pareto-optimal hypersurface can be explored in detail with a view to matching it with an implicit set of planning and policymaking preferences.

This interpretation rests on the postulate that there exists a single set of over-all planning preferences embracing all commodities, all regions, and all time periods. This set of preferences permits trading off *on the preference side* (independently of the production-possibility side) present against future consumptions, consumptions in one region against consumptions in another, consumptions of one commodity against consumptions of another, as well as any cross-combinations of the former. A match of the complete set of preference trade-offs against the complete set of production trade-offs results in the selection of the over-all grand optimum in a straightforward extension of standard neoclassical notions to a dynamic, multiregional, central planning situation. The only remaining task necessary to complete this picture is to treat primary factor supplies symmetrically with consumption, i.e., to unlock the respective parameters and to include them as variables both in the production and in the preference trade-offs.

This postulate implies an absolute centralization of planning decisions; this is, however, not the only possible way of adjoining preferences to the Pareto-optimal production-possibility surface. That other possibilities exist is indicated by the fact that in the former model there is no relationship between factor incomes at shadow prices and optimal consumption levels except at the level of the system as a whole; in other words both the amounts of commodities consumed and the amounts of primary factors supplied by region and by time period are determined solely by central preferences and over-all scarcities.

The opposite extreme is a complete decentralization of decisions on the basis of the shadow price system. Adjoin to the former model a number of individuals and distribute among these individuals claims to the shadow incomes generated by all primary factors and all *initial* stocks. Define the income of an individual in a time period as the sum of the former claims plus new claims generated by stock accumulation, where claims to newly accumulated stocks in each period are distributed in proportion to savings provided by individuals for investment purposes in the same period. As long as there is only one commodity in the model the meaning both of savings and of stock rents is unambiguous. Then in each time period each individual makes a consumption-savings decision subject to the constraint on his total income for the period as defined above; this decision is based on the matching of his income constraint against his time preference between present and next-period consumption. If we are now willing to make the assumption that period-to-period time preferences are independent of consumption possibilities in later periods (i.e., if we are willing to assume a more restricted set of time preferences than in the central decision model) then it is possible to decentralize both with regard to individual time preferences and with regard to production decisions (e.g., by an institutional assumption of perfect competition) since period-by-period optimization of production will guarantee a long-run Pareto-optimum (as discussed in the preceding section) while period-by-period optimization will likewise guarantee (by the above assumption) a long-run optimum with regard to the structure of preferences. If we are not willing to assume this much with regard to the independence of period-to-period time preferences then decentralization on the side of individual preferences is possible only if the latter can be matched against a Pareto-optimal production possibility hypersurface linking all time periods that is generated by central planning computations.[14] In other words the function of planning in the latter context is reduced to the generation and display of a complete representation of the technological possibilities confronting society over time while leaving perfect autonomy of decision to each individual.

When there is more than one commodity it is necessary to make one

[14] The reason for this is that present consumptions cannot be taken as determined unless future consumption possibilities are already known. Only central planning computations are able to generate and display such consumption possibilities extending into the long-run future.

further adjustment in the analysis on the side of preferences. Single-commodity income, consumption, savings, and investment now give way to aggregate concepts weighted by shadow prices. The income constraint of each period can always be replaced by an equivalent wealth constraint in shadow prices linking two successive periods (see Appendix 3 for the derivation of such period-to-period balances for wealth):

$$(P^{t+1} + R^{t+1})H^t = (P^t + R^t)H^{t-1} + W^t Q^t - P^t C^t$$

next-period wealth   present-period wealth   present-period factor income   present-period consumption

Since the consumption of the next period will be taken out of the next period's wealth there is now a trade-off between more consumption in this period and less consumption during the next period; moreover, there is a trade-off between different kinds of consumption during both periods. On the consumption side these trade-offs require knowledge of the same relative commodity valuations that are required on the production side for the determination of the structure of stocks that are accumulated. Decentralization with regard to individual preferences and with regard to production decisions is therefore equally dependent on the availability of these valuations at the time the consumption or production decisions are taken. If we extend the previously mentioned dynamic "invisible hand" theorem to variable consumption and assume that the system is already on an efficient time path of capital accumulation under perfect competition, the theorem will guarantee that the system will stay locked on a single path, but it offers no explanation of how this path came to be selected from among infinitely many possible efficient time paths. We are thus forced to accept one of three possible interpretations:

1. The efficient path has been chosen at random, but this does not matter since all preferences are satisfied at all times; thus even though the system drifts blindly toward a terminal condition the exact nature of this terminal condition is a matter of indifference.

2. The terminal condition is *not* a matter of indifference to individuals; therefore, contrary to assumption, their period-to-period time preferences are not independent over the long run. In this case, we arrive at the same conclusion of having to match individual preference against a Pareto-optimal production-possibility hypersurface generated by central planning computations that we already encountered in the one-commodity case.

3. The terminal condition does not enter individual preferences but is a matter of *social* concern. In this case we have to select a given efficient time path that will lead to the prescribed terminal condition, i.e., the system has to be switched from its historic path to another path at the beginning of the planning period, and the shadow prices corresponding to this path have to be given initially in order to lock the system onto the new path. The required shadow prices, however, can be computed even by central planning methods only if the preference functions of all individuals in all periods are known in advance.

Interpretation 2 appears perhaps somewhat less unrealistic than the others, but it has to be admitted that this entire analysis based on a deterministic view of the future is highly unsatisfactory. Savings-investment decisions inherently have a probabilistic element that is inescapable even in these highly formalized models as soon as we get to the terminal period, since terminal stock valuations are proxies for post-terminal consumption possibilities that extend into the future in an infinite regress. Therefore, unless we wish to follow the road of determinism to its bitter end with the formulation of infinite-period models with finite preference levels, we have to face up to the broader implications of indeterminacy. This task, however, falls entirely outside the limits of the present paper.

In addition to the interesting match between a representation of production possibilities over time that are generated by central planning and perfectly decentralized individual decisions, the above analysis also demonstrates the indifference of the individual to the physical nature of the stocks to which he has a claim, thus naturally leading to the notion of capital in the abstract, without reference to any particular collection of stocks. This can be seen as follows: A change in the consumption of any good can be traded off against the formation of any stock of equal shadow value, $P^t H^t$, in the same period; no matter what the nature of this stock is, the zero-profit condition on all actually utilized stock-holding activities guarantees that wealth in the next period at shadow prices will exactly equal the shadow value of the stock in this period:

$$(P^{t+1} + R^{t+1})H^t = P^t H^t$$

Thus while the structure of stocks is of paramount importance to the system as a whole it is of no importance to the individual as long as his claims are small in relation to total stock holdings in the system, since under equilibrium the period-to-period payoffs are equalized on all stocks. We can therefore conceive of a decentralized system that operates as follows: All savings decisions (as well as decisions pertaining to the structure of consumption and factor supply) are arrived at in a completely decentralized fashion; all savings are pooled and invested under central management; [15] central planning computations determine and display the entire production-possibility surface in such a manner that individuals can adjust their preferences to a known set of present and future production possibilities. For the system to be determinate rather than taking on the nature of a strategic game the preference functions of individuals have to be independent of changes in the production-possibility surface and the preferences of other individuals, as required by neoclassical theory.

An intermediate stage between complete centralization and complete decentralization of decisions is also possible, namely, decentralization to the regional level. In this case regional incomes and wealth are defined as indicated in the section Interrelations Between Time Periods, above, and Appendix 3, except that an export surplus of given shadow value in any period is treated as a capital export, giving rise to a corresponding claim to the wealth of an import-surplus region in the following period. Unless the doubly unrealistic assumption of a single commodity and no transport costs is insisted upon, the Pareto-optimal production-possibility surface will now, for the reasons discussed above, have to be generated by central planning. Regional decentralization of decisions with regard to consumption, savings, and factor supply can, however, be accomplished as before, with regions taking on the role of individuals in the former analysis. In particular, an important result that carries over from individual to regional decisions under this model is the pooling of savings: Under the assumptions of this model these are always distributed between the regions merely on the basis of capital productivity and factor limitation criteria regardless of their regional origin. It can be demonstrated with the aid of the single-commodity model discussed in the previous section that a region that insisted on investing its savings locally when this was contrary to over-all investment criteria would reduce its own accumulation of wealth, since this wealth is composed indifferently of stocks invested at home and abroad. An important difference from full decentralization, however, is the following. The independence of preference functions from

---

[15] After a long-run solution has been obtained by central planning computations, the execution of production decisions is in theory compatible with an institutional arrangement of perfect competition once the system has been locked onto the desired efficient path of capital accumulation by means of planned and administered first- or second-period shadow prices.

production possibilities can be taken as far less assured in the case of regions than in the case of individuals, because regions often represent a sufficiently large fraction of the supply or demand of a resource to affect noticeably the outcome of the optimal solution following autonomous changes in the corresponding regional supply or demand behavior. Thus restricting the supply of a regional factor can under suitable conditions capture a larger wage bill for this factor than would otherwise be possible, but only at the cost of a generally larger than compensating drop in system income, as discussed in the previous section. Assuming, for example, that the entire capital stock of the region in question was under claim by other regions, this would unequivocally increase regional income.

The above three ways of adjoining preference functions to the Pareto-optimal production-possibility surface are mutually exclusive, since each covers the entire range of available choices and it is known that in general there exists no way of synthesizing composite preference functions from individual ones.[16] There appears to be no reason, however, why different levels of preference functions could not govern different domains of social decision provided only that they either operate in nonoverlapping decision ranges or that they are subject to rules of precedence in case of conflict.

This whole area requires much further study. It is nonetheless clear that the levels at which decisions are exercised imply definite consequences with regard to the structure of incentives. Full decentralization of the decision process creates economic incentives for individual effort and for the supply of individual savings by tying changes in the income and wealth of individuals directly to the shadow prices of their factor supplies and the rent on their capital. Full centralization breaks such links almost completely except for an over-all social constraint imposed on all individuals collectively. Intermediate stages of decentralization can evidently operate effectively by defining the disposable incomes of individuals by means of suitable transfers that are determined on the basis of social preferences. In social systems where the means of production are in public ownership, the link between shadow rents and individual incomes can be completely broken without thereby necessarily eliminating economic incentives for individual effort; in this case, however, savings-investment decisions have to be controlled through political channels. As a general proposition, to the extent that areas of economic decision are exempted from the operation of individual prefer-

---

[16] See Arrow (1951).

ences they have to be subjected to higher-level preferences, to be determined by political processes that have to be different from the logically prohibited synthesis of composite preference functions.

While the abstract structure of preference is a useful analytical tool for the exploration of issues pertaining to decentralization and to multi-level decisions, it is recalled that preference functions are regarded as empirically all but useless. Therefore, wherever fully decentralized market decisions by individuals are excluded, a realistic planning strategy has to replace them by a two-step process: (1) The relevant decision range is approximately located by means of functional relationships that act as *proxies* for the preference functions, i.e., savings ratios, consumption ratios, supply and demand relationships; and (2) within the relevant decision range, the Pareto-optimal production-possibility surface is explored in detail for the purpose of applying an *implicit* set of planning-policymaking preferences to the alternatives so disclosed. The savings relationships built into the previously discussed Rahman-Dorfman model will now be inspected from this perspective and particularly the issues concerning the structure of incentives will be analyzed in more detail.

The Rahman-Dorfman model makes the assumption that savings are transferred between regions without setting up corresponding claims to future incomes; in other words the surpluses of a region are centrally appropriated without compensation except for such future development as might be channeled toward the region itself as a result of a preferred terminal weighting. The savings ratio in each region is assumed to be a constant fraction of current income. These assumptions imply, first of all, a set of central planning preferences for the system as a whole that subordinate the path of development in each region to the objective of maximal terminal stock accumulation; the development of individual regions is considered as an end in itself only as a terminal condition realized by the assignment of regional weights to terminal stocks. In terms of the behavior of the model that has been previously discussed this amounts to a preference for growth in the short run no matter how this growth is distributed between the regions, tempered only by the objective of arriving in the long run at a regional distribution that is considered equitable. Secondly, the constancy of regional savings coefficients independently of direct immediate benefits to a region resulting from this saving implies either that central preferences are imposed on a region, overriding the preference structure of the latter, or that the interregional political consensus assigns great weight to maximal short-run growth subject to an equitable long-run distribution of benefits.

The contrary assumption with regard to preferences in the context of the Rahman-Dorfman model would be to postulate that regional savings give rise to corresponding claims against future income. This amounts to a decentralization of the savings decisions to the level of the regions. Savings are now no longer exacted by central coercion or contributed under an interregional political consensus but are motivated by the returns that accrue to the region as a result of these savings. Since under this assumption savings generate income for a region no matter in what geographical location they are invested, there is now no longer any reason to prefer investment in regions with high savings rates even though their capital-output ratios might be unfavorable. The regional distribution of investments thus becomes independent of the regional saving rates and is determined by the interaction of the capital-output ratios with terminal weightings; if the latter are equal, the capital-output ratio becomes the sole criterion of regional investment.[17]

The above two versions of the structure of preferences of the Rahman-Dorfman model can be generalized to multifactor, multicommodity models by the techniques already discussed in previous sections, without materially affecting the conclusions except for substantially relaxing the extreme concentration of investments into a single region that is a consequence of operating with a single constraint in every period. A more interesting generalization from the point of view of preferences, incentives, and growth possibilities can be obtained by relaxing the assumption concerning the constancy of saving rates.

SOME REFORMULATIONS

What happens when savings rates in the regions are made variable in response to central investment decisions?

In terms of preferences such a situation can be interpreted as the interaction of two preference systems: the central supraregional preference system and the decentralized regional preference system.

[17] A question can be raised concerning the legitimacy of maintaining terminal weightings in a model where the savings decisions are decentralized to the level of the regions. In a multicommodity model terminal weights assigned to stocks that differ by commodity and by region are required for the representation of posthorizon growth possibilities; thus the terminal stock weights can be regarded as genuine indicators of the intrinsic worth of the stocks to any individual or region that may have a claim on them. In a model aggregated by commodities, such as the Rahman-Dorfman model, the same interpretation can be put on terminal weights if they represent solely future productivities rather than central preferences with regard to long-run regional development.

Assume a central decision-making process such as is postulated in the first version of the Rahman-Dorfman model, i.e., regional savings are appropriated by the central decision-making authority without crediting the region with claims against future income. Savings are now, however, no longer assumed to be a constant fraction of current regional income but are determined in response to an autonomous preference structure operating within each region. In making the central investment allocations the supraregional authority therefore has to take into account the reactions of the regions to these central allocation decisions.

This simple change in the formulation of the model has far-reaching implications since it opens the door to the inclusion of a new set of behavioral relations into regional resource allocation models, with important consequences for the issue of regionally balanced versus unbalanced growth.

Tables 4, 5, and 6 are simple illustrations of the changes in behavior that can be introduced into the Rahman-Dorfman model by allowing regional savings to respond in a specific manner to central allocation decisions or to exhibit an autonomous behavior trend of their own.

Table 4 shows the basic model with constant savings ratios. This model will serve as a standard of comparison for two alternate reformulations presented in Tables 5 and 6. There are two regions, A and B, with constant savings ratios of 20 per cent in either; the regions differ only in regard to their capital-output ratios, which are taken to be 4 and 3, respectively, in all periods. If terminal stock weightings are assumed to be equal in both regions then the maximization of either terminal income or terminal wealth for the two regions requires the transfer of all savings from A to B. In the tables, only incomes are shown; the increase of capital in each region or in the two regions jointly can be obtained by adding successive investments. In Table 4 the time profiles of incomes, savings, and investments are derived for the two regions for five successive periods on the assumption that the savings transferred from A to B equal none, half, or all of the savings in A. In accordance with the previous analysis the highest income growth is obtained when all of A's savings are transferred to B.

In Table 5 the assumption of constant savings ratios is replaced by the assumption that savings in a region in each time period will equal the investments *in the region itself* during the preceding time period. This assumption introduces incentive effects of savings in each region that require a special interpretation.

This interpretation rests on the assumption that savings decisions in each region are arrived at by a process of planning that takes into account so far unquantified effects and is responsive to popular pressures. It is assumed that people in general expect the payoff to sacrifices of present consumption to take the form of development within the region itself. While some awareness of systemwide benefits that accrue to savings channeled to other regions need not be ruled out, it is nevertheless highly reasonable to postulate an asymmetry in the popular recognition of benefits that are near and tangible and reflect themselves in visible material progress within the region, as against benefits that are far off and that have to be accepted on the verbal assurances of political leaders. This interpretation can thus be regarded as in a sense intermediate between the two savings assumptions discussed earlier.

One extreme assumption, it is recalled, was the independence of savings decisions from the regional location of investments. For the latter assumption to have any claim to a degree of realism we have to postulate one of several alternatives.

1. Savings may originate with individuals, who deposit them in a banking system that is under central control and allocates investments purely on the basis of interregional efficiency criteria. In practice, however, a banking system will often show a local bias in investments due to problems of communications and control.

2. Savings may originate in capitalist enterprises: These could in theory exhibit a genuine indifference between the location of reinvestments, but in practice most enterprises, especially the smaller ones, have a strong bias toward local reinvestment due to the problems of cultural differences, communications, and control that often have to be overcome when investing in other regions.

3. Savings may originate with regional government. Now even if the institutional possibility existed of investing these savings in other regions and obtaining corresponding benefits in future time periods in the form of interest receipts from these other regions, the assumption of a systematic long-term trend for the government of a region to accumulate savings and lend them out on interest to other regions is far-fetched indeed.

4. Savings might be accumulated in a region by means of an over-all planning and decision-making system within the region that goes beyond the ordinary housekeeping operations of government. Now while the models analyzed earlier indicate that the highest payoff on such savings could be obtained if these were invested purely on the basis of the interregional efficiency criteria that follow from these models, in practice there are a number of considerations that create a bias even in this case toward local as against extraregional development investments.

TABLE 4   Interregional Growth Model 1

Constant Savings Ratios, A: 20%, B: 20%

Constant Cap/Output Ratios, A: 4, B: 3

Total	Income		Savings Ratio		Savings		Investment		Investment Ratio		Income Change	
ΣY	A YA	B YB	A SRA	B SRB	A SA	B SB	A IA	B IB	A IRA	B IRB	A ΔYA	B ΔYB
No Transfers: IB(t) = SB(t)												
0 200	100	100	20	20	20	20					5	6.667
1 211.667	105.000	106.667	20	20	21.000	21.333	SA = IA	SB = IB	Not	Required	5.250	7.104
2 224.021	110.250	113.771	20	20	22.050	22.754					5.513	7.577
3 237.111	115.763	121.348	20	20	23.153	24.270					5.788	8.082
4 250.981	121.551	129.430	20	20	24.310	25.886					6.078	8.620
5 265.679	127.629	138.050	20	20								

Transfer ½A → B: $IB(t) = SB(t) + \frac{1}{2}SA(t)$

t											
0	200	100	100	20	20	20	20	10	30	2.500	9.990
1	212.490	102.500	109.990	20	20	20.5	21.998	10.250	32.248	2.563	10.739
2	225.792	105.063	120.729	20	20	21.013	24.146	10.507	34.653	2.627	11.539
3	239.958	107.690	132.268	20	20	21.538	26.454	10.769	37.223	2.692	12.395
4	255.045	110.382	144.663	20	20	22.076	28.933	11.038	39.971	2.760	13.310
5	271.115	113.142	157.973	20	20						

(annotation between columns: "Not Required")

Transfer All A → B: $IB(t) = SB(t) + SA(t)$

t											
0	200	100	100	20	20	20	20	0	40	0	13.320
1	213.320	100	113.320	20	20	20	22.664	0	42.664	0	14.207
2	227.527	100	127.527	20	20	20	25.505	0	45.505	0	15.153
3	242.680	100	142.680	20	20	20	28.536	0	48.536	0	16.162
4	258.842	100	158.842	20	20	20	31.768	0	51.768	0	17.239
5	276.081	100	176.081	20	20	20					

(annotation between columns: "Not Required")

TABLE 5 Interregional Growth Model 2

SYMMETRICAL INCENTIVE EFFECTS ON SAVINGS

SR(t) = IR(t - 1) in Both $\underline{A}$ and $\underline{B}$

Constant Cap/Output Ratios, A: 4, B: 3

	Income		Savings Ratio		Savings		Investment		Investment Ratio		Income Change	
Total ΣY	A YA	B YB	A SRA	B SRB	A SA	B SB	A IA	B IB	A IRA	B IRB	A ΔYA	B ΔYB
A. - No Transfers: IB(t) = SB(t)												
0 200.000	100	100	20	20	20	20	SA = IA	SB = IB	20	20	5	6.667
1 211.667	105	106.667	20	20	21.000	21.333			20	20	5.250	7.104
2 224.021	110.250	113.771	20	20	22.050	22.754			20	20	5.513	7.577
3 237.111	115.763	121.348	20	20	23.153	24.270			20	20	5.788	8.082
4 250.981	121.551	129.430	20	20	24.310	25.886			20	20	6.078	8.620
5 265.679	127.629	138.050	20	20								

B. – Transfer $\frac{1}{2}$ A → B: $IB(t) = SB(t) + \frac{1}{2} SA(t)$

t				20	30	20	30	10	30		
0	200.000	100	100								
1	212.490	102.500	109.990	10.250	34.660	32.997	38.122	5.125	5.000	2.500	9.990
2	226.466	103.781	122.685	5.189	36.775	42.523	45.118	2.595	2.500	1.281	12.695
3	242.139	104.430	137.709	2.611	37.723	50.642	51.948	1.306	1.251	0.649	15.024
4	259.765	104.757	155.008	1.311	38.146	58.474	59.130	.656	0.626	0.327	17.299
5	279.619	104.921	174.698	.						0.164	19.690

C. – Transfer All A → B: $IB(t) = SB(t) + SA(t)$

t				20	20	0	40	0	40	0	
0	200	100	100	20	20	0	40	0	40	0	0
1	213.320	100	113.320	0	45.328	0	40	0	40	0	13.320
2	228.414	100	128.414	0	51.366	0	40	0	40	0	15.094
3	245.519	100	145.519	0	58.208	0	40	0	40	0	17.105
4	264.902	100	164.902	0	65.961	0	40	0	40	0	19.383
5	286.867	100	186.267	0		0	40	0	40	0	21.965

Functional Issues

TABLE 6   Interregional Growth Model 3

AUTONOMOUS GROWTH OF SAVINGS RATIO

TOGETHER WITH INCENTIVE EFFECTS ON SAVINGS

SR(t) = Min (SR(t - 1) + 2,   IR(t - 1) + 2,   30)   in Both A and B

Constant Cap/Output Ratios,   A: 4,   B: 3

Total	Income		Savings Ratio		Savings		Investment		Investment Ratio		Income Change	
ΣY	A YA	B YB	A SRA	B SRB	A SA	B SB	A IA	B IB	A IRA	B IRB	A ΔYA	B ΔYB
A - No Transfers: IB(t) = SB(t)												
0 200.000	100	100	20	20	20	20	20	20	20	20	5	6.667
1 211.667	105.000	106.667	22	22	23.100	23.467	23.100	23.467	22	22	5.775	7.815
2 225.257	110.775	114.482	24	24	26.586	27.476	26.586	27.476	24	24	6.647	9.150
3 241.054	117.422	123.632	26	26	30.530	32.144	30.530	32.144	26	26	7.633	10.704
4 259.391	125.055	134.336	28	28	35.015	37.614	35.015	37.614	28	28	8.754	12.525
5 280.670	133.809	146.861	30	30								

B - Transfer ½ A → B: IB(t) = SB(t) + ½ SA(t)

0	200	100	100	20	20	20	20	10	30	10	30	2.500	9.990
1	212.490	102.500	109.990	12	22	12.300	24.198	6.150	30.348	6.000	27.592	1.538	10.106
2	224.134	104.038	120.096	8	24	8.323	28.823	4.162	32.985	4.000	27.466	1.041	10.984
3	236.159	105.079	131.080	6	26	6.305	34.081	3.153	37.234	3.000	28.406	.788	12.399
4	249.346	105.867	143.479	5	28	5.293	40.174	2.647	42.821	2.500	29.845	.662	14.259
5	264.267	106.529	157.738	2.5	30								

C - Transfer All A → B: IB(t) = SB(t) + SA(t)

0	200.000	100	100	20	20	20	20	0	40	0	40	0	13.320
1	213.320	100	113.320	2	22	2	24.930	0	26.930	0	23.765	0	8.968
2	222.288	100	122.288	2	24	2	29.349	0	31.349	0	25.635	0	10.439
3	232.727	100	132.727	2	26	2	34.509	0	36.509	0	27.507	0	12.157
4	244.884	100	144.884	2	28	2	40.568	0	42.568	0	29.381	0	14.175
5	259.059	100	159.059	2	30								

There is the factor of *risk* that is not absent even in the most highly co-ordinated interregional planning system: Development investments within the region itself cannot be readily removed, but the claims to the proceeds of extraregional investments might have to be surrendered in the face of some systemwide or extraregional emergency. There is also the question of *indirect benefits due to local production activities* that are not quantified within the models so far discussed. Even a high level of consumption does not necessarily create a condition of economic development, since the latter is a cultural phenomenon that depends on the simultaneous presence of many factors, among them a highly organized and well-functioning production apparatus that is capable of generating its own supply of human skills and technological advances.

In sum under almost any kind of institutional assumption it is realistic to postulate a strong bias toward internal as against external investments of regional savings.

The other extreme assumption was that of constant regional savings ratios in the face of supraregional planning decisions that channel these savings to other regions. In practice a greater or lesser loss of motivation toward savings in a region is likely to result whenever these savings are removed from the region. Bank deposits by individuals are probably the least sensitive to this factor, but in the less developed regions these are likely to be small. Surplus captured in a systematic way by the central government in the form of income or turnover taxes, etc., may not be strongly affected in the short run by the regional allocation of this surplus, but the required impositions will meet greater political and administrative (tax evasion) resistance if they are popularly resented as a form of draining off resources from the region in question. The reinvestment of the profits of capitalist enterprises under central planning direction may be bitterly resisted if the enterprises are small and backward. If they are large and rational and if a good basis for cooperation exists between these enterprises and the central planning authorities—a quite realistic assumption for certain European countries or Japan—a favorable basis might exist for escaping from the consequences of the extraregional diversion of savings. To the extent, nevertheless, that regional planning organizations exist that have an influence upon planned savings decisions within the region and that are subject to the considerations mentioned in the previous paragraph, they will again tend to create a negative force in regard to savings if the latter are channeled outside the region. In sum it is reasonable to postulate that whenever savings are channeled outside a region, a negative force will be exerted on these savings. The assumption that regional savings will be limited to the amount of regional investment in the previous period is perhaps an excessively strong representation of this negative force, but it is considered as an acceptable first approximation for the purposes of defining a simple illustrative model.

While the regional savings-investment relationship postulated above may have large components that represent private rather than planned savings, *the role of planning in this postulated relationship is crucial,* since it is indispensable for assuring that there will always exist regional investment opportunities corresponding to regional savings. The relationship is thus assumed to operate in a general atmosphere of capital shortage characterizing accelerated economic development rather than in an atmosphere of effective demand limited by profitable investment opportunities. Thus while under limited effective demand *ex ante* savings schedules are often not filled because of the scarcity of investment opportunities, under the postulated relationship *ex ante* savings schedules for a region as a whole can always be automatically adjusted upward or downward to regional investment allocations. Such an adjustment presupposes a considerable degree of planning.

One might suppose that the incentive effects with regard to regional savings that have been discussed above would lead to a more uniform distribution of interregional investment allocations, since the benefits of channeling savings from regions with lower to those of higher productivities would be counteracted by a drop in the savings rate in the regions whose savings are removed. A comparison of Table 4 with Table 5 embodying the indicated incentive effects shows, however, that just the opposite is the case: The transfer of savings from A to B results in faster over-all system growth in the presence of incentive effects than in their absence. A little reflection will reveal why this should be so. Since incentive effects are symmetrical between regions the loss to the system due to the lowering of A's savings rate is more than offset by the gain due to the *raising* of B's savings rate, which operates on a more favorable capital-output ratio.

Incentive effects can lead to an equalization of regional development only when they are asymmetrical between the regions that participate in capital transfers. The question now arises: Are incentive effects likely to be symmetrical between regions and, if not, under what conditions can asymmetrical incentive effects be expected to occur?

An asymmetrical incentive relationship for savings that may be highly realistic under the conditions characterizing economic development in many parts of the world is obtained when the former savings-investment relationship is supplemented by an autonomous growth trend of the savings rate up to a fixed practical limit. This autonomous growth trend is postulated as the *outcome of conscious planning efforts* in the face of the usual difficulties and resistances encountered in underdeveloped countries that make it practically impossible to introduce abrupt upward changes in the savings rate without excessive political cost. The specific form of the relationship adopted for illustrative purposes is a period-by-period autonomous rise of 2 percentage points up to a limiting rate of 30 per cent.[18] This autonomous trend holds only while no savings are drained off to other regions. If the latter loss of savings occurs, however, the previous disincentive relationship takes over: The savings rate (SR) drops to the investment rate (IR) and thereafter continues its gradual rise from this low point. Such a relationship can be expressed by the equation

$$SR\,(1) = \text{Min}\,[SR(t-1) + 2, IR(t-1) + 2, 30],$$

where the savings rate of a region is expressed as the smallest of three quantities: the autonomous growth trend starting from the savings rate of the previous period, the autonomous growth trend starting from the investment rate of the previous period, and the limiting savings rate. Table 6 shows the development of the two regions as well as of the system as a whole under these conditions, with the usual assumptions of transferring none, half, or all of the savings of A to B.

The case where no savings are transferred from the less productive to the more productive region is now clearly superior to either of the two alternative transfer patterns. Thus whenever it is realistic to postulate the presence of strong asymmetric incentive effects of this kind, the usual conclusions with regard to the advantage of concentrating investment in the more productive regions have to be replaced by a strategy of permitting each region to develop on the basis of its own self-generated capital resources.

Whether the illustrative case of Table 6 can be taken as representative of the relationship of advanced to backward regions in general is open to some question, since less developed areas at times exhibit favorable capital-output ratios.[19] The illustrative case also shows an unrealistically large sudden increase in the investment ratio in region B that is surely inconsistent with the absorptive capacity for investment that might reasonably be expected to exist in almost any region. The purpose of

[18] Both of these magnitudes are chosen for illustrative purposes only without a claim to the representation of realistic orders of magnitude for particular instances.

[19] In Tables 4–7, the *backward* region has been assumed to have the *less favorable* marginal capital-output ratio in order to explore the possibilities of growth (and perhaps eventual income) equalization under the most difficult conditions. To the extent that the reverse is the case, the task is considerably easier.

the illustration is to demonstrate the kind of asymmetry that is required in order to reverse the usual conclusions with regard to the concentration of investment in productive regions, rather than to furnish a realistic representation of all the limiting factors involved in decisions concerning the transfer of savings from one region to another.[20]

The autonomous growth mechanism of the savings rate that has been postulated as one feature of the asymmetrical savings-investment relationship is not only a powerful disincentive to interregional transfers but also a most effective motor of economic development in the backward regions once certain constraints that hold back the development of these regions are eliminated. If the backward region is, for example, held back by its inability to convert savings into investment due to the inadequate growth of its traditional exports on the one hand and scale limitations on the domestic production of investment goods on the other, then the advanced region can easily help to break this constraint and set into motion a self-accelerating process of growth in the backward region by simply *planning* to draw upon the backward region as a source of supply of certain commodities in addition to traditional exports, thereby enabling the backward region to buy more investment goods. This requires no capital transfer of any kind whatsoever from the advanced to the backward region, but of course it presupposes an institutional environment of active planning efforts in the backward region as well as both the ability and intention on the part of the advanced region to include the development problems of the backward region within the compass of its own planning processes. Table 7 furnishes a simple numerical illustration of this kind of assistance to the backward region that will be recognized as an example of the "trade-not-aid" approach to international development problems. Under the latter arrangement the growth rate of the backward region, previously limited to approximately 3 per cent per annum, rapidly rises toward an eventual 7.5 per cent per annum.[21]

[20] For the purpose of this illustration the autonomous advance of the savings rate was taken to be determined solely by the difficulties of appropriating the surplus of the backward region rather than by limitations on the absorptive capacity for investment that generally furnishes a simultaneous constraint. The latter can be as binding or at times more binding than the constraint on the generation of appropriable surplus; in the latter case, accordingly, the advance of the savings rate in a region will be governed by the slow expansion of absorptive capacity for capital investment rather than by resistances to the expansion of reinvestible surplus.

[21] The detailed behavior of this model raises interesting points in regard to the financing of the expansion of nontraditional exports and in regard to the evaluation of development projects related to this export expansion in region A which cannot be discussed further here.

TABLE 7 Interregional Growth Model 4

AUTONOMOUS GROWTH OF SAVINGS RATIO

SR(t) = MIN(SR(t-1) + 2, IR(t-1) + 2, 30)
Constant Cap/Output Ratios, A:4, B:3
Situation 1 - Income Elasticity of Imports (B) = 0.7

TOTAL	Income		Imports	Savings Ratio		Savings		Investment		Income Change		Income Growth		Import Growth
ΣY	A YA	B YB	B MB	A SRA	B SRB	A SA	B SB	A IA	B IB	A ΔYA	B ΔYB	A ΔYA/YA	B ΔYB/YB	B ΔMB/MB

SITUATION 1 - LIMITED TRADITIONAL EXPORTS

	ΣY	YA	YB	MB	SRA	SRB	SA	SB	IA	IB	ΔYA	ΔYB	ΔYA/YA	ΔYB/YB	ΔMB/MB
0	200	100	100	10	10	30	10	30	10	30	2.5	10	2.5	10	7
1	212.500	102.500	110.000	10.700	10.439	30	10.700	33.000	10.700	33.000	2.675	11.000	2.610	10	7
2	226.175	105.175	121.000	11.449	10.886	30	11.449	36.300	11.449	36.300	2.862	12.010	2.721	10	7
3	241.137	108.037	133.100	12.250	11.339	30	12.250	39.930	12.250	39.930	3.063	13.310	2.835	10	7
4	257.510	111.100	146.410	13.108	11.798	30	13.108	43.923	13.108	43.923	3.277	14.641	2.950	10	7
5	275.428	114.377	161.051	14.026	12.263	30	14.026								

SITUATION 2 - "TRADE-NOT-AID"

	ΣY	YA	YB	MB	SRA	SRB	SA	SB	IA	IB	ΔYA	ΔYB	ΔYA/YA	ΔYB/YB	ΔMB/MB
0	200	100	100	10	10	30	10	30	10	30	2.5	10	2.5	10	23.000
1	212.500	102.500	110.000	12.300	12	30	12.300	33.00	12.300	33.000	3.075	11.000	3.0	10	20.171
2	226.575	105.575	121.000	14.781	14	30	14.781	36.300	14.781	36.300	3.695	12.010	3.5	10	18.280
3	242.370	109.270	133.100	17.483	16	30	17.483	39.930	17.483	39.930	4.371	13.310	4.0	10	16.999
4	260.051	113.641	146.410	20.455	18	30	20.455	43.923	20.455	43.923	5.114	14.641	4.5	10	16.113
5	279.806	118.755	161.051	23.751	20	30	23.751						7.5		

NOTE. Assumptions:
a. No capital transfers; exports = imports
b. Region A produces no capital goods
c. Region A uses all of its foreign exchange to import capital goods
d. Situation 1: limited traditional exports from A to B.
   Situation 2: planned imports in B to limit of savings growth in A.

CONCLUSION

The autonomous growth tendency of the savings rate postulated in the foregoing illustrations is not the only possible phenomenon of its kind. Similar autonomous growth tendencies can reasonably be postulated for such factors as the evolution of skills, the development of an indigenous technology capable of generating its own advance, and in general the evolution of an integrated, self-contained cultural pattern that we associate with the notion of a high level of economic development. Likewise, in addition to the incentive effects of the transfer or regional utilization of savings there are many other kinds of possible behavioral relations of a similar nature including the one that is probably the most important, namely, the effect of the level, rate of advance, and acceleration of economic development itself upon the supplies of all factors, the supplies of savings, and the productivity coefficients characterizing the technology of a region.

The simple numerical illustrations that have been given at a highly aggregated level can do no more than open up an area that requires a great deal of further study; they suggest nevertheless that a view of economic development as an essentially autonomous growth process that is frustrated by a series of specific constraints can be made operational by the formulation of precise mathematical models for the investigation of these phenomena. This approach holds out the promise of extending the use of mathematical programing development models from the present formulations that are centered almost exclusively on technological interrelations to formulations that give a considerably wider scope to relationships involving human motivations and behavior.

APPENDIX 1

The Correspondence Between Price-type and Quantity-type Control
Instruments in the Reconciliation of Regional Development Objectives

The correspondence between (a) the weighted sum of two
objectives and (b) a single objective function with one additional constraint
representing a secondary objective, can be demonstrated graphically in
two dimensions.

By reference to Figure 1, assume that the space of feasible
solutions is OAP_1P_2B, determined by technical constraints. Assume
further that the maximization of X_1 and of X_2 are separate objectives.
Then any positive weighting of these two objectives will carry the
system to an optimal solution along the boundary AP_1P_2B.

If the weighting is such that its slope corresponds to the
slope of the line FF, the optimal solution is P_2. It is asserted that
FF may be replaced:

a. either by the maximization of X_1 subject to a proper
constraint replacing X_2 in the weighted objective
function;

b. or by the maximization of X_2 subject to a proper
constraint replacing X_1 in the weighted objective
function.

In the first case, the proper constraint is $X_2 \geq D$. With
this constraint, the feasible region shrinks to P_2DB; maximizing X_1
over this region yields P_2, as required. In the second case, the
proper constraint is $X_1 \geq C$. With this constraint, the feasible zone
becomes $AP_1 P_2 C$; maximizing X_2 over this zone yields again P_2,
as required.

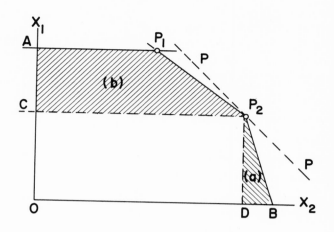

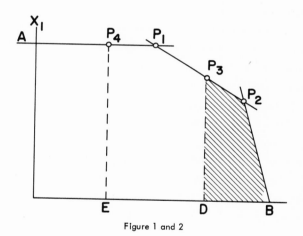

Figure 1 and 2

If the weighting is such that the slope of FF coincides with the slope of P_1P_2, all points of the line segment P_1P_2 will be optimal. By a proper choice of C or D in the inequalities above, any one point of the segment P_1P_2 may be made optimal in the corresponding transformed problem. Thus in Figure 2, P_3 is made optimal by maximizing X_1 over the region DP_3P_2B. Note, however, that in this case of multiple optima C or D cannot be chosen so as to duplicate the entire multiple optimum P_1P_2 in a single equivalent problem, but rather, to each one of the multiple optima there corresponds a transformed problem.

The above demonstrates one side of the limited correspondence between price-type and quantity-type control instruments in the reconciliation of independent objectives, namely the replacement of a weighted optimum by a single objective plus a constraint. Conversely, it can be demonstrated that the optimal solution attainable by a single objective plus a constraint can be replaced by a combined objective with properly chosen weights. By reference again to Figure 2, replace the maximization of X_1 subject to the technical constraints plus the constraint $X_2 \geq D$, by a weighted maximum in X_1 and X_2, after omitting the last constraint. This can evidently be done if the weights are chosen so that the slope of the combined objective function coincides with the slope of the line segment P_1P_2. To P_3, the optimal solution of the original problem, there corresponds now the multiple optimum over the segment P_1P_2 in the transformed problem, which contains the point P_3, as required. It should be noted, however, that this is not a perfect equivalence because the transformed problem has many solutions that are not solutions to the original problem, and some of these are not even feasible in the original problem, e.g., the points of the segment P_1P_3 excluding P_3 itself.

If the original problem is chosen with the constraint $X_2 \geq E$ (See Figure 2) it will have multiple optima along the line segment P_4P_1. The corresponding transformed problem will now also have mutliple optima along this line segment, and also along the line segment AP_4 which is infeasible in the first problem, except for P_4 itself.

In sum when either of the corresponding problems has mutliple optima, there is no perfect equivalence, but in every case, the corresponding problems have at least one optimal solution in common.

The above demonstration can be generalized in the following ways:

1. The positive weighting of the separate objectives is not essential to the correspondence. With negative weightings allowed, the gradient of the combined objective function may point in any direction rather than only into the positive quadrant, as above. The only change required now is to reverse the inequality in the constraint replacing a negatively weighted individual objective.

2. The individual objectives need not be X_1 and X_2 alone, but may be any two linear functions in these variables, with the combined objective being a weighted sum of the two functions. Such a weighted sum is always equivalent to another weighted sum in terms of the two variables X_1 and X_2 alone; thus the correspondence established for the latter will hold for the former.

3.   The correspondence also holds for convex nonlinear
problems, i. e., convex constraints with concave
objective functions, where the latter are equivalent
to convex sets of "acceptable" points. The latter are
defined as points which are equal or preferred to an
auxiliary variable signifying a constant value of the
objective function. With the aid of this auxiliary
variable any problem having a nonlinear concave
objective function can be transformed into an equivalent
problem with a linear objective function (which is identical
to the auxiliary variable mentioned above); this linear
objective function is maximized over a convex point set.
When there are two nonlinear objectives, each of these
can be subjected independently to the above transformation,
and the problem now becomes one of demonstrating the
correspondence of the weighted objectives and a single
objective with an additional linear constraint, over a
convex nonlinear point set. By reference to Figures 1
and 2, the demonstration does not rely on the linearity
of the boundary of the feasible point set, only on its
convexity; thus the generalization is immediate. Moreover,
when the boundary has no linear segments the possibility
of multiple optima does not arise and there exists a perfect
equivalence rather than a limited correspondence as in the
linear case where the possibility of multiple optima has to be
taken into account.

4.   In more than two dimensions multiple optima may occur
      not only along line segments but also along planes or
      hyperplanes. For a generalization to these cases the
      above argument can be framed in purely algebraic
      terms which yields an extension to n dimensions.

A straightforward application of the above principles to
the reconciliation of regional development objectives might consist
in establishing a correspondence between (1) the maximization of a
weighted objective, e.g., the sum of regional products for two regions,
and (2) the maximization of a single objective, e.g., the product of
region A, subject to the attainment of a prescribed minimum level of
the product of region B. It often happens, however, that it is desired
to establish another kind of correspondence that is slightly different
from the one discussed above, namely a correspondence between (1)
a weighted maximization where the weights are unequal and (2) a
weighted maximization with equal weights, subject to the attainment
of a minimum level of the objective of one or the other region. For
example, it may be desired to replace (1) the maximization of national
wealth (which is an equally-weighted sum of the wealth of several
regions), subject to regional distribution constraints, by (2) the
maximization of an unequally weighted sum of regional wealth in the
several regions. (The problem of assigning terminal weights to
capital stock in different regions is encountered in multi-period
regional allocation models.)

By reference to Figure 3, P_1 is the optimal solution to
the unequally-weighted maximum problem, and P_2 is the optimal
solution to the qually-weighted maximum problem. If it is desired

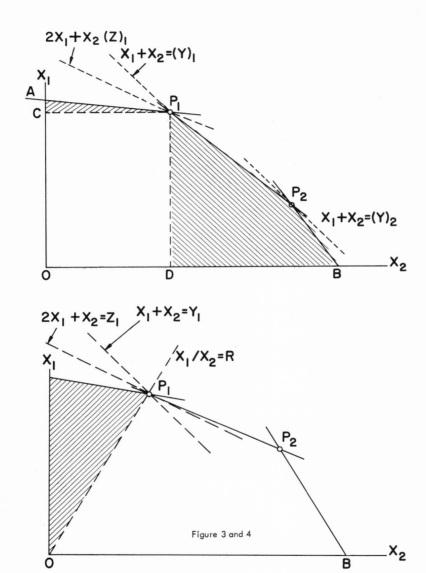

Figure 3 and 4

to reformulate the first problem so as to replace its objective by an equally-weighted objective plus a proper constraint, it is found that the symmetry between the constraints $X_1 \geq C$ and $X_2 \geq D$ no longer exists. Only the first of these constraints will assure that $X_1 + X_2$ attains its maximum at P_1; the other constraint will not prevent the system from going to P_2, the maximum of the equally-weighted objective. In other words, the constraint has to be imposed on the income of the lagging region, X_1, as is intuitively obvious, otherwise the system will go to the maximum P_2 implying an unacceptably low value of X_1.

    In Figure 4, another reformulation is shown in which the income of the lagging region, X_1, is constrained to be a minimum proportion of the income of the leading region, X_2. Here again, we encounter an asymmetry in that the constraint must operate in the proper direction, otherwise the system will go to the maximum P_2. Finally, the two incomes may be constrained to the line representing the exact ratio R, in which case the feasible region collapses to points along the segment OP_1, with the optimum again at P_1.

    By reference to Figures 3 and 4, the unconstrained, equally-weighted maximum P_2 corresponds to a higher level of $(X_1 + X_2)$ than the maximum of the same objective function subject to regional distribution constraints, P_1; in other words, $(Y)_2 > (Y)_1$.

APPENDIX 2

Notation, Formal Interpretation and Transformation Rules for the
Model Presented in Table 1

A. Notation

1. Variables

All variables are given two-letter names, to be interpreted as single symbols, not as algebraic products.
In Table 1, all variables are vectors, except as indicated
below:

Primal principal variables

$XX_j^t \equiv \left[(XX_j^t)_1 \ldots, (XX_j^t)_n \right]$, level of production activity j at time
t in each region $1, \ldots, n$

$XZ_i^t \equiv \left[(XZ_i^t)_{11}, \ldots, (XZ_i^t)_{1n}, (XZ_i^t)_{2i}, \ldots, (XZ_i^t)_{2n}, \ldots, (XZ_i^t)_{n1}, \ldots, (XZ_i^t)_{nn} \right]$
level of **transport** activity for commodity i at time t from
each region $1, \ldots, n$ to each region $1, \ldots, n$

$XH_i^t \equiv \left[(XH_i^t)_1, \ldots, (XH_i^t)_n \right.$, stock-holding activity for commodity
i at time t in each region $1, \ldots, n$

XO,   a scalar, level of exogenous supply/demand activity,
pre-set to unity

Primal **slack** variables

$SB_i^t \equiv \left[(SB_i^t)_1, \ldots, (SB_i^t)_n \right]$, surplus of stock of commodity i at
time t in each region $1, \ldots, n$

$SF_i^t \equiv \left[(SF_k^t)_1, \ldots, (SF_k^t)_n \right]$, surplus of flow of primary factor
k at time t in each region $1, \ldots, n$

$SA_i^t \equiv \left[(SA_i^t)_1, \ldots, (SA_i^t)_n \right]$, surplus of flow of commodity i at
at time t in each region $1, \ldots, n$

SO,   a scalar, weighted sum (value) of terminal stocks,
to be maximized. May be interpreted as a surplus,
since no prescribed demands exist.

Dual principal variables

$YR_i^t \equiv \left[(YR_i^t)_1, \ldots, (YR_i^t)_n \right]$, shadow <u>rent</u> per period on stock of commodity i at time t in each region $1, \ldots, n$

$YW_k^t \equiv \left[(YW_k^t)_1, \ldots, (YW_k^t)_n \right]$, shadow <u>price of primary factor</u> k at time i in each region $1, \ldots, n$

$YP_i^t \equiv \left[(YP_i^t)_1, \ldots, (YP_i^t)_n \right]$, <u>shadow price of commodity</u> i at time t in each region $1, \ldots, n$

YO, a scalar, <u>valuation of terminal stocks</u>; pre-set to unity, it can be interpreted as the numeraire of the shadow price system

Dual slack variables

$DX_j^t \equiv \left[(DX_j^t)_1, \ldots, (DX_j^t)_n \right]$, <u>shadow loss</u> (negative profit) <u>on production</u> activity j at time t in each region $1, \ldots, n$

$DZ_i^t \equiv \left[(DZ_i^t)_{11}, \ldots, (DZ_i^t)_{1n}, (DZ_i^t)_{21}, \ldots, (DZ_i^t)_{2n}, \ldots, (DZ_i^t)_{n'}, \ldots, (DZ_i^t)_{nn} \right]$,

<u>shadow loss on transports</u> activity for commodity i at time t from each region $1, \ldots, n$ to each region $1, \ldots, n$.

$DH_i^t \equiv \left[(DH_i^t)_1, \ldots, (DH_i^t)_n \right]$, shadow loss on <u>stock-holding</u> activity for commodity i at time t in each region $1, \ldots, n$.

DO, a scalar, <u>shadow loss on exogenous supply/demand activity</u> (see formal interpretation). Dual objective is the minimization of (-DO).

2. Parameters

The parameters enumerated are vectors or matrices.

(a) <u>Parameters which represent initial or terminal values of certain variables</u> (vectors)

$H_i^0 \equiv \left[(H_i^0)_1, \ldots, (H_i^0)_n \right]$, zero-period value of XH_i^t, initial stock endowment of commodity i in each region $1, \ldots, n$.

$P_i^4 \equiv \left[(P_i^4)_1, \ldots, (P_i^4)_n \right]$, fourth-period value of YP_i^t, post-horizon shadow price of commodity i in each region $1, \ldots, n$.

$R_i^4 \equiv \left[(R_i^4)_1, \ldots, (R_i^4)_n \right]$, fourth-period value of YR_i^t, post-horizon one-period shadow rent for stock i in each region $1, \ldots, n$.

(b) <u>exogenous supply and demand parameters</u> (vectors)

$Q_k^t \equiv \left[(Q_k^t)_1, \ldots, (Q_k^t)_n \right]$, exogenous supply of primary factor k at time t in each region $1, \ldots, n$

$C_i^t \equiv \left[(C_i^t)_1, \ldots, (C_i^t)_n \right]$, exogenous demand of commodity i at time t in each region $1, \ldots, n$

(c) <u>technical coefficient matrices</u>

$$I \equiv \begin{Bmatrix} 1 & & \\ & \ddots & \\ & & 1 \end{Bmatrix}$$, identity matrix of order n

$$B_{ij}^t \equiv \begin{Bmatrix} (B_{ij}^t)_1 & & \\ & \ddots & \\ & & (B_{ij}^t)_n \end{Bmatrix}$$, diagonal matrix of stock input

coefficients for stock of commodity i used in activity j at time t in each region $1, \ldots, n$.

$$F_{kj}^t \equiv \begin{Bmatrix} (F_{kj}^t)_1 & & \\ & \ddots & \\ & & (F_{kj}^t)_n \end{Bmatrix}$$, diagonal matrix of

primary factor input coefficients for factor k used in activity j at time t in each region $1, \ldots, n$.

$$A_{ij}^t \equiv \left\{ \begin{matrix} (A_{ij}^t)_1 & & \\ & \ddots & \\ & & \ddots \\ & & (A_{ij}^t)_n \end{matrix} \right\} , \text{ diagonal matrix of commodity output}$$

(if positive) or intermediate input (if negative) flow coefficients for commodity i produced or used in activity j at time t in each region $1, \ldots, n$

(d) <u>transfer matrices</u>

T_i^t, the transfer matrix for commodity i at time t, from each region $1, \ldots, n$ to each region $1, \ldots, n$, has the form shown below:

index of transport activity:

		1 1	12 ... ln	21 22 ... 2n	...	n1	n2 ... nn
i-th	1)	0	-1 -1	1		1	
commodity balance in	2)		1	-1 0 ... -1			1
this region :			⋱		⋱		⋱
	n)		1	1 ... -1	-1 ...	0

In this matrix a unit of commodity i imported to a region appears as (+1), a unit exported appears as (-1).

(e) <u>transport</u> cost matrices

$$L_{ie}^t \equiv \left\{ \begin{matrix} (L_{ie}^t)_{11}^1, \ldots, (L_{ie}^t)_{1n}^1, \ldots, (L_{ie}^t)_{2n}^4, \ldots, (L_{ie}^t)_{n'}^1, \ldots, (L_{ie}^t)_{nn}^1 \\ \vdots \\ (L_{ie}^t)_{11}^n, \ldots, (L_{ie}^t)_{1n}^n, (L_{ie}^t)_{21}^n, \ldots, (L_{ie}^t)_{2n}^n, \ldots, (L_{ie}^t)_{n'}^n, \ldots, (L_{ie}^t)_{nn}^n \end{matrix} \right\}$$

Matrix of <u>stock requirement</u> coefficients at time t for the stock of commodity i used in the transport of commodity e, the stock belonging to each region $1, \ldots, n$ (vertical dimension of matrix) and the transport activities connecting each region $1, \ldots, n$ with every other region $1, \ldots, n$ (horizontal dimension of matrix).

M^t_{im} Same indexing as above, **M, m** substituted for L, e   <u>primary factor</u> requirement

coefficients

N^t_{in} Same indexing as above, **N, n** substituted for L, l   <u>commodity flow</u> requirement

coefficients

B. Formal Interpretation

The linear programming problem in Table 1 is set out by means of Tucker's condensed format as explained below (Tucker in Graves and Wolfe, 1963). Primal variables appear in the top margin, primal slacks at the left, dual variables on the right, dual slacks at the bottom. The equations of the primal problem are derived by setting equal the primal slacks to the matrix products of each row in the table by the variables in the upper margin. The equations of the dual problem are correspondingly derived by setting equal the dual slacks(with their signs reversed) to the matrix products of each column in the table by the dual variables in the right-hand margin. All variables are restricted to non-negative values, with the exceptions noted below. Any row may be chosen as the primal maximand: the corresponding primal slack may be of any sign, and the corresponding dual variable must be set to the fixed value of unity. Likewise, any column may be chosen as the dual minimand: the corresponding dual slack may be of any sign, and the corresponding primal variable must be set to the fixed value of unity.

All outputs in the table are positive, all inputs negative. The rows are interpreted as resource balances, and the primal slacks as resource surpluses. One of these is maximized <u>as activity scales vary</u>, subject to all others being non-negative. This resource, with unit valuation, is the numeraire resource of the system. The

columns are interpreted as economic activities, and the dual slacks
as losses (with their signs reversed: as profits). One of these
profits is minimized as resource valuations vary, while the others
are restricted to being nonpositive. The corresponding column is
the (unit) fixed-scale activity of the system, e. g., in the present
problem the vector of the exogenous parts of the primal resource
balances. Note that the above profit minimization is undertaken as
prices, not quantities, vary. This implies assigning the smallest
possible weighted valuation to the scarce exogenous input resources
and the largest possible weighted valuation to the exogenous demands
of the system consistent with the no-profit stipulation for the other
activities. (The latter stipulation can be thought of as an analogue to
perfect competition.) In other words, the prices are to be such that
they reduce the scarcity of the scarce resources and raise the reward
value of the prescribed consumption as much as possible.

Both activities and resource balances are distinguished
by time periods. There are four kinds of activities: production,
transport, stock-holding, and an activity specifying exogenous supplies
and demands; and three kinds of resources: commodity flows,
commodity stock levels, and primary factor flows. Primary factors
cannot be produced or transported. For convenience in presentation
the model has only two commodities and three productive activities
at each location and in each period. All activities and resource balances
are distinguished by n locations; locational distinctions are, however,
left implicit in the notation of Table 1 by grouping the corresponding
marginal entries of the table into vectors and the inner entries into
submatrices. For example the A_{ij}^t elements denote diagonal

submatrices of coefficients for $\underline{n}$ locations; these are production coefficients of flow inputs (if negative) or outputs (if positive) at time $\underline{t}$ of the $\underline{i}$th resource in the $\underline{j}$th activity. The B_{ij}^t and F_{ij}^t elements likewise denote diagonal submatrices of stock and factor requirement coefficients. The T_i^t elements denote a complete set of transport connections pairwise between the $\underline{n}$ locations; as seen in Table 1, there is one such T_i^t element for each flow-type resource. It can also be seen in Table 1 that the transport activities have coefficients L_{ie}^t, M_{im}^t, N_{in}^t which denote stock factor and flow requirements for performing transport activities: these are thus generalizations of transport costs in terms of explicit resource utilizations.

C.   Transformation Rules

In this format all variables in the top and right-hand margins (except the ones fixed as unit level) are regarded as non-basic, i. e., to be set to zero; consequently the first column gives the numerical values of all basic primal variables while the last row gives the numerical values of all basic dual variables (with signs reversed).

In a transformation of the tableau (a Gaussian elimination process) the variables corresponding to one column and one row are interchanged, and all numerical entries of the tableau are recomputed by the following rules:

Definitions.   Pivot $\underline{p}$: element of the tableau at the intersection of the interchanged row $\underline{i}'$ and column $\underline{j}'$: $p \equiv a_{i'j'}$

Pivot - row element	$\underline{r} \equiv a_{i'j}$, $j \neq j'$
Pivot - column element	$\underline{c} \equiv a_{i,j'}$, $i \neq i'$
General element	$\underline{e} \equiv a_{i,j}$, $i \neq i'$, $j \neq j'$.

Transformation Rules

Element	Short notation	Full notation
pivot	$p \rightarrow 1/p$	$a_{i', j'} \rightarrow 1/a_{i', j'}$
pivot-row element	$r \rightarrow -r/p$	$a_{i', j} \rightarrow -a_{i', j}/a_{i', j'}$
pivot-column element	$c \rightarrow c/p$	$a_{i, j'} \rightarrow a_{i, j'}/a_{i', j'}$
general element	$e \rightarrow e - r \cdot c/p$	$a_{i, j} \rightarrow a_{i, j} - a_{i', j} \cdot a_{i, j'}/a_{i'j'}$

Note:

A tableau in Tucker's general format can be rewritten with the negative signs shifted from the bottom margin to some other margin; in the latter case the sign-reversal rule may be interchanged between the pivot-row and pivot-column element transformations.

APPENDIX   3

Accounting Concepts and Current Prices

In this Appendix we shall discuss the definition of accounting concepts based on the model of Table 1 including national and regional product and income; the evolution of stock value (wealth) from period to period; and the relationship between shadow prices, current prices and the rate of interest.

The accounting concepts to be dealt with are based on the "accounting values" of coefficients in the model. To derive the accounting value associated with a coefficient the latter is multiplied both by the corresponding activity scale and by the corresponding shadow price in the optimal solution. Accounting values add to zero both by rows and by columns as a consequence of the law of complementary slacks, well-known in linear programming.

1. Notation

In designating the optimal-solution values of primal and dual variables the "X" or "Y" part of the double symbol is dropped. In addition an expression such as

$$P^1 . A^1 . X^1$$

where the subscripts of the variables are dropped designates the sum of all accounting values involving the A^1 coefficient group, i.e.,

$$P_1^1 . A_{11}^1 . X_1^1 + P_1^1 . A_{12}^1 . X_2^1 + P_1^1 . A_{13}^1 . X_3^1 + P_2^1 . A_{21}^1 . X_1^1 +$$
$$+ P_2^1 . A_{22}^1 . X_2^1 + P_2^1 . A_{23}^1 . X_3^1 .$$

2. National Income and Product

(a) Sum to **zero** the accounting values of rows having the index of a given time period $\underline{t}$:

$$R^t . I . H^{t-1} \quad -R^t . B^t . X^t - R^t . L^t . Z^t \qquad = 0$$
$$W^t . Q^t . 1 \qquad -W^t . F^t . X^t - W^t . M^t . Z^t \qquad = 0$$
$$-P^t . C^t . 1 + P^t . I . H^{t-1} \underbrace{+P^t . A^t . X^t}_{=0} + \underbrace{P^t . (T^t - N^t) . Z^t}_{=0} - P^t . I . H^t = 0$$

(b) Sum the above expression by columns. Since the third and fourth columns above contain all the non zero entries for a complete column in Table 1, they have to sum to zero, as indicated. The other summations give:

$$-P^t . I . (H^t - H^{t-1}) - P^t . C^t . 1 + R^t . I . H^{t-1} + W^t . Q^t . 1 = 0$$

(c) Dropping I and 1 coefficients and rearranging, we get:

$$P^t . (H^t - H^{t-1}) + P^t . C^t = R^t . H^{t-1} + W^t . Q^t$$

Investment   Consumption   Rentals   Wages
at time t at time t at time t at time t

National product   National income

The above demonstrates the identity between national income and product. (For the definition of the latter in current prices see sec. 6 below.)

3. Regional Income and Product

Repeat the above operations using only the rows referring to a particular region h. Now column 4 no longer sums to zero since a transport activity always has coefficients involving other regions than h (otherwise there can be no transfer of a commodity from region h to k or k to h) and the latter are omitted in the summation. In addition there can be stock and factor inputs from regions other than h in both transport and regional production activities; these also will have the effects of preventing the respective columns from summing to zero.

Method of dealing with foreign-region coefficients: treat the accounting values of all positive ones as exports from region h, of all negative ones as imports to region h. A little algebra will show that the summation of the accounting values of region h in the columns corresponding to production and transport will yield net exports from region h with sign reversed. Upon rearranging the summation as under heading (c) above, net exports will appear to gether with consumption and investment as part of regional product. Regional income will be analogous to national income and will consist of payments to regional stocks and primary factors.

4. Period-to-Period Evolution of Stock Value

(a) In the expression for the national income/product identity isolate $P^t . H^t$:

$$P^t . H^t = (P^t + R^t) . H^{t-1} + W^t . Q^t - P^t . C^t$$

(b) From the accounting values of the columns of stock holding activities, express $P^t . H^t$:

$$P^t . H^t = (P^{t+1} + R^{t+1}) . H^t$$

(c) Substitute into expression under (a):

$$(P^{t+1} + R^{t+1}) . H^t = (P^t + R^t) . H^{t-1} + W^t . Q^t - P^t . C^t .$$

From this expression it is evident that with $Q^t = C^t = 0$ for all t, stock valuation is constant from period to period, and thus also between the starting (zero) period and the terminal period. By progressive substitution we similarly derive for the general case:

$$(P^t + R^t) . H^{t-1} = (P^{t-1} + R^{t-1}) . H^{t-2} + W^{t-1} . Q^{t-1} - P^{t-1} . C^{t-1}$$
$$= (P^{t-2} + R^{t-2}) . H^{t-3} + W^{t-1} . Q^{t-1} + W^{t-2} . Q^{t-2} -$$
$$P^{t-1} . C^{t-1} - P^{t-2} . C^{t-2}$$
$$\vdots$$
$$= (P^1 + R^1) . H^0 + W^{t-1} . Q^{t-1} + \ldots + W^1 . Q^1 - P^{t-1} .$$
$$C^{t-1} - \ldots - P^1 . C^1,$$

where t can be the terminal period, T.

5. Current Prices and the Rate of Interest

The relationship between shadow prices, current prices and the rate of interest is derived from stock holding activities connecting two successive periods:

$$(P_i^{t-1})_h \le (P_i^t)_h + (R_i^t)_h$$

where the equality holds when the stock of commodity i in region h is held in non-zero amounts.

In order to create a system of current prices,

(a)   The rate of interest r is defined by an ordinary discounting formula that connects current prices and shadow prices:

$$(\pi_i^T)_h = (P_i^T)_h \left(\frac{1}{1+r}\right)^{t-T}$$

$$(\rho_i^T)_h = (R_i^T)_h \left(\frac{1}{1+r}\right)^{t-T},$$

where π and ρ are current flow prices and stock rents, T is the index of any time period, and t is the index of the base time period for the current price system. Substitution into the earlier given shadow price relation yields:

$$(\pi_i^{t-1})_h (1+r) \le (\pi_i^t)_h + (\rho_i^t)_h,$$

and

$$r = \frac{(\pi_i^t)_h - (\pi_i^{t-1})_h}{(\pi_i^{t-1})_h} + \frac{(\rho_i^t)_h}{(\pi_i^{t-1})_h}.$$

(b)   A value standard commodity (in a specific region) has to be selected whose current price remains unchanged from t-1 to t:

$$(\pi_{i'}^{t-1})_h = (\pi_{i'}^t)_{h'},$$

where the value-standard commodity is commodity i' in region h'.

As an immediate consequence the rate of interest is revealed as the current rent on the value-standard commodity provided that finite non-zero stocks of the latter are being held in the optional solution.

6.   National Income, Product   and Wealth in Current Prices

If we transcribe the national income/product identity into current prices we get (remembering that in period t current and shadow prices are equal):

$$\pi^t . (H^t - H^{t-1}) + \pi^t . C^t = \rho^t . H^{t-1} + \omega^t . Q^t,$$ where $\underline{\omega}$ is a current wage.

The defining relationship for the rate of interest from Sec. 5 can be restated in terms of accounting values that sum to zero:

$$-P^{t-1} . H^{t-1} + P^t . H^{t-1} + R^t . H^{t-1} \qquad = 0$$
$$\therefore \quad -\pi^{t-1} . H^{t-1} . (1+r) + \pi^t . H^{t-1} + \rho^t . H^{t-1} = 0$$

Expressing $\rho^t . H^{t-1}$ from this relationship and substituting we obtain:

$$\pi^t . (H^t - H^{t-1}) + \pi^t . C^t = ((1+r) . \pi^{t-1} - \pi^t) . H^{t-1} + \omega^t . Q^t$$
$$= \pi^t . H^{t-1} . r - (\pi^t - \pi^{t-1}) . H^{t-1} + \omega^t . Q^t,$$

where $\pi^t . H^{t-1}$ is the value of all stocks available for production in period $\underline{t}$, and $\pi^t . H^{t-1} . r$ is the total interest imputed to the former; while $(\pi^t - \pi^{t-1}) . H^t$ is the net value increase on all stocks between period $\underline{t-1}$ and $\underline{t}$. Thus in terms of the interest rate, stock rents are replaced by the difference between interest income and stock appreciation.

We can redefine both national income and investment (and thus national product) by adding the stock appreciation to both sides of the identity:

$$\pi^t . (H^t - H^{t-1}) + \pi^t . C^t + (\pi^t - \pi^{t-1}) . H^{t-1} = \pi^t . H^{t-1} . r + \omega^t . Q^t$$
$$(\pi^t . H^t - \pi^{t-1} . H^{t-1}) + \pi^t . C^t \qquad = \pi^t . H^{t-1} . r + \omega^t . Q^t.$$

National income thus redefined is the sum of wage and interest incomes, while investment in national product is redefined as the difference of stock values at time $\underline{t}$ valued at the prices of time $\underline{t}$, and stock values at time $\underline{t-1}$; i. e., the difference of aggregate stock values in current prices.

A rearrangement of the last equation yields the following relation for the evolution of national wealth (national aggregate stock value):

$$\pi^t . H^t = \pi^{t-1} . H^{t-1} . (1+r) + \omega^t . Q^t - \pi^t . C^t,$$

i.e., aggregate national wealth in current prices at time $\underline{t}$ equals the same concept at time $\underline{t-1}$ increased by the interest accrued, plus the difference of aggregate wages and aggregate consumption.

Bibliographical Note

After this paper was finished I learned of the existence of a study addressed to the same over-all problems of locational-regional goal setting in economic planning and had an opportunity to exchange ideas and to inspect a preliminary version of the paper resulting from the latter study (T. A. Reiner, "Sub-National and National Planning," to be published in *Regional Science Association, Papers,* 1966). While the principal problems identified in my paper correspond closely to those in Reiner's, the analytical approaches taken are quite different. Reiner's paper contains a detailed literature survey and many practical examples of particular problems. The two papers are complementary rather than overlapping.

The basic reference on methods of regional and locational economics is Isard *et al.* (1960). A more recent survey of regional economics will be found in Meyer (1963). A number of articles on regional economic planning will be found in Isard and Cumberland (1961). The *Papers* of the Regional Science Association and the *Journal of Regional Science* contain much valuable material closely related to the topic of this paper.

The basic reference on mathematical programing in relation to economic problems is Dorfman, Samuelson, and Solow (1958). Standard references on linear programing include Dantzig (1963), Gass (1958), Hadley (1961), and Simonnard (1962); on nonlinear programing see Kuhn and Tucker (1951) and Wolfe (1963).

The first discussion of a mathematical programing approach to locational problems apart from simple transport problems was by Samuelson (1952). Such models have been developed further by Beckman and Marschak (1955), Vietorisz (1956), Moses (1957), Lefeber (1958, 1959), Isard (1958), Stevens (1958, 1959). A survey of interindustry models with a regional dimension, including both input-output and linear programing, is given in Chenery and Clark (1959, Chap. 12). The effects of economies of scale are explored in Vietorisz (1956, 1964) and Vietorisz and Manne (1963); the externalities arising from the fact that locations cannot be shared between several production processes are explored by Koopmans and Beckman (1957).

Applications of locational linear programing models to the study of particular industries will be found in Fox (1953, 1955, 1963), Henderson (1955, 1956, 1957, 1958), Snodgrass and French (1958), Koch and Snodgrass (1959), Heady and Egbert (1963), and Marschak (1963).

The handling of transport in the models given in Tables 1 and 2 in the text of the present paper is simple but highly sketchy; alternative ways of handling transport and a discussion of the merits and disadvantages of these alternatives appear in Stevens (1958), Lefeber (1958, 1959) and the discussion by Henderson (1958).

On interindustry growth models, see, for example, Dorfman, Samuelson, and Solow (1958), Solow (1963), and Koopmans (1964). The latter reference contains a detailed survey of the history of such models and in particular of the celebrated "turnpike theorem." A discussion of interregional growth models without interindustry detail will be found in Rahman (1963; see also the Comment by Dorfman, 1963), and Ward (1963). A regional interindustry growth model for a single region appears in Moore (1955).

REFERENCES

Arrow, K. J., *Social Choice and Individual Values,* New York, 1951.

Beckman, M., and T. Marschak, "An Activity Analysis Approach to Location Theory," *Kyklos,* 1955.

Chenery, H. B., "Development Policies and Programs," *United Nations Economic Bulletin for Latin America,* March 1958, pp. 51–77.

——, "Patterns of Industrial Growth," *American Economic Review,* September 1960, pp. 624–54 (mimeo. appendix on data and methodology is available from Research Center, for Economic Growth, Department of Economics, Stanford University).

Chenery, H. B., and K. A. Kretschmer, "Resource Allocation for Economic Development," *Econometrica,* October 1956, pp. 365–99.

Chenery, H. B., and P. G. Clark, *Interindustry Economics,* New York, 1959.

Dantzig, G. B., *Linear Programming and Extensions,* Princeton, N.J., 1963.

Dorfman, R., "Regional Allocation of Investment—Comment," *Quarterly Journal of Economics,* February 1963, pp. 162–65.

Dorfman, R., P. A. Samuelson, and R. Solow, *Linear Programming and Economic Analysis,* New York, 1958.

Fox, K. A., "A Spatial Equilibrium Model of the Livestock-Feed Economy in the United States," *Econometrica,* October 1953, pp. 547–66.

——, "Spatial Price Equilibrium and Process Analysis in the Food and Agricultural Sector," *Studies in Process Analysis,* eds. A. S. Manne and H. M. Markowitz, Cowles Foundation Monograph 18, New York, 1963, pp. 215–33.

Fox, K. A., and R. C. Taeuber, "Spatial Equilibrium Models of the Livestock-Feed Economy," *American Economic Review,* 1955, pp. 584–608.

Gass, S. I., *Linear Programming: Methods and Applications,* New York, 1958.

Hadley, G., *Linear Programming,* Reading, Mass., 1961.

Heady, E. O., and A. C. Egbert, "Spatial Programming Models to Specify Surplus Grain-producing Areas," *Studies in Process Analysis,* eds. A. S. Manne and H. M. Markowitz, Cowles Foundation Monograph 18, New York, 1963, pp. 161–214.

Henderson, J. M., "A Short-run Model for the Coal Industry," *Review of Economics and Statistics,* November 1955, pp. 336–46.

——, "Efficiency and Pricing in the Coal Industry," *Review of Economics and Statistics,* February 1956, pp. 50–60.

Henderson, J. M., "The Utilization of Agricultural Land—A Regional Approach," *Regional Science Association, Papers and Proceedings,* 1957, pp. 99–114.

———, *The Efficiency of the Coal Industry—An Application of Linear Programming,* Cambridge, Mass., 1958.

———, "Discussion—Interregional Equilibrium and Linear Programming," *Regional Science Association, Papers and Proceedings,* 1958, pp. 87–89.

Isard, W., "Interregional Linear Programming—An Elementary Presentation and a General Model," *Journal of Regional Science,* Summer 1958, pp. 1–59.

Isard, W., *et al., Methods of Regional Analysis: An Introduction to Regional Science,* Cambridge, Mass., and New York, 1960.

Isard, W., and J. H. Cumberland (ed.), *Regional Economic Planning— Techniques of Analysis,* Organization for European Economic Cooperation, Paris, 1961.

Koch, A. R., and M. M. Snodgrass, "Linear Programming Applied to Location of and Product Flow Determination in the Tomato Processing Industry," *Regional Science Association, Papers and Proceedings,* 1959.

Koopmans, T. C., "Economic Growth at a Maximal Rate," *Quarterly Journal of Economics,* August 1964, pp. 355–94.

Koopmans, T. C., and M. J. Beckman, "Assignment Problems and the Location of Economic Activities," *Econometrica,* January 1957, pp. 53–76.

Kuhn, H. W., and A. W. Tucker, "Nonlinear Programming," *Proceedings of the Second Berkeley Symposium on Mathematical Statistics and Probability,* ed. J. Neyman, Berkeley, Cal., 1951, pp. 481–92.

Lefeber, L., "General Equilibrium Analysis of Production, Transportation, and the Choice of Industrial Location," *Regional Science Association, Papers and Proceedings,* 1958, pp. 77–86.

———, *Allocation in Space,* Amsterdam, Holland, 1959.

Marschak, T. A., "A Spatial Model of U.S. Petroleum Refining," *Studies in Process Analysis,* eds. A. S. Manne and H. M. Markowitz, Cowles Foundation Monograph 18, New York, 1963, pp. 75–135.

Meyer, J. R., "Regional Economics—A Survey," *American Economic Review,* March 1963, pp. 19–54.

Moore, F. T., "Regional Economic Reaction Paths," *American Economic Review,* May 1955, pp. 133–48.

Moses, L. N., *An Input-Output, Linear Programming Approach to Interregional Analysis,* Report, Harvard Economic Research Project, 1956–57, Cambridge, Mass., 1957.

Rahman, M. A., "Regional Allocation of Investment," *Quarterly Journal of Economics,* February 1963, pp. 26–39.

Reiner, T. A., "Sub-national and National Planning—Decision Criteria," *Regional Science Association, Papers and Proceedings,* 1966.

Samuelson, P. A., "Spatial Price Equilibrium and Linear Programming," *American Economic Review,* June 1952, pp. 283–303.

Simonnard, M., *Linear Programming,* Paris, 1962.

Snodgrass, M. M., and C. E. French, *Linear Programming Approach to Interregional Competition in Dairying,* Lafayette, Ind., 1958.

Solow, R. M., *Capital Theory and the Rate of Return,* Amsterdam, Holland, 1963.

Stevens, B. H., "An Interregional Linear Programming Model," *Journal of Regional Science,* Summer 1958, pp. 60–98.

————, "Interregional Linear Programming," unpublished Ph.D. thesis, Massachusetts Institute of Technology, 1959.

Tinbergen, J., *Economic Policy—Principles and Designs,* Amsterdam, Holland, 1956.

Tucker, A. W., "Combinatorial Theory Underlying Linear Programs," *Recent Advances in Mathematical Programming,* eds. R. L. Graves and and P. Wolfe, New York, 1963, pp. 1–16.

Vietorisz, T., "Regional Programming Models and the Case Study of a Refinery-Petrochemical-Synthetic Fiber Industrial Complex for Puerto Rico," unpublished Ph.D. thesis, Massachusetts Institute of Technology, 1956.

————, "Industrial Development Planning Models with Economies of Scale and Indivisibilities," *Regional Science Association, Papers and Proceedings,* 1964.

Vietorisz, T., and A. S. Manne, "Chemical Processes, Plant Location, and Economies of Scale," *Studies in Process Analysis,* eds. A. S. Manne and H. M. Markowitz, Cowles Foundation Monograph 18, New York, 1963, pp. 136–58.

Ward, B., *Problems of Greek Regional Development,* Athens, Greece, 1963.

Wolfe, P., "Methods of Nonlinear Programming," *Recent Advances in Mathematical Programming,* ed. R. L. Graves and P. Wolfe, New York, 1963, pp. 67–86.

COMMENT

Alan S. Manne, *Stanford University*

Plausible-looking linear allocation models display a disconcerting tendency to arrive at optimal solutions of an all-or-none character. For example, with the assumptions underlying Samuelson's substitution theorem, it will be optimal to produce all of a commodity via a single technique of production and none by any other technique. Other examples of all-or-none optimal solutions occur in the warehousing model of Charnes and Cooper and the minimum-time-to-balanced-growth model of Stoleru. Similarly, the Rahman-Dorfman multiperiod interregional growth model implies that in each time period all of the funds available for reinvestment should be absorbed by a single region, and none by any others.

To a policymaker concerned with equity between regions, this form of optimal solution will undoubtedly be unacceptable, and Dorfman himself has commented: "The resultant plan is a little outrageous, though suggestive, and should not be taken literally." Vietorisz has not taken the Rahman-Dorfman results literally. Most of his paper is devoted to discussing the qualifications that might cause a more realistic multiperiod interregional growth model *not* to have these unacceptable extreme solutions. Some of the qualifications suggested by Vietorisz are rather straightforward, e.g., that there might be upper bounds on the levels of individual activities so that there could be positive levels of investment in several activities (i.e., regions) within a single time period.

To this reader, perhaps the most appealing modification to the Rahman-Dorfman model is Vietorisz's hypothesis that there will be incentive effects operating to bring about a positive correlation between the current rate of savings in a region and the past rate of investment in that region. If this type of incentive effect is really operative, then the optimal policy need no longer be of an all-or-none character. Typically, it will be optimal to invest simultaneously in more than one region, and indeed there will be a strong presumption in favor of a policy of self-financing for each region. Self-financing constraints are anathema to those who are impressed with the workings of perfectly competitive capital markets—as well as to would-be global optimizers. It will take more than casual introspection to establish whether Vietorisz's savings incentive hypothesis is an empirically tenable one.

References

Charnes, A., and W. W. Cooper, "Generalizations of the Warehousing Model," *Operational Research Quarterly,* December 1955.

Dorfman, R., "Regional Allocation of Investment: Comment," *Quarterly Journal of Economics,* February 1963.

Rahman, M. A., "Regional Allocation of Investment," *Quarterly Journal of Economics,* February 1963.

Samuelson, P. A., "Abstract of a Theorem Concerning Substitutability in Open Leontief Models," *Activity Analysis of Production and Allocation,* ed. T. C. Koopmans, New York, 1951.

Stoleru, L. G., "An Optimal Policy for Economic Growth," *Econometrica,* April 1965.

Techniques of Project Appraisal

ARNOLD C. HARBERGER

UNIVERSITY OF CHICAGO

In this paper, I attempt to bring into focus what I believe to be some of the important practical issues that face development planners in the field of project appraisal. I shall try, insofar as possible, to recognize the handicaps under which planners operate, most importantly the handicaps imposed by imperfect foresight and by the virtual necessity of decentralized decision-making. To elaborate briefly on these handicaps, I think we must take it for granted that our estimates of future costs and benefits (particularly the latter) are inevitably subject to a fairly wide margin of error, in the face of which it makes little sense to focus on subtleties aimed at discriminating accurately between investments that might have an expected yield of 10½ per cent and those that would yield only 10 per cent per annum. As the first order of business we want to be able to distinguish the 10 per cent investments from those yielding 5 or 15 per cent, while looking forward hopefully to the day when we have so well solved the many problems of project evaluation that we can seriously face up to trying to distinguish 10 per cent yields from those of 9 or 11 per cent.

Moreover, in what follows, I shall try to bear in mind the virtual necessity of decentralized decision-making. Rules and procedures can be imposed which assure a certain rough harmony among the decisions taken in such vastly different areas as roads, irrigation projects, and educational investments, but one cannot realistically expect all investment decisions to be funneled through a single office or authority that exercises more than a general supervisory power. Most of the real work connected with project appraisal must, I believe, be done "close to the ground"; this fact alone limits the range of workable procedures to those in which a substantial amount of power can in fact be delegated to decentralized bodies.

Within this general framework the focus of the paper is mainly on the fact that the relevant prices may change through time. The first section discusses the problem of real wage changes. The second section discusses the problem of future changes in the discount rate; the third section, the choice of a time path for the discount rate; the fourth section, the choice of the level of the discount rate. The fifth section discusses shadow prices for labor and capital, again coming to rest on the problem of selecting time paths. Finally, the sixth section discusses time paths of other prices and of demand functions.

The Problem of Real Wage Changes

Most discussions of project evaluation note that expected price changes should be taken into account, but little more than lip service is paid to this idea when working procedures are outlined. Insofar as the relative prices of commodities are concerned, this neglect of expected changes is understandable. "On the average," our best guess is likely to be that relative prices will remain as they are; cases where we have good reason to believe they will change can probably be regarded as somewhat exceptional, and project analysts can perhaps be presumed to deal with these exceptional cases as they arise.

When, however, we come to the price of labor, the story is very different. A rise in the real wage rate is one of the essential features of economic development, and this means a rise in the price of labor relative to the general price level of the economy. If we normalize on the general price level, we can therefore say that the typical investment is likely to be one in which the price of the product to be produced is expected to remain constant while the wages paid to labor rise. If a private entrepreneur leaves out of account the expected rise in wages (relative to the general price level), he does so at his peril, for this fact can readily turn a potentially profitable project into an unprofitable one.

Consider a case in which the price and volume of the output of a project and the prices and volumes of material inputs are expected to remain constant into the indefinite future, yielding an amount of value added, gross of depreciation, that is expected to be constant at R_0 per year. Assume wages are also constant, amounting to L_0 per year. Then the present value of the income stream acruing to the capital invested in the project will be $(R_0 - L_0)/r$, where r is the rate of discount used. If we assume that the capital cost is equal to this present value, it is a barely acceptable project when evaluated at r per cent. But now suppose that the wage rate is expected to rise at λ per cent per year, while the product price and materials prices are expected to remain constant. Then, in the first place, the project life ceases to be infinite, as the value of direct costs $L_0(1 + \lambda)^t$ will at some time come to exceed R_0, and the operation will not be worth continuing. Defining the life of the project, N, by $L_0(1 + \lambda)^N = R_0$, we have as the present value of the income stream accruing to the capital invested in the project

$$\left[\frac{R_0}{r} - \frac{L_0}{r - \lambda} \right] \left[1 - \frac{1}{(1 + r)^N} \right]$$

This falls short of the present value obtained in the previous case by

$$\frac{\lambda L_0}{r(r - \lambda)} + \left(\frac{R_0}{r} - \frac{L_0}{r - \lambda} \right) \left(\frac{1}{1 + r} \right)^N$$

This can more conveniently be expressed as

$$\frac{L_0}{r} \left[\frac{\lambda}{(r - \lambda)} - \frac{r}{(r - \lambda)(1 + r)^N} + \frac{R_0}{L_0 (1 + r)^N} \right]$$

To guess at the importance of this element, we must evaluate the term in square brackets for alternative plausible values of its parameters. Let us assume a rate of increase (λ) of real wages equal to 3 per cent per annum. The result then will depend only on the ratio R_0/L_0, from which N can be derived, and on the rate of discount, r. Table 1 presents some results that illustrate how important the "wage-increase adjust-

TABLE 1

Reductions in Present Value (ΔPV) Assuming a 3 Per Cent

Annual Increase in Wages as Against a Zero Rate of

Increase, Expressed as a Fraction of the Present

Value (L_0/r) of Wages Bill Assuming a Zero

Rate of Increase of Wages

R_0/L_0	1.159	1.344	1.558	1.806	2.094	2.427
Implied value of N (years)	5	10	15	20	25	30
$r \Delta PV/L_0$ assuming $r = .06$	.369	.634	.816	.941	1.021	1.074
$r \Delta PV/L_0$ assuming $r = .10$	.264	.384	.457	.482	.485	.484
$r \Delta PV/L_0$ assuming $r = .15$	.206	.272	.284	.274	.268	.261

ment" is in different cases. As can be seen there, for the cases examined, the adjustment ranges from 20 per cent to over 100 per cent of L_0/r, the present value that would be computed for wage outlays if the wage rate were assumed not to change. For what I consider to be the most relevant part of the table—$r = .10$ and R_0/L_0 ranging between 1.5 and 2.5—the adjustment is consistently between 45 per cent and 50 per cent of the present value of wages estimated, assuming the wage rate to be constant. Clearly this is not a negligible factor; I think the conclusion is obvious that the anticipated growth of real wages should be built into project analyses as a matter of normal operating procedure.[1]

Future Changes in the Discount Rate

The discount rate used in cost-benefit analysis should reflect the marginal productivity of capital in the economy as a whole. Obviously, a fully optimal situation would require that the marginal productivity of capital be the same in all applications within the economy, and problems are created when, because of capital market imperfections, differential rates of taxation among activities, or other reasons, rates of marginal productivity vary from sector to sector. Let us waive these difficulties for the moment, however, so as to be able to concentrate on variations in the discount rate over time. Thus, in this section we will be assuming a well-functioning capital market without significant imperfections.

The key element that enables us to take account of variations in the relative scarcity of investible funds is a discount rate that changes as we move through time. If funds are particularly scarce this year, but are expected to be relatively abundant in subsequent years, this fact might appropriately be reflected in, say, a 12 per cent rate of discount applying to this year's flows of benefits and costs, and a more modest 8 per cent

---

[1] The example above assumes that the amount of labor required to produce a given output from the project in question remains constant through time, and is not reduced as a consequence of improvements in "productivity." This is the case for many types of projects, in which labor and materials requirements are established by the initial design of the project and its associated capital equipment. However, it is certainly possible that for some projects one might reasonably forecast a gradual improvement in labor productivity; in such cases the labor requirements should be projected independently, and the wage rate should, as in the example above, reflect the expected trend of real wages for the relevant categories of labor. Even where productivity on the project is expected to rise through time, there are no grounds for assuming that, project by project, the increase in productivity will just offset the anticipated rise in real wages.

rate applying to future flows. The present value of a project (PV) would then be found by the formula

$$PV = \sum \frac{N_t}{\displaystyle\mathop{\pi}_{i=1}^{t} (1 + r_i)}$$

where N_t represents the estimated excess of benefits over outlays in year t, and r_i is the rate of discount applicable to flows accruing during the year i.

This formulation also brings out clearly the method of analyzing the benefits or costs associated with the postponement of a project. Assume the project costs $1 million and yields a stream of benefits (net of current costs) of $100,000 per year in perpetuity starting in two years. Let the discount rate for all years from next year onward be 8 per cent, and let the discount rate appropriate to this year be 20 per cent. Then the present value of net benefits, evaluated as of next year, will be $1.25 million, and brought back to this year will be $1.04 million. Benefits thus exceed costs, if the project is undertaken this year, in the amount of $40,000.

But suppose it would also cost $1 million to do the project next year, and that in that event benefits would begin to accrue three years from now. In this case the present value of net benefits evaluated two years from now would again be $1.25 million, but brought one year from now they would be $1.16 million. From this sum we must deduct the project cost of $1 million, and discount the difference of $160,000 back to this year at 20 per cent in order to obtain the present value of the project if undertaken next year. This yields a present value of $133,000—clearly higher than is obtained under the option of doing the project this year, and it thus pays to postpone the project for one year. It does not pay to postpone the project for two years, however, for in this case the net present value of the project must be discounted for an additional year at 8 per cent, yielding a value of $123,000.

Actual problems of project postponement are likely to be more complicated than that above, for postponement is likely to alter the size and time shape of the stream of net benefits, and also the capital costs of the project, rather than just displacing both benefits and costs through time. But the principle of evaluating benefits and costs under alternative assumed timing patterns remains valid when these complications are taken into account.

The Choice of a Time Path for the Rate of Discount

I should like to begin the discussion of this problem from a different starting point than is usually taken. What should be r_{10}, r_{11}, r_{12}, . . . , r_{20}, etc.? That is, what should be the one-year discount rate applicable to flows 10, 11, 12, . . . , 20, etc., years in the future? One answer is surely clear: We have very little specific information on which to base such a judgment. But it is worthwhile to add a second statement: The limited information we have is very unlikely to lead us to judge that r_{10} should be .08, r_{11} should be .14, r_{12} should be .10, etc. Even though we know that there will be cyclical and other short-term variations in the relevant rate of discount in the future, we do not know when they will occur, so our best guess as to the relevant rate for year 11 will not be very different from our best guess as to the relevant rate for year 10, etc. Thus we can conclude that the relevant rate for years in the far‹ distant future will move, if at all, only as the result of the operation of basic secular forces.

Obviously, the marginal productivity of capital will be affected by many factors: the rate of capital formation, the rate of labor-force growth, the nature and degree of "neutrality" or "nonneutrality" of technical advance, the nature of changes in the pattern of demand, particularly of relative shifts toward or away from capital-intensive industries, etc. Some of these prices by themselves would work to produce a secularly rising rate of marginal productivity, others to produce a secularly declining rate. One obviously cannot be dogmatic about which set of forces will dominate in the long-term future, but I think that our past experience is relevant here. If we have had steady downward trends in series that we might take as reasonable indicators of the marginal productivity of capital, that would give us some basis for projecting a secular downward trend in the future. But I do not believe that the evidence can be read in this way. Whether one looks at interest rates, at rates of return on corporate capital, or at ratios of the rent of property to its value, no case can be made for a significant downward (or upward) secular tendency. In the face of the historic sluggishness of these series, I believe it is reasonable to project far-future rates of discount, for the purposes of cost-benefit analysis, to be constant and to be somewhere near the historical average of the most directly relevant past series.

This judgment greatly eases the burden on the project evaluator. He has basically three questions to answer: (1) What is the relevant long-term future rate of discount? (2) What is the relevant rate for the current year? (3) By what path will the relevant rate move from its current to its expected future level? We have already hinted at the answer to the first of these questions, so let us set that aside for a moment and turn to the second and third questions. A general answer is easy: When investible funds are relatively scarce this year and in the near-term future, relative to what is expected for the long-term future, the near-term rates of discount should be above the rate for the far future, and vice versa when investible funds are relatively abundant. Obviously, relative scarcity here incorporates both demand and supply factors, and I think that it should be fairly easy for project evaluators to have a good sense of whether they are in a year of glut or famine in this sense. Where really good capital markets exist, one can get a direct indication of the ease or stringency of the current relative to the expected future situation from the relationships of short-term relative to long-term interest rates. From the yield curve of loans and bonds by term to maturity, one can derive implicit expected one-year rates for each year in the future. This observed pattern can then be compared with the "average" pattern of the past to see what "abnormalities" exist. Where current short-term rates are relatively high, the difference $(r_t - \bar{r}_t)$, where r_t is the expected one-year rate applicable to the year t and $\bar{r}_t$ is the average of past expected rates applicable to times t years in the future, will tend to look like curve A in Figure 1. Where the situation is normal, the difference $(r_t - \bar{r}_t)$ will tend to look like curve B, and when the situation is one of current glut, a curve like C will be likely to apply.

Although, for reasons to be indicated later, the level of interest rates

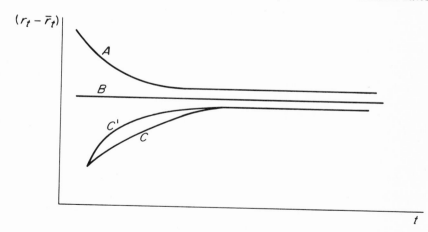

Figure 1

on bonds and loans is likely to be a poor indicator of the level of the relevant discount rate for cost-benefit analysis, the use of bond market information can give us clues as to the intensity of stringency or glut of investible funds in a given year, as to the length of time that the stringency or glut is likely to last (this being the length of time before the curve has effectively leveled out), and as to the expected pace at which the stringency or glut will be eased (compare C and C'). All of this information will be helpful to the planning authority in setting the time path of discount rates for cost-benefit work.

The Choice of the Level of the Rate of Discount

We now return to question (1), above, distinguishing between the time-shape of curves representing the discount rate to be applied to flows in year t and their general level, perhaps best summarized by the common level of longer-term future one-year discount rates. I have already indicated that I believe this level should be set at approximately the average of the relevant rates in the past. But we do not have data on the marginal productivity of capital itself, and it certainly is not equalized across industries. I would choose here the average rate of return to capital for the economy as a whole, at least in cases in which this rate appears to have been relatively constant. In textbooks, when the average rate is constant, the marginal rate must equal the average, but we are dealing here with a considerably more complicated problem than the textbook example from which the above statement was drawn. It is not by any means necessary that the marginal rate of return from capital should have always been equal to the average, just because the average rate has been historically constant, and I must emphasize that the choice of the past average rate entails an element of judgment. What we can be dogmatic about is that one should use the marginal social rate of productivity of capital as the discount rate, that this rate includes taxes paid on the income from capital, as well as any other external effects not perceived by the individual investor, and that largely for the above reasons (principally the inclusion of taxes) the relevant rate is likely to be quite high compared with the observed rates on bonds, mortgages, etc.

One must recall that the purpose of the discount rate in cost-benefit analysis is to be a guide to decision-making. Suppose that we took some average of bond rates as the relevant one; virtually automatically, almost any corporate investment would pass the test of yielding a positive present value of benefits minus costs. This would be so because the benefits counted by corporate investors are net of tax, while the benefits relevant for social decision-making are gross of tax. Thus any corporate investment found privately acceptable at the market rate of interest, for example, would be socially an excellent investment; and many projects rejected by corporations because they fail to yield the market rate of interest net of tax would nonetheless have to be adjudged socially acceptable after including the tax component of benefits. Virtually no privately undertaken project would fail to pass the market-rate test, and many more would be added that would pass the market-rate test once taxes (let alone other social benefits) were included in the analysis. I cannot imagine that funds would be forthcoming from any source (private or public) to finance the volume of investments that would pass the market-rate test once we count social as well as private benefits.

On the other hand, if we use as the social rate of discount the rate including taxes, for example, existing private sector projects would "on the average" pass the test, but some (with less-than-average taxes and normal post-tax yields, for example) would have negative present values while others (with higher-than-average taxes and normal post-tax yields, for example) would have positive present values. The decision rule implied by a tax-inclusive rate of discount would call for shifts in the allocation of investment from low-tax to high-tax fields—as well it should—but it would not normally call for any long-term major alteration in the propensity of the community to save.

Some writers appear to argue for a rate of discount reflecting social time-preference in some sense. Without attempting to argue the case in depth, let me note that such a procedure does not run into practical difficulties if one is able to generate a sufficient volume of savings so as to be able in fact to set in motion all the projects that pass the present-value test using such a rate. But I find it hard to support a policy that would force from the community the savings levels that would be required to do, say, all investments passing a 4 per cent test, and difficult to believe that this would be possible to do even if desirable.

There is an argument for eliciting from the community more savings than it currently undertakes on the ground that, because of taxes and other possible "externalities," the social yield of investment is higher than the private yield. But this argument would not justify extracting (perhaps by taxes) more savings from the community than it would be ready to make voluntarily if faced with a private yield equal to the social marginal productivity of capital—and the available studies of savings behavior do not show any powerful responsiveness of private savings to the private rate of return. Thus some supplementing of private savings by public savings appears to be justified, but not nearly so much as would be required to pull the typical rate of marginal productivity of capital in the economy down very substantially.

Other arguments that sometimes arise in discussions of this general point are (1) that the market mechanism fails to give a vote to future generations and therefore generates too little savings, (2) that private investors excessively discount the far future on grounds of risk, and (3) that private individuals would like to provide better for future generations than they do, if only this were done collectively, as they know that individually they can have little effect on future generations' standards of life. These arguments are discussed by Robert Strotz in a recent paper.[2] Strotz emphasizes, and I have long agreed, that the integeneration comparison, as a normative problem, arises only if we expect future generations as a whole to be poorer than we are. There is no normative reason for making the present (poor) generation save more than it wants to in order to make future, richer generations still richer. On the risk-premium argument, Strotz notes that there are ample possibilities for risk-pooling, and that yields in industries of differential riskiness do not diverge widely from each other.[3] I would add that yield curves give us an even better way of isolating the relative discounts placed on the far-future as against near-future income, and that they provide no presumption of an excessive discount of the distant future. Consols have not gone begging for a market in this world, nor have 30- or 40-year bonds!

Argument (3), best reflected by Sen and Marglin,[4] smacks of charity. It already rests on a rather weak reed if it is assumed that future generations will in fact be better off than the present one. Such compassion as nonetheless exists for future generations is, however, dissipated because each individual's saving will presumably be reflected in negligibly small increments in the future welfare of many individuals. To avoid this a concerted effort of the present generation is needed, each individual's contribution being contingent upon those of the rest. My reaction to this is simple: Any individual who wants to help others and make sure that his contribution is not dissipated can do so by selecting one or more people of the present generation to help. By so doing he can be sure that the object of his charity is needy, and that all his

[2] Robert H. Strotz, "The Social Rate of Time Discount," mimeo., 1964, pp. 2–6.
[3] Strotz here cites the results reported in George J. Stigler, *Capital and Rates of Return in Manufacturing Industries,* Princeton, N.J., 1963.
[4] See A. K. Sen, "On Optimizing the Rate of Saving," *Economic Journal,* September 1961; and Stephen A. Marglin, "The Social Rate of Discount and the Optimal Rate of Saving," *Quarterly Journal of Economics,* February 1963.

charity will reach the desired object. Moreover, it is clear that by helping the youth of the present generation more fully to reach their productive potential and their human potential as individuals, one is likely to do much more for the generation of the year 2000 than by setting up a generalized trust fund in their favor.

I am thus left with recommending the observed past average social rate of return to capital as the best first approximation of the rate desirable for cost-benefit analysis. This rate should, of course, be modified whenever there are good reasons to expect that in the future the typical rate of social marginal productivity of capital will differ from that observed in the past, and for the present and near-future years should be modified whenever there is evidence of an abnormal scarcity or glut of investible funds.

Shadow Prices for Labor and for Capital

It has come to be generally accepted that when prevailing prices do not reflect the true scarcity value of goods or services, one should substitute for them "shadow prices" that in fact do so. There are many ramifications of this simple statement, and I shall not go into all of them here. For the moment let me focus on the shadow price of labor and on the shadow rate of return to capital.

The shadow price of labor should in some sense reflect the opportunity cost of such labor. When there is a substantial pool of unemployed labor, it is likely that the shadow price of that factor will be below the market price, and it is sometimes sustained that when there is really widespread unemployment in the economy, the shadow price of labor should be at or near zero.

Let me begin by attacking what is surely a straw man. Suppose an economy in which we can take it for granted that the shadow price of labor is zero. The wages bill of the nation is then, in effect, not a required payment to labor because of its scarcity-induced productivity, but rather a sort of transfer payment out of the "true" marginal product of capital. If, for example, we have a capital stock of $30 billion and a national income of $10 billion divided equally between labor and capital, the full $10 billion should be counted as representing the social marginal product of capital, and the estimated rate of social productivity of capital should be 33⅓ per cent, not the 16⅔ per cent that we would estimate using the observed return to capital.

The point of this example is to emphasize that to the extent that we set the shadow price of labor below the market wage, we are obliged also to set the social marginal rate of productivity of capital above that which we would compute by counting all wages paid as true economic costs. As one pushes the shadow wage to zero, one simultaneously pushes the shadow rate of productivity of capital toward the ratio of national income to capital stock in the economy. With this come some rather embarrassing implications: A rate of discount as high as the income-capital ratio is virtually a kiss of death for projects with long gestation periods or long economic lives. Waiting cannot well be afforded at a $33\frac{1}{3}$ per cent rate of discount, and far-future incomes are virtually worthless when discounted back to the present at such a rate. Moreover, as one looks at the full equilibrium of an economy with a zero shadow wage, one finds that the appropriate prices for all goods are proportional to their capital-service components; that is, in such a full equilibrium, the ratio of net value added to capital would tend to be equal in all industries and sectors. I shudder at what this means for house rents, electricity prices, road charges, and the prices of the outputs of other similarly capital-intensive activities; and I doubt that any who may momentarily believe that a zero shadow price for labor is truly relevant for any given economy will continue to sustain this view after they follow through its full implications.[5]

In practice, the shadow wage for labor is, I venture to assert, never zero for the entire labor force and rarely zero for any significant part of it. But it certainly may fall below the actual wage for some occupations in many industries and for many occupations in some industries. To the extent that it does, the excess of the actual over shadow wage bill in any industry or sector should be attributed as part of the true economic yield of capital, and should thus tend to produce a discount rate for cost-benefit analysis that is higher than the observed gross-of-tax rate of return to capital.

But—and this is an extremely important point—it is hardly something to be hoped for that the shadow wage should forever remain below the actual wage. Unemployment, underemployment, market imperfections, all the forces that make for a discrepancy between actual and shadow wages, are things that one would hope and expect to be substantially reduced if not eliminated as an economy develops successfully. This has important implications for cost-benefit analysis, which I shall try to bring out in a simple example. For this example, let me assume that we can take, for each year, the ratio of estimated shadow

---

[5] I have dealt with this subject at some length in "Cost-Benefit Analysis and Economic Growth," *Economic Weekly,* Annual Number, February 1962, pp. 207–21.

income from capital to total capital stock as the relevant shadow rate of return to capital applicable to benefit and cost flows during that year.

Let us start with the prospective total national income stream shown in the last two columns of Table 2, divided between labor and capital according to market prices, and with a ratio of shadow wage to actual wage expected to move from a current level of .70 to a level of .99 in ten years.

TABLE 2

Year	National Income	Labor Share at Market Prices	Capital Share at Market Prices	Shadow Wage as Per Cent of Market Wage	Labor Share at Shadow Wage	Capital Share at Shadow Prices
1	1,000	600	400	70	420	580
2	1,060	640	420	75	480	580
3	1,120	680	440	80	546	574
4	1,180	720	460	84	605	575
5	1,250	760	490	88	669	581
6	1,320	800	520	91	728	592
7	1,400	850	550	93	790	610
8	1,480	900	580	95	855	625
9	1,560	950	610	97	922	638
10	1,650	1,000	650	99	990	660

In Table 2 the returns to labor and capital are evaluated at shadow prices. Now assume the series in Table 3 for the prospective level of capital stock in each year. This series was so selected as to yield a market rate of return (gross of taxes, of course) to capital of 10 per cent in each year.

The re-estimation of the shadow rate of return to capital, year by year, to take account of the expected gradual elimination of the discrepancy between shadow and actual wages obviously has the effect of bringing the shadow rate of return to capital gradually into correspondence with the market rate of return. Moreover, it leads to a decision rule which is much less discriminatory against capital-intensive or long-lived projects than a rule based solely on the initially prevailing shadow wage and the initially prevailing shadow rate of return to capital.

The technique just outlined of obtaining the time path of the shadow

TABLE 3

Year	Capital Stock	Capital Share at Shadow Prices	Market Rate of Return to Capital (per cent)	Shadow Rate of Return to Capital (per cent)
1	4,000	580	10.0	14.5
2	4,200	580	10.0	13.8
3	4,400	574	10.0	13.0
4	4,600	575	10.0	12.5
5	4,900	581	10.0	11.8
6	5,200	592	10.0	11.4
7	5,500	610	10.0	11.1
8	5,800	625	10.0	10.8
9	6,100	638	10.0	10.5
10	6,500	660	10.0	10.2

rate of return to capital is appealing in other ways as well. First, it is consistent with the over-all approach that was recommended above for a situation in which market prices were taken as a guide; in effect the 10 per cent market rate of return to capital could be the observed past average of that rate, or that average adjusted in the light of prospective market developments. Second, it develops the shadow rate of return to capital on the basis of macroeconomic magnitudes of the type likely to be estimated by development planners. And third, it recognizes that the setting of the shadow rate of return to capital as something distinct from the gross-of-tax market rate of return should be based on the discrepancy between the wages bill for the total economy valued at market prices and the wages bill for the total economy valued at shadow prices, rather than on these magnitudes by individual industries.

To elaborate a bit on the last point, assume that in Sector A the shadow wage is equal to half the market wage, while in Sector B the shadow wage and market wage are the same. Suppose the market rate of return to capital is 10 per cent in both sectors, but that by imputing half the wages bill of Sector A to capital in that sector, we would thereby increase the computed rate of return to capital to 20 per cent in that sector. It makes no sense at all to proceed with project evaluation in this case by using a 20 per cent rate of return for projects in Sector A and a 10 per cent rate of return for projects in Sector B. The same rate must be used in both sectors, and the above procedure would estimate the approximate rate by, in effect, obtaining a weighted average of the 20 per cent return imputable to capital in Sector A and the 10 per cent return of Sector B. Projects of Sector B would (and should) be burdened by being required to meet the test of a higher rate of return than the 10 per cent market rate, while wages paid in B would be fully counted as costs. On the other hand, projects in Sector A would benefit from being allowed to exclude from costs half of their wages bill and include that amount as imputed income from capital, while being required to meet a 15 (not 20) per cent test of capital yield at shadow prices.

The treatment of capital and labor in the above example is obviously different, and for a good reason. Discrepancies between shadow and market wages vary by skill of labor, by region, and by industry sector, among other things. Shadow prices should discriminate in favor of projects that actually draw into employment workers whose opportunity cost is less than the wages paid them, and should discriminate (at least in a relative sense) against projects that do not do so. This is done by assigning a share of the wages bill to capital in the former class of projects—a share that varies from project to project in accordance with the degree of discrepancy between their shadow and market wage bills. Once this is done, the accounts have been rectified, so to speak, and the projects should be free to compete for available capital funds by being required to meet the same rate-of-return or present-value test.

The main weakness of the procedure used in the tables above is that it requires one to specify—in advance, so to speak—the time path by which the gap between over-all shadow and actual wage bills will be reduced. Obviously, this time sequence cannot be drawn out of thin air or assumed at will; on the contrary, its estimation is a serious responsibility of the macroeconomic planners. Without attempting here to go into detail as to reasonable ways of guessing at this time path, let me just note that the most common alternative procedure also makes such a guess—by assuming that the shadow wage remains constant through time. The procedure advocated here simply makes explicit that a guess is required—and suggests that it be the best guess possible in the face of all available evidence and judgment.

Time Paths of Prices and of Demand

Let me begin this section by focusing on a particularly important price— the exchange rate—to indicate how its role differs from that assigned to the wage rate in the preceding section. The key point of the preceding section that is relevant here is that a shadow wage below the market wage had a direct implication with respect to the rate of return to capital. The situation is not nearly so clear when we consider a shadow exchange rate (defined as the price in local currency of foreign currency) different from (generally above) the market rate. A rise in the rate of exchange will enhance the profitability of export industries through its effect on their product prices. It may or may not enhance the profitability of import-competing industries, depending on whether imports were previously restricted (e.g., by licensing) to a volume determined by foreign exchange availabilities (in which case the effective internal price of imports might decline as a consequence of the rise in the exchange rate together with a relaxation of restrictions), or whether imports were freely admitted at the pre-existing exchange rate (in which case their price would surely rise). The rise in the exchange rate, on the other hand, would tend to reduce the profitability of investment in industries using imported materials and also in industries using imported capital equipment. The net effect of all these forces is uncertain in that there is no presumption that the introduction of a shadow exchange rate in place of a (lower) market rate will either typically raise or typically lower the shadow rate of return to capital.

The exchange rate differs from the wage rate in another important respect as well. Whereas the labor market imperfections that require the use of shadow as distinct from actual wage rates tend to be rather fundamental phenomena—not possible to eliminate quickly—there is no corresponding excuse for the use of shadow pricing with respect to the exchange rate. A simple act of devaluation can put into effect as the market rate whatever value one would choose to set as the shadow price of foreign currency. I feel that the policy of allowing the exchange rate to reflect the scarcity value of foreign currency is virtually essential for good project evaluation—as well as being good for other reasons. It obviates the need for readjusting a whole set of internal product prices and for revaluing amounts of capital actually invested. Moreover, even if the exchange rate is allowed to reflect the scarcity value of foreign currency, it still presents substantial problems for the project evaluator and the planner whenever it is expected that the rate will have to change through time. As in the case of investible funds, we may face circumstances of abnormal scarcity or glut of foreign currency that would require different expected exchange rates to be applied to different future years. I see no merit at all in compounding these problems by following exchange rate policies that require a complete reshuffling of the accounts for the present year as well.

Much of what has been said about the exchange rate applies to other prices as well. If the shadow price of a product is different from the actual price, this fact is not likely to have a profound effect upon the shadow rate of return to capital for the economy as a whole. But it does introduce serious problems in that purchasers of the product guide their own decisions by the actual price, while we would like them to guide their decisions by the shadow price. It may take ingenuity to make the actual price reasonably reflect the shadow price in some cases, but as the experts of Electricité de France have shown, the job can be done well even in some very complicated cases.

Finally, just as with the exchange rate, even if we do permit market prices to reflect scarcity values on a current basis, we still have the substantial problem of estimating the future path of prices. With respect to this problem, there is one principle which is crucial to good project evaluation. One often hears projects justified, in practice, on the basis that even if they are not profitable today, they will become profitable in the future because of the growth of demand. There can indeed be such a justification for particular projects, but when this is the case it is more subtle than many people think. Almost any investment made today would become profitable with time if no competing investments were made in the future. But that does not say by any means that all such investments should be made today. In the first place, their postponement might result in their having even higher present value, and this should be taken into account in the process of analysis and decision-making. In the second place, and probably much more important, is the fact that the "profitability" of today's investments should be estimated on the assumption that all "profitable" future investments will also be made. This kind of consideration must of necessity enter into investment decision-making in a competitive industry, where one can more or less be sure that someone will undertake those investments that become profitable in the future even if they are inimical to the profitability of one's own investment of today. It is properly reflected, for example, by forecasts of declining prices where rapid technological advance is foreseen. In public-sector decision-making, one cannot rely on the expectation of "someone's" future action to force upon the project analyst a pattern of a declining future price in the face, for example, of a rapidly rising total demand for the good or service in question. Here, of necessity, the project analyst himself has to estimate an expected time path of the price —not on the assumption that his project stands alone, nor on the assumption that future projects will be held up in order to "protect" the profitability of his current project, but on the much more rigorous assumption that future investments will be made on their own merits and without consideration to their effect on the profitability of any past investments. All this can in most cases be summarized in the expected price path of the product through time, but it must be realized that the expected price path here means more than just a guess about future prices—it means rather a guess as to the prices that will be generated in the future by an essentially optimal investment policy or, perhaps better put, by the continuous application in the future of valid investment decision rules.

What has just been said about prices can be translated into corresponding statements about consumers' surplus. For simplicity, I shall represent this problem by a simple supply-and-demand diagram (Figure 2), but it should be borne in mind that the principle involved extends to much more complicated cases. Assume that the demand function for a product shifts, through time, from D_1 to D_2 to D_3, etc. Assume, furthermore, that in each period the installation of new capacity of 1,000 units is expected to be justified, following a valid decision rule.

The benefit stream attributable to the first year's investment will be (1) in the first year, (2) in the second, (3) in the third, (4) in the fourth, etc. It will not be $EFCO$ in the second period, $GHCO$ in the third, and $IJCO$ in the fourth, because in these successive periods additional

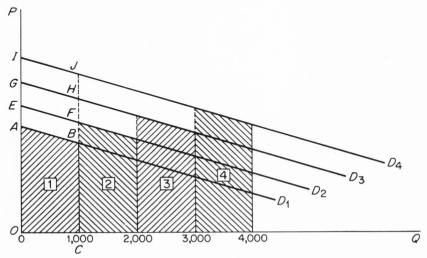

Figure 2

amounts of capacity of 1,000, 2,000, and 3,000 units must be assumed to be installed. Similarly, in evaluating the second year's investment, the benefit stream should be (2), (3), (4), etc.

One can, on occasion, count *ABCO, EFCO, GHCO,* and *IJCO* as the benefit stream from the first investment, but that only occurs if no further acceptable investments will be generated as demand grows through time—a condition that can be presumed to be highly unlikely.

The general principle involved here is that in assessing the contribution of any unit of capacity, it should be considered as the marginal unit in each year of its operation. Inframarginal benefits, which would have accrued in any event as a consequence of subsequent additions to capacity in the absence of, say, the first year's project, should not be attributed to part of the benefits of that project. Indeed, one can go further, for no benefits should be attributed to any given project which are greater in present value than the lowest alternative cost of achieving the same benefits. Following this principle, it is quite possible that the shaded areas in Figure 2 might overstate the benefits properly attributable to the first year's project. We can be sure, however, that they do not understate the relevant benefits.

COMMENT

Frederick T. Moore, *RAND Corporation*

In his paper, Professor Harberger has very perceptively chosen to focus attention on the effects of uncertainty (imperfect foresight) on project appraisals. This is a most important topic and one that is rarely recognized or accounted for in practical cases. Typically, a project appraisal treats the information as though it were known with certainty, with the result that the calculations are carried out in great detail. This paper attempts to provide an antidote for that procedure. Under this heading the paper focuses primarily on the implications of changes in one particular price, that is, the level of and changes in the discount rate.

One other aspect of project appraisals is briefly mentioned, the "virtual necessity of decentralized decision-making." It is true that in most cases project appraisals are performed by ministries, public corporations, and similar bodies, and there is a need to regularize the procedures that they use. This is particularly true when projects are relatively small in scale; very large projects usually receive a great deal of attention not only from the ministry involved but also from the planning body and from various other interested agencies. But the general point is well taken.

These comments raise certain questions about the development of the topic as presented in the paper, but it is also necessary, it seems to me, to consider whether some of the most critical elements in project appraisal are in fact covered by the paper. Consequently, some brief additional remarks on this point are appended.

Our attention is first directed to the necessity of adjusting for real wage changes in project appraisals and a generalized formulation of the problem is given. But there seems to be some confusion here between changes in the wage rate and in the total wage bill. As development proceeds we expect that the real wage rate will rise, but this does not necessarily mean that the wage bill for any project will also rise. Wage rates rise because of increases in productivity, and at the project level the total labor force may be so adjusted to compensate for this rise that the wage bill stays the same. Alternatively, if the total labor force on the project is maintained, we would expect that total revenues would increase rather than remain constant as is postulated in the example. Consequently, it would appear that the problem is rather more complicated than it is presented in the paper.

The extended discussion of the appropriate choice of rates of discount provides a number of practical suggestions to the analyst. There are only a few minor comments that might be made. First, it is suggested that the information derived from capital markets may be useful in determining an appropriate discount rate. This is certainly true, but as a practical matter most underdeveloped countries have extremely weak or nonexistent capital markets; so they do not provide any satisfactory source of information. As a brief digression I might mention one specific instance in which such information appears to lead to a wrong decision rule. The regulations adopted by the Agency for International Development on this matter make a distinction between local currency costs and dollar costs. In the absence of any other information the regulation states that local currency costs shall be discounted at 6 per cent and dollar costs at 3½ per cent since this approximates the rate on U.S. government bonds. Clearly the decision rule is faulty. The 3½ per cent rate does not reflect the marginal productivity of investment in the United States nor in the underdeveloped country. Moreover, the use of two different rates suggests that there is a difference in the productivity of local currencies and dollars. That may in fact be the case, but if so the evidence is mostly to the effect that the productivity of dollars is higher; so a higher rate (not a lower rate) should be used. This is simply one illustration of the difficulties of obtaining appropriate information from the capital markets.

The paper also comments somewhat unfavorably on the argument that "private investors excessively discount the far future on grounds of risk" and says that there are "ample possibilities for risk-pooling" (citing approvingly a paper by Strotz). On this I am skeptical. Where are the possibilities for risk-pooling in underdeveloped countries, and if they exist why are they not better used? Basically the tendency to discount the future heavily is directly related to the investor's perception of the degree of uncertainty, both political and economic, associated with his investment. This is a "play it safe" strategy which makes a good deal of sense to the individual investor. In the long run the problem is to try to reduce those uncertainties, and in the short run a solution may well require higher public participation.

The necessity of adjusting market prices to reflect the scarcity value of inputs is discussed generally, and an illustration is provided. There can be no quarrel with the desirability of undertaking such corrections. The problem is how to find appropriate measures for the shadow prices and how far to push the process of correction to the inputs. The illustration presents a case where the correction is applied only to labor and not to capital. It must be assumed that the market price and the shadow price are the same for the latter. This leads to some curious conclusions. It must be assumed that the labor input is the same (in quality) in Sector A and Sector B, but in Sector A the shadow wage is only half the market wage whereas in B they are the same. Alternatively, this says that the productivity of labor in Sector A is half that in Sector B, and the capital-labor ratio in A is twice that in B when both are computed at their shadow prices. The paper concludes that "shadow prices should discriminate in favor of projects that actually draw into employment workers whose opportunity cost is less than the wages paid them. . . ." In the context of the example this suggests that increased employment is the criterion, but if that is so the appropriate strategy in this example is to increase projects in Sector B where one unit of capital provides twice the employment that it does in A. In short, omitting consideration of the scarcity of capital involves confusion and probably a wrong decision rule.

If the admonitions and suggestions contained in the paper were followed by project analysts, a substantial improvement in the appraisals would most certainly result, but in many cases the difficulties of choosing an appropriate discount rate are completely swamped by uncertainties with respect to other prices and costs. Gross errors are typically found in the estimates of both the investment and operating costs of projects. These errors can sometimes be greater than 100 per cent. Ministries consciously or unconsciously present the most favorable case for projects for which they are responsible. Projections of demand are typically overoptimistic; estimates of labor productivity are too high; delays in project implementation lead to rapid cost increases; and project designs do not adequately reflect investment costs. Perhaps most importantly of all, projects are not systematically compared to alternatives in the same sector. It is not enough to consider the individual merits (including the appropriate rate of discount) of double-tracking a stretch of railway; the question is whether this is the best way to increase capacity or whether some alternative methods (such as block signaling, increased length of trains, etc.) might not be better. This lack of attention to alternative investment opportunities and the absence of any sensible priority system is one of the major defects of project preparation in underdeveloped countries. While the points raised in the paper are obviously significant for project appraisal, major improvements are likely to require some workable solutions to these other problems.

Some Implications of Planning for Trade and Capital Movements

DON D. HUMPHREY

THE FLETCHER SCHOOL OF LAW AND DIPLOMACY
TUFTS UNIVERSITY

Introduction

Planning has been the enemy of foreign trade. This is true, moreover, though not equally true, of socialist planning and that of less developed countries. In each camp the current trend of thought is toward correcting the bias which planners have had against trade. It seems doubtful, however, that this salutary trend away from the extremes of balanced growth will eliminate the prejudice against export investment. The nineteenth century model of trade as the mainspring of growth is out of fashion. The age of mass production caters to stable and homogeneous markets. Export markets are uncertain for both economic and political reasons, and the tendency is to cut the risk.

The influence of the Soviet model, distaste for the enclave economy, and the revolt against colonialism have each played a role. But the preference of planners for balanced growth is also derived from analytical economics—the emphasis on complementaries, external economies, elasticities, and the terms of trade. The planned neglect of exports together with inflation diverts supplies from export markets to home consumption and, similarly, diverts factors to production for the domestic market. Overvalued currencies, in effect, tax exports and subsidize imports. While one may cite experienced advisers on development planning whose works do not mention foreign trade, others have stressed the positive effects of imports on industrialization.[1]

---

[1] Notably, Albert O. Hirschman, *The Strategy of Economic Development*, New Haven 1958, p. 121. "The advocates of protection and industrialization have also been reluctant to notice the connection between imports and industrialization. . . . As a result underdeveloped countries, always ardently protectionist, have

In addition to the swing from exports to import substitutes, development planning has had negative implications for private foreign investment and the automatic transmission of technology that goes with it. The substitution of government for private sources of capital is a corollary of massive intervention with the market which encompasses planning in the very broadest sense. The consequence of intervention, exchange controls, and less respect for the sanctity of contract is that private foreign investment in developing countries is reduced to minor proportions as compared with the nineteenth century rate of lending relative to saving.

Rather than documenting the intellectual history of planning and trade, the point regarding their limited compatibility can be illustrated by the European experience since the Second World War. The chief criticism of the Marshall Plan has always been that investment planning for the efficiency of Western Europe as a whole was unacceptable. But will anyone now argue that investment planning would have produced anything like as much growth as had been realized by the market stimulus to export-oriented investment? It is hard to imagine that planners would have dared to predict the increase of trade and productivity that has been realized.

Less Developed Countries

In the mixed economies of the West, planning has many faces ranging from the design or strategy of growth to the process by which governments and their agencies prepare to mobilize resources. Planning in less developed countries is typically associated with an environment of direct controls, especially the rationing of imports for the deliberate purpose of accelerating industrialization. Planning in the broad refers to the processing of information and the policy decisions by which governments mobilize resources to promote development.

often adopted a policy that is self-defeating. . . . By restricting imports too severely, they have been shutting out the awakening and inducing effect which imports have on industrialization" (*ibid.*, pp. 123–24). Cf. the papers on comparative costs and economic development by Wilfred Malenbaum, Walter A. Chudson, Werner Baer, and Isaac Kerstenetsky in *American Economic Review,* May 1964, with discussion by Albert O. Hirschman, Wolfgang F. Stolper, and Raymond Vernon. Nurske was concerned with reconciling the conflict between balanced growth and international specialization in *Patterns of Development,* Stockholm, 1959, reprinted in *Equilibrium and Growth in the World Economy: Economic Essays by Ragnar Nurske,* ed. Gottfried Haberler, Cambridge, Mass., 1961.

That strong emphasis on import substitution is not dead is indicated by Hiroshi Kitamura, "Foreign Trade Problem in Planned Economic Development," *Economic Development with Special Reference to East Asia,* ed. Kenneth Berrill, New York, 1964.

Balance-of-payments problems have played a major role in shaping the programs of many countries, but export levels were often not re-examined in the light of projections for extensive import substitution. Systematic calculation of the resources required to earn or save foreign exchange has, apparently, not been the rule of development planning, at least in its earlier stages The lack of information permits serious disagreement as to the importance of external effects associated with policies of balanced growth.

Until recently the development plans of many countries were based on partial projections. These are being replaced by macromodels for testing internal consistency.

The appeal of the planning process to the governments and intellectual leaders of underdeveloped countries draws sustenance from many streams of thought and feeling. First, due mainly to unfavorable conditions, the international mechanism of trade and investment has failed to transmit automatically the opulence of the rich to the poor regions of the world. The attitudes, practices, and social structure of underdeveloped countries may block development and keep the response to foreign trade within narrow channels and may themselves withstand transformation by economic forces alone. An enclave established by foreign investment will not be translated into a self-sustaining process of development unless many other conditions are fulfilled. But if these conditions are not fulfilled, the potential effect of economic planning is likely to be stultified.[2]

Secondly, the fear of dependence born of colonial experience turned the latent energies of new nations inward and fostered national planning which has inverted mercantilism by making import substitution, rather than exports, the source of wealth. Thus, nationalism seeks a sheltered environment for leaders more concerned with the visible symbols of economic power than with the invisible discipline of competition and foreign trade. Thirdly, the successful Soviet experience stands as a symbol of planned industrialization and casts a long shadow over the alternative of planned or unplanned trade expansion as an engine of growth. It would be ironical if the non-Communist countries of Asia, Africa, and Latin America should continue to follow the antitrade bias of the Soviet model now that most Communist countries are devoting a great deal

[2] "That the nineteenth century process of growth-transmission works rather differently nowadays is not in dispute. . . . In the middle of the nineteenth century that growth averaged about 13 percent annually, the total volume trebling within thirty years largely as a result of the inflow into Europe of primary produce from countries overseas" (A. K. Cairncross, *Factors in Economic Development,* London, 1962, pp. 215–19).

of effort to developing analytical tools with which to free themselves from the crippling effects of massive underspecialization.

DIVERSIFICATION AND FLEXIBILITY

In a changing environment, efficiency without flexibility spells overspecialization. It has long been said, for example, that survival of the species calls for enough inefficiency to reserve some energy for adapting to changes in the external environment. As regards trade, the Bhagwati model of "immiserizing growth" shows that an exporting country which is unable to re-allocate increasing factor supply may suffer because productivity gains are more than offset by terms-of-trade losses if price elasticity is low. Overexporting, according to Sir Arthur Lewis, results when labor for export crops remains cheap, because the only alternative is subsistence farming where its marginal product is zero. By a similar argument, pecuniary external economies may lead to overinvestment in primary production for export.[3] In the same vein, Kindleberger explains his empirical finding that the terms of trade have favored the developed against the undeveloped countries, rather than manufacturers against primary producers, by the difference in capacity to adjust. Factor immobility impedes exit from old lines and entry into new ones, which results in lower levels of welfare.[4] Swings in the terms of trade are a rough indicator of the relative factor mobility of trading countries.

That flexibility, rather than diversification per se, is the key to trade adjustment is supported by an empirical study of the effect of diversification on export stability. The study provides scant support for the view that industrialization is a means of reducing the variation in export earnings.[5] But the fact that neither diversification nor the degree of industrialization appears to explain much of the variation in export earnings does not preclude other benefits. Mere diversification is not enough if the structure of production remains inflexible owing to higher costs.[6]

---

[3] For a statement of assumptions and comparison with other models within a brief compass, see Richard E. Caves, *Trade and Economic Structure*, Cambridge, Mass., 1960, pp. 249 and 267.

[4] Charles P. Kindleberger, *The Terms of Trade: A European Case Study*, New York, 1956, pp. 227–31, 253–56; see the same author's contribution to J. J. Spengler (ed.), *Natural Resources and Economic Growth*, Washington, D.C., 1961.

[5] Benton F. Massell, "Export Concentration and Fluctuations in Export Earnings: A Cross-Section Analysis," *American Economic Review*, March 1964, pp. 47–63.

[6] This seems to be consistent with a study of the role of raw materials in international trade from the late 1920s to mid-1950s, which found that semi-industrialized countries experienced less favorable development than the pure raw material exporters (Karl Gustav Jungenfelt, "Raw Materials in International Trade," *Ekonomisk Tidskrift*, March 1964, pp. 1–25.

The object is to improve the elasticity of the country's response to change, whether of external or internal demand.

The case for diversification is little more than the need for greater bargaining power. Other things the same, the exporting country's bargaining power will be greater, the larger and more elastic its home consumption and production. For the more readily export supply can be transformed into new products by consuming more and producing less of the traditional product, the greater is the country's ability to improve its well-being, and vice versa. Similarly with regard to imports, the country's bargaining power is greater the more easily consumption can be shifted to import substitutes and the more readily their production can be expanded.

THE POOR-COUNTRY DILEMMA

The poor-country dilemma is that domestic resources are not readily convertible into either imports or import substitutes at constant terms. The attempt to speed up development by planning is certain to shift aggregate demand from domestic to foreign supply and to put pressure on the exchanges. This is conducive to overvaluation of the currency —in effect, exports are being taxed and imports subsidized. Foreign exchange is worth more than the market price, and demand must be shifted from foreign sources of supply back to domestic resources. The balance-of-payments disequilibrium requires export expansion or import restriction. Adjusting the exchange rate has the virtue of offering equal price incentives to expand exports and restrict imports but is unpopular in an era of planning.

Optimum tariff considerations and apprehension over export prices favor import restriction. The choice, however, is between the rising costs of import substitution or less favorable terms from export expansion (unless exports remain insignificant relative to world demand). In either case, the real rate of return on investment declines or, stated differently, the quantity of investment goods which can be obtained from rising rates of saving is less than if domestic resources were convertible into foreign resources at constant terms. The rising costs of deliberate import substitution, often associated with a questionable interpretation of the infant-industry argument, make the export option increasingly attractive. Investment planning must cope with the poor-country dilemma—for successful development, as distinguished from the initiation of growth, depends on the productivity of investment as well as the rate of saving.

Formal growth models typically focus on the allocation of labor and capital between investment and consumption in order to obtain the output proportions for turnpike growth; the country's welfare function determines the rates of saving and investment over time. Development planning, by contrast, introduces external financing and is concerned with foreign exchange allocations in a transitional period of accelerating growth. As a result "there has been little carry-over from the optimal growth paths derived from general theory to policy for developing countries. Since capital goods are largely imported, the problem of allocating resources to earning or saving foreign exchange largely replaces the problem of determining the share to be allocated to investment goods." [7]

Borrowing to finance capital imports permits an underdeveloped economy to grow initially at a rate limited by its ability to invest rather than by its ability to save.[8] The policy problem is then to transform the economy by shifting demand from foreign resources back to domestic resources as rapidly as the increase of savings will permit.

PLANNING CRITERIA VS. MARKET FORCES

Chenery's illuminating examination of the conflict between growth theory and comparative costs concludes that, "to most economists, a survey of the procedures actually followed in designing development policy would probably suggest that balance is overemphasized and the potential gains from trade are often neglected." [9] The principle of comparative advantage was not readily absorbed by emerging, and sometimes conflicting, growth theories because marriage of the two must reconcile trade improvement for external balance with internal disequilibrium and productivity changes over time. The work of Chenery and associates marks a milestone on this path, bringing comparative costs into development planning.[10]

[7] Hollis B. Chenery and Arthur MacEwan, "Optimal Patterns of Growth and Aid over Time," Conference on the Theory of Design of Economic Development, Iowa State University, 1965, mimeo.

[8] "The allocation of resources between trade-improvement and normal production takes the place of the allocation between investment and consumption in closed models. 'Trade-improving' investment is identified with output which either increases exports or substitutes for goods presently imported" (*ibid.*). Whether the commodity produced is cotton, steel, or machinery is irrelevant.

[9] Hollis B. Chenery, "Comparative Advantage and Development Policy," *American Economic Review*, March 1961, p. 48.

[10] See H. B. Chenery, "The Interdependence of Investment Decisions," Moses Abramovitz, *et al.*, *The Allocation of Economic Resources*, Stanford, 1959. I. Adelman, and H. B. Chenery, "Foreign Aid and Economic Development: The Case of Greece," *Review of Economics and Statistics*, forthcoming. H. B. Chenery, and K. Kretschmer, "Resource Allocation for Economic Development," *Econometrica*, October 1956. H. B. Chenery, and M. Bruno, "Development Alternatives in an

The attack on comparative advantage has concentrated on the risk of specialization in primary exports and the failure of trade theory to include various nonmarket elements. The four assumptions separating growth theory from comparative costs have been advanced as reasons for planned industrialization.[11] These are:

1. Internal structural imbalance with divergence of factor prices and opportunity costs
2. Expected changes in the quality and quantity of inputs
3. Internal and external economies of scale
4. Dominance of complementarities with regard to commodity supply and demand

Under favorable conditions of elastic demand and technological improvement, internal and external economies of scale arising from multi-sector expansion may confer significant market-expanding, cost-reducing benefits on each sector which would be unattainable to a single industry. The problem is to define growth criteria under realistic conditions. Development policy has often suffered from going ahead without satisfactory theoretical guidance or quantitative information, assuming that this could be justified by the advantage of an early start even though investment was inefficient.[12]

The showing that all less developed countries cannot achieve satisfactory growth rates by specialization in primary exports should not be used to argue against selective specialization by any primary producer. Neither the low income and price elasticity of demand for primary products nor their instability seriously damages the case for comparative

Open Economy: The Case of Israel," *Economic Journal,* March 1962. H. B. Chenery, and A. M. Strout, "Foreign Assistance and Economic Development," A.I.D. Discussion Paper No. 7, June 1965. A. S. Manne, "Key Sectors of the Mexican Economy, 1962–72," Research Center in Economic Growth, Stanford University, Memorandum No. 41, August 1965. A. S. Manne, and J. Bergsman, "An Almost Consistent Intertemporal Model for India's Fourth and Fifth Plans," Research Center for Economic Growth, Stanford University, Memorandum No. 40, August 1965. W. Tims, "Growth Model for the Pakistan Economy: Macroeconomic Projections for Pakistan's Third Plan," Planning Commission, Karachi, March 1965. J. Sandee, "A Long-Term Planning Model of India," New York, 1959.

[11] Cf. Gunnar Myrdal, *An International Economy,* New York, 1956, p. 279. I have adopted the phrasing of Chenery ("Comparative Advantage," p. 21) rather than Myrdal. For a selected bibliography and critical examination of the doctrines of trade and development see Gerald M. Meier, International Trade and Development, New York, 1963, especially Chaps. 6 and 7, and pp. 195–202.

[12] Cf. "The Growth and Decline of Import Substitution in Brazil," and Santiago Marcario, "Protectionism and Industrialization in Latin America," *Economic Bulletin for Latin America* (United Nations), March 1964.

costs.[13] The market value of export receipts can be reduced to cover these risks, and the social value of the stream of marginal revenue may then be used to compare investment in primary exports with other alternatives. The adjusted yield of export investment may well justify continued specialization because of the rising costs of import substitution and, also, because extra foreign capital may be attracted which would not otherwise be available.

The theory of comparative advantage is easily reconciled with the cost of labor training, which is an investment in human beings and, like any investment, involves a temporary sacrifice. Hence, the divergence of private and social costs in the infant-industry case justifies taxing consumers of protected products if producers are unwilling to invest without protection. The long-run reduction of costs justifies social investment in education. This implies extending protection to those industries which need the least protection for the shortest time and argues for a uniform tariff. Modest protection may also find limited justification in the need for diversification, provided that a broader economic base leads to greater flexibility and elastic factor supply.

What we find, however, is that this case for limited protection has been generalized and shelter extended to almost every conceivable sector with the possible exception of aircraft and certain heavy investment goods. The reasons for this doubtless stem from the risk of exports markets, the elasticity of home demand, the quest for external economies, and other problems—theoretical, quantitative, and political—of reconciling balanced growth strategy with comparative costs. Import statistics provide a map of internal demand while a strong preference for industrialization and for emulation of the rich and powerful nations lead in the direction of protecting a national "infant-economy." In short, the certain and elastic home demand offers a captive market for high-cost production of inferior quality, and industrialization, as a symbol of power, is preferred to the risks implied by specialization.

The "growth-package" approach to investment planning involves a radical departure from market criteria and precludes comparing individual alternatives on the scale of capital-labor intensity or comparative costs. But introduction of growth criteria into the investment package does not justify the neglect of exports that has characterized so many

---

[13] One thesis is that the terms of trade of the "periphery" decline, and its growth is retarded, because the periphery has a high income elasticity of demand for imports, while that of the center is low. This, however, justifies protection only under extremely limiting conditions (M. June Flanders, "Prebisch on Protectionism: An Evaluation," *Economic Journal*, June 1964, pp. 305–26).

development programs. This calls for three sorts of observations: the method of linking growth criteria to comparative costs, information problems, and the assessment of economic environment and political efficiency.

Since the market is not relied on to balance supply and demand in the face of structural change, allocations must provide for consistency of production levels with commodity demand and factor supply. "The technique of linear programming is designed to combine the test of consistency with the test of social profitability of a given resource use." By this method, trade improvement can be linked with efficient resource allocation, combining increased exports or import substitutes with the consistency test. This approach permits comparison of growth strategies provided that the criteria can be quantified. "Although it cannot be applied very extensively in underdeveloped countries as yet, the programming methodology serves as a guide to improved practical measures." Chenery looks forward to the inclusion of external effects, such as labor training, savings effects, and the social overhead costs of urbanization. "In formal terms, it is also quite easy to extend the programming model in time and to compute future prices for commodities and factors. The measurement of social profitability could then be made against a pattern of changing future prices." [14]

In the presence of dramatic scarcities and failure of the automatic mechanism, for whatever reason, to spread opulence from the center countries to those on the periphery via trade and investment, it is difficult to quarrel with planning as a principle. Since successive stages of one-period efficiency may result in a suboptimal growth path for the long period, development planning offers more distant horizons than are recognized by the market and, usually, advances more ambitious goals under conditions where private profits do not maximize social benefits.

If growth criteria can be quantified, the choice of governments can be illuminated by use of sophisticated models. But model building may outrun the supply of information, external economies are elusive under realistic conditions, and the side effects of extensive market intervention by weak governments and untrained officials are often neglected. For both theoretical and practical reasons, the pursuit of external economies is fraught with uncertainty and, since the policymaker usually knows little of their quantitative importance, it may be impossible to determine whether a production process should be expanded or contracted. "The

[14] "Comparative Advantage," pp. 48 and 39.

planner's task may be compared to an attempt on a foggy day to get to the highest point on what, for all he knows, may be the top of a ridge or the rim of a crater. Just going uphill may well take him in a very wrong direction." [15]

When the practical limitations on information and analysis are recognized, the tension between growth criteria and comparative advantage is increased by the uncertainties of a radical departure from the market. It is the growth path of imports that needs to be economized and, since long-term planning must anticipate future import demand, the current list of imports is no longer the best guide to import substitution; in the context of optimal growth paths, it may be more efficient to provide substitutes for potential imports for which demand will be created by the acceleration of growth. As has been learned from costly experience, moreover, import-substituting industries were often heavy processors of imports; so development policy may be self-defeating if resources are diverted from exports.[16] The familiar argument against exports has "a limited validity when we speak of a comparatively long time where mistakes are as likely to be made in estimating domestic demand and supply as in gauging foreign demand and supply, where at least the law of averages would apply with somewhat greater force. Similarly, the superiority of import substitution over exporting cannot be established merely by reference to the fact that at any given time existing exports face a somewhat unresponsive international market. In the context of long-term growth, the resources that go into import substitution can equally be diverted to the creation of new export opportunities. . . ." [17]

[15] William J. Baumol, "External Economies and Second-Order Optimality Conditions," *American Economic Review*, June 1964, Part I, p. 369. "If marginal social benefit exceeds the marginal private benefit . . . it would appear that, from the point of view of society, an increase in the activity must necessarily be beneficial. . . . We get into trouble only if we proceed one more step and argue that the optimal output is necessarily larger than the equilibrium output. For there is one very obvious reason why this result may not hold—the second-order maximum condition may just not be satisfied. In these circumstances there are likely to exist local maxima in the social welfare function, and a move that increases net social benefits may then well lead us toward one of those little hills in the welfare function and away from its global optimum" (*ibid.*, p. 359).

[16] Carlos F. Diaz-Alegandro, "On the Import Intensity of Import Substitution," *Kyklos*, 1965, pp. 495–511. Because demand for imported inputs is a derived demand, the author argues against the presumption of high price elasticities.

[17] I. G. Patel, "Trade and Payments Policy for a Developing Economy," *International Trade Theory in a Developing World*, eds. Roy Harrod and Douglas Hague, New York, 1963, pp. 315–16.

OBSERVATIONS ON ENVIRONMENT

If development planning is guided by growth criteria outside the market, the more successful it is in improving the elasticity of factor supply and produced factors, the greater will be the opportunity for realizing external economies. The factor-producing industries of transportation, power, and capital equipment are especially important in poor countries. Yet it is characteristic of underdeveloped countries that capital equipment operates far below capacity because of the inelastic supply of inputs associated with factor-producing bottlenecks and import rationing.

Perhaps the most striking aspect of the capital shortage in underemployed economies is that their industrial plants operate well below capacity. Output is typically 65 to 75 per cent of capacity, and the operation of more than one shift is the exception rather than the rule. Inventories are much higher in underdeveloped than in advanced countries owing to poor transportation and communications and to hoarding, which is encouraged by price controls and direct allocation of materials. Undercapacity levels of production result from multiple bottlenecks: poor highways, crowded rail facilities, congested ports which delay the turnaround of ships, long delays in getting spare parts, rationing of electric power, or coal of a quality for which the boilers were not designed, and above all—import rationing with fixed exchange rates.

The significance of environment for reliance on growth criteria may be illustrated by reference to Marcus Fleming's theoretical treatment stressing the importance of elastic supply for balanced growth: "the chances are much better for a 'vertical' propagation of external economies, from customer industry to supplying industry, and especially from supplying industry to customer industry, and . . . developments in industries at different stages in the same 'line' of production are more likely to afford each other mutual support than those in different lines of production." [18] A realistic assessment of environment, however, suggests that vertical integration is often "forced" by the inelastic supply of inputs associated with import rationing.[19]

[18] "External Economies and the Doctrine of Balanced Growth," *Economic Journal,* June 1955.

[19] For example, a foreign-owned tire plant was saddled with high-cost domestic nylon, while the synthetic rubber plant operated below capacity because supplies of alcohol depend on the price of sugar cane, controlled by the government, which was not competitive enough to provide sugar mills with adequate supplies of cane (Wilfred Malenbaum, "Comparative Costs and Economic Development," *American Economic Review,* May 1964, p. 396).

A recent survey of "The Impact of Underdevelopment on Economic Planning" argues that the most important obstacles which frustrate the efforts to accelerate growth are the "lack of various kinds of information which planners need, the lack of suitable projects worked out in sufficient detail for inclusion in a plan, and the lack of qualified and properly motivated personnel." [20] The contribution of planning to development depends not only on the information which is provided for policymaking but also on the environment in which decisions are carried out. The information provided must not only be better than that of the market, the climate in which decisions are made and executed must produce results without negative side effects that are important enough to offset the superior information.[21] We cannot hold planners responsible for the political diversion and bungling decisions of governments or the incompetence of their officials. But can we entirely absolve the planning process from the climate that multiplies opportunities for mismanagement and waste? The incorporation of growth criteria may be important. But whether the net effect of interdependence outside the market will be positive or negative depends not only on the design of sophisticated models and the scraps of information fed into them, but also on the political efficiency with which resources are mobilized and whether cost calculation is equivalent to a competitive environment.

Execution of the program, moreover, depends on how quickly the society can adjust to cultural and political change. Some economists consider the use of linear programing as premature. "Given their present circumstances, most countries might benefit more from the sound application of fundamental elementary principles. . . . The temptation to use the highest level of analysis also reinforces the tendency to neglect the non-economic components of the development process. . . .

[20] "One of the cruel ironies of economic life is that the societies that most want comprehensive economic planning are those least prepared to benefit from it. . . . But since no one dares take the responsibility for inaction, over-all plans continue to emerge. These plans are concocted by methods which bear little scrutiny, and which are, in fact, almost never discussed in the literature of economic development. . . . The process of making plans, as distinct from the principles of planning, has not been regarded as an important area of study" (Andrea M. Watson and Joel B. Dirlam, *Quarterly Journal of Economics,* May 1965, pp. 167–68).

[21] "Planners thus face a dilemma. On the one hand, any important contribution of economic planning to the forecasting done by firms depends upon the possibility of constructing detailed models; on the other, the probability of error in forecasting increases with the amount of detail" (Fernand Martin, "The Information Effect of Economic Planning," *Canadian Journal of Economics and Political Science,* August 1954, pp. 328–42). The reference is to the mixed economies of advanced countries.

For a country that is still in only an early phase of development, it is especially important that attention first be given to whether the total environment is favorable for development, before concentrating on the purely economic factors." [22]

FACTOR IMBALANCE

Factor imbalance has been used to justify the protection of manufacturing from Manoilesco to Hagen. [23] It is examined here as an example of the lacunae in the empirical and analytical foundation for protectionism in development planning. Haberler's well-known article, using production-possibility curves, conceded the possibility that protection may increase welfare in case of external economies or factor immobility combined with price rigidity. He warned, however, that it is infinitely more difficult to assess the importance of such cases for policy, and his most recent contribution rejects such policy implications of pecuniary external economies on the ground that they misinterpret the role of entrepreneurs and the functioning of markets in the face of uncertainty and change. [24]

Although the meaning and significance of disguised unemployment have been widely debated as a justification for industrialization, the structural case for protection remains unsatisfactory from a cosmopolitan point of view. [25] In the first place, what counts is not the amount of underemployment in agriculture, but the rural-urban wage differential adjusted for the cost of labor training and social overhead investment required by urbanization. Assuming that the wage disparity exceeds these costs, it is true that the real income of a single country may be raised as long as the direct and indirect cost of protection is less than the additional income of factors moving from agriculture to protected industries. What has been overlooked, however, is that the same factor imbalance is characteristic of advanced countries which export manufactures. The wage disparity argument for industrial protection is generally unacceptable if all countries suffer from the same internal

[22] Gerald M. Meier, *Leading Issues in Development Economics*, New York, 1964, p. 563.

[23] *Theory of Protection and International Trade*, English edition, 1931.

[24] Gottfried Haberler, "Some Problems in the Pure Theory of International Trade," *Economic Journal*, June 1950, pp. 223–40; and "An Assessment of the Current Relevance of the Theory of Comparative Advantage to Agriculture Production and Trade," *International Journal of Agrarian Affairs*, April 1964. Haberler concludes that comparative advantage is relevant to the modern world including modern agriculture.

[25] For selected readings on underemployment, see Meier, *Leading Issues*, pp. 74–84.

disequilibrium. In the theory of second best, one country's wage differential may offset another's. After surveying the empirical evidence on this question, Hagen wrote: "The agriculture-urban [wage] differential exists in underdeveloped and economically advanced countries alike; the available evidence suggests that it does not disappear, or even diminish, in the course of development. It is a persistent long-run phenomenon. While the evidence is not absolutely conclusive, the presumption is very strong." [26]

Wage disparities are the natural result of labor immobility and inelastic demand for food in a growing economy. This implies that almost every country is underproducing manufactures. Hence, the structural case for import restriction falls wide of the mark, for it would seem to justify almost worldwide protection of manufactures which, by restricting consumption, would contract the manufacturing sector.[27] In the general case, only subsidies expand manufacturing relative to agriculture.

SCALE

Except for textiles, the home market of underdeveloped countries is seldom large enough for mass production industries. Yet in the Communist and non-Communist world alike, and in both developed and underdeveloped countries, high-cost automobile production is a status symbol. As regards size, the cost constraint is of two sorts—technological and monopolistic—and the rate of demand expansion is also quite relevant. Home markets which are too small to take the full-capacity output of one plant of optimum size establish a technological basis for foreign trade. But even if the market is large enough to absorb the output of at least one such plant, it may still be too small or not growing fast enough to provide the incentive for building a single plant of optimum size.

A fairly large number of small-scale, high-cost plants is not unusual even in rich countries—one thinks of Canada, for example.[28] This means that technological economies of scale are available before the market is large enough to provide an effective competitive response.

[26] Everett E. Hagen, "An Economic Justification of Protectionism," *Quarterly Journal of Economics,* 1958, p. 503; and *ibid.,* February 1961, pp. 145–51. Hagen returns to this theme in a forthcoming book on technical advance and economic theory. He concludes in favor of subsidies.

[27] In a well-stated argument for dual exchange rates to promote exports of manufactures while protecting the traditional sector, Nicholas Kaldor rests his case on factor imbalance as well as infant industries ("International Trade and Economic Development," *Journal of Modern African Studies,* December 1964).

[28] Cf. Harry C. Eastman, "The Canadian Tariff and the Efficiency of the Canadian Economy," *American Economic Review,* May 1964, pp. 438–48.

"Economically, therefore, an economy is too small if it fails to provide the competitive conditions necessary to spur the utmost efficiency and to lead to establishment of the technically most efficient plants." [29] Although in principle this may provide some justification for investment planning by small nations, the national planning process has, typically, failed in this respect.

As regards scale, the problematical aspect of external effects is still further complicated by the importance of industries producing intermediate products. A domestic market large enough to provide internal economies of scale for final consumer goods may be suboptimal with respect to raw materials, intermediate products, and servicing. Hence, vertical integration may result in external diseconomies. In sum, the realization of internal and external economies of scale is likely to depend on markets which are larger and expanding more rapidly than is implied by requirements of technical efficiency.

Moreover, the isolation of small markets from foreign competition is not conducive to risk taking. Businessmen of consequence who could raise large capital sums often have personal relationships conducive to "letting sleeping dogs lie." In his essays on European economic integration, Scitovsky concluded that the effect of an increase in competition would be more important than the expansion of trade. His eloquence regarding the beneficence of a competitive climate is far more relevant to underdeveloped countries: "The most successful institutions are likely to be imitated in countries that do not yet have them; the better industrial and commercial practices are likely to displace inferior ones; and the behavior and habits of thought of the more ambitious, more imaginative, more pushing and more ruthless are likely to prevail and be adopted also by their more easy-going competitors." [30]

In addition to policies of massive import substitution, a serious blow to exports, actual and potential, has been struck by the failure to appreciate fully the cost-increasing effect of protecting inputs by tariffs and, even more, by import rationing in an inflationary environment. Until recently, economists have failed to provide essential information on the wide disparity between nominal tariffs and the real rates of protection which they provide. The negative implication of protected inputs for internal and external economies of scale has also received scant attention.

[29] Tibor Scitovsky, "International Trade and Economic Integration as a Means of Overcoming the Disadvantages of a Small Nation," *Economic Consequences of the Size of Nations,* ed. E. A. G. Robinson, New York, 1960, p. 283.
[30] *Economic Theory and Western European Integration,* London, 1958, p. 23.

NEGLECTED ASPECTS OF PROTECTION

Protection is not measured by the duty on imports. While tariffs are are imposed and revenue collected on the total value of imports, this results in seriously misleading information as to the amount of real protection provided to processors. Protection is calculated by relating nominal tariff rates to the *value added* by manufacture. A duty of 20 per cent on cotton cloth, for example, provides protection of 40 per cent to the manufacturer if raw cotton accounts for half the cost and is unprotected.[31] Thus, the amount of protection is revealed by the difference between the tax on finished goods and the tax on their raw materials, intermediate products, and component parts. A uniform rate of duty is the equivalent of dual exchange rates favoring exports over imports.

The measurement of protection in relation to value added has three significant implications.[32] First, the degree of protection is higher than the duty when inputs are taxed at lower rates than finished imports. Secondly, protection of materials, intermediates, and components reduces the protection of processing industries, and if protection (including the effect of import rationing) is higher on inputs than on output, the result is negative protection for industries using protected inputs. Thirdly, real protection is represented by nominal rates only in case of

[31] "For a grain mill that buys grain for 75 cents and sells the product for one dollar, the incidence of a 20 percent duty would be 20 cents divided by 25 cents (the value added by milling), or 80 percent. In this case, protection to the milling industry is four times the rate of duty, because the milling of grain accounts for one-fourth of the total value of the product. By contrast, an industry paying 20 cents for materials that are fabricated and sold for one dollar receives protection of 25 percent (that is, the duty of 20 cents divided by 80 cents) from an import duty to 20 percent" (Don D. Humphrey, *The United States and the Common Market, a Background Study*, New York, 1962, pp. 60–63). Cf. James E. Meade, *Trade and Welfare*, London, 1955, Chap. X; Clarence L. Barber, "Canadian Tariff Policy," *Canadian Journal of Economics and Political Science*, November 1955, pp. 513–30.

[32] Harry G. Johnson is responsible for the formula measuring real protection: "The proper theoretical formulation entails using a formula in which the demand elasticities are weighted by the ratio of consumption to imports and multiplied by the nominal tariff rates, and the supply elasticities (in individual processes) are weighted by the ratios of value added in the country of imports and multiplied by the effective rates of protection of value added" (*U.S. Economic Policy Towards the Less Developed Countries, A Survey of Major Issues*, Brookings Institution, forthcoming). For estimates showing that real protection is higher than nominal protection, see Bella Balassa, "Tariff Protection in Industrial Countries: An Evaluation," *Journal of Political Economy*, forthcoming. For estimates of U.S. protection on the value added by labor, see G. Basevi, "The U.S. Tariff Structure: Estimates of Effective Rates of Protection of U.S. Industries on Industrial Labor," *Review of Economics and Statistics*, forthcoming.

a uniform tariff, provided that there are no direct import restrictions or natural protection from location or other invisible barriers to trade—assumptions which are, of course, wholly unrealistic.

The significance of the first proposition is that import-competing industries in most advanced countries have higher protection than is indicated by nominal duties and, further, that the same nominal rate may provide a wide range of protection to different industries. The second proposition is important for exports, especially those of underdeveloped countries. The general practice of restricting imports of materials and other inputs, whether for balance-of-payments reasons or to encourage home production, means that the opportunity for exporting manufactures may be seriously crippled by uninformed or inept policies.

For that matter, it may be doubted whether most countries have an approximate conception of the degrees of real protection that they are extending to various levels of processing from materials to finished manufactures. As a matter of theoretical interest, excessive protection of inputs may restrict processed exports more than imports.[33] When the combined protection of tariffs and import-rationing forces processors to produce their own inputs, the implications of protection for export restriction become a practical concern, especially since officials administering import controls are unlikely to be fully aware of the indirect effect of their actions. It seems doubtful if program planning has taken into account the uncertainty introduced by extending protection to inputs and the negative effects of *ad hoc* import controls for balance-of-payments reasons. The uncertainty of delivery dates because of exchange controls is itself sufficient to divert the energies of producers to the scramble for supplies of import substitutes because disequilibrium conditions place a high value on assured dates of delivery. In sum, the market interference associated with planning may exacerbate the divergence of private and social costs in attempting to correct it.

The prospect of realizing internal and external economies of scale is impaired by a vicious cycle which is started by the overextension of import substitution, reinforced by inflation and import rationing, and compounded by a further round of import substitution resulting from rigid exchange rates and the diversion of resources away from exports. Instead of a rational policy of both export stimulation and import substitution, the typical practice is to ration imports and maintain the ex-

[33] Hence, removal of protection does not necessarily imply currency devaluation (Harry A. Johnson, "A Model of Protection and the Exchange Rate," forthcoming).

change rate, thus extending a broad umbrella of protection to producers of materials, intermediate products, and component parts.

Witness that the voice of Raul Prebisch has now been raised against the high cost of import substitution. Extensive protection "has had unfavorable effects on the industrial structure because it has encouraged the establishment of small uneconomical plants, weakened the incentive to introduce new techniques, and slowed down the rise of productivity. Thus a real vicious circle has been created as regards exports of manufactured goods. These exports encounter great difficulties because internal costs are high, because, among other things, the exports which would enlarge the markets are lacking. . . . Finally, excessive protectionism has generally insulated national markets from external competition, weakening and even destroying the incentive necessary for improving the quality of output and lowering costs under the private enterprise system. It has thus tended to stifle the initiative of enterprises as regards both the internal market and exports." [34]

PREFERENTIAL TRADE AMONG LESS DEVELOPED COUNTRIES

Since the small markets of less developed countries suffer from an excess of protectionism, preferential trade may be a means of overcoming this obstacle. This may depend, however, largely on whether preferential tariffs are employed to reduce the protection of established industries or to establish new industries. This brief section qualifies the case for preferential trade and emphasizes the problems of equity and efficiency that result from the extension of protection to partner exports. The substitution of high-cost partner supply for imports from the cheapest source is a fundamental weakness of preferential trading systems. A similar dilemma of the East European bloc results from the fact that the internal prices of a preferential system may be unenforceable.

The case for preferential trade is strongest in respect of high-cost industries already established, especially those in which the region is nearly self-sufficient, because these offer the greatest gains from trade creation within the region and the least loss from trade diversion outside the area of preference.[35] This qualified case for preferential trade is stronger for less developed than for advanced countries because their markets are smaller and more highly protected. Governments, however, are likely to be more interested in establishing new industries than

---

[34] *Toward a New Trade Policy for Development* (United Nations), New York, 1964, p. 22.
[35] Johnson's *U.S. Economic Policy* makes this point.

in improving the efficiency of those already established—an adjustment involving losses to the less efficient producers.

In the light of their policies favoring industrialization in spite of the cost of protection, it can be argued that many less developed countries are prepared to sacrifice efficiency for the sake of industrial expansion.[36] On the other hand, it seems plausible to suppose that policymakers may have deceived themselves regarding the extra capital costs of protectionism which may stall the accumulation process before it becomes self-sustaining.

Customs unions, free trade areas, and other preferential arrangements have one thing in common: They extend protection from import-competing industries at home to partner exports. The net effect depends, therefore, on whether trade is created, by the contraction of high-cost production in the importing country, or is diverted at the expense of low-cost imports from third countries.

As regards new industries, preferential protection is bound to divert trade from the lowest-cost source of supply. The dynamic case, based on internal and external economies of scale, is subject to the dangers already discussed plus the additional risk that preferential access to partner markets may be cut off suddenly for balance-of-payments reasons or because of dissatisfaction with the distribution of benefits. About all one can say is that a strategy of balanced growth is less risky for a region than for a nation. The elasticity of demand will be greater within protected regions than in national markets, and the rate of growth may be as important as the size of the market for making the leap from suboptimal plants to those of optimum size.[37] Moreover, the greater elasticity of demand is more likely to attract outside capital. It bears repeating, however, that preferential trade will contribute to successful development over the long run only if, in fact, costs are reduced enough to yield adequate social returns on investment.

By extending home-market protection to partner exports, the stronger country stands to benefit not only from the freer trade created between partners, but also from the injury inflicted on third countries. The importing partner loses from trade diversion which substitutes high-cost

---

[36] By treating the "values" of industrialization as a collective consumption good, it is argued that protection is a rational policy. Harry G. Johnson has developed theories to explain this and related phenomena of nationalism ("An Economic Theory of Protectionism, Tariff Bargaining, and the Formation of Customs Unions," *Journal of Political Economy,* June 1965, pp. 256–83; and "A Theoretical Model of Economic Nationalism in New and Developing States, *"Political Science Quarterly,* July 1965).

[37] Scitovsky, *Economic Theory,* p. 116.

partner supply for imports from the cheapest source. Thus, the stronger country will grow at the expense of the less developed member, which is saddled with the obligation of importing high-cost partner supplies. The loss becomes visible immediately in the loss of tariff revenue. Thus, trade diversion results in transferring the revenue which is or could be collected on imports from the cheapest source to the producers of the exporting partner. Buyers in the weaker country pay for the protection of industry established in the stronger country. This is the rock on which preferential blocs are likely to founder.

In any unified market, a few centers tend to attract an agglomeration of industry, and development spreads but slowly from these growing points where social overhead capital and other supplies are available.[38] This is precisely what less developed countries are complaining about, and it may happen within a protected region as well as in the world at large.[39] The alternative, which is to plan regional specialization by investment allocations or similar measures, is likely to face the other horn of the high-cost dilemma. Deliberate measures to disperse, prematurely, the establishment of new industries away from the centers of growth will postpone the critical point at which external economies pay off on the investment, and the stronger country may be saddled with the obligation to import at higher costs than those at which the product could be produced at home. Once one rejects the market, it becomes extremely difficult to negotiate international specialization, as the Communist countries have found.

CAPITAL MOVEMENTS

The chronic payments problem and regime of controls surrounding planned development inhibit the inflow of private capital which, under favorable conditions, might relieve the acute shortage of exchange, supplement domestic savings, and expand trade. Partly because of the unfavorable climate in many less developed countries, private foreign investment plays a less important role in the transmission of growth than in the nineteenth century.[40] Two major changes in the character of capi-

[38] A. J. Brown, "Customs Union Versus Economic Separatism in Developing Countries," *Yorkshire Bulletin of Economic and Social Research,* May and November 1961, p. 88.

[39] For a proposal to encourage competitive specialization by classes of manufactures, see P. G. Elkan, "How to Beat the Backwash: The Case for Customs-Drawback Unions," *Economic Journal,* March 1965, pp. 44–62.

[40] Contrasting the earlier role of Britain as a foreign investor with that of the United States today, Cairncross notes that "in the forty years before the First World War about two-fifths of additions to the stock of capital owned in the United Kingdom consisted of investments abroad. There were years when more than

tal movements are, first, the shift from private investment to intergovernmental loans and grants and, secondly, the rising importance of equity capital from minor proportions to about two-thirds of total private foreign investment.

The preference of underdeveloped countries for loan capital is frustrated by overvalued currencies which repel portfolio investment.[41] The negative effect of fixed exchanges on direct investment arises from the rationing of imported materials and the risk of price controls. Otherwise, inflation is favorable to profits, and currency overvaluation may permit an excessive repatriation charge on the host country.

Direct foreign investment offers several kinds of special benefits to underdeveloped countries. The commonly overlooked advantage is the tax revenue collected by the host government on foreign equity investments.[42] Even though foreign investment is unattractive to entrepreneurs unless it is expected to produce higher net profits than home investment,[43] the gross return includes a social benefit in the form of tax revenue. Secondly, the knowledge and organization of foreign entrepreneurs may improve the host country's access to world markets. Finally, direct

half of current British savings went to the finance of foreign assets. It is unimaginable that what was then true of the United Kingdom could now apply to the United States. To yield such a result, the flow of investment from the United States would require the entire Marshall Plan to be carried out at least thrice a year" (*op. cit.,* pp. 39–40). Nonetheless, a comparison of capital movements with trade expansion since 1913 indicates that the one has kept pace roughly with the other.

[41] The developing countries argue that for some industries, e.g., electric power, techniques are now so standardized and well known that loan capital is the appropriate means of finance, while equity capital should be restricted to industries for which the technical knowledge is not readily available.

[42] Paul B. Simpson, "Foreign Investment and the National Economic Advantage," *United States Private and Government Investment Abroad,* ed. Raymond F. Mikesell, Eugene, Oregon, 1962.

"Parallel analysis of the effects of foreign investment on the investing country, however, suggests that foreign investment may frequently be to that country's disadvantage, both because as a result of double taxation arrangements its government loses the tax revenue paid to the foreign country, and because investment in competing production facilities abroad reduces the market for its exports and consequently its gains from trade." In addition, "U.S. tax law in the postwar period has in effect subsidized U.S. foreign investment by giving it favourable tax treatment in a variety of ways" (Harry G. Johnson, *The Canadian Quandary,* Toronto and New York, 1963, pp. xvi–xvii).

[43] The disadvantage of foreign investment to the lending country includes not only the loss of tax revenue, but also the loss of indirect benefits in the form of productivity gains and higher wages. It is by no means clear that the marginal return on foreign investment exceeds that of home investment by enough to compensate for the loss of these benefits (Marvin Frankel, "Home Versus Foreign Investment: A Case Against Capital Exports," *Kyklos,* 1965, pp. 411–33).

investments bring technology and know-how which are indispensable to economic progress and are a means of creating a competitive environment. Since the supply of intergovernmental loans is limited, private capital is a means of redressing the internal factor imbalance and accelerating growth, which in turn is limited by the country's capacity to absorb investment rather than by its capacity to save.

A System in Transition

The invitation of this conference to deal with the role of planning and critical policy decisions affecting the allocation of resources seems broad enough to include international capital movements under a system of fixed exchange rates. The reserve-currency system of international payments bears the marks of a system in transition. It consists of three components: the planned institution of the International Monetary Fund, unplanned and uncharted practices regarding the supply and demand for reserve currency, and an historical remnant of the gold standard. Although Bretton Woods did not distinguish the role of the dollar from that of other currencies, the dominant position of the United States as a source of capital gradually established the dollar as a reserve currency.

The problem of the reserve-currency center has been intensified by two subtle changes developing out of postwar history. One is the growing disposition to resist adjustment of the exchange rate in the face of fundamental disequilibrium. The other casts central banks in a more important role. We have witnessed an increase in international monetary cooperation among central bankers, with greater reliance being placed on monetary reserves and official lending, without a consensus being reached at the government level on the means of correcting disequilibrium.

The Marshall Plan with its salutary emphasis of self-help and European unity has turned out to have more far-reaching effects on international monetary plans than was evident at the time. Creation of the European Payments Union with its automatic credit facilities fostered rapid trade expansion, which stimulated economic growth by making nondollar trade multilateral. The Bank of International Settlements found new scope for its energies, and there emerged a body of knowledge and common opinion in Western Europe which, by supplementing or displacing the influence of the IMF, increased the weight of European opinion in the world at large.

Fortified by the solid achievement of convertibility, the original IMF design of "cooperation between governments to reconcile national economic policies with a smooth mechanism of international payments has tended to give way to a technical cooperation of central banks which, though appearing to grow in flexibility, has in fact been fastening upon governments a more rigid monetary framework than was ever intended at Bretton Woods." [44]

A regime of rigid exchange rates has increased the need for international monetary reserves and opened the doors to controversy.[45] Since the goal of full employment and stable prices leads surplus countries to resist inflation and deficit countries to resist deflation, the result is a resort to direct controls during prolonged periods of adjustment. "In effect, adjustment under the present international monetary system depends on the inability of policy in the surplus country to resist inflationary pressure and of policy in the deficit country to maintain employment at the desired level. This mechanism of reluctant adjustment is bound to take considerable time and to generate continual mutual recrimination, while the size of the payments imbalance involved in the process of slow adjustment inevitably exerts pressure for the increasing use of interventions in international trade and payments to reduce the magnitudes of deficits and surpluses, and especially for the use of restraints and controls on private capital movements." [46]

The conflict over foreign payments has been exacerbated, first, by misunderstanding and disagreement over the role of the United States as world banker and financial intermediary and, secondly, by the fact that prolonged dollar deficits provide surplus countries with an opportunity to gain leverage over U.S. foreign policy. As regards foreign investment, the heart of the controversy is whether the United States in its role of financial intermediary is to be allowed to invest long while borrowing short by means of key-currency financing. A significant volume of U.S. foreign investment involves no transfer of real resources because the

[44] R. S. Sayers, "Cooperation Between Central Banks," *Three Banks Review,* September 1963.

[45] Surplus countries are likely to regard their enlarged reserves as normal if not permanent, while deficit countries regard their loss of reserves as temporary and something to be put right again in the future. Fritz Machlup concludes that "most central bankers start fussing when the reserve ratio declines. . . ." I conclude that the "need" for reserves is determined by the ambitions of the monetary authorities. I submit we ought to see to it that they get foreign reserves in amounts sufficient to be happy and satisfied; in amounts, that is, that will keep them from urging or condoning policies restricting imports or capital movements ("International Monetary Systems and the Free Market," *International Payments Problems,* Washington, D.C., 1965, p. 100).

[46] Johnson, *U.S. Economic Policy,* Chap. 7.

United States provides liquidity which, indirectly, has permitted foreign savers to hold short-term assets, while the United States provided long-term loans and equity financing. The role of the United States can be characterized in two very different ways: Thus, it may be said that the liquidity of European money markets was made possible by the long-term financing of the United States, or, alternatively, that Europe, by holding short-term dollar assets, has financed long-term American investments in Europe.[47] The basic problem is that balance-of-payments equilibrium is incompatible with the role that the United States plays as world banker.

The two faces that can be placed on the American role as supplier of liquidity are easily seen by contrasting the periods before and after 1958. For about a decade after initiation of the Marshall Plan, Europe restricted dollar imports while accumulating dollar reserves, with the result that the United States did not transfer real resources in the full amount of Marshall Plan assistance and other foreign payments. But there was no charge at that time of using key-currency borrowing to finance the Marshall Plan. The flow of dollars to Europe served "as a stabilizing and sustaining element in world payments which allowed most countries to exploit their growth potentiality fully without external restraints or deflationary shocks." [48] The return of convertibility was made possible by this liquidity. Since that time, however, France, in particular, has voiced strong objections to direct American investment, partly on nationalistic grounds, but supported also by the charge that Americans were gaining control of European industry through the resources provided by the automatic borrowing mechanism. The German central bank and others have been more concerned with what they term the inflationary implication of continued dollar liquidity which, in effect, says that the deficit country must bear the burden of adjustment for which surplus countries assume little or no responsibility.[49]

The conflict appears, also, in connection with interest rates. The United States, in the face of unemployment, was constrained from a

[47] Charles P. Kindleberger, *Balance-of-Payments Deficits and the International Market for Liquidity,* Princeton Essays in International Finance, No. 46, Princeton, N.J., 1965, p. 12. Kindleberger, correctly, insists that Europe cannot have it both ways. That is to say, if the United States is to provide long-term financing because of the preference of European savers for short-term assets, then the central banks of surplus countries will have to accommodate moderate key-currency borrowing by the United States.

[48] Angus Maddison, *Economic Growth in the West,* New York, 1964, p. 171.

[49] Regarding the charge of inflation and the danger of controls, see Gottfried Haberler, "The International Payments System: Postwar Trends and Prospects," *International Payments Problems,* pp. 5–7, 10–16.

policy of extremely low interest rates in the early 1960s because more capital would have moved to Europe where high interest rates prevailed in order to restrain excess demand. Foreign deficits and domestic unemployment pose the dilemma of how to serve two masters. The European prescription is that monetary policy should be used to protect the foreign balance while a flexible tax policy is used to serve domestic objectives. While it is true that conflicting objectives require two instruments of policy, the prescription applies equally to surplus countries. If monetary policy is to serve external balance, then surplus countries need lower interest rates to avoid attracting unwanted capital and taxes to avoid inflation.

The European prescription of sacrificing monetary policy to protect the foreign balance is many times more costly for the United States than for Europe because U.S. trade is so very much smaller relative to domestic production. The fact that European trade is a very much larger percentage of production than that of the United States also explains why the adjustment process works so slowly in the American case. European investment is much more responsive to export expansion because exports account for a very much larger share of production.

The key to Europe's balance-of-payments strength has been heavy investment in the export industries, stimulated by the liberalization of intra-European trade and reinforced by cost-reducing technology.[50] When U.S. payments for economic assistance and military purposes increased in the mid-1950s, resources were not fully transferred because the Atlantic productivity gap had been narrowed without a commensurate increase of European wage costs. Private American capital was also attracted both by Europe's productivity gains and by the shelter of a preferential trading area in order to compete on equal terms inside the Common Market.[51]

The foreign policy issue was whether Europe would permit the United States to pay for its foreign economic aid and military commitments, especially those to Europe, by means of multilateral trade which would allow the nations receiving dollar payments to import from the cheapest source. The answer has been "no"; the surplus countries were reluctant to accumulate dollars while allowing sufficient time for market forces to restore equilibrium. The Common Market countries were unwilling to

[50] On the reinforcing tendency of export-led growth with cost-reducing technology and wage lags, see A. Lamfulussy, *The United Kingdom and the Six,* New Haven, 1964, especially Chap. IX.

[51] Tariff discrimination, incidentally, violates the rule of good behavior which says that surplus countries should not impose fresh restrictions on their imports from debtors.

sanction any positive steps which would enable the United States to increase its large surplus on current account at the expense of their balance of trade. The implication is that Europe sought a measure of control over American foreign policy expenditures as the price of monetary cooperation or that its central banks acted independently.[52]

The result has been a resort to the inefficiency of controls over trade and payments which it is the object of an international monetary system to avoid. The givers of foreign aid are now inhibited by concern with balance-of-payments effects and the receivers are denied access to the cheapest market. Restrictions on direct foreign investment and access to the American market are awkward controls to administer because the free flow of capital is more important to the growth of some countries than to others. Moreover, the effect on the growth of borrowing countries is far more serious than the loss of income to the lender. Unfortunately, innocent third countries are injured by the conflict between the deficit and surplus countries which has resulted in the interest equalization tax and other restrictions on the outflow of U.S. capital.

The significance of these developments for the planning of international monetary institutions is that the International Monetary Fund was but ill equipped for the task of providing European liquidity, a role performed with remarkable success by the key-currency system. Events have conspired to put a great deal of power in the hands of European central banks with a corresponding reduction in the influence of the fund, where the United States and Britain have greater voting strength. A regime of rigid exchange rates and reluctant adjustment have exacerbated the conflict between surplus and deficit nations and opened the door to nationalism.[53] Basically, the debate over international monetary reform is whether the plan places major responsibility for adjustment on deficit or surplus countries—essentially a choice between a more or less expansive international monetary system. It seems predictable that most European countries will prefer arrangements outside the IMF which give them control over future changes in liquidity.[54]

---

[52] "On their side, the Europeans have neatly segregated the contexts. Their financial officials wash their hands of tariff and trade policies, agricultural protection, defense and aid appropriation, and their government's budgets. Any European failings on these counts are facts of life to which the United States must adjust, rather than reasons for more patience or more credit" (James Tobin, "Europe and the Dollar," *Review of Economics and Statistics,* May 1964, pp. 124–25).

[53] See Hans O. Schmitt, "Political Conditions for International Currency Reform," *International Organization,* Summer 1964.

[54] This point is made in Harry G. Johnson's lectures, *World Economy at the Crossroads,* Montreal, 1965, p. 20.

This poses the question of whether the United States should continue to provide the services of a key-currency center for those countries which want the service and, if so, whether the United States should consider the partial demonetization of gold, if necessary in order to make evident the strength of the dollar.[55]

Centrally Planned Economies

That central planning is inherently hostile to foreign trade is quite evident. Commodities are not "convertible," pricing is not suitable, and trade requires an active political decision in contrast to the market economies where trade is spontaneous unless suppressed by the state. Central planning is biased against the risks of external dependence.

The relationship among currencies of Communist countries is also unfavorable to economic integration. It represents an extreme form of *independence* with resistance to either *integration,* as illustrated by convertibility at fixed exchange rates or dominance as illustrated by the pound sterling in the nineteenth century and the dollar during the period of dollar shortage after the Second World War. Even if Soviet currency were convertible at meaningful exchange rates, one can hardly believe that it would be held by trading partners on the scale that Europe holds dollars. Moreover, the economic relationship of bloc countries to Russia is unusual in several respects. First, the dominant power and mother of socialist states is poorer than some members of the bloc; this creates tension with regard to capital flows and the avowed objective of equalizing the national income of socialist states. Secondly, except for Poland, "the USSR plays *vis-à-vis* the area the typical role of a raw-material hinterland rather than that of a supplier of industrial commodities—a role which strikes one as unusual for a politically paramount power." [56] Thirdly, the trading problem is not so much to find a market in the Soviet Union as to obtain the range of manufactures which are desired in exchange.

In one respect the socialist states may be regarded as more rational than the capitalist states and that is in the consistency with which they export in order to import. For this reason one might suppose that intrabloc trade would flourish freed of the main obstacle which restrains export-led growth in the West, namely, the greater risk of foreign markets

[55] Emile Despres has not published his views on the partial demonetization of gold (see Haberler, "International Payments System," p. 9).

[56] Alfred Zauberman, *Industrial Progress in Poland, Czechoslovakia, and East Germany, 1937–1962,* London, New York, Toronto, 1964, p. 303.

as compared with home markets. In other words, why is it not comparatively easy for centrally planned economies to plan foreign trade on a scale that is unattainable by market economies because of protectionism and the risk of devaluation. The irrationality of prices for trading purposes is doubtless an important factor, but this does not get to the root of the matter. Foreign trade is the least "plannable" sector of centrally planned economies, partly because the tools of analysis have to be developed, but also because of the character of the bureaucracy.[57] It is planners who have to aggregate the apparent gains from trade, based on efficiency coefficients, and to assess the new alternatives. A built-in rigidity in favor of adherence to actual trade flows has been observed.[58]

Although a highly restricted volume of trade implies larger gains per unit of trade, there are reasons for supposing that centrally planned economies may benefit less than market economies in a comparable position. Their commerce has been confined largely to intrabloc exchange, and traded goods were restricted, mainly, to basic products essential to the growth of nations committed to very similar strategies of development. By the design of their growth strategy, their demand for imports has tended to be competitive rather than complementary. The fundamental conception of "proportionate planned development" seems incompatible with comparative-cost specialization. Moreover, Communist countries have lacked the analytical tools for obtaining the optimum benefits of trade.

Socialist pricing undervalues capital-intensive and resource-intensive goods and can scarcely be satisfactory for foreign trade, for it favors the export of these products and the import of labor-intensive goods. The Soviet growth model raises questions as to whether the countries committed to it are prepared to specialize in the export of raw materials and intermediate products, an issue which may be complicated by the awkward fact that the Soviet Union is both a net importer of machinery and a leading exporter of primary products.[59] At the administrative level,

[57] On planning and organization, see Frederick L. Pryor, *The Communist Foreign Trade System,* Cambridge, Mass., 1963, Chap. II.

[58] "For a national 'material balance,' the fact that production is the starting line tends to induce a certain automatism in allocations: uses are put down for the same shares year after year . . . In planning the allocation to, and within, foreign trade, something of the same fossilization is apparent" (Michael Kaser, *COMECON: Integration Problems of the Planned Economies,* New York, London, Toronto, 1965, pp. 35–36). This study became available too late for more than a marginal reference.

[59] The long overdue emergence of socialist microeconomics may be hastened by the COMECON pipeline. See Jan S. Prybyla, "Eastern Europe and Soviet Oil," *Journal of Industrial Economics,* March 1965, pp. 154–67.

pressures and bonuses for fulfilling plan targets concentrate import demand near the terminal date of planning periods, precipitating awkward short-term demands in a system that does not recognize scarcity rents.

By adopting the Soviet model, the leadership of other Communist states placed on excessive value on diversification and the development of all major sectors. A bias against foreign trade is a corollary of this type of national planning because of the strong aversion to the risk of external dependence and a built-in priority in favor of balanced growth. Trade was also restrained by bilateralism and the rule that the current account should not be greatly out of balance. As the European Communist states came to appreciate the excessive costs implied by the Soviet model adopted by smaller countries, their efforts to expand trade have been constrained by the inadequacy of socialist economics, the bias against trade inherent in the bureaucracy of central planning, and the problem of developing new institutions to cope with inconvertible currencies and multilateral trade. Even with growing sophistication, the optimization of trade remains a shadowy goal.

The extreme stress on national sovereignty and the development of a diversified economy in each country make the political and economic risks of excessive specialization loom large in the minds of both the political leaders and the planners. It is likely that a planner who makes a mistake in providing for too much autarky is less likely to suffer in terms of power or prestige than a planner who errs in the other direction. The inability to measure gains and losses with any accuracy, the lack of an adequate theory of the division of labor, and the danger of placing excessive reliance on other planned economies for timely deliveries of high quality goods—all create further biases against extensive specialization. The lack of flexibility of adjustment to unforeseen circumstances in centrally planned economies raises the specter that extensive specialization could lead to serious disruptions in national plans.[60]

So long as prices remain divorced from scarcities, Communist countries can hardly know what to export if their economies are to be integrated. Since import needs are determined by the materials-balance method of planning, the need for a guide to "export efficiency" leads to extensive computations, which provide some insight into the recent evolution of socialist economics.[61] Numerous indexes were developed, comparing production expenditures with export receipts. The first, a

[60] Egon Neuberger, "International Division of Labor in C.E.M.A.: Limited Regret Strategy," *American Economic Review,* May 1965, p. 511.
[61] Analysis of the "comparative purchasing power" of some 2,000 consumer goods was started in mid-1963 (Stanislaw Albinowski, *Polish Perspectives,* Vol. 6, No. 6, p. 7).

simple bookkeeping ratio, fails to disclose the relative efficiency of different industries in earning foreign exchange. The second, a gross foreign exchange index, takes no account of the import content of exports. The third, a net foreign exchange index, adjusts for the import content of exports and was used by countries importing materials and exporting finished goods. However, since this overrates the benefits of exports made with exportable domestic materials, still a fourth index was needed. The absolute net foreign exchange efficiency measurement was devised to show whether further processing of exportable materials is productive of foreign exchange. As regards socialist economics, it seems curious that not one of the four indexes brings out the value added by labor (as distinct from materials) clearly enough to show the relative labor cost of the exchange-earning "efficiency" of various exports. To overcome this deficiency, a foreign exchange equivalent of labor was devised for the final stage of production and, finally, a global index, which included labor costs at earlier stages.

Although the bloc countries have not attached so much significance to analysis of "import efficiency," "One shudders to think of how many highly skilled people must be tied up in this sort of work. . . ." [62] Such a vast effort confirms the obvious, among other things, that use of world prices for intrabloc trade does not tell a country what to export. Patently, the automatic trade restrictions built into central planning and bilateral state trading are less of a handicap to continental USSR and mainland China than to fragmented Eastern Europe where the economics of foreign trade is being revived. It is still difficult to see how the shortfall of the planning error can be resolved by trade, except by market prices which embody scarcity rents. The greater obstacle to effective integration, however, is probably the fear of dependence on foreign markets. [63] Socialist growth strategy places a high value on the development of all major sectors, and this implies underspecialization by design.

[62] J. Wilczynski, "The Theory of Comparative Costs and Centrally Planned Economies," *Economic Journal,* March 1965, pp. 70–75. The practical value of these studies so far has been limited, but immensely complicated models are being evolved. Cf. Alfred Zauberman, "The Criterion of Efficiency of Foreign Trade in Soviet-Type Economies," *Economica,* October 1964.

[63] Richard M. Bird, "COMECON and Economic Integration in the Soviet Bloc," *Quarterly Review of Economics and Business,* Winter 1964, pp. 37–49. This survey concludes that it is unlikely that the key steps needed for economic integration of East European bloc countries will be completed for a long time to come. For a narrow conception of integration, based on the use of international prices within the bloc, see Edward Ames, "Economic Integration in the European Soviet Bloc?", *American Economic Review,* May 1959, pp. 113–24; "International Trade Without Markets—the Soviet Bloc Case," *AER,* December 1954.

The built-in bias against trade will not be easy to reverse, for the institutions of central planning, no less than those of private property, develop their vested interests.

In order to obtain optimum benefits, the Communist countries will need: first, a meaningful system of prices, including an acceptable principle for dividing the gains between buyers and sellers under changing conditions; secondly, a more flexible organization for the integration of production and foreign trade; thirdly, a multilateral clearing system and convertible currencies.[64] A socialist substitute for an organized capital market would help. These measures need analytical tools which require some revision of socialist economics and, also, a great deal of mutual confidence.

The East bloc of centrally planned economies is a preferential trading area with a difference. Preference for partner trade is derived primarily from political motives. While the members' distrust of dependence on the West is greater than their aversion to dependence on each other, evidently the commitment to bloc loyalty differs substantially among its members. In addition, the cohesion of the bloc as a preferential trading area is subject to the erosion of *rapprochement,* permitting a reconciliation of the two Europes.

Like any preferential system, the bloc suffers the disability that imports from third countries may be cheaper than those from partners. Unless each member overcharges the other by an equal amount, as compared with world prices, the exporting country is, in effect, taxing the importing country. Since the degree of preference for bloc trade differs among members, some are less willing than others to import at higher costs for the sake of bloc integration. These conditions are an obstacle to multilateral trade and, more importantly, third-country trade must be a constant threat to the system.[65]

[64] On the organizational structure of COMECON, see Andrzej Korgonski, *International Conciliation,* September 1964. The International Bank for Economic Cooperation, created in late 1963, was charged with the development of multilateral clearing, but officials recognize that this depends on exchange rate and price reform. Kaser's historical treatment of COMECON refers to these issues. The text of a 1957 agreement attempting to make trade multilateral is given in Laslzo Zsoldoes, *Economic Integration of Hungary into the Soviet Bloc,* Columbus, Ohio, 1963. This work provides an extensive bibliography. The essay by Soviet writer V. P. Sergeyev, "Economic Principles of the Foreign Trade of Socialist States," *International Trade Theory in a Developing World,* is disappointing.

[65] "Any set of sovereign nations intent on economic integration must develop its own set of enforceable intra-bloc prices, different from the prices of the outside world, if this economic integration is to proceed very far" (Frederick L. Pryor, *American Economic Review,* May 1964, p. 522).

Economic integration of the East bloc requires that members act like a customs union, free trade area, or, at least, like a preferential tariff bloc. In market economies, preferential treatment expands partner trade in two ways: Trade is created by the production-contracting, consumption-expanding effect in the importing country; and partner trade is also expanded by the diversion of imports from third countries, which may be the cheapest source. But, since trade creation between centrally planned economies has to be planned and negotiated, the prospect of trade creation at the expense of home production is uncertain. And since preferential pricing is unenforceable, trade diversion at the expense of third-country trade is not automatic. To the contrary, the system is threatened by the alternative of lower-cost imports from third countries. Clearly, this uncertainty increases the risk of long-term investment planning with the objective of intrabloc specialization.

Since the mid-1950s, apparently, world prices have been used as a starting point for negotiating intrabloc trade. This may be owing not only to the irrationality of internal prices, but also because preferential treatment on a basis of domestic prices proved unacceptable. World prices, however, can scarcely be satisfactory to planned economies which do not adjust their internal costs to world markets. The implication seems to be that price serves mainly as a basis for dividing the gains from trade between importer and exporter.[66]

In 1962, per capita foreign trade of the East bloc stood at about one-fourth that of the Common Market. The trade of most members is far less than that of market economies of similar size at comparable stages of development. Pryor estimates that no bloc nation realized half of its "potential" for trade.[67] From this low base, there is no apparent reason

[66] The empirical evidence on pricing does permit definitive answers to the more important questions. The Economic Council for Europe interpretation was that sellers of scarce goods managed to get more than the world price (*Economic Survey of Europe*, 1957, p. 28). Mendershausen's calculations suggested that the USSR exploited partner trade. But this is not proved by favorable terms of trade between the USSR and other bloc members, as compared with the West, for as Holzman pointed out, each bloc member may receive more favorable terms on partner trade than on trade with the West (Horst Mendershausen, *Review of Economics and Statistics*, May 1959 and May 1960; Franklyn Holzman, "Soviet Foreign Trade Pricing and the Questions of Discrimination: A Customs Union Approach," *Review of Economics and Statistics*, May 1962). Pryor suggests alternative interpretations (*Communist Foreign Trade*, Chap. V, especially pp. 142 ff.). Kaser's reservations regarding "the comparison of prices in East-West trade with those in intra-Comecon trade by no means imply that members would not, on the whole, do better by trade with the rest of the world" (*COMECON*, p. 145).

[67] *Communist Foreign Trade*, p. 27; see also Wilczynski, "Comparative Costs," p. 65, and Kaser, *COMECON*, p. 122.

why their trade should not continue to expand—possibly at somewhat higher rates than income. Despite intensified efforts to expand trade, however, central planning remains a serious handicap to trade and one finds little basis for supposing that it is likely to become as important for centrally planned economies as for the market economies of the West.[68]

COMMENT

James C. Ingram, *University of North Carolina*

Just as the forecasting of a balance of payments seems to pose exceptional difficulties to the Western economist, so the incorporation of international trade in economic plans seems to pose special difficulties for economists everywhere. The desired amounts of trade seem to emerge only after a long chain of reasoning and a long series of calculations. First of all, planners must specify general objectives, such as (1) to maximize the increase in real income, (2) to achieve a given degree of autarky, or (3) to maximize the rate of growth in capital formation, or some combinations of objectives. Once objectives are fixed, a general strategy of development must be decided upon. Next, outputs required in the various industries must be calculated, taking account of projections of demand and cost, changes in technique, influences of the production pattern on savings, and incentives to effort; and allowing for external economies and other divergences between private and social cost. If all these were accurately done, a rational planner could finally make some comparative cost calculations to determine the desired amounts of exports and imports. Even if autarky were a prime objective, trade might be the quickest route to it, and trade might play an important role in the plan.

Unfortunately, the information required for all these calculations is not available. As several papers in this conference have emphasized, the planner must do his work with very limited data. I was particularly impressed by Professor Harberger's remarks on the rough-and-ready character of project appraisal. For proper treatment of the foreign sector, such projections of home cost must be compared with external prices and with estimates of future price trends. Small wonder that planners, whose biases are usually toward autarky in any case, tend to underrate foreign trade! Furthermore, since project appraisal must be "close to

[68] Zauberman agrees with Viner that it is more difficult to integrate socialist than capitalist economies without the loss of national identity ("Criterion of Efficiency," p. 330).

the ground," as Harberger emphasized, the decentralized administrative unit is not likely to recommend trade instead of a project in its district.

Professor Humphrey's paper is primarily concerned with the general strategy of development and the place foreign trade occupies in developmental planning. His paper is not directly concerned with techniques of project appraisal, with the specific methods that might be used to fix the composition and level of exports and imports, or with the way in which trade is incorporated in the planning apparatus. What we have to discuss, then, is *not* a technical paper on planning techniques in an open economy, but a broad survey of the relationship (past and present) between planning and trade. It is doubtful, in fact, that much could be said at this stage about planning techniques in an open economy. Planners seem to regard trade as an activity to be used only as a last resort, not one to be systematically incorporated into the plan. I think it is fair to say that Humphrey's paper tells us much more about the reasons why planning has this negative bias than it does about the technique of planning. The paper contains many insights and many suggestive comments about a wide range of topics. Many of these remarks are speculative, representing not so much the results of a technical study of planning and trade as the considered judgments and observations of a trade specialist who is casting a reflective eye over the field. As such, the paper is a rich lode indeed, full of ideas that would need lengthy study to follow up.

One comes away from the first two parts of Humphrey's paper with the strong impression that both central planning in the Soviet bloc countries and the looser developmental planning of the less developed countries (LDC's) have been characterized by mistrust of trade, and that both have been antagonistic toward it. As Humphrey says, "planning has been the enemy of trade." But why? Several reasons are stated or implied in Humphrey's paper, but I was especially impressed by the role played by nationalism. Nationalism has tended to make planning hostile to trade in both groups—bloc countries and the LDC's— though perhaps its influence has had a different basis in the two. This point will come up again below.

In Soviet Russia itself, the reasons for distrust of trade in the early years are obvious, but what is interesting is that after almost twenty postwar years the bloc countries still have a strong bias against trade, even among themselves. Since the concept of exports as the cost of imports is clearly recognized, it would seem that rational planners would rely on trade. Humphrey says they cannot because "any shortfall of output below target is very likely to be reflected in exports," and trade is therefore highly uncertain. This argument reverses the usual point. I should have thought that central planners could hold to the export targets if they wanted to, as in the well-known examples of grain exports during famine. Trade with the West would still be subject to uncertainties, e.g., about price and political factors; but if bloc countries were willing to meet export targets, why should intrabloc trade be subject to any uncertainties?

The answer seems to be political—the reflection of a nationalism that makes the attitude of planners toward intrabloc trade sharply different from their attitude toward interregional trade. After all, interregional trade in the USSR is planned without qualms, though perhaps not without occasional shortfalls. We can invoke the familiar analogy between interregional and international trade for planned economies as well as market ones. Planners appear to use the national boundary to distinguish between "us" and "them," and they may be glad to have both the Soviet precedent and ideological underpinnings to justify the distinction.

Humphrey's interesting argument that centrally planned economies will resist economic integration (i.e., specialization and interdependence) is related to the above discussion. His argument is an extension (and in part an explanation) of the "strategy of limited regret." That strategy, which calls for maximum diversification in order to avoid the risks of dependence upon outsiders, is itself a clear manifestation of nationalism. Just exactly why the penalties to a planner for too much trade are greater than the penalties for too much autarky is not clear to me, but I am not in a position to dispute the claim. (Also, how is "too much" measured?) In any case, the risk aversion applies to bloc members as well as other foreigners. Humphrey suggests that an additional constraint on preferential trading and on the development of specialization within the bloc is that a country has no way to protect itself against excessive prices charged by partner countries for their exports. The point is strongest where complete specialization occurs, since if a country retains some capacity in the line it would have a "yardstick" for comparing prices and costs. (A similar risk exists between market economies when complete specialization occurs in industries where "natural" barriers to entry are great.) Here again, however, interregional specialization occurs readily enough, and the crucial factor seems to be the national boundary.

As long as a bloc nation has the alternative of trading with the West, intrabloc specialization and trade can occur only at world-market prices. Integrated economic planning, which would seem to be the planner's preferred path to economic integration, seems to be an unpopular notion, to say the least.

Fundamentally, the planners' mistrust of planned trade and specialization implies a mistrust of planning itself, and they are therefore unwilling to accept it for decisions that involve external transactions.

Most of the above points apply with equal force to capital movements in centrally planned economies. Since interest as a price paid for the use of capital encounters doctrinal objections, each nation wants to avoid a current-account surplus unless such surplus is settled in convertible currencies. Here too we find bloc nations using Western pricing, with liquid exchange reserves being held in Eurodollars to get a favorable return. Capital transactions are of course doubly difficult because of the pricing problems discussed above; with no currency to use as a standard of value and with no economically significant prices for goods, a lender has no way to ensure that his loan will be repaid in full. Lending cannot flourish in such circumstances. The difficulty, be it noted, lies in satisfying both parties that the bargain is fair; there is no reason why the plan could not incorporate an inflow of capital.

Less developed countries share with bloc countries a bias against trade. In the LDC's this antitrade bias seems to reflect distrust of the market mechanism, a distrust arising from three related sources. First, nationalistic reactions against colonialism nurtured a suspicion that the market mechanism was somehow rigged to favor the advanced countries. Second, the influence of the Soviet model of economic growth encouraged autarkic tendencies. Third, analytical criticisms of free trade resource allocation developed greater weight and cogency, and thus lent support to planners' efforts to allocate investment to suit potential comparative advantage positions rather than those indicated by present prices, level of technique, and the like.

Humphrey's section on developmental planning is mostly concerned with the third source of bias against trade. He especially emphasizes the risk of export markets and the need to utilize home demand in order to achieve external economies, economies of scale, diversification, and the associated improvement in adaptability of resources. Humphrey seems in general agreement with the broad consensus which has emerged in recent years, in which traditional comparative cost theory has been modified to allow for infant industries, external economies, and various divergences between social and private cost.

The problems are clearly recognized, if not resolved: The domestic market may not be large enough to yield external and internal economies; planners may seek balance, both geographically and sectorally, so eagerly that investments are spread too thinly to achieve efficient levels of output; planned development may simply build in inefficiency, chronically overvalue the currency, and never achieve the goal of competitive output.

Humphrey does not discuss technical planning techniques or other devices that might be used by planners to guide their difficult choices. His discussion runs in terms of the broad strategy of development.

The avoidance of risky export markets makes it difficult for the LDC's to provide a market large enough to yield economies of scale, etc. Humphrey endorses preferential trading groups among LDC's as a way to resolve this conflict. Preferential trade has the effect of extending protection to exports (of a single member nation) as well as to import-competing industries. This advantage is also a weakness, as Humphrey shows us in his demonstration that preferential trade has redistributive effects (through the tax burden) that may prevent its adoption. Here again the role of nationalism comes to the fore. Regions of a single nation encounter this redistributive effect as a matter of course, but they can accept it more easily than nations can. Since we now discourage the forcible formation of larger preferential trading areas through conquest, perhaps the most promising way to confer scale benefits upon LDC's is to provide them guaranteed access to Atlantic community markets for a selected group of manufactured goods. LDC planners could then treat demand as almost perfectly elastic and concentrate their attention on supply. The Puerto Rican case seems relevant, even though Puerto Rico had still other advantages not likely to be found in LDC's. The fact that Puerto Rican producers had free access to the vast U.S. market meant that feasibility studies could focus on cost, and also that government could proceed with more confidence to the provision of social overhead capital. To produce at competitive costs is difficult enough, but it is a great relief to the planner to be free of worry about demand.

In my opinion, this now-familiar proposal for guaranteed access to advanced-country markets is very promising. It would facilitate an overall expansion of world trade along comparative-advantage lines, since LDC's can be counted upon to spend any additional export proceeds for badly needed imports. Incidentally, with relatively low tariff rates on many manufactures in Europe and the United States, I wonder if export markets are really as risky and unstable as is often suggested. LDC's and their planners may be too quick to apply experience gained in the export of primary products to prospects for development of exports of manufactures. In any case, I do not think we should automatically assume that the export alternative means exports of primary prod-

ucts by LDC's. Also, we should keep in mind Harrod's point that a
deterioration of 10 per cent in a nation's terms of trade will still leave
exports preferred to import-competing products if the latter require 20
per cent tariff protection. It appears that less developed countries have
erred on the side of underemphasizing exports in recent decades, and
it seems likely that greater attention to export expansion would improve
their prospects for economic growth.

Humphrey calls for a new code of behavior to permit greater use of
foreign capital, both direct and portfolio. He is more sympathetic than
I am to complaints about repatriation of profits and principal. Since
profits are paid from increases in output, and since the host country does
possess taxing power, I do not regard repatriation as a major problem,
though obviously it can be made one through unwise financial policies.
In Puerto Rico, profit rates of 100 per cent on invested capital are not
uncommon, with ten-year exemption from taxation on top of that, but
the profits are largely generated from export sales, and no exchange
problem is created. The real problem is to achieve productive use of
capital. If it is wasted on inefficient projects, repayment can become
an impossible burden.

Humphrey does not discuss planning in Western Europe, perhaps because its role seems less important. But it is likely that in Sweden, Norway, France, and Italy the planner's actual role is as great as in most
LDC's, though perhaps the aspiration is less. It would be particularly
interesting to have an account of the way in which capital imports (and
the servicing of external debt) are incorporated in the national plan.

The third part of Humphrey's paper, which contains a discussion of international monetary problems, is not concerned with economic planning
in the usual sense of the term. This part contains some extremely interesting points, however, and I am unable to resist the temptation to make
a few brief remarks about it.

Humphrey says the dollar is overvalued, a condition caused by increased U.S. military and aid commitments in the 1950s and by a
narrowing of the Atlantic productivity gap unmatched by European
wage increases. Now, if the presence of a payments deficit is proof of
overvaluation of a currency, there can be no argument. But the term
has pejorative connotations and implications for policy that are in my
opinion not justified. Since 1958 the United States has held prices
stable, restrained wage increases, and tolerated uncomfortably high
rates of unused capacity. At the same time we have sought to transfer
larger amounts of aid and capital than our current-account surplus
warrants. Thus we have provided Europe with the opportunity to en-

large her absorption of real output, but Europe has declined to accept the opportunity either through increased wage rates or through significant reductions in barriers to imports. While we can understand the reluctance to increase money wages in economies already facing inflationary threats, the reluctance to accept larger real income through expanded imports is less easy to understand.

Even if European governments are unwilling to permit a rise in absorption, the payments problem could still be solved by permitting the private sector to acquire foreign assets. Some steps have been taken in this direction, but it is clear that a great many obstacles still prevent such capital flows. Having blocked both current- and capital-account adjustment, Europeans then complain that we are somehow cheating them by "lending long and borrowing short" or "financing the purchase of capital assets at 3 per cent." Although these are descriptively accurate statements, the implication of flimflam is absurd.

This brings us back to the sense in which the dollar can be said to be overvalued. If Europeans refuse current-account and capital-account adjustment at present exchange rates, what grounds have we for thinking they would accept these adjustments through exchange-rate change? I agree with Humphrey that Europe should dose with its own medicine: lower interest rates and higher taxes, or, even better, freer imports of goods and securities. But I do not agree that the dollar is overvalued, except in a definitional sense, or that U.S. direct investment in Europe is a misallocation of resources.

Humphrey properly emphasizes the political element in exchange rates and payments balances. While this emphasis often points to the crucial aspect of the matter, I think it also tends too much to *personify* nations with respect to some transactions and thus to lead us astray. Economists are overly fond of their interpretation of European dollar holdings as short-term *loans* to the United States. In a given community, some individuals have demand deposits in a commercial bank, other individuals borrow from the bank. If we locate all these individuals and group them together, we can say that the bank is borrowing short and lending long vis-à-vis that group, but we do not ordinarily claim that the bank is thereby taking unfair advantage of the group. To the extent that foreign firms and individuals voluntarily hold dollar balances, the personification of countries may lead us to an erroneous interpretation of the whole transaction. Involuntary accumulations by official holders are of course another matter. I have suggested already that the governments concerned can, if they so desire, take action to cause their dollar balances to pass into the private sector and be converted into goods or financial assets. If they do not take these actions, then we can of course negotiate the terms on which they may lend to the United States. We can fund these debts into longer-term form at an agreed interest rate. This is what Roosa bonds are all about. Humphrey recommends greater use of such negotiated loans.

The trouble is, settlement of the deficit with negotiated loans prevents any *mechanism* of adjustment from emerging. It also emphasizes the political aspects and the sense in which the balance of payments is subject to discretionary control by authorities. However, I agree that in the present stalemate we may prefer to negotiate loans at higher cost and thus buy a greater degree of freedom to pursue domestic and foreign objectives than we have had. We should recognize that this course of action may involve price discrimination (in interest rates) and a kind of compartmentalization of the capital market. For example, bonds issued to France may have to pay 6 per cent interest while long-term governments yield 4 per cent at home.

V Lewis Bassie, *University of Illinois*

There can be no greater joy for an economic planner than to sit on a slightly overheated economy with an undervalued currency. A comfortable surplus eliminates the need for any unpleasant decisions designed to restrict purchases from other countries. Practically everybody is happy, and incentives are ample to induce cooperation with plans for expansion. If potential competition from abroad is restrained by "legitimate" trade barriers and by self-imposed traditions of "financial responsibility" in other countries, so much the better.

These points are effectively developed in Humphrey's article and receive an assist from Kindleberger. Ingram enters a partial dissent, stating that the dollar is overvalued in a definitional sense only, and not in the basic sense that would lead to pursuing the policy appropriate when overvaluation is acknowledged. It seems to me that this difference of opinion warrants further discussion.

Potential Overvaluation of the Dollar

A significant feature of the postwar situation may be delineated in terms of the distinction between the countries that have made rapid progress and those that have lagged. In general, the former have been the strong investors and the daring spenders. The latter have been sober meeters-of-obligations; they include the key currency countries.

The former have channeled a high proportion of output into investment; they have imported and adapted technology; they have built new plants and industries to make the best use of the new technology. This has resulted in what Humphrey calls the narrowing of the productivity gap. But these countries have also spent freely. They have expanded credit, have tolerated a certain amount of inflation, have adopted other measures to create high profits as incentives, and have borrowed abroad or permitted huge private capital imports.

According to traditional gold standard theories, these policies should have brought a day of reckoning. They have not, and there are still no signs of an adverse fate. Since 1958, as Ingram points out, prices in the surplus countries have been going up while ours have held steady. The Administration hopes that the differentials will soon eliminate the U.S. balance of payments deficits, but so far the prospect is not favorable.

When exchange rates were set just after World War II, most countries wanted them high enough to restrict dollar imports, and U.S. business did not care if the dollar was overvalued, because no other country could produce much anyway and competition appeared to be remote. When foreigners became able to produce, however, they were in a position to compete effectively. The mere shift from the "dollar gap" to our payments deficit shows that "world" prices were to their liking. They clearly had an advantage that could only be wiped out by persistent relative inflation. Since the size of the original margin is unknown, it is impossible to say that moderate differences in price trends could eliminate it in a few years.

The original undervaluation of foreign currencies, however, is only part of the story because some of the forces that brought about the relative expansion and shift in competitive position are continuing to operate. Labor supplies usually proved expansible. Rapidly rising productivity itself freed labor, especially from agriculture, and the domestic wage structure facilitated shifting of workers into high productivity industries. It does not matter that the wages of low-cost labor were rising faster than prices. As long as labor was still available at a price well below the higher wage rates in the more productive industries, expansion could continue without loss of competitive position. The restraint of rising wage rates could become fully effective only when the whole income structure was inflated and this is a very slow process indeed. Again, the initial difference in relative wages was very important.

The competitive imbalance deriving from such differences was aggravated by the concentration of expansion in the newer, more productive industries. Over-all productivity rises much faster from transfers of resources into these industries than it could from trends in any of the industries taken by themselves. These are also export-oriented industries, and their growth helped avert balance-of-payments deficits. The faster growth in productivity that goes along with high rates of investment and innovation could then keep the rapidly expanding country ahead of competing countries with more stable incomes and prices for a long time, if not indefinitely. If protection from imports is added, as Humphrey indicates for Common Market policy, the possibility of correcting a disequilibrium becomes even more remote.

What is the likely response of the successful European planner to all this? We may assume that he wants to preserve the advantageous position which has developed. He will, therefore, give no credence to the idea that his currency is undervalued. He will attribute success to the competence and aggressiveness of his businessmen and to the astuteness of public policy. Such attitudes not only give him maximum support at home but exploit the guilt reactions of countries who are less successful and must try to explain away their deficiencies.

The Use of Key Currency as Reserves

If the story ended here, a clear decision would have to be rendered in favor of the overvaluation case made by Humphrey. Unfortunately, the countries that have been unsuccessful, having balance-of-payments difficulties as well as low growth rates, are the key currency countries. It seems to me that two points arising from this fact should be given greater emphasis.

The first is that the key currency position makes a record of payments deficits much less definitive as an indication of overvaluation. It is in any case difficult to tell whether the failure of a country's businessmen to develop a full measure of export trade is due to lack of interest and effort or to lack of adequate incentives because exchange rates are unfavorable. When the deficits may be due to the desire of other countries for reserves rather than to lack of competitive position, the case is well-nigh hopeless.

Maintenance of value is, of course, one of the characteristics of a good reserve, and this requires relatively stable prices in the key currency country. The traditional view holds gold to be the most stable reserve of all, but its so-called intrinsic value is one of those myths which fails to recognize that its value is determined by its use as a monetary reserve. In the last few years, U.S. prices have been satisfactorily stable. The relative price stability keeps the dollar looking, in that curious inversion of economic logic, "as good as gold." Thus, the price trends that make our goods more attractive also make our currency more attractive as reserves. But additions to the latter tend to keep our payments balance unfavorable and may continue to do so in a world of increasing affluence whose citizen-capitalists seek security in accumulations of monetary reserves. So the question of exchange disequilibrium is confused.

The second point is that a U.S. payments deficit under current conditions is a deflationary factor for our economy. This is true whether dollar balances are accumulated or the holders insist on converting them and taking gold. In either case, the amounts withheld reduce demand correspondingly and contract the income flow. The magnitude of this deflationary influence was at first small and, although larger now, it can still be carried for the time being, but if the situation changes, it will contribute to deepening the setback.

If we were incurring the payments deficits by living beyond our means, purchasing goods and services we were unable to pay for, the traditional fears, pressures, and policy prescriptions might be justified. Clearly, that is not the kind of situation with which we are confronting foreigners. Not only can we afford to pay, we should be glad, by doing so, to have a deflationary factor removed so that our economy could operate nearer to capacity. It would be in the interest of other countries, as Ingram states, to accept payment and enjoy higher real incomes through imports, and it would be in their interest again to have world markets expanded by a higher rate of activity here.

In popular discussions, one frequently hears that it is our government expenditures abroad, or our capital exports, or some other particular payments item that "causes" the disequilibrium. The fact is that all our payments contribute dollar for dollar to the opportunity to purchase goods here, and if foreigners do not choose to make such purchases, it must be concluded that the goods are less attractive than the additions to reserves. Until we are relieved of the key currency responsibility, there will be no sure way of telling whether the reserves are desired, or our goods are made unattractive by being priced too high, or, in the case of official holders, there are other reasons for temporarily "sterilizing" the dollars that have been made available.

Again, consider the European planner's point of view. At the beginning of the postwar period, he wanted reserves but wanted other things more. Later, as he succeeded, with some assistance, in building a basis for acquiring reserves, his need for them began to dwindle. He could, as Humphrey points out, consider his holdings as "normal if not permanent," and he could see no particular advantage in adding to them.

His problem had changed. Now his continued success was tied up with the preservation of a very touchy situation. He could not afford deflation and did not want imports that would depress domestic industry. Nor could he afford to let greater inflationary pressure develop, whether excessive rates of investment were being initiated at home or from abroad. He knew his control was imperfect and did not want it further restricted by U.S. expenditures in Europe which gave him nothing but reserves he did not need. Taking gold was one way to apply pressure. Another was to accuse the United States of using its key currency position to borrow at low cost in order to expand its long-term capital holdings abroad.

Traditional Policies Inapplicable

We cannot afford, of course, to accept the distortion of interpretation implicit in the thesis that we are borrowing to gain an advantage in economic position. The choice is clearly on the other side. We make funds available, and we give holders of dollars access to our active money markets, where they are able to convert them into earning assets. To concede that the banker who accepts a deposit is seeking a loan from the depositor verges on a form of apologetics and is, as Ingram observes, absurd.

So long as the interest earned on dollar reserves exceeds the rate of dollar price increase (in this case practically zero), there is a definite advantage in holding reserves in this form. The only risk is that the dollar might be devalued, and the interest may be regarded as compensation for carrying this risk. For the time being, the risk is made small by our unthinking attachment to dogma about "the integrity of the dollar." Assuming that we continue to lose gold from our reserves as time goes on, the risk of devaluation will increase and the compensation will be inadequate. Then the holders of dollars will seek to gain the best of everything by converting their holdings into gold. Our only counter to this is to impose on them another risk, namely, that we shall not be willing to repurchase the gold at all.

Part of the confusion arises from the failure to distinguish between financial and real capital. We are buying goods, services, and real capital assets and paying for them in part with financial assets, mainly short-term securities and gold. This smaller part, the deficit in our balance of payments, is blown up out of all proportion to its real importance and leads to proposals that we should make unacceptable modifications of our objectives or policies—for example, by restricting capital exports and raising interest rates.

Since the great, positive contribution we can make in a developing world depends on exports of real capital, cutbacks based on the thesis that we cannot afford to sustain the volume of those exports would threaten world progress. The measures we have adopted so far—the interest equalization tax and the tying of aid funds to purchases here —are not aimed at real capital but at financial transfers that might add to our short-term liabilities.

Countries that rely on planning are willing to accept real capital imports, especially if new technology goes with them, when they believe the results will be favorable. This is generally the case under conditions that afford some control over operating policies, the nature and level of output, its contributions to foreign exchange, the location of new plants, and the disposition of profits. Where any of these conditions is not met, obstacles may be imposed.

When this is done, the reason is likely to be political rather than economic. In complaining about "borrowing short, lending long," the planners are objecting to certain kinds of financial transactions, but most of all to those by which our businessmen acquire greater control over their industry. Our growing power to influence industrial decisions in their economies is a rival power, and their control over it is subject to limitations that might put them on the spot in the event cooperation is not forthcoming. At the same time, his own capitalists are made more independent by acquiring the option of becoming, if necessary, well-heeled expatriates. The planner's opposition to foreign domination of his industry and to more than ample foreign assets in the hands of his own businessmen is a natural consequence of the situation in which he finds himself.

Another technique of "adjustment," prescribed by some European officials and widely advocated by financial executives in this country as well as abroad, is the proposal that we raise interest rates further in order to restrict gold outflows. We could indeed increase the "risk premium" against devaluation in this way. We might even put the rate high enough to exceed the marginal efficiency of many investments available to foreign holders.

As Ingram states in his conclusion, temporizing in this way will not produce a solution. To my mind, opposition should be unequivocal. We can better afford to lose the gold than to withstand any additional deflationary effects from restrictive monetary policy. Besides, this policy, even if it is carried out by means of longer-term funding, is merely playing with fire financially. By promoting further accumulation of dollar reserves, it opens the door to speculative crises.

The handwriting on the wall is all too easy to read. The United States will not be able to negotiate cooperative defense of the dollar over the long run. We shall in any case be forced to give up the role of world banker, and we can do this most constructively by moving for further economic integration through the cooperative establishment of an international credit institution to perform world monetary functions. Such an institution is needed because the world has outgrown gold; because the United States should be relieved of the penalties involved in providing reserves for other countries; and because no one country should be left in an exposed key currency position from which, in some future crisis, it might be pulled down alone.

Toward a Higher Level of Planning

Although nobody has been willing up to this point to accept the interdependence which this kind of proposal involves, the need for reforms in the present system is making most countries willing to consider new arrangements. The current situation is posing a dilemma for the planners who wish to maintain autonomy on national or regional lines. Insistence on fixed exchange rates itself implies a high degree of economic integration, and efforts to maintain or establish advantages for national economies come increasingly into conflict with the international cooperation and progress needed in order to achieve any country's goals. Humphrey's article makes its greatest contribution in pointing out these inconsistencies.

I should like to add that there is an urgency to try to eliminate these inconsistencies by approaching economic problems in the broadest perspective. We have been living in a period of extraordinary boom conditions everywhere. The forces that generated and sustained the boom are still at work but will tend continually to lose their vigor. Deflation in any major economy will now threaten deflation everywhere. The biggest mistake the planners of any country can make is to think that their welfare can be preserved in the face of serious weakness in the rest of the world.

Nationalism in planning, as described by Humphrey, can only help to bring on the instability it is supposed to avert. No country can build its strength and grandeur by weakening somebody else. All of us can best progress through interchanges with others who are also progressing.

For the United States, consistent pursuit of expansionary policies at home and aid to developing countries will best serve the needs of the world. We should not try to buy the right to pursue these policies by arrangements designed only to permit us to retain our gold, but should push ahead with the willingness to do things that has been shown by the daring spenders in other parts of the world. True, this might bring on a crisis in world finance a little sooner. But it will be far easier to deal with an emergency of international finance than one of international deflation.

The problems of world finance have reached a state where they cannot be solved by national actions. If the threat of another crisis is needed to force international cooperation, events are sure sooner or later to force it on everybody's attention. Improved international financial arrangements cannot by themselves eliminate the possibility of cyclical or other interruptions in the course of steady progress, but they could do much to prevent financial factors from aggravating a cumulative pattern of recession. Specific aims, in addition to the usual monetary and banking functions, would be twofold: first, to permit adjustments for countries that would be forced into deflation by existing international arrangements which require fixed exchange rates and rule out both export subsidies and import restrictions, and, second, to insulate the finances of expanding economies from shocks originating elsewhere. Continuing as well as advance planning would be needed to achieve these objectives, but world finance is definitely a field in which planning can be effective only by moving up to the international level.

Planning Public Expenditure

W. ARTHUR LEWIS

PRINCETON UNIVERSITY

The welfare economist is at his happiest with a model economy where all goods can be produced at constant or rising cost for sale to individual consumers. He can then operate with the proposition that each consumer should have as much of any good as he is willing to pay for. This is a crude formulation of a principle which has been subjected to much mathematical refinement. At sophomore level we teach it in the form that marginal rates of substitution must equal marginal rates of product transformation. At higher levels we modify this to take account of indivisibilities, of the interdependence of consumer preferences, or of the interrelationship between demand and income distribution; and in so doing, deprive the proposition of most of its logical foundation. But having completed these theoretical exercises, economists usually return to this proposition in their advisory work because they have nothing better to offer.

The economic theory of public policy begins where production by private entrepreneurs in response to market demands would not, in the absence of public intervention, yield the right allocation of resources. There are many classes of case, but they fall into two major categories, one which is in line with the basic assumptions of economic theory and another which is not.

The basic assumptions of economic theory are that each consumer knows just what he wants, independently of other consumers, and that satisfying individual preferences is the object of production. Given these assumptions, the allocation problem could always be solved in theory if we had a machine for reading consumers' minds, even though the free market might not give the right answer. Public production is a substitute for the private market in many instances. We confine ourselves to two of these cases, both stemming from indivisibility. One is the indivisibility which gives rise to decreasing costs, and leads to the theory of public utilities. The other indivisibility is the indivisibility of benefit, which has appeared in economic literature under different names ("collective consumption," "public good") but which is analytically a form of joint supply with fixed proportions. Indivisibility of benefit is illustrated by the problem of how much to spend on ridding an area of mosquitoes. The more one spends, at increasing cost, the smaller the chance for each citizen of being bitten by a mosquito. The benefit is indivisible since everybody gains from marginal expenditure. The problem cannot be solved by the market, since the market cannot force all who gain to contribute to the cost. But it could be solved by a public authority equipped to read the mind of each citizen, and discover what his preferences are for protection against mosquitoes as against consuming other goods or services.[1]

In allocation theory the treatment of indivisibilities is the same whether one is dealing with decreasing costs or with indivisible benefits. After the consumer has been charged separately with any costs which supplying him separately imposes on the system, the remaining "fixed cost" has to be allocated to all consumers in some fashion such that none pays more than his consumer's surplus. Whether the investment should be undertaken in the first place is decided by comparing the fixed cost with the sum of the consumers' surpluses of the group who will be benefited; at the margin, the last dollar of fixed cost must equal the sum of the consumers' surpluses on this marginal benefit.[2]

Thus in all cases where the consumer has definite preferences, and where the purpose of public action is to satisfy these preferences, the correct allocation of resources can be determined in theory, whether or not there exists in practice any means of discovering what these preferences are.

The other category of public action is concerned with cases where the consumer has no definite preferences, or where there are thought to be good reasons for acting contrary to his preferences. Here the government exercises the function of leadership. Since economic theory starts from consumer preferences, it cannot produce any guidance for

[1] See R. A. Musgrave, "The Voluntary Exchange Theory of Public Economy," *Quarterly Journal of Economics,* February 1939; and P. A. Samuelson, "Diagrammatic Exposition of a Theory of Public Expenditure," *Review of Economics and Statistics,* November 1955.

[2] To arrive at the consumers' surplus on one commodity, one must take all other prices as given. Hence, one is in increasing difficulty as the number of indivisibilities increases. However, as we noted in the first paragraph of this paper, any exploration of consumer preferences as a guide to policy formation leads into a morass. Economists use welfare economics because they have nothing better.

action in spheres where individual preferences do not exist or are not to be followed.

These cases can be classified into four types. In the first, the object is to encourage people to consume more (subsidized education, milk, housing, etc.) or less (narcotics, alcohol, obscenity) than they would prefer. Secondly, the individual citizen may have no preference because he does not know what is involved, and may consider that the government is the appropriate authority to decide (e.g., defense). Thirdly, the citizen's preference may merely be to do what others do, and he may wish to have the government set the pattern ("I am willing to pay my share to charity—to the incapacitated or to foreign aid— if somebody neutral tells me what my share is"). Finally, the government may deliberately violate Pareto optimality in order to make one group of citizens (class, race, creed, or region) better off at the expense of others; if this were done by transferring money, Pareto optimality would not be violated, but the government may prefer to supply goods for one of the other three reasons.

Thus some government activities may be in the category of finding out what the individual consumer would like and trying to satisfy him; for these a machine which could read individual consumers' minds would yield the answer. In the other category the government has to decide what to do in the light of other considerations, beyond anything that such a machine might reveal. This approach to the problem comes naturally to the economist, but most other social philosophers must find it strange. Economics is a by-product of individualist philosophy, which is a form of extremism. At this pole society is nothing but a collection of individuals, and special reasons have to be invented to justify collective action. At the opposite philosophical pole, individuals are only the particles of which society is built; like the family, the team, the church, or the university, it exists before, beyond, and after the individual; it has its own life and interests, to which he must subordinate himself, even in extreme cases unto death. Most sensible persons see validity in both these claims, recognizing areas where the individual's wants are paramount, and others where they are secondary.

When the government operates in spheres where it is trying to meet individual wants it is acting like a performer of music; when it is making up its own mind in other spheres, it is acting like a composer. The performer's job is to decipher what other men have written; he is allowed some individuality of expression, but the text is supposed to be sacred. The composer makes his own tunes; in order to please his public he has to stay within a certain framework of rules, but this framework is wide enough to permit infinite choice. Economic theory has some guidance for the government acting as a performer, but is quite irrelevant to the government's actions as a composer. This is essentially why an "economic theory of public expenditure" is a contradiction in terms.

Following the Tune

In this section we assume that the individual's preferences are definite and independent, and that the government's sole object is to satisfy them. We also confine ourselves to market imperfections arising out of indivisibility, whether decreasing cost or indivisible benefit.

We do not examine the question whether the government should become a producer of all goods which the private market allocates incorrectly, or of any other goods. The respective merits of private and public enterprise cannot be established in terms of economic theory. We merely assume that the government is producing some goods involving indivisibilities, and ask what policy it should follow in allocating resources.

There are two problems: to find out what the individual wants, in the absence of a mind-reading machine, and to devise a levy based on consumer's surplus.

The first principle is to isolate the group which benefits from the particular expenditure, and put it on a self-financing basis. Thus, if the citizens of Princeton want to build themselves a service with heavy indivisible costs, they must be willing to meet these costs by one means or another from their own resources, or do without. Surprisingly, this proposition, which seems obvious to the man in the street, has not appealed to some welfare economists. Following Hotelling,[3] many have argued that indivisible costs should be paid by the central government. When asked why the citizens of Princeton should be favored in this way, they reply that if everybody is treated in this way the subsidies will cancel out; or if they do not the resulting distribution of income is not necessarily any worse than would have occurred if some different policy were followed.

This attempt to distinguish between what the buyer should pay for divisible and what he should pay for indivisible assets is based on a

[3] Harold Hotelling, "The General Welfare in Relation to Problems of Taxation and of Railway and Utility Rates," *Econometrica,* July 1938. The argument of the next three paragraphs is elaborated in my *Overhead Costs,* especially Chapters 1 and 2.

logical fallacy. The theory of allocation tells us that divisible output should be carried to the point where marginal utility equals marginal cost, and indivisible investment to the point where the sum of the marginal utilities of the beneficiaries, measured in money, equals the marginal indivisible cost. Allocation theory cannot tell us what price to charge, since levying a price is an act not of allocation but of distribution; "price must equal marginal cost" means "we must take from the buyer enough income to cover marginal cost." Such a statement is not any easier or more difficult to derive from allocation theory than the statement "we must take from the buyers as a group enough income to cover indivisible cost." Neither statement can be derived logically from allocation theory. The man in the street believes that people should pay whatever cost they impose on society, divisible or indivisible, and this ethical proposition is the only foundation for statements about price policy.

Given that the group must meet all costs, a system of levies must be devised. If some of the costs can be attributed to the individual and some cannot, some kind of multipart charging is indicated—a part or parts based on the separable costs, and a residual part based on consumer's surplus. The residual part is normally levied proportionately to consumer's surplus or some index thereof ("charging what the traffic will bear"). Since there is no machine for reading the consumer's mind, some arbitrary index of benefit has to be taken such as (in transport) the value-weight ratio of the traffic or (in local authority services) the value of the house in which the consumer lives or (in central government services) the citizen's income.

The group may decide that collecting a separate levy from each consumer is not worth the cost. For example, where water is cheap, it does not pay to install a meter in each house and send men round to read meters every month. In such cases there is a single levy, not based on consumption; or the cost of the service is merely absorbed into the general budget. This is most appropriate where elasticity of demand is low and the cost of charging for consumption high. It is also appropriate if the government especially wishes to encourage consumption, but that case is outside the assumptions of this section. How much to raise by fixed charge and how much by a price per unit consumed raises many interesting problems which are normally discussed in the literature of two-part tariffs, and into which we need not enter here.

Since the main problem in planning investment is to guess how much of the service the public would be prepared to pay for out of consumers' surplus, the main policy rule is to take decision-making as close to the consumers as possible, by decentralizing the service as much as is feasible, having regard to economies of scale. This leads to one of the most important principles of public administration, viz.: The federal government should not do anything which the state could do equally well; the state, anything which the county could do equally well; or the county, anything which the borough, township, or village authority could do equally well.

This principle runs into three kinds of opposition. Those who accept its spirit may nevertheless dispute in any given case whether it is done "equally well." The spirit is rejected by those who do not accept in some particular case that each community should decide for itself what it wants, but prefer to impose uniform standards determined at the center. And it is also rejected, in authoritarian states, by those who wish to centralize power, even though they might claim that they would use this power to give the consumer what he wants; these object to decentralization not because of its effects on the service, but because decentralization enables political rivals to acquire power in those parts of the country where they have a large following.

For one or other of these reasons, the current trend is away from decentralization. In most parts of the world the central government grows stronger at the expense of subordinate authorities.

In some of the new African states the situation is acute. Most expert visitors to the continent consider that the subordinate authorities are much too weak; too much is decided at the center (an inheritance from colonial days); and the building up of provincial and other local authorities would greatly improve administration. This is resisted for political reasons, from fear that decentralization gives scope to political enemies, and also prevents the adoption of uniform standards. Decisions about the allocation of investments are therefore made by men who live at a great distance from the places where the investments are to be made.

The problem is compounded by premature adoption of the principle that basic necessities should be supplied free of charge. In many parts of Africa the villager assumes that the central government will provide water, schools, hospital service, roads, and even electricity free. If decentralization were in vogue, the village could be told that it can have as much water or electricity, or as many roads as it is willing to pay for out of village taxes; and the principle of "free" supply would not then give rise to such unlimited demands. The clear connection between quantity of service and village taxes would be beneficial at both ends: keeping down demand, and increasing the willingness to pay taxes. When the service is on the central budget, the connection between demand and taxes is tenuous; nobody wants to pay taxes to a distant central government, whose use of them is neither known nor approved; but the demand for immediate installation of services is unlimited. Governments are then saddled with insoluble problems. The public's demand for service grossly exceeds the willingness to pay taxes. Installing services in some places merely inflames the demand in others. And if there are 10,000 villages, but only enough money over the next five years to give water supplies to 1,000 villages, which 9,000 are to be excluded?

The problem is not strictly insoluble, since it could be solved by decentralizing all services which exist primarily to satisfy individual consumer needs. But this solution cannot be adopted until administration and politics begin to be separated from each other.

The Art of Composition

Even if the government desired only to give the citizen what he wants, it could not always discover what he wants, because the mind-reading machine has not yet been invented. Hence over a wide sphere of public action, philosophical demonstration that a Pareto optimum exists conceptually is of no value to the decision-maker. Action in this sphere imposes on the government the same obligation to decide what is desirable that falls upon it when dealing with its second category of cases, where the consumer has no definite independent preferences, or where these preferences are to be disregarded.

How governments decide what is desirable is studied not by economists but by political scientists. How governments ought to decide, taking everything into account (what is known or guessed about preferences, keeping the peace between hostile groups, ensuring orderly political succession, looking two or three steps ahead into the future, exercising leadership, etc., etc.) would be an essay in philosophy rather than in science, and gives scope for wide divergence of opinion. Every political leader has to balance the myriad forces as he sees best, and the citizens judge him only to a limited extent by his accordance with their preconceived ideas. Rather, a great political leader is judged like a great composer; one looks to see what he has created, and surrenders part of one's individuality in the process.

A theory of public expenditure, which would enable the right decisions to be derived out of an electronic computer, is no more feasible than a theory of composition which will get great works of art out of an electronic computer. And this is the basic reason why economists, recognizing the limitations of their science, have written almost nothing on this subject.

Actually, the politician's task in planning public expenditure is much less formidable than it sounds. To begin with, the scope for maneuver from one year to the next is very narrow. Redistribution of existing expenditures is nearly impossible, whether because of vested interests in jobs or because of pressure from those who value the services that would be cut. Adding without cutting is also difficult. However small public expenditure may be, in relation to national income, a large increase from one year to the next is ruled out by the impossibility of getting away with large changes in tax rates except during such crises as war. Over a five-year period one might with determination increase tax revenues by two points, say, from 15 to 17 per cent of gross domestic product; in the absence of windfalls, such as improved terms of trade or a big increase in mining, more than this is improbable.

Then, much of the expected increase in revenues is already doomed to be swallowed up by existing commitments. The teachers will make their annual demand for salary increases. The hospital built last year will now have to be staffed. Population will increase by, say, 12 per cent over the five years; so, merely to maintain existing standards of public service, the public service will have to be expanded in approximately the same ratio. Most prime ministers take up office with big ideas as to what they can achieve, and are sadly disillusioned within a few months, unless their accession to office happens to coincide with some economic windfall (usually either the expansion of mining output or a rise in the price of exports).

At the administrative level, the planner begins by estimating normal growth arising out of existing commitments. Rather, one should say "should begin," because, astonishingly, the great majority of development planners concentrate on the capital budget and never make an item-by-item forecast of the likely growth of recurrent expenditure on existing commitments. As a result, expenditure grows faster than was estimated when assessing how much money the government would have for capital expenditure, and the plan runs into a crisis within two or three years. Discussion of foreign aid has tended to focus attention on the importance of capital; but in the public sector the limitation tends to be recurrent expenditure rather than capital; over five years the recurrent expenditure on a school is more than twice the capital cost.

The next step is to assess the cost of new commitments. Some budget items are linked to items appearing in the part of the plan which relates to the private sector. Others are independent public policy decisions.

The projected rate of growth of the private sector has implications for public expenditure in many fields, notably roads, ports, telecommunications, water supplies, electricity, research institutions, geological service, technical education, and secondary education. Working out what this involves is relatively easy; education will be used as an example in the next section.

However, in all these spheres, public policy goes much further than merely supplying the needs of industry. Most regimes take for granted that public services should be planned to meet whatever need may be forthcoming from industry. The practical problem is how far to go in meeting consumer demands. As we have seen already in the preceding section, this problem could be minimized by greater decentralization, which would leave it to each village to decide what it was willing to pay for. Given centralization, and the resulting gross excess of demand over possible supply, the central government has to make up its own mind what to include in the plan and what to postpone.

The rule which has been suggested as a way out is that in the poorer countries public expenditure should concentrate at this time on building up those services which contribute most to productive capacity. This seems sensible at first sight, but is not in practice very helpful. For almost any public service can be defended on the ground that it contributes to productive capacity. The main effect of this orientation is to send supporters of each service scurrying to find arguments and statistics which will prove that their service is not "consumption" but "investment."

Very little operations research has been done on the public services. Something will be said in the next section about the work of this kind on education and public health. The most successful work has been done on roads and irrigation projects, assessing how far the opening up of new lands or increased productivity of existing investments would pay the cost of new works. Naturally, much of this is guesswork, but the operation has been done so often that the practitioner at least knows what features to look out for. Another possible area is defense expenditure; a good deal has been done in this area in developed countries; so similar work in underdeveloped countries might be fruitful.

However, it is idle to expect operations research to decide how big the budget can be. No doubt it can contribute in the area of defense. It has also a marginal contribution to make in the sphere of general and economic administration. But the group which grows fastest in the budgets of most underdeveloped countries, and now accounts for more than half the expenditure of many, is the social service group, including education, health, and welfare services. Here the proposition that expenditure be confined to what is demonstrated to increase productive capacity is a nonstarter with the citizen, however much it may appeal to the administrator. The citizen wants education and health and welfare services for their own sakes, and in most countries wants more than can be demonstrated to be profitable in terms of increasing future yields.

Another guide is to make international comparisons. This is done all the time, as a check on standards. Countries compare the number of policemen per 100,000 of population; the ratio of teachers to students; the ratio of agricultural extension agents to farm population; the ratio of army officers to other ranks; the infant mortality rate; and so on. The paper by this author and Miss Martin, comparing sources of revenue and objects of expenditure in seventeen countries in relation to gross domestic product, is alleged to have been found useful in some ministries of finance.[4] Such comparisons are obviously of limited value. They are relevant only in cases where most countries have the same proportion or where differences can be clearly related to some measurable index. Even then they are merely suggestive; if your country's proportion is very different from what the index suggests, you do not conclude that it is wrong, but merely start trying to discover what accounts for the difference.

The principal fact revealed by national income comparisons is that countries do not differ widely in the proportions of gross domestic product (GDP) which they spend on general and economic administration; the big differences are in social services, defense, and public debt charges. In the majority of countries the recurrent cost of general and economic administration lies between 5 and 7 per cent of GDP. The proportion spent by the less developed tends, if they are ambitious, to exceed the proportion spent by the more developed. The latter have better administrative services and relatively more people engaged in them. But in the less developed, because of the shortage of educated persons, the ratio of the salary of a civil servant to per capita national income is much higher. As countries grow richer, these two factors tend to offset each other, keeping the proportion spent on administration within narrow limits. Social services are much more flexible and therefore range more widely.

The various guides we have indicated—calculating the rising cost of

4 W. A. Lewis and Alison M. Martin, "Patterns of Public Revenue and Expenditure," *Manchester School of Economic and Social Studies,* September 1956.

existing commitments, making provision for new commitments, operations research, and international comparisons—all help to indicate what the plan for public expenditure should be. But there always remains a residual area for judgment—and for political pressures and bargaining. The musicologist talks about all the various ingredients of the symphony, but in the last analysis the composer has to fall back on his own power of creation.

One should note, finally, that the welfare economist's search for an "optimum" which represents "equilibrium" is quite out of place. In politics one does not try to make progress on all fronts simultaneously. The government is engaged in an exercise of leadership, persuading the citizens to pay more taxes for various services. This has to be done by concentrating on one or a few things at a time. Perhaps the leader's present concern is defense; he has some support, but also much opposition. Getting this program through takes a lot of time and much organized effort; he may succeed, and yet be so exhausted or mauled by the process that his further usefulness is diminished. At another time the emphasis may be on education; at some other time on measures to increase agricultural productivity. To try to win on all fronts simultaneously would almost certainly invite defeat, since it would arouse the maximum of enmity. "Unbalanced growth" is the secret of political strategy. Hence the question is never "have we got the equilibrium distribution of public expenditure between all the various categories," but only "where is the need most urgent, and are we progressing toward meeting it?"

Suite for Small Ensembles [5]

In this section we assemble some random remarks about various objects of public expenditure. These are based to some extent on experience as a consultant, and are therefore mainly matters which have struck this author's attention. They relate exclusively to the problems of underdeveloped countries.

THE ROLE OF SERVICES

The attitude to services has passed through a number of phases. When development planning began, at the end of the Second World War, the emphasis was on the public services. This was defended by asserting that infrastructure was the key to economic development. After a while

[5] Some of the material in this section will appear simultaneously in my new book, *Development Planning*.

the assertion began to be doubted. Governments were expanding their public service commitments faster than public revenue, without this necessarily resulting in greater output of other goods and services. They were therefore now advised to concentrate instead on measures designed directly to stimulate the output of commodities in general, and export commodities in particular. "Production" (meaning commodities) must come before "consumption" (meaning services). Development plans which concentrated mainly on public service programs were held inferior to those which were full of arithmetical targets for agriculture and manufacturing industry. Then came a counterattack in which services were taken out of the category of "consumption," and defended on the ground that they are "investment in human resources and just as productive as investment in physical resources." Ministers of finance find this disputation not a little confusing.

Let us begin with exports. In terms of value added, the income elasticity of demand for services is about 1.05, while that for commodities is about 0.95. The elasticity of supply of services is very high, while the elasticity of supply of commodities taken as a whole is rather low. If income is increased by producing more commodities, the demand for services will expand in a slightly greater proportion, and will be met by an expanded output of services (the elasticity of supply of labor to the market economy is very high). The situation is asymmetrical. If income is increased by producing more services, the demand for commodities will expand nearly in the same proportion, but the output of commodities will not. Hence there will be a deficit in the balance of payments and deflation in the home market. The expansion of services will not prove viable. From this it follows that the practical problem in planning is to expand commodity output; services will look after themselves; to concentrate on services instead of commodities must lead to trouble. But while this statement of the practical problem is good shorthand, a complete statement recognizes that the framework is one of balanced growth; services and commodities are equally important.

Actually, while this analysis applies to services in the private sector, it does not apply to public services financed by taxes. If private entrepreneurs open up hotels, hospitals, schools, and other services they or other service entrepreneurs will go bankrupt for the reasons indicated (unless there is an influx of tourists, i.e., the services are for export). But if the government expands services, and takes in as much again in taxes, imports of commodities remain unaffected. Personal income increases by the value of the additional services, but personal income net of taxes remains as before. Hence there is no balance-of-payments limitation on the expansion of public services financed by taxes; these do not have to keep step with the growth of commodities in any balanced way. The only financial limitation on the expansion of services financed by taxes is the unwillingness of the public to pay more taxes.

If the balance of payments is an unreal bogey, what about investment? Must public services be curtailed unless they can prove themselves to be a form of productive investment?

This question has to be taken in two stages. First, if the level of investment is already decided, the competition is not between services and investment, but only between services and commodities for consumption. Here economists are on familiar ground, since this controversy was settled nearly a hundred years ago. Commodities and services have no advantage over each other; both yield utility. Men require both commodities and services; so the only question is whether the proportions in which they are supplied correspond to the proportions in which they are demanded. Since public services are paid for out of taxes, this question reduces to whether the public is being asked to pay more or less in taxes than it would spend on public services if these could be financed through sale in the market. We know that in most underdeveloped countries the demand for public services greatly exceeds the supply, but whether this situation would continue if the link between services and taxes were clearer is very doubtful. As we have seen, the only practical way to solve this problem is greater decentralization of the financing and administration of public services.

The second stage of the problem is to assume that the proportion between services and commodities offered for consumption is correct, and consider whether consumption as a whole is not too great; and therefore whether the supply of public services (as well as of consumable commodities) should not be restricted in the interest of greater saving.

This is the stage where defenders of public services rush to prove that they are not consumption but investment in human resources. The defense cannot be sustained (see below) because the demand for services, especially for education and health, exceeds considerably anything that might be defended on these grounds. But is this defense really necessary? Just as the previous attack implied that commodities are superior to services, now this attack implies that saving is superior to consumption.

What economic mathematics says about the optimum rate of saving does not take us far. By making arbitrary assumptions about a capital-output ratio, one can calculate what rate of saving would maximize consumption, say, in ten years from now, or the total of consumption over the next ten years, or the present value of the total of consumption over the next ten years. For example, if the capital-output ratio is 3:1, consumption in year 10 would be maximized if the rate of saving were about 64 per cent of national income. This is obviously not feasible (even ignoring the unreasonableness of the capital-output assumption), since it requires an absolute fall in present consumption. If absolute consumption cannot fall, and saving is now 9 per cent of income, consumption would be maximized in year 10 by increasing the absolute amount saved at a rate of 13 per cent per year, bringing the savings ratio to 20 per cent in year 10. This high rate of growth is also not feasible; it assumes that the rate of growth of output depends only on the rate of growth of saving, and not on the rate of growth of consumption. Total consumption over ten years would be maximized by holding constant the absolute amount saved. This is a slower rate of growth than can be achieved, and the rate of saving which would maximize the present value of consumption over ten years would be still lower.

An alternative approach is to start from the link between the rate of growth of output and the rate of growth of consumption which is required to achieve it. Economic development cannot take place without an increase in consumption. Growth requires inducements; workers must move to higher-paid occupations; farmers must adopt more profitable methods; and as the incomes of some producers rise, incomes of other mobile or powerful groups will also rise, even though their per capita output is not increasing—especially in the rapidly growing service industries, where wages keep pace with industry but productivity lags. An increase in per capita output unaccompanied by a sizable increase in per capita consumption is therefore inconceivable, except perhaps in a police state.

It is not merely inconceivable, but also undesirable. Economic growth creates disturbing tensions in society, which can be resolved only if the increased output is used to secure more equitable distribution. Men migrate from villages where they have been sustained in time of want by the obligations of extended family systems. In the towns they take sick, or become unemployed, and it falls to the public authorities to look after their welfare. Other men are deprived of their living by technological changes which make them poor but others rich. Some are by-passed by opportunity, but are made envious by the good fortune of neighbors or relatives, and associate with others in unions or other societies to try for a share of the obvious increase in national riches. The early stages of economic development are always a time of tension and unrest. Narrowly conceived economic interest may seem to point in the direction of holding down consumption as long as possible; but the interest of creating a healthy society with tensions and injustices moderated and limited requires that welfare be given equal priority with growth right from the beginning.

The growth of stark poverty through the explosion of towns, unemployment, and the breakdown of family relationships is one of the most terrible features of the early stages of economic development. It demands that the government go into the welfare business right from the start if society is not to be deeply scarred. To provide a framework of services for the unemployed, the aged, the orphaned, and the handicapped is just as important as saving to build factories to produce more radios or bicycles.

More saving and more growth are desirable, but not at the expense of social or welfare services. On the contrary, the universal experience is that as income per capita increases, both saving and the public services increase their relative shares of the national income at the expense of personal consumption. How rapidly to proceed is part of the art of politics. Those who have accepted the advice of impatient economists have found themselves with riots on their hands.

The following suggestion is made. Since growth requires inducements, the minimum allowable rate of growth of personal consumption is tied to the rate of growth of output. Thus one can devise a rule of thumb. Suppose that per capita consumption must grow at least 60 per cent as fast as per capita output, and that personal consumption is currently 75 per cent of output. Then if per capita output grows by 1.0 per cent, the ratio of consumption to output falls by 0.3 per cent of output (i.e., from 75 to 74.7 per cent). If per capita growth is 2.0 per cent, the ratio falls by 0.6 points. In practice, in the absence of windfalls from mining or the terms of trade, most underdeveloped countries cannot increase per capita output by more than 2 per cent per annum over a long period because of the backwardness of their agriculture, and should not plan on raising the share of taxes and saving combined by more than three percentage points over five years.

Economists have often debated whether there is a limit to taxable capacity. The question is unsettled, but is in any case irrelevant in underdeveloped countries, for their tax collections are far below any reasonable definition of taxable capacity. A much more important limit is the feasible rate of change. Many factors determine this; the present suggestion is offered as a contribution to understanding.

EDUCATION

Poor countries cannot afford to pay for as much education as richer countries. They have therefore to establish priorities in terms both of quality and quantity.

The cost of education is higher in poor countries, for two reasons. First, because of the higher birth rate, the school-age population is relatively larger. The proportion of the population aged 5 to 14 is only 15 per cent in Great Britain, but it is over 25 per cent in the typical underdeveloped country. Secondly, because of the relative scarcity of educated people the ratio of a teacher's salary to per capita national income is much higher in poor countries—two to three times as high. For these two reasons together, whereas universal primary education costs a rich country rather less than 1 per cent of national income, it would cost a poor country from 2 to 4 per cent of national income.

The cost of university education is particularly high in Africa, since more than two-thirds of the teachers have to be imported from Western Europe and America. Inducement allowances, plus the cost of transporting them and their families to and fro and on leave, makes the cost per student 50 to 100 per cent higher than the cost of maintaining universities in Western Europe. Since tuition fees in Europe are very low, an African government can send two or three students to Europe on scholarships for what it costs to maintain one student in a university at home, even without bringing the high capital cost of the universities into the account. Africa needs her own universities to do research into her own problems, but (except in parts of Francophone Africa where France pays the running cost of the university) it is good strategy to tailor the size of the local university to the size of staff required for local research, and send additional students overseas if they can be placed. Whatever may be the special advantages of going to college in one's own country (and these are grossly exaggerated), from the social point of view it is better to educate two men overseas instead of one at home at the same cost.

In rich countries the core of educational planning is to use census figures and vital statistics to estimate how many children will need places over the next twenty years. In poor countries such exercises are secondary, since one knows in advance that the number of children will exceed the number of places that can be afforded. The strategy is rather to begin by estimating the demand for skills, and to try to provide at least as many places as are required to meet the demand for persons with different levels of schooling.

The earliest manpower surveys were made by visiting employers and asking them how many people they expected to employ in different kinds of jobs in five years' time. This is obviously unsatisfactory. Nowadays the starting point is to project several years ahead (say, ten) what the structure of the economy will be, and deduce the number of skilled persons from tables relating skills to industrial classification. If there is a good census, cross-classifying industry, occupation, and education, it will show existing numbers and their distribution; published cross-classifications are rare in underdeveloped countries, but the data

TABLE 1

Educational Requirements, Jamaica, 1964

(per cent)

	University	Secondary	Skilled	Other
Agriculture				
Large-scale	0.4	2.0	3.5	94.1
Small-scale		0.6	0.1	99.3
Mining	4.0	10.0	25.0	61.0
Manufacture				
Complex	4.0	10.0	25.0	61.0
Simple	2.0	5.0	15.0	78.0
Workshop	0.1	1.0	12.0	86.9
Construction	0.2	1.7	50.0	48.1
Communications	1.5	6.0	10.0	82.5
Commerce	1.5	11.0	1.0	86.5
Domestic service				100.0
Other services	4.5	35.0	2.0	58.5

can sometimes be run off from the census cards. However, there is constant upgrading of educational requirements for jobs; so in calculating recruitment one needs to know not only the educational level of the present holders of jobs, which the census may show, but also the educational level now expected of new recruits. The latter is discovered by on-the-spot investigation. For example, Table 1 shows for each Jamaican "industry" the proportion of jobs for which a college degree would now be required, the proportion requiring secondary education with or without further specialized training (excluding college), and the proportion requiring primary education plus at least one year of intensive training (including on-the-job training).[6]

[6] For details, see my article "Secondary Education and Economic Structure," *Social and Economic Studies,* June 1964.

For the Jamaican economy as a whole current requirements are: university, 0.9; secondary schooling, 6.0; and skilled, 7.0 per cent. These figures are based on aspirations rather than on achievement. Thus against the secondary and university requirement of 6.9 per cent, we must set the fact that the proportion of the population over 20 which had actually completed secondary or higher education was only 3.4 per cent. On the other hand, the proportion that had received some secondary schooling was 6.4 per cent, the dropout rate being very high.

Jamaica has a relatively advanced economy. Similar figures for West Africa in 1960 would have shown less than 1 per cent having received secondary education, and not more than 3 per cent of jobs requiring it, even with upgraded educational requirements. However, what matters for policy is not how high the figures are, but the gap between the proportion who now have secondary education and the proportion now required to have it. The gap in secondary education is the greatest drawback to African development because of the crucial roles in society of people with this kind of training. There is also a great shortage of university people, but the number required is small—only about one-eighth of the number with secondary schooling—so it is feasible to import university graduates from other countries. The number required with secondary schooling is so large, and the cost of importing them so high, that there is no feasible alternative to concentrating the educational effort at this stage on expanding secondary rather than university or primary education.

Calculating the demand for skill gives the answer so long as the demand substantially exceeds the number of skilled persons likely to be produced, but ceases to help when the number of places already exceeds the jobs. Such calculations are based on employers' current practices in hiring staff, but these practices are themselves partly derived from the current market situation. What qualifications employers expect when hiring will depend partly on what the market has to offer. If there is a shortage of secondary school graduates, they will hire primary school graduates to be stenographers. Expectations are also conditioned by relative prices. If the salaries of secondary school graduates were lower relative to those of primary school graduates, employers would prefer to hire secondary school graduates for jobs as salesclerks. Employers' expectations are therefore elastic.

If educational requirements and relative prices were a simple function of the level of economic development, one would get a good correlation between economic structure and education. This relationship has been tested by comparing countries in respect of the proportion of the male population aged 25 and over which has received four years of secondary education, and the proportion of the occupied population engaged in agriculture.[7] The result was

$$x = 26.1 - 0.37a$$

where x = percentage of males aged 25 and over who left secondary school after reaching age 15

a = percentage of the occupied population engaged in agriculture

This formula was subject to the restriction that x should not be less than 3.0. The formula relates to the stock of educated people in existence.

TABLE 2

Required School Enrollments for Given Levels

of Agricultural Employment

(per cent)

Occupied in Agriculture	Completing Secondary School	Completing Higher Education
70	6	0.8
60	9	1.1
50	13	1.6
40	18	2.3
30	21	2.6

Annual enrollment is a function both of wastage and of changes in the desirable level of the stock resulting from changes in the proportion of the occupied population engaged in agriculture. A series of further assumptions (detailed in the same article) suggested the enrollment percentages shown in Table 2, for each level of economic development, taking boys and girls together.

These suggestions are highly tentative. The original statistics are rather shaky, and do not fall into a neat pattern. Several countries had many more (apart from the United States and Canada) and several had many

[7] *Ibid.* In that article the population aged 15 and over is used instead of the occupied population. Conversion is made here by multiplying by 0.55.

fewer persons with secondary education than such a formula would require. Departures from the formula were not obviously associated with productivity. What emerged was that commerce serves as a reservoir for the products of secondary schools. If a liberal educational policy is pursued, the proportion of salesclerks who have had secondary education is high, while the proportion is low where opportunities for secondary education are restricted. There is no obvious correlation between productivity and the extent to which salesclerks have received a secondary education.

The main conclusion of attempts to link education with economic structure is that a country can absorb almost any number of educated persons by varying the qualifications for jobs and adjusting relative earnings. The demand for various skills serves as a target for the educational planner while he is still in the stage where demand exceeds places; but as soon as the number of places catches up, he has to look behind employers' demands to more fundamental factors.

Recently American economists have tried to measure the productivity of education on an economywide basis for the U.S. economy by correlating income statistics with educational attainments.[8] Such exercises can hardly be translated to underdeveloped countries, for three main reasons. First, the assumption that the pattern of earnings reflects differences in productivity seems rather doubtful; in Jamaica an unskilled laborer earns three times as much in the bauxite industry as in the sugar industry; such "anomalies" are too numerous in underdeveloped countries for earnings to be accepted as a guide to productivity. Secondly, even if earnings reflect productivity, education is so highly correlated with other causes of high productivity (especially intelligence, patience, persistence, and ability to persuade) that one would have to be able to distinguish these other factors before reaching conclusions; attempts have been made to do so, but they are not convincing. Having regard to the irrelevance of what is taught in schools (even at the college level, not more than 30 per cent are trained in scientific or technological skills) employers probably pay more for educated men not because of what they have learned in school, but because ability to survive the tests imposed by schooling is as good a test as any of the kind of personal qualities which employers are seeking. Thirdly, this kind of correlation would not be useful in underdeveloped countries because of the big difference between average and marginal earnings. In most of Asia, where there is acute unemployment of educated persons, a correlation

[8] For a summary see a paper by a leading pioneer, T. W. Schultz, "Investment in Human Capital," *American Economic Review,* March 1961.

between education and marginal income might well lead to the conclusion that the marginal productivity of higher education is negative.

Less ambitious exercises take one occupation at a time and study how changes in education would affect efficiency. This is being done all the time, especially by those who have the responsibility for determining professional qualifications, but also by educational planners and by employers or their associations. The most important unanswered question in underdeveloped countries is how much difference universal primary education would make to agricultural productivity, when compared with spending more money on establishing a better system of agricultural extension and adult education focused on practical needs. Universal primary education is much more expensive. It is also rather disturbing, since graduates of primary schools do not at present want to return to the farms, but tend to congregate in towns, where there is not enough work of the kind they seek, and where their high unemployment rate creates social and political problems. If it could be shown that adult education is nearly as productive in the countryside as primary education, there would be a strong case for expanding primary education more slowly (e.g., planning to get from 20 to 90 per cent of children in school in thirty years instead of ten).

The practical problem can therefore be summed up as follows. It is fairly easy to estimate what the demand for the educated will be at current prices. It is also fairly easy, using the census and birth and death statistics, to estimate how many children there will be at different ages, and using one's knowledge of trends, to estimate how many of these will be demanding education. If the demand by employers exceeds the supply, priority should be given to expanding educational facilities. However (except for secondary and higher education in Africa), most developing countries have passed or are passing into the stage where the number demanding education exceeds the number of foreseeable jobs, and their problem is how far to go in satisfying this surplus demand.

This question the economist cannot answer. We can point out that a surplus of educated can only be a temporary phenomenon. Any economy can absorb any number of educated: The premium for education falls, and the qualifications for jobs are upgraded, and so everybody finds work. Being ourselves educated and teachers, we incline to the view that education of any kind must have some productivity; but we cannot demonstrate that the marginal product of investment in education is bound to exceed the marginal product of investment in other resources. We further point out that education does not have to be productive to justify itself; even as pure consumption it has value, and giving young people more education is not inferior to giving them bicycles or radio sets. When we have said all this we have said very little. There is no reason why the public should not have as much education as it is willing to pay for; the real problem is to make people see the connection between cost and taxes, so that if they really want more education they will bear more taxes cheerfully. This is part of the art of politics.

Most African politicians have come to power with education as the number one priority. All now have second thoughts, first because of the unexpectedly heavy burden of education on their budgets, and secondly because of the tensions created by young people pouring out of primary schools looking for jobs which do not exist. Like any other composer, each must do the best he can, having regard to his own inner compulsions and the public which he serves.

HEALTH

Expenditure on health is productive in three ways: First, it increases the number of man-hours of work; secondly, it improves the quality of work; and thirdly, it makes possible the use of natural resources which would not otherwise be usable.

Much statistical work has been done on the cost of sickness.[9] Correlating expenditures on health with man-hours saved by better health, or by an increase in the population, is very difficult. Much of the expenditure on health is ineffective in that the patient would have improved or got worse equally rapidly without medical attention. Also, the cost of treating different diseases varies enormously. To make progress one would have to cross-classify different diseases in terms of the amount of debility each causes if not treated, how much difference treatment may make to the progress of the disease, and how much the treatment costs. Some treatments would prove to be highly productive on this count; but when one remembers how much is spent on colds and mental troubles, one may hazard the guess that in the most advanced countries more than half of medical expenditure costs more than it yields in extra man-hours.

Insofar as the yield of health expenditure is man-hours, its value depends on the marginal productivity of man-hours. Here the viewpoint of the individual and of society diverge. Most underdeveloped countries have a good deal of underemployment. The farms experience full employment for a few weeks during the planting and reaping seasons; extra man-hours outside those seasons yield no product. The towns never have full employment because they have a large population living by

---

[9] For a survey see S. J. Mushkin, "Health as an Investment," *Journal of Political Economy,* Supplement, October 1962.

casual employment, working on the average perhaps two or three days a week (dock workers, construction workers, transport workers, jobbing gardeners) and also have a good deal of disguised unemployment among the self-employed (petty traders, dressmakers, taxi drivers, etc.). If one man falls ill, the amount of work done does not diminish; someone else takes his place. From the individual's point of view the yield of medicine is extra income earned, but from the social point of view the yield is zero.

Reducing the death rate increases the population. The individual is interested in the income he gets, but society's calculation is based on the marginal productivity of labor. The situation varies widely. In much of Africa and Latin America the land could carry more people without a fall in average productivity, whereas in most of Asia an increase in the population reduces the average level of living.

One cannot rest the case for medical expenditures in underdeveloped countries primarily on extra man-hours. More promising is the effect in enabling people to use existing resources more productively by reducing lethargy and inattentiveness. Here one has in mind those diseases which remain in the body, not preventing work, but diminishing effort; most notably, malaria, sleeping sickness, and bilharzia. Finally one must add diseases which make land uninhabitable. To get rid of these adds physical resources, as well as man-hours and attentiveness; so this type of health expenditure is the most productive of all.

There is a vast difference between the productivity of public health measures and the productivity of curative medicine. The spectacular fall in the death rate over the past hundred years owes very little to curative medicine. The great killers have been wiped out at relatively small cost, using the services of only a handful of doctors, either by improvements in the water supply—cholera, typhoid, dysentery—or by environmental sanitation—malaria, yellow fever, tuberculosis—or by vaccination—smallpox, diphtheria, poliomyelitis. One can see this by comparing developed and underdeveloped countries. The death rate is now about the same in Jamaica as in the United States. But the United States has four times as many doctors per thousand as Jamaica. What do the other three do? They see fewer patients per head; Jamaican patients spend hours queuing in doctors' offices. American doctors know their patients more intimately, and give them more spiritual comfort. There are more specialists, and a number of complicated conditions are handled more skillfully. But as far as concerns general practitioners, the marginal productivity of doctors in the United States, in terms of healthy man-hours, must be close to zero.

In underdeveloped countries how much to spend on public health is not the problem at issue. Most governments realize the productivity of this type of expenditure, and this is why death rates are falling so rapidly toward the levels of advanced countries. The real problem is how much to spend on curative medicine, especially on hospitals and on clinics. This is the part of the medical service with which the public comes most into contact; this is what the public wants most; it costs most, and achieves least, in terms of productivity.

Productivity is not a helpful approach—the modern tendency to defend services only in terms of productivity must be rejected. Men value health for its own sake, as they value consumer goods. They value it above most other goods or services, being willing often to mortgage all they possess in search of health. They value medical attention even when it does not bring health, and so spend much money on the chronically ill, including those who will never again be able to work. If a government is trying to give people what they want, it seems right to conclude that they want health more than they want anything else.

The practical problem is the cost of loading on to the budget the cost of the general practitioners' service. The budget can bear the cost of public health measures quite easily. Hospitals are more of a strain, but their use can be controlled, and if finance is decentralized to municipalities and provinces, the clear link between cost and taxes will keep the demand for hospital facilities in check. The demand for general practitioners, however, is virtually unlimited. Countries which now have 1 general practitioner to 20,000 of population could easily use twenty times as many as they have if there were uncontrolled access at zero price.

At present, most countries have compromised. A skeleton general practitioner service is available on terms which make it attractive only to the poorest people. There are relatively few offices; so the patient must travel far, wait long, and receive very rapid and often superficial attention. This allows private practitioners to cater profitably to those who can afford to pay substantial fees. Medical insurance is beginning, but is not popular, because the trend of these countries is so markedly toward loading services on the budget instead of encouraging individual payment. The atmosphere of the second half of the twentieth century is not favorable to the economist's theory of prices.

HOUSING

The trouble with houses is their expense. Nobody has discovered how to build a small but acceptable urban working class family house or apartment out of wood, brick, or cement to cost less than $1,200 without land. The annual cost of such a house is about $120. If a worker paid 10 per cent of his income in rent, he would need an income of $1,200 a year. Even if he paid 20 per cent he would need $600 a year. And the percentage of workers who earn $600 a year in Asia or Africa is small.

Rural houses cost much less because lower standards are accepted. The density of rural houses per acre is low, even in villages, and houses built of local clays at low density are accepted. Densities are much higher in towns; suitable clays are not so easily available; and even if available, are more likely to be regarded as an eyesore by those who make public opinion. Housing is therefore urgently a problem of towns rather than of villages; and this is a blessing, since dealing with the towns is hard enough without taking on the villages as well.

Since labor is half the cost of a cheap house, self-help building schemes appeal to the administrator. Here a team of, say, six men collaborate in building six houses under supervision. When the houses are built they draw lots, and over twenty years each repays his share of the cost of materials and supervision. Some schemes are doing well, but they are tiresome to organize, and not so appealing to ministers who want to build publicly owned working class houses.

Housing policies are almost always wrong. The number of houses the government can afford to build is a drop in the bucket. Hence the problem can be solved only by encouraging other people to build houses, whether for owner occupation or for rent, and whether by subsidizing development of sites, or subsidizing interest rates, or supporting building and loan associations by guaranteeing mortgages. Typically one finds, on the contrary, measures which discourage private building, such as rent controls without interest subsidies; or enough subsidized housing is built to make private building unattractive, but not nearly enough to meet the demand. Meanwhile, nearly everywhere the slums are multiplying.

The housing problem is probably insoluble because it arises from governments wanting people to live in more expensive houses than they can afford, while not having the money to subsidize the difference. This being so, it would be better to think less about the houses themselves and more about their environment—developing attractive sites, controlling density, looking after streets, water supplies, garbage disposal, and lighting—since what makes slums is not that houses are built of clay, but that the environment is overcrowded and ill-provided. A town of well-spaced clay houses, washed in different colors and properly serviced with utilities, is well worth having, and is inexpensive. Con-

trol of building is much more important for the government than building itself. Also important are measures to prevent the explosion of
towns, by making it more attractive for people to remain in the countryside—but this goes far beyond our terms of reference.

CODA

The quantity and quality of government activity which underdeveloped countries now demand for themselves cannot be provided (taking
central and local authorities together) for less than 20 per cent of gross
domestic product, even when defense and debt charges are excluded. Recurrent expenditure on general and economic administration takes 6
per cent; education, 3 per cent; health, 2 per cent; and welfare services,
2 per cent. Capital expenditure is also heavy; public works (including
roads, schools, and hospitals) take 3 per cent, and at least 4 per cent is
required for government enterprises (water, transport, ports, housing)
or for lending to private enterprise through the government's financial
agencies (industrial banks, agricultural credit, housing mortgages).
Some of the government's capital needs can be met by borrowing at
home or abroad; but private saving is so low that the government itself
has to be a large saver. Taxes and other revenues must come to at least
17 per cent of GDP if it is to do what is expected of it.

Quite a few underdeveloped countries have passed this level, through
having rich mines to tax or windfalls in the terms of trade. Most are
still far away, and embarrassed by the gulf between what their people
expect and the taxes they pay. Bridging this gulf by teaching the people
to pay more taxes is their chief fiscal headache.

We have already suggested that decentralization is one of the best
ways of persuading people to pay more, since it enables them to see
clearly the connection between what they pay and what they get. The
purpose of this coda is to make another, less orthodox, suggestion with
the same objective.

Several governments seeking financial support for new services have
adopted the strategy of imposing a new tax whose proceeds are tied
to the new service. This ought to appeal to economists because the link
between tax and service increases the likelihood that the quantity of
the service will be in line with the preferences of the public. The system,
on the contrary, is condemned by Anglo-American fiscal experts because it reduces fiscal "flexibility." They are not always consistent, since
the same man will recommend a tax on wages tied to financing social
security, but oppose a tax on beer tied to financing education. Inconsistency apart, the condemnation seems out of place. At this time the

principal problem is not greater flexibility but making it easier for people newly emerging to sovereignty to learn the connection between taxes and services and, therefore, to learn to pay more taxes. By the time this major objective has been achieved it will not be difficult to explain why flexibility requires that the practice be discontinued. Reconsideration of the experts' inconsistent and inflexible position is invited.

COMMENT

Emile Despres, *Stanford University*

Professor Lewis's essay on planning public expenditure in underdeveloped countries is rich in penetration, wisdom, and good sense. It is to be hoped that it will be read—not merely tasted but also chewed and digested—by planners, advisers, officials, and finance ministers in underdeveloped countries. The theoretical introduction is cogent and provocative, but it is the subsequent distillation of "practical" insights, drawn largely from the author's experience as adviser or administrator in Africa and in Jamaica, which gives the paper its distinctive value. Although some of the observations and recommendations reflect the special circumstances and problems of the countries in which he has served, most are of quite general applicability.

According to Professor Lewis, the gap between the appetite for increased public services and the willingness to bear increased taxes is particularly wide in the underdeveloped countries, and his paper is addressed to the problem of dealing, or coping, with this gap. He emphasizes the constraints within which the budget maker must proceed in his efforts to bridge the gap, and avoids the economist's temptation to recommend unrealistic and extreme measures. On the side of revenue, the scope for tax increases is limited by the necessity of reserving a major share of the increments of national product—he suggests 60 per cent as a rule of thumb—for increased private consumption. On the expenditure side, extreme austerity in public services is both impracticable and undesirable. Although heavily discounting the currently fashionable "investment in human capital" justification for large expenditures on education or health services, Professor Lewis nevertheless maintains that, even if viewed chiefly as consumption, public services should be accorded high social priority. I agree both with this formulation of the budgetary problem of underdeveloped countries and with most of Professor Lewis's specific recommendations.

A strong case is made for fiscal decentralization, partly on general theoretical grounds but more specifically because of the special need in underdeveloped countries to establish popular awareness of the link between increased taxes and expanded governmental services. This is undoubtedly good doctrine, but it is important to recognize that in most countries increased local financing of government services can, at best, proceed only slowly. Fiscal decentralization implies administrative decentralization, and the necessary local administrative apparatus is usually nonexistent. The central governments usually are not well fitted to administer education and health services, but, for better or worse, theirs is the only administrative apparatus which exists. Progress in building up local revenues and local administration is likely to be least difficult in major cities and the advanced sector, although in rural areas emphasis on fiscal decentralization might provide a means of reviving land taxes, which in real terms have declined almost to the vanishing point in many countries. It must be recognized that the transfer to local financing of such services as education and health implies marked inequalities between city and country and between advancing and backward regions in the scope and quality of services, and that a substantial contribution from central revenues to the cost of these services is essential if these inequalities are not to become unacceptably large. Since popular pressures for reducing regional disparities are very strong, the role of central government financing must remain considerable.

Professor Lewis's proposal for earmarking of particular taxes to specific services deserves serious attention. Although this device is already much employed today, its use could undoubtedly be further extended. Whether, in fact, such earmarking brings the quantity of the service more into line with public preferences is debatable, but its adverse effects are far less great than those of the tying which results from separation of revenue and capital budgets. The present practice of building schools without teachers and hospitals without doctors or nurses might not cease if the distinction between revenue and capital budgets were abolished, but this practice might become somewhat less common. Improvidence in public construction combined with neglect of the recurrent costs of maintenance and operation is one of the worst features of public expenditure planning in underdeveloped countries. The separate capital budget, under which borrowed funds are used only for capital outlays, does little or nothing to limit and much to distort outlays.

With respect to specific types of expenditure, Professor Lewis's recommendation that it is more efficient to send students abroad for university education than to provide higher education at home is more clearly valid for small African and Caribbean countries than for under-developed countries as a whole. Education abroad undoubtedly contributes to the serious "brain drain" from underdeveloped countries, and this must be reckoned as one of its costs. On the general question of costs of education and health services, there is need for greater information on the extent to which these services are subject to economies of agglomeration. Is it not much cheaper to provide education and health services of given quality in cities and towns than in rural areas?

In his analysis of major expenditure categories, Professor Lewis did not comment upon the typically large outlays for the military establishment and other expenditures for ostentation and prestige—new national capitals, pretentious public buildings, international airlines, overextended diplomatic establishments, and so forth. In these fields of expenditure, the wants which are gratified are frequently those of the political leaders, civil servants, and military officers themselves. The government, in its role as composer, often plays tunes for its own enjoyment, and the opportunity for economies in military and ostentation expenditures is particularly great.

Perhaps of greatest interest to builders of programing models is Professor Lewis's proposed rule of thumb that the marginal tax plus saving ratio should not exceed 40 per cent, partly for incentive reasons and partly because growth of output goes hand in hand with an upgrading of labor from lower-income to higher-income activities. Large earnings from mining, favorable movements in the terms of trade, or a succession of favorable harvests would raise this ratio, but it is probably true, as this rule of thumb implies, that an initial decision regarding the feasible marginal ratio of taxes plus saving to output is the best starting point in framing a development plan. For many countries, a marginal ratio of 40 per cent is still unattainably high.

PART II

*Evaluation of Planning
in Individual Countries*

Development Strategy and Planning: The Soviet Experience

ALEXANDER ERLICH

COLUMBIA UNIVERSITY AND RUSSIAN RESEARCH CENTER,
HARVARD UNIVERSITY

Introduction

The First Soviet Five Year Plan was officially launched almost exactly thirty-five years ago. The hallmarks of the period that was ushered in therewith were rapid extension of social ownership beyond the limits of the modern urban sector, with the full-scale collectivization of agriculture virtually completed by the mid-thirties; the establishment of an all-embracing system of centralized planning; and a remarkably high over-all rate of economic growth. The architects of the system have been insistent in postulating a three-way connection between these elements. Without centralized planning, it was argued, there would be no comparable rates of growth; without extensive social ownership no effective centralized planning would be possible; and without thorough-going modernization and concentration of production in the wake of rapid economic growth, both planning and social ownership would lack a firm basis and would eventually either be subverted from within or destroyed from without.[1]

NOTE: The author gratefully acknowledges the support of the Russian Research Center of Harvard University and of the Russian Institute of Columbia University in the preparation of this paper. He is also indebted to Mr. Abbott Gleason and Professor Donald Keesing for valuable suggestions.

[1] Cf. the preamble to the First Five Year Plan for a very explicit statement of this view:

"The great task of the five-year plan for the development of the productive forces of the Soviet Union through rapid industrialization and steady strengthening of the socialist elements in national economy is to attain and to surpass the economic level of the advanced capitalist countries in the next historical period, and thus to assure the triumph of the socialist economic system. . . . This makes it imperative to secure, with the aid of the colossal natural re-

In the context of the present inquiry, obviously enough, it is the first of these three propositions that deserves examination, although the other two are by no means irrelevant. Few Western economists would disagree nowadays that the Soviet planning has been "about growth," to paraphrase Professor W. Arthur Lewis's well-known remark, and that it cannot be properly appraised without a clear notion of its performance in the realm of long-range development. It seems, therefore, appropriate to begin by surveying this performance.

The Development Strategy

THE OVER-ALL VIEW

In order to keep things in proper perspective right from the start, let us reveal an important part of the plot in advance. In Table 1 are shown some of the most recent Western measurements of Soviet development trends through 1958.

It is, of course, impossible to discuss here the full implications of these figures. Some of them will become clear in the subsequent sections of this paper.[2] A few words of comment are nevertheless in order at this point:

1. The Soviet rate of growth of net national product has unquestionably been high. More specifically, it is well above the U.S. rate of growth over the same period (2.9 per cent during 1929–57), and it exceeds, although by an extremely small margin, the U.S. rate of growth from 1869–78 to 1899–1908 (4.6 per cent); in both cases, the difference is significantly higher when the Soviet series is presented "as

sources of the Soviet Union, the advantages afforded by the system of an organized and planned national economy and the latest technical achievements, a higher rate of economic development than that yet attained by modern capitalist countries" (*The Soviet Union Looks Ahead,* New York, 1930, p. 7; the translation has been slightly corrected).

[2] An extensive analysis can be found in Professor A. Bergson's paper "National Income," which contains Table 1, as well as in Professor Simon Kuznets' "Summary Appraisal," both in *Economic Trends in the Soviet Union* (hereafter cited as *ETSU,* eds. Abram Bergson and Simon Kuznets, Cambridge, Mass., 1963.

The general problem of the reliability of the underlying data and the reasons for not using official Soviet indexes must be likewise bypassed. The reader is referred to the abundant literature on the subject, more particularly, to Abram Bergson, *The Real National Income of Soviet Russia Since 1928,* Cambridge, Mass., 1961; Alexander Gerschenkron, *A Dollar Index of Soviet Machinery Output, 1927–28 to 1937,* Santa Monica, Cal., 1951. Gregory Grossman, *Soviet Statistics of Physical Output of Industrial Commodities,* Princeton for NBER, 1960. G. Warren Nutter, *Growth of Industrial Production in the Soviet Union,* Princeton for NBER, 1962.

TABLE 1

USSR: Net National Product, Factor Inputs, and Productivity,
Average Annual Rates of Growth for Selected Periods, 1928-58

(per cent)

	1928-58	1928-58 (effective years)[a]	1928-40	1940-50	1950-58
Net national product					
In 1937 ruble factor cost	4.1	4.8	4.2	1.9	6.8
As composite, 1937 base[b]	6.0	7.0	9.3	1.7	6.8
Employment: number of workers (adjusted for nonfarm hours)	2.0	2.3	3.7	0.7	1.2
Reproducible fixed capital					
In 1937 rubles	7.0	8.1	9.8	0.5	11.2
As composite, 1937 base	7.1	8.2	11.0	−0.2	10.9
Farm land acres	1.5	1.8	1.6	−1.3	3.7
Livestock herds (1937 rubles)	−0.2	−0.2	−1.9	−0.8	3.2
Selected inputs (1937 weights)	{ 2.9 / 2.4 / 2.9	{ 3.4 / 2.8 / 3.3	{ 4.2 / 3.8 / 4.1	{ 0.6 / 0.6 / 0.5	{ 4.0 / 2.7 / 4.0
Net national product					
Per worker (adjusted for nonfarm hours)					
Output in 1937 ruble factor cost	2.1	2.4	0.5	1.1	5.6
Output as composite, 1937 base	3.9	4.5	5.4	0.9	5.6
Per unit of reproducible fixed capital					
Output in 1937 ruble factor cost and capital in 1937 rubles	−2.7	−3.1	−5.1	1.3	−3.9
Output and capital as composite, 1937 base	−1.0	−1.1	−1.6	1.9	−3.6
Per unit of selected inputs					
Output in 1937 ruble factor cost and inputs with 1937 weights	{ 1.2 / 1.7 / 1.2	{ 1.4 / 1.9 / 1.4	{ 0.1 / 0.5 / 0.2	{ 1.3 / 1.2 / 1.3	{ 2.7 / 4.0 / 2.8
Output as composite, 1937 base, and inputs with 1937 weights	{ 3.0 / 3.5 / 3.1	{ 3.5 / 4.1 / 3.6	{ 4.9 / 5.3 / 5.0	{ 1.1 / 1.0 / 1.1	{ 2.7 / 4.1 / 2.8

[a]Excluding four war years.

[b]Comparison with 1937 in terms of the ruble factor cost of the given year.

Source: Abram Bergson, "National Income," in *Economic Trends in the Soviet Union,* ed. Abram Bergson and Simon Kuznets, Cambridge, Mass., 1963, p. 6.

composite, 1937 base." [3] The U.S. output during 1869–78 to 1899–1908 is measured in 1929 dollar prices; a consistent recalculation in terms of prices of an earlier year might decisively alter the results of the comparison of the Soviet 1937 factor cost series with the U.S. series for 1869–78 to 1899–1908 (although it should be remembered that in the context of Soviet development, the 1937 factor cost was definitely not an early-year weight). Moreover, even if such a possibility were disregarded, the Soviet tempo (when measured in 1937 ruble factor costs, at any rate) would not be entirely unprecedented. It has been exceeded, during periods of roughly comparable length, by Australia as well as by the United States (when the years 1869–78 to 1884–93 are considered) in the second half of the last century; and the very high Soviet growth in 1950–58 was more than matched by West Germany and Japan during the same time span. [4] These calculations are undoubtedly of interest. Yet the margin of non-Soviet superiority is low (within one percentage point) in all cases cited, and meaningful comparisons are therefore difficult, not only because of the refractory nature of the statistical material but also in view of the wide differences in the external settings and in the size and resource structures of the respective economies.

2. The divergences in the Soviet rates of growth during the three subperiods are striking. In the period 1928–40 the rate of growth, high by any standard, varies sharply depending on the kind of measurement used—a disparity reflecting the extremely drastic and nonrecurrent change in the product mix during these years, with the "composite, 1937 base" method being better suited for indicating how much more efficient the Soviet economy was toward the end of the subperiod at producing the 1937 mix than at producing the old mix of 1928. (For a proof of this proposition, see Bergson's *The Real National Income of Soviet Russia Since 1928,* Chapter iii, cited above.) The very high rate of 1950–58 (with the alternative ways of measurement cited above making no difference) is determined in part by the fact that this period encompassed the five most successful years which Soviet collectivized agriculture ever had. (The post-1958 years which are not covered by the calculations of Table 1 show a marked slowdown in growth, due largely, although not exclusively, to the stagnation in Soviet agriculture.) The low rate of the forties is clearly due to wartime developments.

3. The high rate of decline in the productivity of reproducible fixed capital can be viewed as the result of an extremely rapid increase of this

[3] Bergson, *ETSU,* p. 7.
[4] See Kuznets, *ETSU,* pp. 335, 339 (Table VIII.3), and 355 (Table VIII.14).

capital in relation to the employed population—a point repeatedly stressed by Professor Bergson. But, as he indicates, this may not be the whole story. On the face of it, the time-honored law of diminishing returns can be (particularly for a "latecoming" country) effectively counteracted by internal and external economies of scale, the opening up of new areas, and the increasing ability to absorb and generate modern technology. True, it could be argued that in the Soviet case the capital accumulation had been proceeding too rapidly for its effects on returns to be offset in such a way. But it is also not inconceivable (a) that some of these "offsets" were less than fully operative while others were being rapidly exhausted; (b) that the Soviet economy was suffering from certain built-in inefficiencies which proved less tolerable in more advanced stages than in the early ones, and (c) that the unusually rapid increase in capital stock reflected, in part, the urgent desire to compensate for some of these inefficiencies and to make up for the "corner-cutting" in the past. As will be seen later, these obiter dicta are not entirely devoid of substance.

4. The two points presently to be made border on the obvious. As has been explained time and time again, quantity indexes, even if constructed with the utmost care, tend to understate the rate of growth since they do not take fully into account the changes in quality; as a result, they are bound to favor an economy relying in its growth (as compared with other economies) more on rapid multiplication of broadly similar and highly standardized items, a large part of which could be used for purposes of self-reproduction, and less on continual improvements in quality. (It is not suggested that an attempt to allow for such a purely statistical advantage is likely to reduce large differences between the observable rates of growth to insignificance.) Lastly, and, in the present context, more importantly, the index numbers can give us a general notion of the speed with which the economy under review has been moving northeast (or southwest) on the production possibilities map. They cannot, and are not meant to, tell us whether the economy was "on the curve" at a particular point of time, that is, whether or not the familiar optimum conditions were fulfilled, or more generally, whether the route chosen was the most efficient one from the viewpoint of the decision makers' objectives. It goes without saying that a summary discussion of the underlying developments and policies cannot provide anything like conclusive answers to these formidable questions. It may nevertheless help to establish a prima-facie case.

INVESTMENT POLICY

It is sufficient to glance at the capital stock series in Table 1 in order to realize the crucial importance of investment in the Soviet strategy. The proportion of domestic resources directed toward capital formation under the Five Year Plans has been notably high. Still more remarkable is the rate of speed at which this proportion rose from its initial level. According to the source already cited, the share of gross investment in the national product (measured at 1937 ruble factor cost) went up from roughly 12 per cent in 1928 to nearly 26 per cent in 1937.[5] During the fifties and early sixties, following the precipitous fall during World War II and the fast climb of the recovery years, the increase was decidedly slower, although by no means negligible; according to Professor Bergson's unpublished estimates, the present Soviet rate of gross investment is about 33 per cent. How are we to interpret these figures?

Let us begin with what may look like an overlong digression into *Dogmengeschichte*. It has been customary for the Soviet system's directors (to borrow a term from Professor Bergson) as well as for their leading ideologists to invoke the two-sector model of Marx in support of their development strategy, and with perfectly good reasons on the face of it. True, Marx set up the "reproduction schema" of Volume II of *Capital* in order to lay down conditions for a macroeconomic moving equilibrium on the basis of full-capacity output and not for maximizing (or optimizing) the rate of growth. But it was entirely legitimate to infer from his analysis that, other things being equal, economy A with a larger capital-goods-producing "Department I" relative to the consumer-goods-producing "Department II" was bound to have a higher over-all rate of growth and ultimately also a higher level of consumer goods output than economy B with a lower Department I–to–Depart-

[5] Professor Bergson's estimates, quoted in Kuznets, *ETSU*, p. 352. Professor Kuznets observes that "with the single exception of Canada for 1896–1900 and 1901–10 among the twelve countries for which we have data, in none did the [capital formation] proportion double within a few years [as in the case of the USSR]." As Professor Bergson points out, the rates of *net* (as distinct from *gross*) investment over the period in question were "relatively exceptional" [*The Economics of Soviet Planning,* New Haven and London, 1964 (hereafter cited as *ESP*), p. 317]—a phenomenon easily explainable by the unusually rapid increase of the total investment volume over time and by peculiarities of Soviet replacement policy, still to be discussed. Actually, the initial increase was even more dramatic than the above figures would indicate. The 1937 rate of gross investment was a bit below its level in the preceding years due to the continuous shift toward defense; in fact, it was attained, and even slightly exceeded, by 1932 (cf. Francis Seton, "Social Accounts of the USSR in 1934," *Review of Economics and Statistics,* May 1954, quoted in *ESP,* p. 308).

ment II ratio because the lower share of consumers goods in the A total would be from some time point onward more than compensated for by the growing disparity between the A and B totals, due to the faster rate of addition to capital stock in A.[6]

Consequently, in order to increase the rate of growth, the relative share of capital goods in the total output as well as in the total capital stock of the economy in question would have to be raised accordingly. Furthermore, an increase in the incremental capital-output ratio would demonstrably require a rise in the relative size of the capital goods sector if the existing rate of growth were to be maintained, and a correspondingly steeper rise if the rate of growth were to go up—propositions which could be conveniently stated in terms of the familiar Harrod-Domar equation.[7] No doubt the case for increasing the relative size of the domestic capital goods industry would be weakened if the implicit assumption of a closed economy were relaxed—a point about which Marx was very explicit.[8] But by the same token a country facing sharply

[6] For a rigorous proof, see Evsey D. Domar, *Essays in the Theory of Economic Growth,* New York, 1957, Chap. IX. The path-breaking articles by the Soviet economist G. Feldman, discussed by Professor Domar, are now available in a slightly abridged English translation. See *Foundations of Soviet Strategy for Economic Growth,* ed. Nicolas Spulber, Bloomington, 1964.

[7] The mutual translatability of the Marxian and the Harrod-Domar approaches was made very clear by Mrs. Joan Robinson (cf. her *Rate of Interest and Other Essays,* London, 1952, pp. 91, 95). However, Marx did not make any explicit use of the capital-output ratio in his model building. His "organic composition of capital" could be properly interpreted as an index of the amount of capital per man, and a rise in this index could be compatible, in theory as well as in empirical fact, with an increasing, constant, or declining capital-output ratio, depending on the relative rates of change in the amount of capital per man and in the volume of output per man. (In fact, Marx came close to saying this in so many words; cf. *Capital,* Chicago, 1933, III, 129.) The whole point, incidentally, has a direct bearing on the familiar proposition, according to which the rate of growth of producers' goods must *always* exceed that of consumers' goods in order to ensure the steady growth of the economy as a whole. This thesis, first expounded by Lenin in his *Development of Capitalism in Russia,* was adopted as a guideline by the authors of the First Five Year Plan, and has become one of the cornerstones of Soviet economic orthodoxy, with Stalin restating it in a most dogmatic manner in his last major pronouncement. Actually, this "law" explicitly derived by its originator from the rising trend of the "organic composition" applies only whenever the capital-output ratio, too, is rising, and/or whenever economic growth is not merely steady but accelerating. Yet the practical importance of this overgeneralization in the case under consideration was not great, for reasons which are implied in what has been said already and which will be further clarified as we proceed.

[8] "If a country is unable itself to produce the quantity of machinery which its accumulation of capital allows, it buys it from abroad" (*Theories of Surplus Value,* London, 1951, p. 366).

deteriorating terms of trade for its exports and yet resolved to increase significantly its rate of growth would be bound to rely more heavily on the services of domestic capital goods industries and hence to allot a higher priority to them than if trading prospects had been favorable. The circumstance that in a semideveloped country the capital-output ratio in Department I would tend to be higher than in Department II (owing to the significance of handicraft in the latter sector and to the virtual absence of consumer-durables industries) would add impetus to the shift in priorities. It goes without saying that the Soviet Union on the eve of the First Five Year Plan would fit this general description. It is likewise evident that the policy of rapid expansion of Department I was, in the case in hand, in broad accord with the pattern of the country's natural resource endowment—and the existence of a significant "growth-oriented" nucleus inherited from the prerevolutionary past constituted an important added asset.

In sum, the construct on hand seemed most helpful in providing the argument for a major shift in investment priorities. But granted that the shift was needed, how fast and how far was it to go? This, obviously enough, was the operationally important issue; and here the received theory could lend no aid and comfort to the eventually adopted policy. Indeed, some of the most baffling problems of Soviet development strategy could be conveniently viewed in terms of a deliberate attempt to override the constraints inherent in the model and of the resistance encountered along this path.

To be sure, some of these constraints were not specifically Marxian. The "reproduction schema" clearly implies that the higher the rate of investment, the lower must be, on the assumption of full capacity utilization and/or of full employment, the absolute level of consumption. If this decline in consumption were to be pressed far enough, "other things" would no longer remain equal; the drop in productivity of labor would reduce the size of total income, and "beyond a point this would be true also of the additional income to be obtained subsequently from additional current investment." [9] Furthermore, there were numerous implicit and explicit caveats against unsettling disparities between aggregate supply and aggregate demand which were bound to develop under capitalism as a result of discontinuous increases in investment

[9] *ESP*, p. 304. Soviet economists of the post-Stalin era not infrequently expressed similar views, although they preferred to do it by emphasizing the favorable effects of rising consumption on the rate of growth via the increase in labor productivity (cf. S. Strumilin, "Balans narodnogo khoziaistva kak orudie sotsialisticheskogo planirovaniia," *Voprosy ekonomiki,* November 1954, p. 36).

and which the socialist economy should strive to prevent.[10] Yet the most distinctive contribution of the Marxian model consisted in explicitly relating the total and sectoral output flows to capital stocks which produce them, thus bringing in constraints on the capacity side. Concretely, an increase in the rate of investment requires a widening of the margin in productive capacity of Department I over the replacement needs of the economy; this, in turn, calls for expansion in the capacity of Department I both in absolute terms and in relation to the total capital stock. Yet the logic of the model implies that such an expansion cannot be of the blitz variety; its rate of speed is decisively controlled by the size of Department I at the beginning of the relevant period, as well as by the required amount of capital stock per unit of the increment in capacity, the length of the gestation period of new plant, and the size of the investment demand coming from Department II; assuming that the last-mentioned limitation could be lifted by a highhanded decision, the others would remain in force.[11] A blow-by-blow comparison between a

[10] Cf. *Capital*, II, 361–62, as well as the following passage:

"On the basis of social production, it must be ascertained, on what scale those operations which withdraw labor and means of production from it for a long time without furnishing in return any useful product, can be carried on without injuring those lines of production which do not only withdraw continually, or at several intervals, labor-power and means of production from it, but also supply it with means of subsistence and of production" (*ibid.*, p. 412).

[11] A simple numerical example (or rather an extensive hint at such example) may serve as an illustration. Let us assume that values of the capital stock K, national income Y, and volume of investment I are 300, 100, and 15, respectively, and (for the sake of simplifying our arithmetic) that the capital assets are permanent. On the further assumption that the capital-output ratio V is the same in both departments, we can derive sectoral values from these aggregates; K_1, Y_1, and I_1 would then equal 45 (15×3), 15, and 2.25, and K_2, Y_2, and I_2 would accordingly equal 255, 85, and 12.75, respectively. Following the Harrod-Domar formula, the rate of growth, r, would then be 5 per cent. Suppose now that the economy in question desires to double its r, which can be accomplished only by doubling the $I \div Y$ ratio, provided that V remains constant. But in order to do so, the $K_1 \div K$ ratio must likewise double. It can easily be shown that even if our economy is prepared to go to the extreme of plowing its total investment back into Department I, and thereby foregoing any increase in the capital stock of Department II for the duration, it will take *four years,* counting from the beginning of this relocation, to attain the desired target, and that the choice of a less drastic alternative (such as the Feldman-Domar expedient of fixing the $I_1 \div I$ ratio at the level of the terminal $I \div Y$ ratio for the duration) would lengthen the relocation period. By the same token, the introduction of replacement into the picture would provide an additional degree of freedom: It would now be possible to skip not only the net investment but also the replacement quota of Department II, and this would permit the shortening of the relocation period. (In our numerical example, by adding the over-all replacement quota R of 20 to the same Y and modifying the sectoral proportions accordingly, such a

full-fledged model of this type, with the realistic numerical magnitudes inserted in proper places, and the Soviet long-range plans cannot be attempted here. But even a quick glance at a few selected aggregative targets reveals a monumental divergence. According to the final draft of the First Five Year Plan, fixed capital stock of the economy was to increase by more than four-fifths during five years, the national income was to double, and the gross investment in fixed capital was to more than treble its volume. This herculean feat was to be accomplished by an economy whose fixed capital-output ratio in the base year of the operation equaled 2.9 (with an expected decline to the level of 2.5 in the terminal year), the rate of net investment in fixed capital was 16 per cent, and the average length of construction period of new plants approximated 4–5 years.[12] To make things worse, about 40 per cent of Soviet gross investment on the eve of the First Five Year Plan took place in highly primitive peasant agriculture and was therefore to a large extent technologically incapable of being shifted toward the modern capi-

policy would result in the reduction of the minimum relocation period by one-half.)

We have been thus far assuming the average gestation period to equal one year. What if, say, a three-year gestation period is assumed instead? It could be easily demonstrated that the rate of growth would then be reduced as compared with the previous case, albeit not very significantly. (In our example, r would drop from 5 per cent to 4.8 per cent.) On the other hand, the faster an economy grows, the more pronounced such a reduction will be, because the age group of investment projects reaching the maturation stage will be smaller in comparison with the still incompleted age groups than in an economy growing more slowly. For related reasons, the immediate effect of an *increase* in the rate of investment on the average length of the gestation period (and hence on the rate of growth) would be higher than the sustained effect of the *already established* higher rate. Lastly, the emergence of bottlenecks would obviously affect adversely the gestation period and the rate of growth. (All these points are briefly mentioned in Domar, *op. cit.,* p. 249, footnote.) In the original model of Volume II of *Capital* all these complications are avoided, since the average service life of the "constant capital" *and* the gestation period are taken to equal one year. (This, to be sure, would permit very rapid changes in the structure of capital stock if the whole gross investment were to be "plowed back" into Department I.) Yet Marx was very explicit about the unrealistic nature of these assumptions, and so were his followers.

[12] For data on capital stock, national income, and investment see Gosplan SSSR, *Piatiletnii plan razvitiia narodno-khoziaistvennogo stroitel'stva SSSR,* Moscow, 1929–30, I, 127–28; II, part 2; p. 38. In distinction from Professor Bergson's estimates quoted above the relevant aggregates are measured at 1926–27 market prices, and national income is shown exclusive of services. The data undoubtedly require a good deal of further processing in order to be used in statistical work; this applies with particular force to the capital stock figures. For broadly illustrative purposes, however, the quoted figures are adequate. For data on construction periods, see B. A. Gukhman, "Na rubezhe," *Planovoe khoziaistvo,* August 1928, p. 135.

tal goods sector, particularly in the short run. At the same time the lines of production which were to spearhead the expansion (machine-building and ferrous metallurgy) accounted between them for slightly more than 15 per cent of the total gross industrial output while the whole net output of large-scale industry generated merely 26 per cent of the Soviet national income.[13]

The whole operation looked like putting the cart before the horse on a most monumental scale. The targets of the plan might have been entirely feasible if the capital stock at the beginning of the operation had the size and structure it was supposed to achieve in the terminal year of the plan; they were definitely not attainable with the capital stock actually on hand. As a result, the planned volume of investment was inadequate and excessive at the same time: too small to bring about the desired output increases and too large when measured against the available capacity of the capital goods sector. Only a veritable explosion of "disembodied" technological progress could have slashed the capital coefficients and gestation periods to a level which would have made it possible to carry through the entire program.[14] Barring such a miracle, the grim realities of the situation could not help but assert themselves in a variety of ways:

1. Since the capacity of the capital goods industries proved woefully inadequate for the task, the gestation period of the new plant, which even under the best of circumstances would be very long in view of the kind and size of the new investment projects, was extended still further.

---

[13] Cf. *Piatiletnii plan,* I, 137; II, part 2, p. 22; and TsUNKhU, *Sotsialisticheskoe stroitel'stvo SSSR,* Moscow, 1935, p. 169. Here, too, the figures are quite rough, and (in the case of relative shares of machine-building, ferrous metallurgy, and large-scale industry in respective totals) not fully comparable; but they tell the story.

[14] We say "disembodied," because a capital-saving progress of the embodied kind would clearly not do. If new machines could be produced more cheaply, and more quickly, by the same plants that had been producing the old machines, things could be different. But such a possibility cannot be the rule, least of all with regard to a relatively backward economy. Indeed, assuming a substantial degree of technological discontinuity between the old and the new kinds of machinery (particularly if a change in fuel and energy sources is involved) and given the intent to carry out the modernization on a large scale as well as within a short span of time, the shift to the new technology is likely to entail, during the duration for changeover period, a substantially larger volume of investment and a longer average gestation period than if the old type of technology had persisted. The capital-saving effects of the new technology would then become operative only in the long run. It is not surprising that the problem has attracted the attention of Soviet economists from the eve of the First Five Year Plan to the post-Stalin era. For a perceptive recent discussion, cf. V. Bogachev, "Sovershenstvovanie struktury promyshlennogo proizvodstva i planirovanie kapitalnykh vlozhenii," *Voprosy ekonomiki,* February 1963.

Hence plants dependent on supplies from these projects were either slowed down in their construction or forced to operate at a fraction of their full capacity for a more or less extended period, with the lag in the iron and steel industry behind machine-building as a striking case in point.[15] As a result, the capital-output ratios were increasing all around.

2. While the degree of completion of the investment projects fell far short of the targets, the composition of investment likewise departed from the original expectations; in order to approach the planned increase of the capacity of the capital goods sector as closely as possible, the share of the consumer goods sector in the total investment had to be slashed sharply below the planned level (with one important exception, to be mentioned later). The dramatic underfulfillment of the output plans in the consumer goods area was due, in part, to this decision.[16]

3. The abrupt expansion of construction activity was bound to give rise not only to physical but also to organizational bottlenecks which, in turn, resulted in further lengthening of the gestation period—a phenomenon discussed, in a different context, by Professor Kalecki.[17] And vice versa: A bit of plain arithmetic could show that (with the volume

[15] According to the final version of the First Five-year Plan the output of pig iron was to increase from 3.3 million metric tons in 1927–28 to 10 million metric tons in 1932–33; and the output of ingot steel, from 4.2 to 10.4 million metric tons. (In 1930 the deadline of the plan was moved to 1932.) In other words, two basic branches of an industry characterized by the highest capital coefficient and longest gestation periods in the manufacturing sector, and accounting in the base year for a few percentage points of the total national income, were expected to self-multiply several times within five years and, in addition, to lift the capital stock of the rest of the economy by more than half during the same period. It was hardly surprising that increases in iron and steel output, while substantial, fell far short of the target. Their outputs in 1932 were 6.2 million metric tons and 5.9 million metric tons, respectively. (For Five-year Plan targets, see *Piatiletnii plan,* II, part 1, p. 153; for actual outputs, see Nutter, *Growth of Industrial Production,* p. 420.) The output of basic constructional materials behaved very similarly. It may be worth noting that several leading metallurgical experts who had been openly skeptical about the possibility of producing 10 million tons of steel by 1932 were duly convicted as "wreckers." For a highly informative discussion of the problem of unused capacity in the Soviet machine-building industry during the First Five-year Plan, see David Granick, "On Patterns of Technological Choice in Soviet Industry," *American Economic Review,* May 1962, pp. 149–57.

[16] The 1932 outputs of cotton cloth and of boots and shoes, for instance, remained virtually unchanged as compared with 1927–28, although planned targets called for a near doubling of the first and a more than 40 per cent rise in the second (*ESP,* p. 84).

[17] See his paper, "Czynniki określające tempo wzrostu dochodu narodowego w gospodarce socjalistycznej," in *Zagadnienia ekonomii politycznej socjalizmu,* ed. Oskar Lange, Warsaw, 1960.

of investment determined by the existing capacity of Department I), the longer the technologically given average gestation period, the more investment projects would be in operation at any given point of time; this would mean added organizational difficulties, with feedback effects on the length of the gestation period and on over-all efficiency of the economy.

4. The introduction of technological change into the picture, finally, reveals several new aspects of waste inherent in conditions of over-strain. The phenomenon of delays in completion of projects and of temporary idleness as a result of bottlenecks in complementary lines acquires a new dimension: Plants might become obsolescent very soon after having entered full-scale operation, if not before. The switch from old technology to new, whenever it entailed an extensive reconstruction of plant at the giving and/or receiving end, was made costly and time consuming because the construction processes were slow—a consideration acquiring an added edge in the situation of shortages, with strong built-in pressures to "deliver" as soon as possible. Moreover, managers impelled to add powerfully to their capacity and to show results quickly could ill afford to experiment at length with new technology, to carry out adequate explorations in determining the location of the new plant (a particularly crucial matter in the case of extractive industries), or more generally, "to study everything thoroughly, to weigh all pros and cons, and to avoid rash decisions," as Mr. Khrushchev put it several years ago.[18] (These difficulties, one might add, would lend force to the notion that absorption of new technology cannot be fully effective when carried out in a hurry—a point stressed by Mr. Kaldor in his recent work on the theory of economic growth.) The adverse effects of such corner-cutting, extensively recorded in contemporaneous Soviet writings, proliferated far and wide; and, in virtue of being embodied in durable stocks of productive capital, they could not be treated as a short-run phenomenon.

To be sure, if this were the whole story, it would be hard to see why the Soviet economy did not collapse sometime between 1928 and 1932 or was not forced into a headlong retreat. Are we to conclude that important countervailing factors were overlooked and that there was more "give" in the Soviet economic system than our analysis would suggest? Furthermore, we have been talking until now about the First Five Year Plan only. What about the later period? As will be shown, important relaxation possibilities did exist; but while they helped to pull

[18] Quoted in *Pravda,* January 9, 1963.

the system over the hump and to let it grow, they were unable to transmute a wasteful path of expansion into an efficient one.

FOREIGN TRADE

We noted earlier that foreign trade could, under propitious circumstances, permit an economy bent upon growing to forego a corresponding expansion of its own Department I; but circumstances were far from propitious for the Soviet Union of the late twenties. Actually, the situation was more complex than this observation might indicate. It is true that the Soviet Union's terms of trade during the First Five-year Plan fell from 100 in 1929 to 71.5 in 1933 (in fact, they had been steadily deteriorating since 1925). Yet during 1929–31 the volume of Soviet foreign trade attained its all-time peak of the interwar period. More specifically, the gross imports of capital goods amounted to between 12 and 14 per cent of the Soviet gross investment in these years; and this presumably accounted for about half (or, not inconceivably, more than half) of the value of Soviet investment in equipment and installation which constituted 12 to 15 per cent of Soviet gross investment at that time.[19] Professor Holzman is undoubtedly right in concluding that "if the Soviet economy had been closed completely during the First Five-year Plan, industrialization would have been seriously retarded if not completely stopped for a number of years." [20]

The opportunity to trade, it goes without saying, helped to reduce some of the disproportions noted before; but it could not eliminate them completely, given their extent and multiplicity. It will be recalled, for instance, that basic materials were among the worst laggards; but here the direct contribution of foreign trade was relatively small, although the "underfulfillment" in iron and steel would undoubtedly have been more grave had it not been for large-scale imports of metallurgical equipment. Moreover, the same overambitious plans that made imports of foreign capital goods so vitally important were putting obstacles in their way by generating shortages of some of the most tradable commodities and thus making their large-scale exports a heavy burden. Lastly, the autarkic proclivities of the system's directors tended to keep foreign trade more limited in scope, and to confine its extensive use to a shorter time period than the principle of comparative advantage would require after

[19] For data on Soviet trade, see Franklyn D. Holzman, "Foreign Trade," *ETSU,* p. 305. For data on investment breakdown, see Tsentral'noe Statisticheskoe Upravlenie pri Sovete Ministrov SSSR, *Narodnoe khoziaistvo SSSR v 1958 godu,* Moscow, 1959, p. 620. The figures may not be strictly comparable.

[20] Holzman, in *ETSU,* p. 318.

all proper allowances for dynamic considerations and for security needs had been made. It was therefore not surprising that during the Second Five Year Plan, when the acute crisis stage was over, the share of gross imports in the Soviet gross investment dropped to a mere 2 per cent.[21]

FACTOR PROPORTIONS

At first glance, Soviet policy in the matter of factor proportions would seem bewildering in the extreme. On the one hand, the biggest possible sizes of plant in industry as well agriculture were striven for, and application of the most up-to-date technology was relentlessly pressed forward, even if it entailed high capital-labor ratios. Yet at the same time quite different policies were followed. The highly capital-using housing and railroad transportation sectors were scheduled to expand their capacity at a rate below the all-economy average right from the start— and their actual growth turned out to be even more modest. Auxiliary processes in industry such as repair, packing, and intraplant transportation activities were carried on in a highly labor-intensive fashion. Some of the new equipment did not measure up to high technological standards, but had relatively low resource content and short construction periods. Old plant was being retired, as a rule, not on account of obsolescence but only after becoming physically unusable. Lastly, the degree of planned capacity utilization in industry rose above the planned level, as the increase in the nonagricultural labor force exceeded the target by nearly 100 per cent during the First Five-year Plan and has continued to exceed its targets (although by much more modest margins) ever since.[22] True, this diversity in approach could be interpreted as the "dual-economy" policy, and such a strategy makes good sense whenever a sizable sector with an above-average capital intensity is expanding much more rapidly than the rest of the economy and at least somewhat more rapidly than the capital supply, while large reserves of open or disguised unemployment still persist. The Soviet Union of the Five-Year-Plan period, at any rate in its early stage, was definitely in this class, although, in distinction from the "ideal type" analyzed by Professor Eckaus,[23] some of its low-priority sectors would be highly capital-intensive and therefore could not be pushed far into the labor-intensive range of their production isoquants. Yet while the implicit principle of dualism was sound, its application in the case on hand was

[21] *Ibid.*

[22] See *ESP,* p. 84. The second Five-year Plan was the only exception.

[23] Cf. R. S. Eckaus, "The Factor Proportions Problem in Underdeveloped Areas," *American Economic Review,* September 1955.

highly questionable, to say the least. The system's directors were pushing too far and too hard in each of the directions indicated. But they neglected, or deliberately scuttled, several opportunities to use the dual-economy approach in a much more effective manner, and all these errors of commission as well as of omission were largely (although not exclusively) due precisely to the beating-the-clock nature of the development pattern. We shall attempt to substantiate these assertions by going down the list of major cases as rapidly as possible.

"Giantism." The policy of favoring the construction of plants of unusually large size, known as "giantism," can be dealt with briefly because the salient facts are relatively well known.[24] The typical inefficiencies of the "giants" of the early thirties could be summed up under the following headings: (1) internal diseconomies of a conventional sort, caused by growing difficulties of management, rising cost of intraplant transportation, and the like, (2) external diseconomies reflecting primarily the heavy burden placed on the national transportation system, (3) abnormally long gestation periods, causing the returns from some of the large projects, if properly discounted, to be lower than the returns from quick-yielding small projects that could have been undertaken instead. (In some instances, no doubt, the prospective advantages of the larger plant would be sufficiently pronounced to make the projects in question pass the test of the appropriate time discount if such a test had been applied.[25]) The "giantist" policies were checked and partly reversed in the late thirties when pressing demands of the approaching war made output delays a matter of the utmost gravity. As recent Soviet literature on the subject indicates, however, the old trends are again operative.[26]

In short, the sound notion of skipping technological stages and making extensive use of the economies of scale in a rapidly developing "latecomer" country have often been carried to seemingly absurd extremes. The obvious question to be asked is: Why was this done? The

[24] The most substantial Western work in this field was done by Professor Leon Smolinski. See his paper, "The Scale of Soviet Industrial Establishments," *American Economic Review,* May 1962, and his as yet unpublished Ph.D. dissertation (Columbia University, 1960) on the same subject. Unfortunately, no comparable attention has been given thus far to agricultural aspects of the same phenomenon.

[25] "[Some of] these projects (such as the Magnitogorsk combine, for instance) justified themselves brilliantly. Other projects for which even a correct calculation would have yielded a low percentage rate of effectiveness, did not justify themselves (e.g., the giants of the food industry, some hydrostations which remained underutilized for years, and others)" (L. V. Kantorovich, *Ekonomicheskii raschet nailuchshego ispolzovaniia resursov,* Moscow, 1959, p. 223).

[26] See, e.g., Ia. Kvasha, V. Krasovskii, "Ekonomicheskaia effektivnost kapitalnykh vlozhenii," *Kommunist,* October 1961, p. 71.

foregoing discussion suggests two possible explanations. The actual length of gestation periods in the "giantist" projects was underestimated to a truly fantastic extent, particularly during the early years of Soviet planning. Furthermore, given the stupendous size of the investment program and the firm resolve of the system's directors to push it through, the idea of concentrating the few available managers and skilled workers in a small number of the largest-size plants rather than having them scattered over a much greater number of smaller plants may have seemed appealing even with more realistic estimates of the completion time. As will be seen later on, this was not the whole story, and it is by no means certain that the adopted solution was in fact superior to the rejected alternative. But this merely underlines once more a very basic point: Within the specific framework of Soviet over-all strategy, the possibilities of halfway "rational" decisions in more limited problem areas were nil; it was a matter of choosing the "second worst" rather than "second best."

Economizing on Social Overheads. While a "giantist" policy in a capital-poor country is a clear case of waste, the austerity in outlays for social overheads in a similar situation is parsimony of a double-edged kind. As was pointed out repeatedly in recent writings on the economics of development, capital savings of this sort could, depending on the circumstances, be partially, fully, or more than fully offset in their intended effects by the adverse impact on the over-all efficiency of the system.[27] True, in the case of Soviet transportation there was an important strike in favor of the "economizers." The Tsarist regime had bequeathed to its successors a railroad network of relatively recent vintage, built quite substantially "ahead of demand"; hence its capacity could absorb without undue strain a bigger load than it had to carry by 1928, in spite of the policy of underinvestment in transportation for the benefit of accelerated investment in industry during the mid-twenties. This slack, in all likelihood, could have sustained an effective level of performance in an economy growing at a fairly respectable pace, without any dramatic expansion in the railroad facilities. But—the same problem once again!

[27] Moreover, whatever one may think of the allegedly "dynamizing" repercussions of bottlenecks in social overheads in a totally uncontrolled and typically sluggish underdeveloped economy, a deliberate strategy of "unbalanced growth" would certainly be odd in a system in which major investment decisions with regard to all sectors are made centrally and the decision-makers are, to say the least, quite adequately "stimulated" in matters of growth. As will be seen later on, this does not mean that an "unbalanced" behavior pattern is entirely absent in the Soviet economy; but it constitutes a sign of weakness in the system rather than a source of strength.

—in view of the momentum of the industrialization rush and of the concomitant rise in the volume of shipments as well as in the length of
haul, the idle capacities were filled to the brim within a few years. Worse
still, while the demand for traffic load was growing by leaps and bounds,
the investment allotments to transportation were cut below the planned
level after the over-all investment program had been conclusively revealed as inconsistent with the size and structure of the total capacity
of the economy; and something had to yield the right of way. The results were manifold. The early thirties saw an acute crisis which nearly
became a breakdown, and eventually enforced an increase in the investment allotment as well as in organizational effort devoted to the
transportation sector. Yet while the danger of total collapse was averted,
and did not recur, the state of noncritical overstrain persisted, with a
high cost of transportation and an element of uncertainty about the long-
distance flow of goods as concomitants; these, in turn, gave rise to
counterproductive tendencies toward "self-sufficiency" in particular regions of the country and, more curiously, in individual enterprises as
well. No doubt, the policy of keeping capital outlays on transportation to a very modest share of the grand total released investible resources which made it possible to come close to fulfillment of the plans
for expansion of basic industrial capacity and to keep interindustrial
disproportions within the limits of tolerance. But it is incontrovertible
that some of the major operational troubles of the expanding productive apparatus were attributable to such economizing; and they must be
taken into account when the over-all balance sheet of Soviet development strategy is drawn.[28]

The situation with regard to housing was analytically similar. The
stock of urban housing available on the eve of the First Five-year Plan
could not be described as being in a meaningful sense "ahead of demand" for its services; and the deleterious effects which the increasing
housing shortage had on productivity of labor (largely, although not
exclusively, via rapid increase in the labor turnover) belonged under
the heading of impact of the compressed consumption levels on work
performance.

Substitution of Labor for Capital. The category of relaxation possibilities to which we now turn is certainly not vulnerable to the criticisms
put forward in the preceding sections. Huge reserves of former unemployed (or disguisedly unemployed) thrown into the breach may be
considered a net addition to the productive potential of the economy.

[28] An extensive discussion of the problem can be found in Holland Hunter,
Soviet Transportation Policy, Cambridge, Mass., 1957.

The new entrants into the labor force could be used to raise the degree of utilization of the existing plant and to create components of the new ones with not much more than bare hands, as construction work was highly labor-intensive. Less spectacularly, but more importantly (and, from the viewpoint of the Western marginalist, most appealingly), they could be used not only *in lieu* of capital goods which had yet to be built, but also to release some of the actually existing capital goods to uses in which the elasticity of substitution of labor for capital was low. It cannot be denied that if the planned figure for the nonagricultural labor force had not been exceeded, the over-all output targets of the First Five-year Plan would have fared very much worse than they did. The same held true, if to a much attenuated degree, with regard to the later plans.

However, while the momentous mobilization of labor resources probably saved the day, it could not work miracles. The basic disproportions within the industrial sector lost their explosiveness, but did not disappear. A major influx of labor into construction work could help to expand its volume, but not to shorten the long gestation period; in fact, the spreading of the limited supplies of scarce managerial skills over the rapidly growing number of unskilled laborers had, more likely than not, the opposite effect. Some technological coefficients refused to be "unfixed": Abundant labor was not a good substitute for steel needed in metal-processing, nor was it very helpful in getting more pig iron out of a given blast furnace. Moreover, the social cost of the whole operation was far from negligible: The major entries in the bill of particulars included widespread destruction of equipment during the early years in the process of "learning by spoiling" (as Professor Berliner has called it); [29] a marked increase in the disparity between the rapidly increasing

[29] See Joseph S. Berliner, *Factory and Manager in the USSR,* Cambridge, Mass., 1957, p. 139. In a speech made at a somewhat later date Stalin tried to present this policy as a result of a deliberate decision: "We were confronted by a dilemma: either to begin with the instruction of people in technical grammar schools and to postpone for ten years the production and mass utilization of machines, until technically trained people are turned out by the schools, or to proceed directly to the building of machines and to develop a mass utilization of machines in the national economy so that in the very process of building and utilizing machines people would be taught technique and trained cadres would be turned out. We chose the second alternative. We proceeded openly and consciously to the inevitable outlays and overexpenditures associated with the shortage of sufficiently trained people who know how to handle machines. True, we destroyed many machines at the same time. But at the same time we won the most important thing—time—and we created the most precious thing in the economy—cadres" (quoted in *ibid.,* pp. 138–39 from *Pravda,* December 29, 1934).

In the light of what was said in the text about the labor overfulfillment of the initial labor force target for industry, this sounds like an *ex post* rationalization wage bill and the sluggish supply of consumer goods with mounting inflationary pressures as an inevitable result; and dramatic deterioration of urban housing conditions. In addition, some of the "micro"-policies mentioned before were much less impressive in their implementation than in principle and have met with stern objections in Soviet economic writings. Since these criticisms have not yet received adequate attention in the West, a brief summary of the points raised may be in order:

1. The coexistence of highly mechanized technology in main production processes and of labor-intensive methods in auxiliary work is far from perfect, with the labor-intensive component frequently developing into a bottleneck.[30]

2. The repair work and spare parts supply are fully subject to economies of scale and should be concentrated in large-sized specialized plants rather than be performed in a fairly archaic manner as subsidiary activities of the production enterprises.[31]

3. The cheapness of some of the lightweight machines and the capital savings attributed to slow retirement of old plant appear in a different light if one considers that fully one-third of the total stock of Soviet machine tools was employed in 1962 in repair shops in order to maintain decrepit and inferior equipment in operation.[32]

4. When the postponement of replacement does economize on machinery, it is not always worthwhile because of the heavy strain on supplies of fuel, raw material, and electric power which old equipment consumes in excessively large amounts and which happen to be heavily capital-using.[33]

The strictures, while well taken, seem a bit too harsh. The critics were unwilling to consider the possibility that the condemned policies

plus an understandable attempt to make the best of a disappointing development. Also the sure touch in rigging the argument by overdramatizing the alternatives is worth noting. Actually there is no good reason to assume that the Soviet planners faced an either-or choice between "postponing for ten years the production and mass utilization of machines" and increasing this production and utilization at a backbreaking speed. A less precipitous infusion of unskilled labor into the industry would not only have reduced the wastage of scarce equipment, but would have made it easier for the seasoned workers to tutor the new recruits which would have enhanced the effectiveness of the learning process.

[30] Cf. Akademiia Nauk SSSR, *Voprosy povysheniia proizvoditelnosti truda v promyshlennosti SSSR,* Moscow, 1955, p. 252.

[31] Cf. S. Kheinman, "Promyshlennosti—progressivnuiu otraslevuiu strukturu," *Kommunist,* July 1963, pp. 92–93.

[32] Cf. B. Kapitonov, "O povyshenii kachestva sredstv proizvodstva," *Voprosy ekonomiki,* October 1963, p. 39.

[33] Cf. A. Notkin, "Povyshenie ekonomicheskoi effektivnosti i osnovnye voprosy razvitiia obshchestvennogo proizvodstva v novoi piatiletke," *Planovoe khoziaistvo,* June 1964, p. 2.

need not have been equally wrongheaded in all cases, and that they may have made more sense, or less nonsense, at early stages when they could be interpreted as a way of borrowing against the future; more generally, the connection of these practices with the over-all growth pattern was not made explicit.[34] Yet at the same time a broader point which would have been particularly pertinent for the early period of planning was never brought up, and quite understandably so.

EXIT MIXED ECONOMY

By applying policies described above, the system's directors were, in a sense, substituting not only labor for capital, but also "dual economy" of a substandard sort for a much more sensible sort, that is, for a system in which a private sector comprising small-scale producing units would be operating alongside a publicly owned sector of modern large-scale establishments, and in which there would be a good deal of variety in sizes, levels of technology, and forms of ownership within particular industries as well. This was, to be sure, precisely the setup which existed in the Soviet Union during the so-called New Economic Policy of 1921–28. And although the problem of the proper interrelationship between the two sectors gave rise to intense debates within the ruling party in those years, there was a wide measure of consensus among the Communist and non-Communist experts with regard to fundamentals. The performance of the two-sector system in promoting the economic recovery was rated highly. It was agreed that public ownership had a firm basis in modern industry because of pronounced economies of scale and complementarities prevailing there, and that it could perform a valuable role in promoting the extensive restructuring of the Soviet economy that was on the agenda. But these advantages, it was believed, were less significant in agriculture where the superiority of "bigness" was less striking, the role of incentives rooted in individual ownership very great, and opportunities for increases of efficiency within the limits of existing size distribution and of relatively labor-intensive technology far from exhausted. Hence the two

---

[34] Some of the cited practices could not be regarded as deliberate adjustments to the actually prevailing, or anticipated, factor scarcities. They constituted either *ad hoc* responses to bottlenecks which came into being *after* the construction and output plans had jelled, or attempts to minimize prospective losses on account of uncertainties in supplies by reducing the number of "linkages" and sticking to whatever plant one has got, good, bad, or indifferent. A minor self-reinforcing process might be at work here. Preservation of large blocks of aged plant was likely to lead to sudden collapses every now and then; and this "radioactive depreciation," when occurring at strategic junctures, could have considerable repercussions, thus adding to uncertainty.

sectors were expected to coexist "in earnest and for a long time," as Lenin had put it; the reorganization of agriculture along the lines of collective ownership was to come only after the development of industry had made big strides forward and, more specifically, after the capital goods industries had expanded powerfully enough to be able to supply the needed amount of large-scale farming equipment without prejudice to the needs of the nonagricultural sector. Indeed, the final draft of the First Five-year Plan was explicit in assuming that the dualistic structure would endure well beyond the quinquennium. Yet the "overfulfillment" was monumental. The collectivized sector of agriculture accounted in 1932 for 78 per cent of the total sown area instead of 13 per cent as scheduled, and by 1937 individual peasant farming had virtually disappeared.

In the light of all the foregoing, the logic of this turnabout seems not hard to grasp. Ragnar Nurkse put it well by saying that the main purpose of collectivization was to collect. Considering the speed of industrialization and the drastic nature of the shift of investible resources toward the capital goods sector, the urban demand for foodstuffs was bound to, and did, increase a great deal faster than the volume of industrial commodities available to the peasantry; in fact, the latter presumably declined in absolute terms, at least temporarily. Indeed, the two strongest "relaxation" factors which we have discussed—larger-than-planned increase in the urban labor force and the brief but dramatic spurt in the export of agricultural products—powerfully added to the disparity. In such a situation, to use Marx's phrase, "inequivalent exchange" of a most drastic kind was in order; the peasant had to be prevailed upon to give up more in return for less than, or at best for as little as, before. But it was far from certain that conventional ways of bringing about forced saving—direct taxation and price manipulation—would be effective for the purpose in hand. In fact, the Soviet peasants had repeatedly demonstrated their ability to dodge the first and to resist the second by sharply reducing the marketable share of agricultural output and devoting the unsold balance to use on their own farms. Such massive "withdrawal from the market" would obviously represent a threat to the industrialization program—a contingency which would appear all the more grave when we consider that the marketable share of grain was (as a result of the egalitarian distribution of land in 1917–18) no more than half of its prewar level on the eve of the Five Year Plan. Collectivization which would do away with peasants' power to bolt and would put the state in effective control of the deliveries seemed like a perfect solution. Was it?

The above question, in this writer's opinion, cannot be answered by a clear-cut "yes" or "no" in terms of economic considerations alone. (We refer, to be sure, to the economic considerations relevant for the system's directors and their over-all strategy; from the viewpoint of efficiency of the agricultural sector and of the consumers' preferences the answer would be grimly unequivocal.) The marketable share sharply increased during the period of the First Five Year Plan and has continued to rise ever since. Yet the food ration secured for the urban population was, particularly in the early stages, too low to sustain the desired productivity standards in industrial work, because total agricultural output showed a marked decline (and, in the case of animal products, a catastrophic drop) during the First Five Year Plan, followed by a tortuously slow upward climb later on. Unsatisfactory as this state of affairs was, things would certainly have been much worse if the system's directors had not stepped into the breach created by the slaughter of more than half of the working livestock, and raised the supplies of large-scale mechanized farm equipment to several times the size of the initial targets. But this meant that peasant resistance against the loss of economic independence forced the Soviet leaders to divert large amounts of desperately scarce investible resources, domestic as well as foreign, from the high-priority areas and to channel them into a sector which would otherwise have been a "natural" one for expanding at a relatively low capital cost.[35]

It is hard to say whether or not the advantages of increased marketable share offset these drawbacks. As Professor Bergson pointed out, the system's directors could still have gone a considerable distance in bringing about an increase in the peasants' marketable share without collectivization even though some of the means used would have to be rather severe.[36] Besides, if the need for the rapid mechanization of

[35] It is worth noting, to give just one example, that the tractor industry consumed 50 per cent of the total annual output of quality rolled steel in 1932 (see M. Gardner Clark, *The Economics of Soviet Steel,* Cambridge, Mass., 1956, p. 16). This percentage share declined later on as the rate of increase in the annual output of tractors slackened.

[36] *ESP,* p. 233. The relevant paragraph deserves to be quoted in full: "If the government had never taken its fateful decision in favor of wholesale collectivization and had chosen instead to continue to rely on independent peasant farms, how Soviet agriculture might have performed is conjectural. Students of the Soviet economy (including this one) have assumed that the record achieved regarding marketings could not have been approached. Even without collectivization, however, the government would have been able to fix the terms for marketings. It could also have induced marketings by levying taxes, which it had some power to enforce. Thus it still could have achieved much. Productivity, it is true, might have suffered. But it has suffered much in the collective farm, and this

agriculture had not arisen, some of the resources that went into this crash program could have been used to produce industrial consumer goods for the peasants and thereby strengthen the latter's inducement to sell. But even if the resources thus released had been fully used for the expansion of the capital goods sector either directly or via foreign trade, the "disproportions" within that sector could have been markedly reduced, and fewer extra workers would have been needed to plug the gaps; as a result, a smaller marketable share might have been tolerable, particularly since it would have constituted a lower percentage of a bigger total. Lastly, although the drastic switch was a once-and-for-all affair and the share of agriculture in total investment dropped sharply after 1933, the needs of maintaining, servicing, and further expanding the stock of mechanized agricultural equipment probably constituted a heavier drain on the capital stock goods sector than would have been the case if the old horse-and-plow technology had been supplanted in a less hurried fashion.

However, all this is highly speculative. And this inconclusiveness merely underlines the fact that in an economy forced to expand at a rate heavily overtaxing its capacity, the choice between dualism and forward flight is sometimes very much touch and go on purely economic grounds, and other considerations, still to be discussed, must come into play in order to bring about a final decision.

IS OVERSTRAIN DISAPPEARING?

We are left with an unanswered question. Was not the First Five Year Plan largely unique, and did not things improve later on? If the war and immediate postwar years are disregarded, this was true almost by definition. Because the First Five Year Plan assigned an overriding priority to the capital goods sector, and subsequent plans followed suit, the share of Department I in the total capital stock was increasing from one plan to another. Hence some of the basic disproportions of the early years could be gradually reduced, particularly since the planned rates of over-all output increases did not rise (in fact, they slackened somewhat). Over-all factor productivity has undoubtedly been rising on account of an increase in skills at all levels, the shift of the work force from less productive to more productive occupations, and technological advance. Yet this is only one side of the story. While the capacity for

says nothing of the wholesale losses that attended institution of this form of organization to begin with."

"Still and all, in order to match the record regarding marketings, some sort of war economy probably was unavoidable in early years. But one wonders whether the commitment to the collective farm would have been in order if the system's directors had not also had nonmaterial ends."

growth was increasing, the pressure of competing claims kept mounting too, and some of the compensating factors were getting weaker:

1. It will be recalled that the volume of imports which amounted, within the machinery group, to about half of the apparent consumption during the decisive period of the First Five Year Plan sharply declined later. True, after the war the share of trade in the national income rose again, and according to Western estimates the Soviet Union is at present a net importer of equipment. Yet the ratio of these imports to the apparent consumption is incomparably smaller than it was in 1929–31.

2. A much larger share of the expanded capacity of the capital goods sector is now pre-empted by military demands as the share of defense expenditure in gross national product has risen four- to fivefold since 1928.

3. Labor has become much less abundant than it was at the outset, when "disguised unemployment" was estimated at about 15 per cent of the total agricultural labor force. One of the by-products of this situation is a change in policy with regard to retirement of equipment; obsolescence is no longer being treated as a "bourgeois" foible. Hence, in order to maintain the same rate of net addition to the stock of equipment, its output must increase faster than before. Morever, the average age of the reproducible capital stock is now higher than it was at the end of the 1928–37 period during which quite a few industries had been created virtually from scratch while many others had been greatly expanded and/or thoroughly reconstructed; and this process of aging, strongly influenced by the slowdown in capital formation during the war-ridden forties, is bound to raise the replacement demand more than proportionately to the increase in volume of the capital stock.

4. The industrial expansion during the First Five Year Plan took place to a preponderant extent in areas to the west of the Urals, with capital-consuming social overheads already in existence. Yet still at the time of the Second Five Year Plan, an eastward shift on a substantial scale had begun, and the trend gained momentum after the Second World War. Since most of the Eastern areas are relatively undeveloped, a lot of "building ahead of demand" in social overheads is necessary, and this pushes the capital-output ratio upward—a fact repeatedly noted by Soviet economists during recent years.

5. The rapid urbanization and rise in skills mean that a large and growing segment of the population is no longer prepared to "take" per capita consumption standards which were by 1953 only slightly above the 1928 level, and in some important respects below it. Stalin's successors have realized this. On the face of it, the Marxian-type model would provide a reassuring solution: After the share of Department I in

capital stock had been made consistent with the desired rate of investment (with allowance for difference in capital-output ratios between
I and II and for the sectoral composition of foreign trade) it might seem
perfectly possible to let investment and consumption increase at the
same high rate and make everybody happy. Unfortunately for the system's directors, the key to improvements in living standards is a big
increase in urban housing and a dramatic expansion in chemical fertilizers, both of which happen to have a very high capital-output ratio.
(The relatively cheaper path of agricultural expansion placing main
reliance on the opening of "new lands" in Central Asia was essentially a one-shot affair, with its force largely spent by the late fifties.)
Moreover, since chemicals are a younger industry than, say, steel, and
are expected to grow much faster, the bulk of increase in their output
must come from the newly built plants and relatively little from better
utilization and partial reconstruction of the old ones, particularly when
the output targets were as stupendous as those set by Khrushchev in
1958 (tripling of the output of mineral and chemical fertilizers within
seven years). This is, in fact, another reason why the capital-output
ratio (as well as the share of incompleted projects in the total investment volume) has been rising during the last several years. An attempt
to counter these trends by a still steeper increase in the over-all rate of
investment was bound to boomerang. Its immediate effect would be an
added pressure on a capacity which had been heavily imposed on
anyhow. Moreover, the "revolution of rising expectations" is on the
march, and a marked slowdown (or a reversal) in the rise of living
standards is likely to have undesirable effects on work performance, as
well as unsettling political repercussions.

The conclusion seems evident: While the overstrain in the economy
is appreciably less than in the early period, it is still there, and tensions
are likely to rise sharply if the system's directors should try to restore
the former rate of growth by applying another dose of the old medicine.
The alternative would consist in doing something equally drastic but
quite new, namely, bringing about a radical change in the organizational
system of the economy. And this leads us straight to the concluding
part of the paper.

Planning and Development

While discussing the salient features of Soviet economic development,
we were, in effect, talking about Soviet planning in action. It will now
be our task to follow more explicitly the interplay between the two.

The complexities of the Soviet planning system defy adequate description in the space available here. Fortunately, the predicament is hopeless but not very serious. The phenomenon in question has been with us for a considerable time, and its basic characteristics have become broadly familiar. Moreover, I could add very little, in terms of over-all appraisal, to what has already been effectively stated by others.[37] Specifically, this implies agreement with the following widely accepted propositions: (1) While the Soviet planners did have rudimentary notions of over-all consistency and of the desirability of producing at the lowest possible cost in resources (expressible in terms of "socially necessary labor time"), they have lacked a meaningful and operational criterion for the optimum allocation of resources; (2) the very far-reaching centralization of the decision-making has caused the decisions to be slow in coming and frequently deficient from the viewpoint of feasibility (not to speak of optimality): Extensive delegation of authority to lower echelons helped to avert total chaos but was still leaving the superior agencies stuck with formidable tasks of aggregation and reconciliation; (3) the system has been seriously inadequate in conveying to managers of the individual production units in unmistakable and easily enforceable ways the directives of the planning agencies; prices have been not meaningful and, in varying degrees, none too operative; "success indicators" have proved ambiguous and conducive to waste; and direct commands much too blunt to be effective in situations of normal complexity. I shall argue (1) that distortions inherent in the Soviet development pattern were aided and abetted by the deficiencies of the Soviet planning system, and vice versa; (2) that, nonetheless, this system has been responsible for making the development pattern work and for preventing its disproportions from becoming explosive; but (3) that its economic usefulness to its directors has been by now drastically reduced.

INTERACTION OF INEFFICIENCIES

To be sure, the broad characterization of the Soviet planning system, given above, is no more than a long-winded way of saying that this system in inefficient. To the extent that this is so, the Soviet planning

[37] Reference must be made to Professor Bergson's recent study, the influence of which is in evidence throughout this paper, as well as to the work by Professor Herbert S. Levine. Cf. Levine's "Centralized Planning of Supply in Soviet Industry," *Comparisons of the United States and Soviet Economies,* Part I, Joint Economic Committee, 86th Cong., 1st Sess., Washington, 1959, summarizing the content of his as yet unpublished Ph.D. dissertation, "A Study in Economic Planning: The Soviet Industrial Supply System," Harvard University, 1961. I have also benefited from the already cited monograph by Professor Berliner and from an earlier work by Professor David Granick, *Management in the Industrial Firm in the U.S.S.R.,* New York, 1954.

system would tend to reduce the growth potential of the economy. (This need not mean, to be sure, that the same system could not be favorable to growth in some other respect.) However, certain drawbacks of the Soviet planning system have a more direct and specific impact on growth than this blanket statement would indicate:

1. The effect of inadequacies in the pricing system must be mentioned first. As Soviet economists of the post-Stalin era have been pointing out, the policy of allocating capital to enterprises free of charge provides no incentive whatsoever for speeding up construction. The penchant for "giantism" is likewise reinforced by the lack of an interest charge. Moreover, the absence of the rate of interest and distortions in the relative prices of capital goods contribute to fuzziness in matters of technological choice in general and in the application of the "dual-economy principle" in particular: The choices between full mechanization and partial mechanization or between early and delayed retirement of equipment are inevitably handled in a slapdash, across-the-board fashion.

2. It seems reasonable to assume that, scarce as capital may be in the Soviet economy, the decision-making ability of the central planners constitutes the most important single bottleneck factor. (This observation, it will be noted, is in accord with Professor Hirschman's analysis of the scarcity relationships in an underdeveloped economy, except that in the Soviet case the shortage is largely "system-made.") Harassed members of the planning bodies are vitally interested in cutting down on the number and the complexity of decisions they have to make, particularly since they do not have meaningful prices (explicit or implicit) at their disposal. Hence, the proclivity to make rulings across the board is further strengthened, as is the frequency of garbled applications of a basically sound approach. The strong preference for "fixed proportions," to which Mr. Khrushchev scathingly referred in one of his last public pronouncements, belongs to the same category. It is obviously convenient, after the dramatic transformation in the structure of the economy during the first planning decade, to keep the scheme of investment priorities relatively stable and to change technological co-efficients as infrequently as possible, preferably within the limits of established product groups; witness the tendency to improve on the quality of steam locomotives when an expansion in output of diesels would be more appropriate or, more recently, the resistance against the shift toward chemicals. Only when an innovation seems truly striking and/or when it affects a high-priority area, is it likely to be processed with dispatch. For the same reasons the planners find it easier to deal

with relatively few massive investment projects taking place discontinuously (construction of a new plant or substantial enlargement and full-scale replacement of the old) rather than with much more numerous "modernization"-type outlays which occur continuously and which involve partial but often highly important improvements in the technology of the plants. The "giants" are favored on similar grounds: It is easier to supervise a few huge plants than a large number of large- and medium-sized ones. Lastly, the probability of bottlenecks is enhanced as the inevitably desultory nature of top-level decisions affects some areas more strongly than others, depending on the degree of sensitiveness to hurry-up building methods, and on the substitutability of inferior inputs for better ones.

3. The response of the lower-echelon people to the slowness and blundering at the top compounds the distortions. The "do-it-yourself" principle is the twin brother of overcentralization, and it works all the way from an individual plant which crudely manufactures its spare part supplies to the powerful economic ministry of the pre-1957 period and the not-so-powerful regional economic council of today. All try their best to be as self-contained as possible and to retain some of their most valuable supplies for their own use, with supreme disregard for (and ignorance of) considerations of the social opportunity cost. Moreover, the specific nature of relationships between the planning agencies and the manager tends to encourage the latter to interfere with economic progress in several other ways as well. The plant manager's incentive to improve and innovate is weakened by advantages he can derive from using maximum quantities of costly raw materials in order to boost the size of his "gross value output," and by the circumstance that technological change almost inevitably involves a temporary disarray and slowdown in operations which means underfulfillment of the plan and loss of bonus. The unconcern about assortment, as long as the "gross value" target is met, not infrequently results in shortages of machinery and material of the kind actually needed, with surpluses of unwanted items being at best a poor substitute. Finally, it is deemed advisable to "get into the plan" with a big project rather than with a small one, because the supervising agency is likely to feel more reluctant to cut allowances to an "important" recipient in case of unexpected shortages. As a result, the number and size of the projects in construction are inflated, and this has a feedback effect on the length of the construction period.

4. We have seen that the defects of the planning system tended to

exacerbate the difficulties created by the adopted pattern of growth. Yet the relationship worked both ways; in fact, the chain of causation running in the opposite direction has been given a good deal of attention in Western literature, and we can therefore be very brief. The difficulties of making an imense number of decisions at the top echelon level, serious enough in a relatively static situation, were compounded in conditions of extremely rapid and unbalanced change, as was the margin of error. The "project-makers" propensity to understate the actual cost of new investment when first applying for approval and to submit padded requests for additional appropriation later on, as well as the plant manager's inclination to hoard material and to conceal capacity reserves, were reinforced by the awareness that requisite supplies would be hard to come by and that bottlenecks were likely to develop. Lastly, the sellers' market situation frequently forced the final consumer and the manager to make do with supplies which fell far short of the requirements as to quality and specification. True, such hypertension would not have arisen if the system had been allowed to reduce its over-all scale of operation down to the level of the narrowest bottleneck; but this was precisely what the Soviet planners were up in arms against. It is at this point, however, that qualifications are in order, and elements of strength become visible.

SAVING THE SYSTEM FROM ITSELF?

It would be nothing short of miraculous for a market economy, of the over-all size, structure, and degree of capacity utilization of its Soviet counterpart of 1928, to generate output and investment plans that would add up to something remotely reminiscent of the First Five-year Plan. But even if the miracle should come to pass, it would be virtually certain that such an economy would slide off the "ceiling" at a rather early stage and recoil toward the base line. As has been pointed out in discussions of the analytically similar case of a "mobilizing economy," the clamping down of purely aggregative controls does not suffice. A headstrong expansionary push is bound not only to generate an over-all excess demand but also to produce bottlenecks in areas with relatively low supply elasticities and concomitant excess capacities in other parts of the system, particularly when a drastic restructuring of the economy is aimed at. Yet although increased taxation might reduce the inflationary overhang, it is too blunt and too indiscriminate a device for dealing with sectoral disproportions; at the same time the operation of the market mechanism makes the massive reallocation of resources that is called for a sluggish and "cobweb"-like process.[38] A system of tight centralized controls could be more effective. With major disproportions clearly visible and increasingly grave for the system, the top planners could not afford to stick to their cheery initial drafts; rather they had to exercise their full powers of command, in order to restore a modicum of rough-and-ready consistency to the economy as rapidly as possible. They could do it by strengthening the crucial bottleneck areas, slashing down investment allotments to low-priority sectors while stepping up the intensity of utilization of their capacity, pushing ahead the development of the "guiding links," and letting the relaxation possibilities play their part; and they could refuse to be stampeded into major retrenchment on account of recurrent shortfalls in capacity utilization and delays in the completion of major construction projects. This was precisely what the Soviet planners did in the early days. As a result, they made the system function as a going concern till some of the monumental investment processes could start to come to fruition and reduce the tensions to a more endurable level. As everyone knows, the operation was backed up by the application of outright compulsion and repression on a hitherto unparalleled scale, and could not have succeeded otherwise against popular resistance and the normal slow-motion processes of the bureaucratic "business as usual"; at the same time, more conventional albeit very drastic taxation measures were applied. Yet brute force and a high turnover tax, between the two of them, would not have turned the tide.

In short, the economy did crash through the "ceiling" along a wide front—at an appalling cost, in nothing like the orderly array anticipated at the start, but still in one piece. From the viewpoint of its directors, this was undoubtedly one of the system's two "finest hours," the wartime performance being the second. It is likewise clear that this resilience *in extremis* highlighted some other less dramatic but equally important

[38] Cf. e.g., Tibor Scitovsky, Edward Shaw, and Lorie Tarshis, *Mobilizing Resources for War*, New York-Toronto-London, 1951, especially Appendix II. More generally, an output pattern sharply deviating from optimum cannot be expected to generate "optimum" prices and to be effectively steered toward optimum merely by market-clearing prices. (The latter can no doubt reduce the waste by allocating the nonrational relative outputs in a rational way; but here, too, a qualification is in order because in situations of shortages and quixotic supply flows, the buyers —plant managers as well as final consumers—would not be acting "rationally" from the social point of view either.) For a succinct statement of the proposition, cf. Tjalling C. Koopmans, "Efficient Allocation of Resources," *Econometrica*, October 1951, p. 463. It goes without saying that the point is no less valid when the output pattern not only deviates from "optimum," but fails to meet a much weaker condition of consistency with the existing capacities.

aspects of its operation which made it less hopelessly confused than our long list of deficiencies might indicate. Some of the system's major inefficiencies have kept each other in check and thus have helped to maintain a modicum of consistency without which Professor von Mises's "planned chaos" would have become living reality. The system of centralized allocation of resources within the framework of a fairly rigid priority scheme, ham-handed as it was, did nevertheless prevent the managers from going to extravagant lengths in beefing up their "gross value outputs" by prodigal use of expensive material, just as it precluded the totally haphazard allocation of resources that would have occurred if grossly misleading prices of producers goods had acted as effective allocators. Similarly, the fixed input norms, while exaggeratedly stiff and neglectful of possibilities of factor substitution, were not entirely ineffective as a disciplining factor in conditions of a seller's market, particularly if it is remembered that in a semideveloped economy the element of slack in utilizing productive resources is by no means negligible. The wasteful devices which were used to simplify the planners' task did avert paralysis of the decision-making mechanism, and many big innovations did emerge from the bureaucratic grinder to be applied, owing to the large investment volume, on a vast scale. And this leads us to another and perhaps even more significant point.

It is certainly true that some externalities are more important than others; besides, most of them admit of great variability in their individual components and in lengths of gestation period—and these differences cannot be properly evaluated without the use of meaningful prices and interest rates (to be sure, with the best possible allowance for anticipated future changes in scarcity relationships). Similarly, a planning system greatly overburdened at the top and saddled with massive distortions at the production level must result in inadequate coordination of the interrelated activities—a task which ideally should have constituted its main forte. There is no question that the Soviet planning system was deficient in all these respects. But it is likewise clear that an economy developing a wide range of interrelated industries at a very rapid pace could not help generating such externalities on a large scale and that coordination possibilities were not entirely inoperative. Lastly, the often-mentioned advantage of a longer time horizon (as compared with the ordinary market economy) did exist, and while it was abused often enough, as our discussion of "giantism" has shown, it was not always abused.

Yet while the allowance for all these strengths, both in moments of peril and in quieter times, helps to dispose of the "it-cannot-work" fallacy, it certainly does not constitute a good reason for rushing toward the opposite extreme. To begin with, in the discussion of the preceding paragraphs, as well as in many other discussions of the subject, the net was cast too wide: Were there no other alternatives to choose from than a market economy with a superstructure of strictly aggregative controls and a Stalinist supercentralization? We have seen that the purely economic advantages of collectivization were less than certain even within the context of the adopted over-all growth strategy. It is also arguable that an option in favor of selective and less pervasive direct controls would make Soviet planning less wasteful within the same basic context. The central planners could reserve the authority to make "large decisions" regarding the over-all rate of investment and broad sectoral priorities as well as direct control over short-supply items among major industries, while delegating the rest to the individual managers and letting prices reflect relative scarcities. It is perfectly true, however, that in an economy committed to a jerky and unbalanced pattern of expansion, the scope for effective use of such techniques must be severely limited, on account of poor visibility and the frequency of unexpected shortfalls in output. A recent Eastern European wisecrack to the effect that the Soviet-type planning is highly adept at solving problems which are entirely of its own making may be overly flattering in the first part and somewhat less than fair in the second; but it undoubtedly contains an element of truth. Yet all this raises a much more fundamental problem: Was this pattern of growth as well as the concomitant organizational pattern worth maintaining even from the viewpoint of the system's directors themselves, and if so, in what sense?

An important component of the inevitably tentative reply which emerges from the foregoing can be conveniently stated in terms of Figure 1, which is adapted from Figure II in Dr. Branko Horvat's "Optimum Rate of Investment." [39] The points A, B, C, and D on the solid curve denote rates of growth of income $[(\Delta Y)/Y]$ associated with different rates of net investment (I/Y) which is taken to be an average over a certain period of time in a given economy.[40] As can be readily observed, the $(\Delta Y)/Y$ ratio rises at an an accelerating rate between A and

[39] *Economic Journal,* September 1958, p. 754.

[40] The choice of the appropriate time period is admittedly not a simple matter. The period chosen should not be too short because otherwise a large part of the investment under consideration might still be in the pipeline in case of discontinuous development; on the other hand, economies may undergo, within a long period, strong fluctuations in their investment productivities which will be smoothed over by averaging. We are following Dr. Horvat in accepting a 12-year period as a compromise.

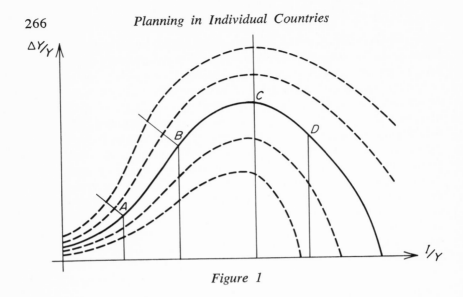

Figure 1

B and at a declining rate between B and C and then begins to decline absolutely. The first of these stages could be taken to reflect significant economies of scale and greatly improved ability to absorb technological innovations; the second—a gradual leveling-off in gains derived from these sources and a correspondingly stronger pull of diminishing long-run returns to capital and of rising short-run investment costs. The declining stage encompassing the *C–D* stretch of the curve can be interpreted as a combined effect of several factors discussed earlier: (1) Fall in productivity of labor in response to compression of consumption and extensive use of low-skilled manpower; (2) smaller volume of completed and fully utilizable (as distinct from total) investment because of long delays in construction and of pronounced "disproportions" reflecting, in turn, a sharply adverse reaction of the capital goods sector to mounting pressure on its capacity; (3) decline in flexibility and in "technological dynamism" as a result of general overstrain. A smaller but still substantial rate of investment corresponding to point *C* rather than to point *D* would be consistent with the capacity of the capital goods sector and entail smaller sacrifices in consumption. Hence it could be assumed to produce, at any meaningful terminal date, a volume of completed investment projects that would be larger in its over-all size, more balanced and technologically superior in composition, operated by a better work force, and consequently more effective in contributing to the further expansion of the productive capacity of the economy.[41] The dotted curves represent loci of increments in income which could be attained at higher or lower levels of allocative and organizational efficiency than those reflected in the solid curve.

In the light of everything we have said thus far, it seems reasonable to assume that the Soviet post-1928 economy was to the right of the maximum-growth point and that it was operating substantially below the highest attainable curve. The first of these propositions applies with particular force to the 1928–40 period encompassing the First Five Year Plan, but the sustained distorting effects of the early "excesses" on the structure of the capital stock and on the quality of work performance, but it is by no means irrelevant also for the post-1950 period, indeed (as was noted above), during the last six years the rate of investment kept creeping upward while the investment productivity was sharply declining. The second proposition is unquestionably valid throughout; in fact its force is likely to have increased over time, for reasons yet to be mentioned. But while the Soviet economy did

[41] It might perhaps be objected that some of the incomplete investment projects might be so phenomenally productive that they could ultimately tilt the scales in favor of D, even after the possibility of reinvesting the proceeds of the completed projects had been duly accounted for. Yet if a "slow" investment opportunity with a spectacular payoff was in existence, the planners could take full advantage of it at C, while still benefiting from the "compounding effect" (to borrow Maurice Dobb's term) of the quicker-yielding investment projects. It is true, however, that such getting of the best of both worlds would be more difficult in an economy operating at B and (a fortiori) at A.

A more serious criticism would consist in noting that in a developing economy with important indivisibilities a complete dove-tailing of projects and full-capacity utilization at any particular point of time is impossible almost by definition—a point made very succinctly by Professor Scitovsky in a more general context (cf. his "Growth—Balanced or Unbalanced?" in *The Allocation of Economic Resources*, eds. Moses Abramovitz *et al.*, Stanford, Cal., 1959, pp. 213–14). Yet this argument, unexceptional as a general proposition, would not take us very far in the particular case at hand. The Soviet planners did expect their output targets to balance—at least in the terminal year of the plan, and within the high-priority capital goods sector. Moreover, the chances of their being right against their own initial judgment appear dim for several reasons. First of all, the indivisibilities in some of the overexpanded lines were not very significant with regard to the relevant areas of the economy, which was, to be sure, already quite large in 1928; hence, a more balanced pattern of growth could be achieved, for instance, simply by building fewer machine-building plants and by postponing increases in output of less strikingly productive kinds of machinery until later. But also when building ahead of demand (or ahead of supply of inputs needed for full-scale operation of the project in question) is justified by the monumental size of the indivisible unit, such a policy can still be carried too far in terms of properly discounted future social benefits, if the said demand (viz., supply) is particularly sluggish in coming forward—a situation which can reflect poor coordination between complementary industries and/or a state of general hypertension. As our earlier discussion has shown, both contingencies would be far from hypothetical with regard to the Soviet economy.

not attain its full growth potential, it was clearly better off in terms of growth (although worse off in terms of investment productivity) than if it had been operating in the neighborhood of *B* either on the solid curve or on a not significantly superior dotted curve. The same would be true a fortiori for the comparison with the position in the neighborhood of *A*, except that in this case, the *D* alternative would be better not only in terms of growth but (with reference to the points on the same curve, at any rate) in terms of investment productivity as well.

A similar diagram could be used to show various economies with different rates of investment and different levels of allocative and organizational efficiency, with each economy represented by a separate family of curves. Here, too, it would be plausible to place the Soviet economy to the right of *C* on the solid curve; the advanced "Western-type" economies could be assumed to operate in the neighborhood of *B*, lying closer to the highest attainable curve; and the underdeveloped market economies would be in the neighborhood of *A*, lying on one of the lower curves. In such a situation, given appropriate values of respective investment rates and investment productivities, it would be entirely possible for the Soviet economy to grow faster than most of the Western-type economies, not to speak of the underdeveloped market economies. As the discussion of the opening section of "The Development Strategy," above, has shown, this was, in fact, the case.[42]

"TIME FOR A CHANGE"

There can be little doubt that the Soviet system's directors would be highly pleased to see their economy operating near the highest of the attainable *C*s. It is equally certain that the massive inefficiencies which prevented this from happening frequently made them feel uncomfortable, to say the least; and it is quite likely that they were genuinely in-

[42] In my view, a hypothetical socialist economy broadly resembling the Lange-Lerner model could be assumed to operate on the highest attainable curve, owing to full utilization of the advantages of the market mechanism plus the absence of monopolies and better allowance for external effects of economic decisions. For the same reasons, it could be expected to maintain the rate of investment at a relatively high level; and it could go further than a standard "Western-type" peacetime economy in overruling the time preferences of individuals. Yet such an economy (or, indeed, *any* economy in which optimization of growth is a matter of social concern) would have no compelling reasons to move all the way toward the peak of the curve. In fact, it would be well advised to stop short of it because the marginal time preferences of individuals in the neighborhood of *C* would be quite high while the incremental productivity of investment would be low, particularly after the risk of obsolescence had been allowed for. (For a full and illuminating discussion, see Amartya Kumar Sen, *Choice of Techniques,* Oxford, 1960, Chap. VIII.) In his quoted article, Dr. Horvat takes the opposite view.

clined, at any rate in the early stages of the process, to expect the impossible from the combination of modern technology, authoritarian discipline, and fiery exhortation. Yet after all is said and done, it remains true that the chosen pattern of growth and planning, seen in retrospect, constituted for Stalin and his lieutenants a sturdy second-best in economic terms and an unquestionable first-best from the viewpoint of noneconomic preferences. It seems high time to say a few words, trite as they may sound, about the latter. The commitment to the principles of social ownership and central planning was obviously important. But it played its part as a necessary but not a sufficient condition for the policy actually adopted, and even this in a qualified sense; there is nothing "in Marx" (or even "in Lenin," for that matter) to justify forcible obliteration of peasant farming by a socialist regime—indeed, one can find there a good deal to the contrary. Sweeping collectivization, with its shattering impact on living standards, centralization pushed to the extreme, and attempts to impose on the economy a rate of growth defying basic human and technological constraints added up to a peculiar sort of "socialism" and a not very efficient way to increase the productive potential of the country. But they certainly made good sense when interpreted as part and parcel of an all-out drive to crush the nuclei of independent decision-making, to extend the range of totalitarian controls as far as possible, and to enhance the system's directors' sense of security with regard to the outside world.[43] It was wholly in accord with the spirit of the undertaking that some of the most stunning accomplishments were achieved not by following the initial blueprint but through an escalatory sequence of attack, resistance, and retribution. Moreover, not only the objectives but also the ways in which they were being attained would represent "something of value" in such a situation. The overstrain, the all-pervading tension, the never-quite-absent risk of partial breakdown that might spread, the atmosphere of smoldering resentment and conflict—all this could be used as a potent device for keeping the society, and above all, its more articulate groups, in a state of constant quasimobilization and *la patrie en danger* mood which

---

[43] We speak of system's directors' *sense* of security because we do not subscribe to the view that combination of beating-the-clock industrialization, overcentralized planning, and searing repression, involving the wholesale purge of the army leadership, represented the most effective way of increasing the military potential of the Soviet Union. But it is, of course, incontrovertible that the Soviet military potential has greatly increased just the same. Here, too, a policy which was no more than "second best" from the viewpoint of meaningful objective criteria, could still be regarded as "first best" in broader terms of reference, given the extent of fear and mistrust of any diversity and autonomy that were inherent in the basic Stalinist attitude toward society.

would help to smother independent thinking, brand every noncon-
formity as treason, and justify the refusal of the dictators to "wither
away." The economics whose spirit was epitomized in such propositions
as "Perish or forge full speed ahead," or "There are no fortresses which
the Bolsheviks cannot take," was dubious not merely from the *natura
non facit saltum* point of view. But it filled a need.

It is understandable that the system's directors have not been eager
to abandon the setup which served them well in the past and which
undoubtedly still appeals to them in important respects. But they know
that modify it they must in order not to be put in a position of
generals fighting the last war, because the situation has changed significantly and irreversibly. The powerful expansion of the Soviet economy
brought forward not only a vast increase in the productive potential,
but also, as was shown earlier, a much stronger pressure of conflicting
claims for its services. The consequences of this state of affairs are
manifold. Costly mistakes on the macroeconomic or microeconomic
level can no longer be papered over after a fashion by throwing in more
manpower or cutting down on the traditional low-priority sectors, because the first is no longer abundant and the latter are in the process
of being upgraded at considerable cost. The old-style capacity reserves
were filled long ago, and the new ones are of little immediate help since
they are, more often than not, due to bottlenecks in complementary
lines rather than to inadequacy of demand. The rough-and-ready nature
of investment decisions is becoming a matter of greater concern than
before. As the technological frontier draws closer for many established
areas, it becomes increasingly difficult to assume that the striking
superiority which new ways of doing things exhibit, over a wide range
of scarcity relationships, will make even a fumbling but bold move
toward the new frontier not infrequently preferable to a cautious grop-
ing along the old one. At present a wrong step is more likely than previously to mean a plain and simple net loss to the economy.[44] But even
a "second-best" gain would not be good enough as further progress

[44] The above proposition could be put in terms of a familiar production function diagram. The striking superiority of the new technology would then be
reflected in a sharp downward shift of the equal-product curve. In such a case
even factor combinations lying to the right or left of the point of tangency between the equal-cost line and the lower equal-product curve, and therefore suboptimal, could be an improvement over any factor combination located along the
higher equal-product curve because the equal-cost lines corresponding to the new
combinations would in all likelihood lie *below* any equal-cost lines corresponding to the old combinations. The situation would obviously be quite different with
regard to a less spectacular change in technology and an accordingly smaller
downward shift of the equal-product curve.

increasingly depends on maximization of such gains rather than on throwing huge amounts of new resources into the hopper: The juxtaposition of "growth" and "choice" is becoming fatuous at this stage.

On the other hand, whenever new technological frontiers do appear, they are likely to be, in an important sense, more difficult to approach than in the old days, since they now compete for resources with some of the well-established high-priority industries, and the institutional as well as physical resistances to rapid and extensive shifts are strong. But as blunders of all sorts tend to become less tolerable, they are also getting harder to avoid, since complexity and specialization within industry are growing by leaps and bounds, while the methods of economic administration and of information processing remain basically unchanged. Moreover, the outside world is not what it used to be. Although the capitalist economies taken as a whole have not been expanding during the last decade at anything like the peak of their growth potential, some of them seem to have come quite close to it, and in others the performance is visibly better than during the thirties, when the stark contrast between the Western depression and the Soviet rapid advance made allocative efficiency appear irrelevant from the viewpoint of "catching up and overtaking."

Last but not least, the system's directors themselves have not remained entirely impervious to developments that have been occurring in their society since Stalin's death. They have, to be sure, not the slightest intention of presiding over the liquidation of their power structure. But they do realize that in order to keep the rate of economic expansion at a level acceptable to them, and to prevent tensions from becoming rampant, they must, with most of the old backlogs gone, turn to the one that still remains, and make use of the stupendous opportunity for improvement in the quality of decision-making in their economy.

It is this combination of reluctance to change and bowing to the inevitable which presumably accounts for the uncertain pace of the economic reforms thus far. While Soviet economic science "has recovered its wind" to a truly amazing extent, and the public discussion of the fundamental issues has been growing steadily bolder, little has transpired in the realm of action. Indeed, the numerous organizational reshufflings that have occurred during the post-Stalin decade seem like elaborate attempts to avoid the necessity of genuine reform; the well-known industrial reorganization of 1957 which transferred authority from all-union ministries to regional economic councils without affecting in the slightest the relation between the planning agencies and the plant managers is the leading example. The slowdown after 1958, and, possibly, a growing restlessness among the forward-looking elements of the managerial and professional intelligentsia have made such a temporizing attitude hard to maintain; the recent reforms in the consumer goods industry are a straw in the wind. It would be rash to make specific predictions at this stage. The forces of the *ancien régime* are still firmly entrenched. Some of its more sophisticated spokesmen are hoping to steal their opponents' clothes: While professing disdain for "bourgeois" theoretical foundations of input-output analysis and linear programing, they strongly advocate use of mathematical computer techniques as an alternative rather than a complement to decentralization—a position which leading men of Soviet mathematical economics have been vigorously opposing. There is no doubt that a dramatic increase in international tension could mean a grave setback to the new trends, and the road ahead cannot be smooth and easy in any case. But barring catastrophic developments and taking all in all, one can feel certain that more changes will come—and that they will bear watching.

COMMENT

Abram Bergson, *Harvard University*

In his very thoughtful paper, Professor Erlich touches on a host of interesting questions, but unhappily for me in my capacity as critic, I find that I am generally rather likeminded with him. Instead of recording my reactions to different points, therefore, I shall try to elaborate somewhat on a cardinal theme to which he refers briefly: the Soviet policy on centralization versus decentralization of decision-making, particularly the nature of the policy, how sensible it has been economically, and its rationale.

As to the nature of the policy, completely to define this might call for a detailed and comprehensive description of the Soviet planning system, but it will suffice simply to underline the familiar fact, referred to by Professor Erlich, that throughout the period of chief interest, that is, the period of the five-year plans, the planning system has been notably centralized by any standard.

I refer especially to three related features:

1. The determination of resource use almost everywhere administratively through a complex of bureaucratic structures.

2. The relatively limited use by superior agencies in these bureaucratic structures of prices and related financial controls as a means of coordinating and directing activities of agencies immediately responsible

for operations, and by the same token the marked degree in which the superior agencies enter directly in one way or another into the determination of the physical process.

3. The tendency of superior agencies even at the highest level to concern themselves not merely with general goals and principles but with details, often of a quite concrete sort.

These features have prevailed under the five-year plans generally. I refer primarily, however, to facets of resource use other than the acquisitions of consumers' goods and offerings of labor by different households. While during protracted intervals in the past these matters too have been dealt with more or less bureaucratically, recourse being had to rationing in one case and to labor compulsion in the other, for some time such procedures have been employed only to a very limited extent. Also, in agriculture, centralized decision-making did not really obtain until after the completion of collectivization, and even since then it has not obtained as fully as elsewhere.

It sometimes is suggested, however, that even since collectivization the degree of centralization has varied markedly in the course of time. Thus, some of the organizational reforms carried out under Khrushchev, particularly the liquidation of industrial ministries in 1957, are said to have entailed a significant decentralization.

Khrushchev's organizational reforms were complex, and are not easy to analyze from the standpoint of centralization. Possibly on balance there was some decentralization, but if so it was not very dramatic. Immediately before Khrushchev's retirement, however, the government took some steps toward a more radical reform, and his successors apparently have now determined to continue along this line. I refer to the recently announced decision to establish new working arrangements for some 400 enterprises in consumer goods branches. Under these arrangements, which stem (though perhaps not quite to the extent often assumed) from proposals of the Kharkhov economist, E. G. Liberman, profitability is to be stressed to a greater extent than hitherto as a criterion of success for managerial personnel. At the same time, such personnel are to be allowed more autonomy for the conduct of the enterprise's affairs. Among other things, they are to be encouraged to negotiate directly with retail trade outlets in respect of the qualities and assortment of goods to be supplied them. Reportedly the new arrangements will later be extended to additional consumer goods enterprises, while similar changes are also contemplated for heavy industry.

As to how sensible the government's policy has been economically, this question is potentially as stupendous as the last, but perhaps I shall have done my duty if I record my agreement with the general impression that the Soviet planning system is often inefficient economically, and that the resultant waste must be quite consequential.

How economically efficient a system is must depend on the end taken as a standard. Waste in the USSR is sizable, I believe, not only from the standpoint of the end usually stressed in the West, "consumers' welfare," but from the standpoint of any "planners' preferences" that we might plausibly impute to the Soviet system's directors, if I may join Professor Erlich in using a phrase I have found convenient elsewhere. I include here planners' preferences in which a cardinal concern is with "growth."

Difficult as it is, we must gauge the extent of the waste under Soviet planning primarily by inquiry into the nature and operating principles of this system. I have recently published such an inquiry, and rely here on its findings.[1] For purposes of gaining further insight into economic efficiency I also tried to calculate the comparative net national product per unit of labor and capital in the USSR and the United States in 1960. Depending on the nature of the measurement, the Soviet net national product per unit of labor and capital turns out to vary from 29.1 to 46.6 per cent of that of the United States. I refer to net national product and labor and capital inputs after the exclusion of certain final services, particularly government administration, health care, education, and military services, for which the type of comparison made is infeasible. For various reasons, I also omit housing services.[2]

Factor productivity as so calculated is, of course, not the same thing as economic efficiency, and I shall not bore the reader with a recital of all the sources of divergence between the two. But I argued previously and still believe that my comparison is illuminating regarding economic efficiency.

Interestingly, despite the Russians' access to the latest Western technology, their factor productivity in 1960 is of the same order as that of the United States sixty years ago during the decade 1899–1908: The latter was 36 per cent of that of the United States in 1960.

The foregoing characterization of Soviet economic efficiency in no way divides me from Professor Erlich, for clearly he holds the same somber view as I on this matter. Indeed, at many points he contributes new insights into it.

---

[1] *The Economics of Soviet Planning,* New Haven, Conn., 1964.
[2] *Ibid.,* pp. 340 ff. I have revised somewhat the figures derived in this study so that the data considered on output refer to *net* national product, as they were supposed to. In my study, I inadvertently referred to data on the gross national product.

Granting that the Soviet planning system has been wasteful, it does not necessarily follow that, given conformity to the imperative of pervasive public ownership, any other system of planning would have been less so. We are concerned especially with the degree of centralization of decision-making. Hence of special interest is the question of whether and to what extent a less centralized system might have been more efficient.

This is also a question which the reader will wish to judge for himself. I take it as almost self-evident that even within the general framework of a basically more or less centralized system the actual degree of centralization in the USSR, involving as it has extensive and often *ad hoc* intervention even by supreme authorities into activities of agencies immediately engaged in operations, has often been economically excessive. Whether and to what extent the Soviet planners might have been able to gratify their preferences better under an alternative system involving heavy reliance on price and related financial controls admittedly is another and more complex matter. Professor Erlich apparently believes that from the planners' standpoint such "market socialism" would have been economically inferior to the system actually employed in the earliest years. Perhaps he is right, though by all accounts the centralized system was flagrantly inefficient in these years.

Professor Erlich stresses particularly the possible advantages of centralization in enabling the system's directors to cope with the structural changes that occurred, and no doubt there were such advantages. The structural changes under the early plans certainly were violent. Even in Western societies, there is usually a shift toward bureaucratic, as distinct from market, controls when a sharp change in structure is required, as in wartime.

In the early years under the five-year plans, it is often said, centralization was also indicated by the scarcity of managerial talent. There must be some truth in this also, but this particular argument could easily be overstressed. While limiting responsibilities of the less competent many, centralization, if carried at all far, easily becomes unduly onerous for the more competent few. The upshot, therefore, may only be to replace many small mistakes by a few big ones. This might occur even if superior posts should indeed fall into the hands of the more competent. It is not at all clear that standards for promotion in the USSR have been such as generally to assure this.[3]

[3] While in Professor Erlich's view the highly centralized system had its virtues for the planners in the earliest years, he considers that a mixed economy in which direct physical controls are employed on some scale along with market processes might also have met the needs of the time. Space does not permit me to pursue this interesting theme.

The violent structural change of the early five-year plans has proved to be a unique episode in peacetime, and managerial talent can no longer be the very scarce factor it was initially. Moreover, the economy in the course of time has become steadily more complex as a result of the increase in the number of interconnecting plants, the ever-expanding variety of products, and the like. The system's directors, who before sought essentially for steel and then more steel, have come to have preferences that also are more complex, and they are now more concerned than they were formerly to cater to the demands of consumers, who themselves have become more choosy. In the circumstances, however effective economically centralization was initially, it surely must be less so now.

To what extent the Russians will gain economically from the sort of reform that they are now initiating, however, is less clear. We still do not know much about this reform. As reported, the new arrangements still seem complex and cumbersome, and the fact that for the present they affect only a limited sector may also prove to be a source of difficulty. While the new arrangements supposedly met with success when employed experimentally for two enterprises in the clothing industry, what will be achieved when they are used on a mass scale, and with managers not so circumscribed as under a highly publicized experiment to be on their best behavior, is another matter.[4]

Coming finally to the rationale of the Soviet policy, I can be brief, for curiously the Russians themselves until recently have had little to say on this very important theme. Indeed, one is led to think that in opting in favor of a notably centralized system the system's directors probably never seriously considered any alternative. Of course, for a time from March 1921 decision-making in the USSR was markedly decentralized, but the government's approach to economic organization during this period of the so-called New Economic Policy reflected in part a decision on a more basic matter: its determination for complex reasons temporarily to limit the scope of nationalization and "cooperatization." Still there was some administrative decentralization even within the public sector, and this represented to some extent a reaction to the extremes of centralization under War Communism. But it is doubtful if

[4] On the planning system as it is on the eve of the reform, see *ibid.* On Liberman's proposals, see Marshall Goldman, "Economic Controversy in the Soviet Union," *Foreign Affairs,* April 1963. The experiment with the Maiak and Bolshevichka enterprises has been discussed extensively in the Soviet press in the past year, and some discussions have been translated in *The Current Digest of the Soviet Press.* See, for example, the issues of November 4 and 11, 1964. On the decree extending the experiment, see *Trud,* January 13, 1965.

anyone was prepared to urge that such decentralization should persist long after the economy has passed through the acute crises into which it has been plunged by world war, revolution, and civil war—after it had been possible to extend once again the scope of public and cooperative ownership and after the government had found the opportunity and acquired the capacity to deal systematically with the great and novel task of creating a planning system appropriate to such ownership.

Interestingly, as the period of the NEP drew to a close, Soviet officials and economists vigorously debated many questions of economic policy. They debated the tempo of industrialization, and they debated the policy to be pursued on agriculture. Especially in the latter context, where the future status of the independent peasant was a cardinal issue, the proper role of market institutions necessarily was in question. But this was considered only secondarily. As for the question of the degree of centralization that was to obtain within the public sector, this seemingly was not debated at all.[5]

If there was always a predisposition toward highly centralized planning, it is not difficult to imagine its possible sources. Even if they have not always been observant Marxists, the system's directors must have been influenced by Marxian views of capitalism, particularly the stress on anarchy of competitive markets. For the government to act to supplant the market with bureaucratic controls thus must have seemed the inevitably right thing to do. And there was little reason, either, to hesitate because of any fear of the complexity of the task. Marx and his followers had had little to say about the problem of resource use under socialism, but they manifestly considered it to be not especially formidable.[6] In the circumstances, it is perhaps not surprising that the Soviet founding fathers often had only an extraordinarily naive and oversimplified view of their economic task; a view which, after all due allowance for possible rhetorical excesses, is clearly exemplified in these famous words of Lenin: [7]

Accounting and control—these are the *chief* things necessary for the organizing and correct functioning of the *first phase* of Communist society.

[5] On economic organization under NEP, and the great debates which brought this period to a close, see Alexander Baykov, *The Development of the Soviet Economic System*, New York, 1947; V. N. Bandera, "The New Economic Policy (NEP) as an Economic System," *Journal of Political Economy*, June 1963; Alexander Erlich, *The Soviet Industrialization Debate, 1924–1928*, Cambridge, Mass., 1960; Nicolas Spulber, *Soviet Strategy for Economic Growth*, Bloomington, Ind., 1964.

[6] See Oscar Lange and Fred M. Taylor, *On the Economic Theory of Socialism*, Minneapolis, Minn., 1938, pp. 130 ff.

[7] *State and Revolution*, New York, 1932, pp. 83–84.

. . . The accounting and control necessary for this have been *simplified* by capitalism to the utmost, till they have become the extraordinary simple operations of watching, recording and issuing receipts, within the reach of anybody who can read and write and knows the first four rules of arithmetic.

It is often said that the system's directors were also influenced by the Germans' experience in organizing their economy in World War I. They were familiar with and obviously were impressed by this experience.[8]

The predisposition toward centralization, however, can hardly have been only of economic origin. As Professor Erlich has stressed, centralized decision-making represents an enhancement in the authority of the system's directors which must be congenial to them. At the same time, their own special status in society only seems the more justifiable in view of the onerous responsibilities they bear.

As explained, the government at long last seems to have begun to decentralize in a consequential way. The ruling circles may not be quite as obsessive as they once were about their own political status, but for reasons already suggested the economic waste of centralization may also be increasing. Such costs must also be more difficult to accept now that the economy is no longer as buoyant as it was formerly, for as even the inflated official statistics show the tempo of economic growth has tended lately to fall. In the circumstances, the system's directors have seen fit to permit propagation of a more sophisticated view of the problem of socialist resource use, and this view now must itself be a source of pressure for decentralization. Yet, for reasons suggested, the system's directors may be disappointed with the results of the decentralization now being introduced. Moreover, as a result of the progress in economics, proponents of centralization paradoxically have now been armed with new weapons to defend their approach, new weapons in the form of mathematical techniques which may facilitate centralized decision-making. And the new techniques are being explored at the same time as a revolution is occurring in methods of information processing which is itself favorable to the use of such techniques. It will be fascinating to observe how in the years ahead these diverse forces make themselves felt on the organization of planning in the USSR.

[8] Bergson, *Economics of Soviet Planning*, p. 173.

French Planning

CHARLES P. KINDLEBERGER

MASSACHUSETTS INSTITUTE OF TECHNOLOGY

This is not a technical paper on French planning. It is assumed that the organizers of this conference were informed and rational when they assigned this topic to what Ragnar Frisch is said to call a "conversational economist." The paper, then, concerns the history, description, delimitation, evaluation, and generality of French planning. Monosyllabically, it deals with what French planning has been, is, and is not; how well it works; and if it could work out of France. French planning is very much *au fait,* so that accounts of its development and present state abound. These aspects will be dealt with minimally. Primary interest attaches then to how planning differs from other aspects of economic policy, to what extent it has been responsible for the remarkable postwar growth of France, and whether it is capable of being transplanted to other jurisdictions.

The Development of French Planning

The origins of French planning lie in the wartime preparation of French emergency needs for overseas assistance after liberation. With liberation achieved, the program was extended, and a special department set up in the Ministry of National Economy. But the requirement of the French mission in Washington for a more systematic statement of governmental intentions and requirements resulted in the consolidation of scattered agencies into a central General Planning Commissariat, in January 1946, under the direction of the chief Washington negotiator, Jean Monnet. The first publication of the commissariat was written in English as well as in French, with the Congress in mind: *Statistical Review of the Economic and Financial Situation of France at the Beginning of 1946.*

NOTE: I am grateful for detailed comments on an earlier draft by Michael Lipton, John Sheahan, and A. Van Nimmen.

A year later, the first four-year plan, covering 1947–50, was adopted. With the change in United States aid from piecemeal to systematic, under the European Recovery Program, the First Plan was extended to 1952 to coincide with the coverage of the Marshall Plan.

The First Plan had a slogan, "Modernization or decadence" (Massé, 1961, p. 211),[1] and chose to concentrate expansion on six "basic" sectors: coal, electricity, steel, cement, agricultural machinery, and transportation. At the time of the extension of the initial four-year period, two further industries were added: fuels and fertilizers. Coal, electricity, and railroad transport were nationalized and could be expanded from within. The others were fairly well concentrated and implicitly threatened with nationalization. In steel, capital for expansion was provided from counterpart funds and other government sources (as in other industries) but on condition of mergers. Government intervention was *ad hoc* in design and in implementation; the emphasis on expansion, modernization, efficiency, and modern management which characterized this intervention, however, was systematic.

The Second Plan, organized with a gap of one year, covered 1954–57, and rested on a more systematic basis in national accounting. The emphasis was still on expansion, but this was now extended from the eight sectors to the economy as a whole. The "basic sectors" of the First Plan were followed by the "basic actions" of the Second (Hackett and Hackett, 1963, p. 27): research, improved productivity, marketing reform, assistance to equipment, and training, that is, programs to produce more, but under competitive conditions of quality and price. The threat of socialization had ended, and the Planning Commissariat was transformed into an agency for forecasting and economizing (Despres, 1963, p. 44). Goals were laid down overall and by sectors, including housing. Most of these were overfulfilled, though not all (machine tools). But the expansive pressure led to price increases and balance-of-payments deficits. Exports grew steadily, but imports grew at a greater rate. The Pinay government chose growth rather than maintenance of reserves, which were allowed to run down virtually to zero by 1957.

The Third Plan ran from 1958 to 1961 and was addressed to growth and the correction of the balance of payments. The need to reduce costs was underlined by the prospective entry into force of the Common Market. The pressure for expansion was maintained, with an increase of 20 per cent projected for the four years (manufacturing, 33 per cent; exports, 70 per cent). Restoration of the balance of payments was to

[1] Full bibliographic details are given in the list of references at the end of this paper.

be achieved in six years. The critical position in internal and external balance meant that the leadership in economic policy in France in 1958 was assumed by monetary and fiscal policy, in which the Planning Commissariat had little voice. Quasi-devaluation occurred in the summer of 1957. The Fourth Republic ended in May 1958, and with the entry into force of the Fifth came more effective authority in the monetary and fiscal field. The 5 per cent rate of expansion sought by the plan gave way to a mere 1 per cent. In December 1958, the Rueff program provided for devaluation of the franc, a cutback of budgetary expenditure, and adjustment of the tax system. The balance of payments righted itself in nine months, rather than six years, and set the stage for a new advance. In 1960, an "interim plan" was adopted for the years 1960 and 1961, to make up for the slowdown of 1958 and 1959. The over-all rate of increase was set at 5.5 per cent per year (7.4 per cent in industrial production). Rapid increases were achieved.

In the Fourth Plan, over the years 1962–65, the rate of expansion was again set at 5.5 per cent a year, raised from the original experts' target of 5 per cent. Whereas earlier plans had been called plans of modernization and equipment, this was one for economic and social development (Perroux, 1963, p. 17). The economic development involved the same prescription as before: expansion, full employment, maximum efficiency, and hence no reduction in working hours. The social side involved heightened pressure for housing and educational capital and attention to urban renewal. In addition, problems of regional balance were explicitly addressed in the plan, to push particularly those regions like Brittany and the Central Massif where industrialization has lagged.

The Fifth Plan, covering 1966–70—five years this time, rather than four—is still in process of formulation as this is written. Newspaper accounts indicate that the projected rate of growth is reduced from 5.5 per cent a year to 5, to prevent overheating of the economy. In five years the increase in over-all production would be 27 per cent, that in private consumption 24 per cent, in public expenditure 39 per cent. Within the total of public expenditure, housing and military equipment outlays were projected at increases of 34 per cent; schools, hospitals, telecommunications, roads and other public projects at 54 per cent. M. Massé's report called for an increase in autofinancing of private investment out of profits—from 60 to 70 per cent; a maintenance of the work week; and an increase in the prices of public services to allow reductions in governmental subsidies (*New York Times,* November 25, 1964).

The Planning Process

Descriptions of the methods of French planning have been provided in great detail (Hackett and Hackett, 1963; Bauchet, 1964, etc.). For our purposes it is sufficient to observe that a given plan begins with an over-all macroeconomic rate of growth agreed between the Planning Commissariat and the Treasury, the economic staffs of which overlap. The Planning Commissariat is divided into three horizontal divisions: Economics, Finance, and Regional, plus 10 vertical sections: Agriculture, Energy, Water, Transport, Industry, Fisheries and Artisans, Construction, Housing, etc., Urban Development, Overseas Territories, and earlier, Algeria. The total permanent full-time staff is small, consisting of no more than 35 professionals, and 140 in all.

For the rest, the plans are elaborated by a series of commissions, which used to meet once for each plan, and now convene annually. The horizontal commissions were two for the Third Plan and five for the Fourth, dealing with General Economics and Finance, Manpower, Productivity, Research and Regional plans. The vertical commissions have expanded from seven in the First Plan, to seventeen in the Third, and twenty-two in the Fourth: Agriculture, Agricultural and Food Industries, Artisans, Buildings and Public Works, Chemicals, Culture and Arts, Energy, Housing, Nonferrous Mines and Metals, Overseas Territories, Oil, Post Office and Telecommunications, Radio and Television, Sanitary and Social Equipment, School, University, and Sport Equipment, Fisheries, Steel, Trade, Transformation Industries, Transport, Tourism, and Urban Equipment (Hackett and Hackett, 1963, Appendix III). The commissions organize working parties to deal with specific problems as they see fit: Under the Fourth Plan that on Transformation Industries had sixty such parties. Some 3,000 persons served with commissions and working parties on the Fourth Plan.

In addition to the commissariat and the commissions, which actually set out the targets and means of their achievement, the plan is submitted to a number of consultative bodies; to the Economic and Social Council, which was provided for in the constitutions of the Fourth and Fifth republics, and is made up of almost two hundred representatives of various interest groups and intellectuals; and to the High Planning Council, composed of ministers of state and heads of various national bodies, such as the chamber of commerce, the employers' federation, the trade union groups, and so on. This numbers sixty. The Economic and Social Council has an Investments and Planning Section which is now brought in early on the choice of the growth rate. Apart from the First and Third plans, which were adopted by administrative order, the plan is submitted to Parliament for ratification. In the Fourth Plan, the debate was a heated one and resulted both in some modification in favor of regional projects and agricultural interests and a change in the order of events. Submission to the National Assembly formerly took place at the last stage; the Fifth Plan, however, was submitted before it had been finally determined, to permit of greater democratization in the planning process.

The planning begins, as noted, with an agreed over-all rate of growth, chosen from among a series, such as 3, 4.5, 6 per cent. After consultation with the Investment and Planning Section of the Economic and Social Council, a growth rate is adopted. At this stage, the government adds directives covering major objectives—balance-of-payments or regional equilibrium, for example—or education, housing, urban redevelopment, etc. The result is a government directive to the Planning Commissariat. Then the commissions within the commissariat go to work to prepare detailed and consistent targets by sectors and industries. Used in the process are national accounts for the final year of the plan estimated by the Services des Études Économiques et Financières (SEEF) of the Ministry of Finance, investment and labor requirements of the horizontal commissions, assisted by detailed industry studies of such organizations as BIPE (Bureau d'Information et des Prévisions Économiques), income elasticities of demand, as calculated by CREDOC (Centre des Recherches Économiques et de Documentations sur la Consommation), the input-output tables of INSEE (Institut National de Statistiques et Études Économiques). Forecasts are made for those elements in the process as are subject to no or only to limited control, such as exports, the prices of imports, the rate of technical progress, etc. End-year targets by sectors and industries are broken down and built up again by an iterative process to obtain consistency, shuttling back and forth between the horizontal and vertical commissions and working parties of the commissariat and the commissariat staff itself. Moving from the preliminary projections with their expression of political choices to the provisional targets for each sector which are to be debated by committees, and back to the writing of a coherent over-all plan is a time-consuming one, using up in present practice a minimum of three years (Wickham, 1963, p. 342).

Implementation

A consistent plan does not ensure implementation, even though industry, agriculture, employers and labor have been consulted in its design.

French planning is indicative, rather than imperative, as is discussed below; that is, it shows the directions in which the economy ought to go, rather than providing specific targets for individual plants and firms. The mechanism for achieving the plan is usually said to be twofold; on the one hand, two-fifths of national income and half of gross investment, at the peaks, have been represented by the national government (public enterprises, 11 per cent of net national product and 30–35 per cent of gross investment); on the other, national savings flow to a considerable extent through government hands, taking into account the nationalization of the major commercial banks and insurance companies and the mobilization of savings deposits through the Caisse des Dépôts et Consignations (to make no mention of the Crédit Foncier and the Crédit Agricole). In addition, the counterpart funds developed by U.S. aid in the early days of the plan were invested by the government through specially created Caisses de Modernization. The private capital market functioned poorly; so firms wishing to expand were dependent upon reinvested profits (autofinancing as the French call it) and government allocations. In addition to these means of ensuring compliance, government policy more generally could be brought to bear on individual firms through the administration of price control, tax measures, and in some cases affecting especially foreign investors, licensing approval. In particular cases, a firm would enter into a quasi-contract with the Ministry of Finance and the Ministry of Industry, an exchange of letters in which the firm would set out a statement of its intention to invest, and the ministries would express their approval and inform the firm of dispositions taken by them in its favor (OECD, 1962, p. 4).

There is some doubt about these means of implementation, however. In the first place, nationalized industries, and even government departments, have not been wholly submissive to the plan. The *force de frappe,* or nuclear deterrent, of the French was not provided for in early versions of the Fourth Plan. The Planning Commissariat's opposition to the tunnel under Mont Blanc and preference for the cheaper Fréjus alternative under Mt. Cenis was overridden (Bolle, 1963). Parliamentary acceptance of the plan does not guarantee voting the necessary credits in the field of public works, which have been considered too important to be fixed rigorously over extended periods of time (Eklund, 1964).

Nor do the nationalized industries help that much. Some of them guard their autonomy better than firms in the private field (Bauchet, 1962, p. 141; Sheahan, 1963, p. 202). The threat of nationalization has been said to have been more potent than nationalization itself (Sauvy, quoted by Despres, 1963, p. 23). Despite its dependence on the state for capital, Régie Renault, its director has asserted, is administered like a private enterprise (Vernier-Palliez, 1956, p. 95), and even a French governmental publication, in calculating the proportions of public investment controlled by the state, "such as those for public works," excludes "certain nationalized enterprises in the competitive sector" (Ambassade de France, 1963, p. 12). The public corporations, especially in railroads, aviation, and electricity, have been among the leaders in increasing efficiency and improving technology. Unlike public corporations in many less developed countries, which have a weakness for wasteful investment programs, they have pioneered in the calculation of efficiency conditions for pricing and investment. To a certain extent, their calculations have become those of the plans. But it is a mistake to regard French planning as using nationalized industries to carry out its designs. Here, as in private industry, where it does not permit itself to be persuaded, it must persuade as much as command.

Even in the field of private business, the plan's powers declined somewhat between 1958 and the 1963–64 inflation with its profits squeeze. Autofinancing picked up and the private capital market as well. Whereas public funds and bank credits accounted for 61 per cent of gross investment of the steel industry under the First Plan, the proportion fell to 11 per cent under the Third (Hackett and Hackett, 1963, p. 169). Control of the supply of capital worked effectively when the economy as a whole was expanded through demand inflation, investment was highly profitable, and savings were in short supply. With cost-push inflation, there may be some profit squeeze in some lines, which would increase the importance of capital availability in the hands of government, but reduce the incentive to expand; and where expansion is maintained at a high pace, with ploughed back profits or access to foreign funds, as in automobiles, the Planning Commissariat is beginning to have doubts that expansion *à outrance* is an optimal policy.

The central fact of the implementation of French plans, as we shall see presently, is that it has not been doctrinaire.

The Need for French Planning

Justification for French planning has been found by different people in a number of aspects of the French economy: in ineffective macroeconomic policy (Wellisz, 1960); in the muddle of democracies with their permanent danger that government will express contradictory preferences (Wickham, 1963, p. 338); in the need for information on the part of French businessmen (Johnson, 1963); in the failure of the price system; and in the need to convert businessmen from restrictionist to expansionist attitudes.

The notion that planning has been a substitute for adequate macroeconomic policy finds particular justification in international economic relations. With an overvalued exchange rate from 1950 or so to 1958, planning called for expansion of exports, and was supported by a variety of devices: special access to credits, special provision of exchange to meet accessory expenses of exporting, credit insurance, insurance against changes in domestic prices, tax adjustments, advances for the purchase of raw materials, concessions on price controls, governmental agreements with industries including, among other aspects, remission of the value-added tax on exports, and the use of funds to advertise abroad (André, 1964). The adoption of a new exchange rate and a monetary and fiscal policy of restraint at the end of 1958 (aided by the end of the Algerian conflict) eliminates much of this Rube Goldberg disequilibrium mechanism. As already noted, the restoration of the balance of payments which the Third Plan thought would take six years was accomplished in nine months.

Outside foreign trade, however, the contention does not stand up. It is true that monetary and fiscal policy have not always been coordinated with planning; it is not clear how annual budgets could be made to conform to a four-year plan originating three years in advance of the initial plan year. But it is possible that planning created more problems for monetary and fiscal policy than the reverse. The rate of expansion in the Second Plan has been mentioned, and lately under the Fourth Plan the pressure on the labor supply, on wages, and hence on prices has been so great as to call for the stabilization measures of the Treasury of September 1963. An initial impression was that it was lucky that the Economic and Social Council had raised the sights of the Planning Commissariat from 5 to 5.5 per cent growth per year, since the higher rate of expansion enabled the French economy to absorb the Europeans returning from Algeria in substantial numbers in 1962 and 1963. By 1963 it appeared that the Planning Commissariat had underestimated the labor requirements of the French economy, which was drawing increasing numbers of North Africans, Spaniards, Portuguese, and Italians, which the plan had not counted on, but was still reflecting sharply rising wages; or perhaps it has overestimated the fluidity of the French labor market and the readiness with which labor could be drawn from areas of excess population like Brittany.

That French government has a propensity to exhibit a muddle is well known and indeed the subject of a thick monograph written before the record of French postwar growth had been firmly established (Baum, 1958—but written in 1952, 1953). The plan may, moreover, have gone some distance to clarify national objectives, as Sheahan puts it, for the public sector as well as for the private, even if the public sector did not always submit to the wishes of the Planning Commissariat. But planning is to be distinguished from *dirigisme* which prevailed in the interwar years—the steady interference of public decisions in response to day-to-day difficulties without systematic, long-term elicited aims (Wickham, 1963, p. 336). The interventions of the authorities are substantial and increasing, and forecasting at a minimum is needed to give them coherence and rationality (Swann and McLachlan, 1964, p. 87).

But while government might perform in an incoherent and contradictory way in the absence of a plan, the real danger as seen by most French observers was in the failure of the price system. Sometimes it was thought that the price system produced the wrong amount, whether too much or too little capacity, as separate firms, making their own forecasts of global demand, followed independent investment programs. In the initial stages, it was thought that capital was scarce and that any investment in excess capacity would be a serious waste (Despres, 1963, p. 27). Later, the fear was general among French economists that private enterprise and the price system tended to lead to underinvestment. This view was subsequently abandoned without modifying the basic distrust of anarchic competition (Wickham, 1963, p. 337). More recently, the European Economic Commission and the French officials which have made representations to it have renewed the view that private pricing leads to excess investment and waste through unemployment. It is, of course, possible to reconcile these views with the position that the price system produces too little investment in noncompetitive industries—through a tacit mutual acceptance of inertia by existing firms—and too much in competitive. In these circumstances, planning calls simultaneously for more competition and less, with each therapy applied separately. It is hard to find an explicit statement of this point of view, but it may well be implicit in the contradictions that abound in writing on the subject.

Among those who believe that the price system fails to produce the right level of investment, the plan is regarded as market research or, sometimes, merely as information. The exigencies of the market and of capitalism demand an informed economy, and a discussed economy, though not a concerted economy (Perroux, 1962, pp. 14–17). In a dynamic economy, large cost-reducing innovations must be based upon a view of the rate of growth (Malmgren, 1961). Uncertainty depresses investment (Johnson, 1963, p. 18).

The record of French planning, however, does not altogether confirm the view that private myopia will depress investment. The First Plan underestimated the growth of demand in electricity, which above other fields should lend itself to accurate forecasting. The Second, using improved methods, such as linear programing, was overly timid: Four-year targets were reached in two years. Concurrently, the Planning Commissariat tried to repress expansion in steel (Sheahan, 1963, p. 184). The record of Charbonnage de France and of the European Coal and Steel Community in coal is one of overestimating demand and the need to expand capacity. In automobiles, the French Plan and the European Economic Community have both been bearish. Wickham states that planning is exhaustive market research, which supports rather than replaces the market mechanism, and thereby generally increases the inducement to invest, although it should probably dampen it in some sectors such as automobiles, steel, wheat, soap powders, shipbuilding, etc. (1963, p. 337).

This is a neuralgic issue, whether the planners replace or supplement the price system, and whether the information or market research provided by the plan increases or depresses the rate of investment which would otherwise obtain. Information removes uncertainty, but collusion removes it more thoroughly, either collusion with government, or with other firms. Simple forecasting—the "onlooker effect" as Frisch puts it (1962, p. 250)—is not enough. To achieve credibility, the forecasts must be confirmed. This encourages the quasi-contract or tolerance of the cartel. It is the great virtue of French planning that it has left individual firms free to experiment, innovate, overexpand and underexpand by restricting its planning to indications rather than commands. Its further virtue is that it has failed to eliminate uncertainty in foreign trade, an area where market research and the provision of information function ineffectively. The uncertainty arising from the openness of the French economy has been a vital element in the success of planning.

If planning is not compensation for faulty monetary and fiscal policy, nor shadow-pricing required by the failure of the price system, nor coherence and rationality in governmental, multifarious, previously inchoate intervention, nor pure market research and the provision of information on demand, what is it? There is room for the possibility that French planning has not been immutable, and that its original essence, of which it retains a large measure, is "promotion," or "pressure for expansion."

In a previous comment on the subject, I suggested that: "Knowledge of income and industry projections and faith in the inevitability of expansion are communicated to firms at intra- and inter-industry meetings. This is perhaps the most powerful effect [of French planning], and one which has a faint resemblance to a revivalist prayer meeting" (Kindleberger, 1963, p. 155).

This passage has been chided for its "faintly derisive tone" (Nossiter, 1964, p. 201), but it is interesting to note an echo of the same note in the most straightforward description of the plan, without a trace of irony: "People have to be convinced, one is tempted to say 'converted' " (Hackett and Hackett, 1963, p. 368). Later, the Planning Commissariat occasionally had fears that its pressure for expansion had overreached itself and that certain industries were going too far, threatening "overequipment," waste, and risks of underemployment (Massé, 1961, p. 18).

The point to note is that French planning is not an exercise in programing or optimizing, but the provision of a flexible framework which is subject to change and adjustment on an *ad hoc* and empirical base. The standard cliché is that French planning is indicative, rather than imperative (to which Streeten adds that British planning is subjunctive, 1963, p. 1164). Bauchet prefers the term "flexible" to "indicative" (1964, p. 24). Massé insists that it should be "active" (1962, p. 6; 1963, p. 15). French economic thought is essentially interventionist, and this characteristic raises the most important issues for economic policy. When the French intervene among domestic firms in their own economy, it is of course their own concern. Readiness to act on a case-by-case basis affecting United States business in France poses larger international questions. But a still more important choice is required if the French attempt to export this interventionist-at-the-particular-level philosophy to the Common Market, or block progress on the Kennedy Round tariff reductions under GATT. Discrimination has been defended as economic by Frisch (1957), and in the case of French planning by Marczewski (1962). There can be no doubt of the need to intervene in particular cases on occasion: The first request to GATT for an exception to the most-favored-nation clause came from the United States, which wanted to discriminate in favor of the Pacific trustee islands; President Kennedy intervened in the U.S. Steel price increase of May 1962, and Secretary Anderson of the Treasury telephoned the Ford Motor Company to request them to postpone or halt the purchase of the minority shares of Ford of Dagenham in the autumn of 1960, backing down, however, when he learned that the arrangements had gone too far ahead to be called off. But here the rule is nondiscrimination, and particular intervention occurs only in exceptional cases.

French economic officials "reject the inhuman fatalism of 'laisser-faire, laisser-passer' " (De Gaulle, 1963, p. 3), and point out the need for "regulating the exercise of economic freedom" (Giscard, 1963, pp. 3, 8). Objection was expressed in August 1962 to the action of General Motors in closing down a Frigidaire plant in Gennevilliers and discharging 685 workers because of the competition of imported refrigerators from Italy, and to Remington Rand's action a month later in dismissing 800 workers at Caluire, near Lyons, as it concentrated its manufacture of portable typewriters in the Netherlands. Applications to invest in France by Chrysler (Simca), Libby, McNeill & Libby (canning), and General Electric (Machine Bull) were all granted, but only after discussion and adjustment of the business arrangements in the latter two cases (Johnstone, 1964; Swann and McLachlan, 1964, p. 99). Other European countries, to be sure, are not above concern in these matters: viz., the Parliamentary clamor in Britain over the Ford purchase in 1960 and the Chrysler acquisition of a minority holding in Rootes in 1964, and the unsuccessful Italian intervention at the EEC to establish rules of competition for American automobile firms operating inside the Common Market. Automobiles present a most interesting case study for future observation of French planning, the Common Market, European Free Trade Association–EEC competition, and the treatment of American direct investment. It will be particularly a testing ground for the principles of customs union and nondiscrimination if the thirteen or so major companies in Europe (four each in Britain, France, and Germany, and one in Italy, to say nothing of the smaller companies in Britain, the Common Market, and EFTA) were to be reduced by competition to three or four, as in the United States market—some of them, perhaps, the same in the two continents.

French justification of special attention to foreign investors is that their sources of capital lie outside the scope of the control of the plan, so that the major instrument of control of French firms, capital allocation, is inapplicable. This overstates the matter. In most direct investment, a great deal of the capital is acquired locally in any event. Moreover, as already noted, the effectiveness of the state's domination over the capital market has varied, declining considerably from its initial substantial height until it rose again under the recent profit squeeze. From this side of the Atlantic it appears that there is more concern for and attention to American firms seeking to establish operations or interests in France than for European firms. There seems to be a disposition on the part of French ministries to regard European competition as suitable in general because of the comparable size of the firms concerned, but American firms as requiring special attention because of their size and power (see the reference by Minister of Finance Giscard d'Estaing to United States firms as "monsters" in *Figaro,* October 17, 1963). Case-by-case intervention is therefore justified as the rule, rather than the exception.

Rapid German economic growth ostensibly based on the operations of competitive markets has made a substantial ingredient of intervention, as Reuss points out (1963), and Wallich before him (1955). This has taken the form largely of fiscal policy, though there are those who attribute an important influence to anticartel policy (Sohmen, 1959). (It is interesting, incidentally, to observe that French policy under the plan favored making bigger firms out of smaller, through mergers, especially in steel and under the First Plan, whereas German anticartel policy, at least under the Allied occupation, and to a degree later, made little ones out of big ones.) But there is this important distinction between intervention through fiscal policy and that through direct contact: The former still operates by means of the invisible hand; the latter, despite the insistence upon an indicative rather than an imperative plan, comes close to ordering. The Citroën plant in Rennes, the Usinor plant in Dunkirk, the electronics plant in Brest, and especially the allocation of quotas in oil come close on the domestic front to the same sort of intervention that seems to apply to United States firms.

It is in the international economic area that French planning faces its most serious dilemma, and one apart from income policy in which it is far from clear what the answer may be in theory and practice. Marjolin (1962) and Massé (1961, p. 18) believe that the logic of planning requires its extension to the Common Market. "Arguments that are valid on a national scale are equally valid on the scale of a group of countries." "Planning, including programme planning, presupposes an economy whose relations with the outside world are limited or can be restricted, should the necessity arise" (Marjolin, 1962, p. 12). Swann and McLachlan believe that the French propose to extend planning to the EEC (1964; see also Hackett and Hackett, 1963, pp. 323 ff.). The Fourth Plan's success has been threatened in different ways by inflation at home and inflation in Italy. The Baumgartner-Pisani "plan" in agriculture, while it is tantalizingly vague on detail, appears to call for planning or programing of production and distribution in agricultural staples on a two-price system, one positive and high and the other zero, on a world basis. Staff members of the Food and Agriculture Organization are beginning to talk of worldwide "programing" for primary commodities (Royal Institute for International Affairs, 1963, p. 1), though in discussion this sometimes comes down to little more than better information, such as the commodity study groups have been providing. It might be possible to contemplate an optimum planning area, analogous to the optimum single-currency or fixed-exchange-rate areas envisaged by Mundell (1961) and MacKinnon (1963). It is worth noting, however, that the Mundell and MacKinnon criteria for a fixed-exchange-rate area differ: Mundell chooses the region within which factor movements are substantial and outside of which they decline sharply, whereas MacKinnon is interested in the openness of the economy, the extent of its trade, and thereby the extent to which it is possible for reductions in the exchange rate to impose level-of-living cuts on factors by means of the money illusion, i.e., rising prices with unchanged money incomes. On Mundell's criterion the optimum area is less than, say, Canada; on MacKinnon's, larger. In planning, the optimum area might again be the region within which factors move, which would make France too big and underline the difficulties faced by France or Britain in planning to correct regional disequilibrium. Or it might be an inward-looking Common Market with a high common external tariff and controls over foreign capital.

Against this is the view that competition from imports was vital in preventing planning by the planned from turning into a cartel. In steel, the resistance of small enterprises was "successfully attacked by the ingenious device of exposing the industry to international competition" (Sheahan, 1963, p. 174). "Foreign competition has proved an essential spur to prevent agreed planning from facilitating the cartelization of the whole system" (Wickham, 1963, p. 341). In a closed economy there was the great risk that the common background of businessmen and government officials and the view of both that companies in the same business shared common interests to which antagonism and competition were foreign would cause targets for industries to become targets for firms (Sheahan, pp. 180, 181; Wickham, p. 342), and planning to become an impediment rather than a spur to progress. Everything here depends on temperament. In the Japanese ten-year plan of 1960, the announcement of the 1970 target of doubling industrial capacity led to serious inflation as each highly aggressive competitor responded to the news by doubling his capacity in a single year. In France, the danger as seen by Sheahan and Wickham is that the target for all would become the target for each, on a fixed-shares-of-the-market basis. The open economy thus either disrupts planning by introducing uncertainty into an area where the need is for market research, information, reduced uncertainty and risk, or prevents planning from turning industry static by requiring the individual firm to go beyond maintaining a share of the market and working to innovate, undertake extra investment, and to hold down costs and expand through price competition.

The French dilemma is illustrated by the fact that most officials come out strongly on both sides of the issue. Massé "readily concedes the tonic value of competition," but holds it is "essential to be able to recognize the dividing line between incentive and waste" (1961, p. 18). Wickham has the Common Market providing checks and balances on one page (1963, p. 341) and making planning difficult on another (p. 347).

The other major dilemma is between planning and macroeconomic policy. It has already been mentioned that planning is not a substitute for adequate macroeconomic policy, except perhaps in the balance-of-payments area. Sound macroeconomic policy may contribute more to planning than contrariwise. The dilemma is this: If planning is to a large degree promotion, or body-English, to sell expansion, and if policing the planning works best in an overheated economy where the power to withhold capital is effective because of a profits squeeze, and mistakes in planning are eradicated by growth in demand, then planning means inflation. Inflation may be stalled off by extra increments of labor on which the planners did not count—*pieds-noirs,* Algerians, Portuguese, Italians, and Spanish, together with women out of the house, farm workers off the farm, and clerical labor out of the inefficient distribution sector. This is fortuitous. High rates of growth can be obtained in a dual economy, where the archaic sector shrinks as resources are transferred to the modern sector. But once the availability of incremental resources for the modern sector dries up, the rate of expansion must slow down, plan or no plan.

Maddison holds that French growth was the result of management of demand and had little or no relationship to planning (1964, pp. 151–53). In his system, demand is all. There can be no doubt but that the maintenance of high demand does encourage workers to leave the farm, or to come out of the household, and that to this extent, demand creates its own supply. It is also possible that planning straightened out some kinks in the supply curve. But the contention of this paper is that French planners underestimated three aspects of over-all supply, which largely canceled out: (1) the resistance of large pockets of domestic labor in regions like Brittany, among housewives, etc.; (2) the mobility of international labor from southern Europe and North Africa; and (3) the increases in productivity implicit in modernization and in the shrinkage of artisanry and small-scale peasant farming. The easy gains from the latter two sources of growth have now been harvested, however, and unless the wave of additions to the labor force from the postwar baby boom makes them good, macroeconomic pressure will find itself exerted against a rising marginal cost curve, instead of a surprisingly flat one.

In these circumstances, income policy is whistling up the wind, as the Dutch found out in 1963. The price system *may* shift the character of investment to greater labor saving, though there is no evidence that the French planners recognized what was happening in this respect in the 1950s, and reshaped their planning in this direction which the German market economy seems to have pursued of its own accord in response to changes. There is more and more talk of the need for planning income distribution, which is normally a function of factor pricing and macroeconomic policy, but little discussion of what may be involved. To plan high rates of growth and high profits, when the rate of innovation, though high (CEPREL, 1963, p. 90), is autonomous and labor is limited is to overdetermine the system. It is well to say that you plan for no increase in leisure, but the Régie Renault will give an extra week's vacation, going from three to four, if a tight market gives labor the bargaining power (Despres, 1963, p. 52). Labor's refusal to enter into the Planning Commissariat on a substantial scale, so as to preserve its freedom of action, is a symptom of the problem, rather than a cause.

Evaluation

Is French planning a success? To ask the question is to pose another: By what criteria should it be judged? Wickham deliberately rejects the rate of growth, and chooses instead stability of the growth rate, conformity of the results with targets, and investment productivity (1963, p. 344). It is hard to see the basis for the first; moderate success on the second may reflect nothing more than that any plan tends to be self-confirming, without indicating whether any single plan is the best possible plan, or better than total absence of planning. Investment productivity is a function of the rate of technical progress, on the one hand, and of the efficiency of resource allocation, on the other. John Despres claims that the lower capital-output ratio in France than in Britain, with roughly the same rate of investment in each, is proof of more efficient allocation of resources under planning because Britain and France presumably use the same industrial technology (1963, pp. 59–61). But this leaps too many steps. With identical allocation and identical technologies, Britain could have a higher capital-output ratio than France because of less efficient firms: There is evidence to suppose that in the nationalized industries such as railroads, coal, and possibly electricity, this has been the case. Or with firms of equal efficiency, and identical technologies, the British aggregate capital-output ratio could be higher because the composition of final investment demand was different. Or with labor relatively scarcer in Britain than in France, it is only normal to expect a higher capital-output ratio. More likely, in my judgment, the technologies have not been identical.

France started the postwar period with a large technological lag (United Nations, Chap. VI, p. 10). This gap was closed, and French innovative capacity in many lines exceeded that of its neighbors, certainly of Britain. To what extent this change in productivity was a direct result of planning and of the activity of the horizontal Commission for Productivity, which was brought into the Planning Commissariat from the Productivity Agency, and to what extent it was an independent phenomenon can be debated. Certainly beginning with the Second, the various plans placed great stress on increasing productivity, including special productivity loans and special financing for the production of new products (*ibid.*, p. 13). But the case can be made that productivity increases bulked larger in the implementation than in the planning. Innovation is a consequence of technical virtuosity, which is unpredictable. It does not proceed at an even pace which can be projected. Planners can provide exhortation to technical progress and incentives, but they cannot summon it into being or claim credit for its time path. The French economy used its scarce resources with great efficiency— more efficiency than almost any other country in Western Europe in the postwar period (United Nations, Chap. II, pp. 14, 20, 33, Chap. VI, p. 7) but whether this is owing to *ex ante* planning or empirical management is impossible to determine, with the latter favored by the record.

In short, it is easy to give French planning high marks for macro-dynamic success, although the growth of the economy seems to have followed more an Abramovitz-Solow model of growth through technological progress than a Harrod-Domar model based on investment. The record on macrostability is so-so—despite Wickham's claim—with no serious setbacks, but with difficulties in the balance of payments and income distribution and with need for macroeconomic policy alongside and occasionally opposed to planning goals. On the microeconomic front, it is difficult or impossible to devise an adequate test: Bottlenecks were broken during the early days, but entrepreneurs ignored the plan's attempt to apply the brakes in some fields, and seem not, as yet, to have suffered from it. Perhaps it is enough to score the macrodynamic success. Planning and growth are associated, even if it be true that causality cannot be established, that growth without planning can be found in other contexts, and perhaps planning without growth. The final question poses itself: Are French planning and its success exportable?

Can French Indicative Planning Be Applied Elsewhere?

The success associated with French planning has established an enormous vogue for it. Belgium adopted planning on the French model in 1959 (CEPES, 1961, pp. 84–94). The establishment of the National Economic Development Council in Britain draws admittedly on the same inspiration. Chancellor Ludwig Erhard in establishing a four-year framework for the annual budget and creating a Council of Economic Advisers felt obliged to uphold "social market economy" and to insist that he was not "pandering to the politico-economical fashion as expressed in the term which by now has become almost a slogan, 'planification'" (Erhard, 1963, p. 14). One German who is now a member of the council, moreover, was prepared to contemplate that the major modifications of the German economic structure, for which he saw a need, would require planning to carry through (CEPES, Giersch, 1961, p. 113). Organizations which had already embraced planning as doctrine were not slow in finding their beliefs confirmed (PEP, 1961; Private Planning Association, 1963). Perhaps the most persuasive voice lifted in its behalf was that of a Washington economic journalist who urged its application in the United States (Nossiter, 1964, Chap. 8).

There is no lack of disagreement. Bankers, businessmen, statesmen, and economists do not hesitate to point out that French planning is more French than planning: Where it abjures price and wage controls, import quotas, consumer rationing or government allocations of labor, materials, and capital, and involves a minimum of interference with private decision-making in the economy, it may not be planning at all (McLaughlin, 1963, p. 1). Economists in the less developed countries who are inordinately impressed with indicative planning have not questioned whether the primary impetus for French growth did not arise from the backlog of technological advancement into an economy with highly developed skills and institutions, and have shown too little awareness of the tradition of centralization and close contact between government and business technicians in France (Collado, 1963, p. 6). More generally, the French system may be seen as squarely in the mainstream of a tradition of cooperation between government and industry which goes back at least to the time of Colbert (Downie, 1963, p. 5). In his presidential address to the American Economic Association, Mason concludes that French planning is irrelevant to the United States (1963, p. 12).

But the relevance of French-type planning to the developed countries of the West which have competition, appetite for income, capacity for innovation and resource reallocation, and reasonably effective monetary and fiscal policies is perhaps not the issue. Where these ingredients of growth are not present, or only latent, some mechanism is needed to call them into being or into action, and planning is as good a mechanism as any other—perhaps better. Whether French-type planning can evoke growth in countries where the listed attributes are missing, as in the less developed countries, or have lost their cutting edge, as in Britain, is another question. The French economy in 1946, poised on the brink of resurgence, could use the stimulus of planning to great effect.

But planning is not the all-purpose weapon. However much it may have contributed to French growth, it has failed to cope with the problem of stability, or rising costs and prices, or income distribution, problems to which the United States must give heed along with growth. Moreover, growth seems to have made progress lately in the United States, as in Germany, though the circumstances of the two economies differ in important respects and it is dangerous to reach hard and fast conclusions on the basis of the response to the 1964 tax cut.

The important issue, to which reference has already been made, is the extent to which intervention in the economy occurs at the level of the firm, and with regard to the specific results of action rather than conformity to general rules of conduct. This is the old issue of "rules vs. authority" in monetary policy. In the United States there will be economic bills of attainder, administrative rulings, appeals to public opinion, pressure, or even laws designed to produce a particular result in a particular situation. They will be exceptional under present circumstances. If indicative planning is adopted, the role of authority will perhaps not expand much, but the likelihood is that it would expand some. The extent of such intervention in France is greater now and likely to increase. When planning gives rise to growth which makes competition more feasible (Sheahan, 1963, p. 242), we have the best of all possible worlds. Where planning is primarily intervention, the gain is less evident. It can be argued that intervention in France has been efficient economically. It can also be argued that it is becoming increasingly regrettable politically.

References

Ambassade de France, Service de Presse et d'Information, *France and Economic Planning,* New York, April 1963.

André, René P., "Government Action and French Exports," unpublished M.S. thesis, Massachusetts Institute of Technology, 1964.

Bauchet, Pierre, *Priorièté Publique et Planification,* Paris, 1962.

―――, *Economic Planning: The French Experience,* New York, 1964 (translated from the revised French edition, 1962; first French edition, 1958).

Baum, W. C., *The French Economy and the State,* Princeton, N.J., 1958.

Bolle, Pierre, "Deux études de cas―Pierrelatte et le Tunnel du Mont Blanc," unpublished paper given at Colloque sur la Planification under Fondation Nationale de Sciences Politiques, Institut d'Etudes Politiques de L'Université de Grenoble, Mai 2–4, 1963.

CEPES (Centre Européen pour le Progrès Économique et Social), *French and Other National Economic Plans for Growth,* report of a conference held under auspices of the French group in Paris, June 1962, distributed in United States by Committee on Economic Development, Washington, D.C., June 1963.

CEPREL (Centre d'Étude de la Prospection Économique à Moyen et Long Termes), *Bulletin du CEPREL,* December 1963.

Collado, E. G., "Economic Development through Private Enterprise," *Foreign Affairs,* July 1963.

De Gaulle, Charles, "President De Gaulle Holds Eighth Press Conference," Ambassade de France, *Speeches and Press Conferences,* July 29, 1943.

Despres, John, "Planning and French Economic Growth," unpublished honors thesis, Harvard College, March 1963.

Downie, J., "What Can the U.S. Learn from Foreign Experience," paper prepared for a University of California Conference on Unemployment and the American Economy, at Berkeley, Cal., April 18–20, 1963 (mimeographed).

Eklund, Per, "French Indicative Planning and Uncertainty," unpublished paper at the Fletcher School of Law and Diplomacy, April 1964.

Erhard, Ludwig, government statement made by the chancellor on October 18, 1963, *News from the German Embassy,* Washington, D.C., October 25, 1963.

Frisch, Ragnar, "On the Need for Forecasting a Multilateral Balance of Payments," *American Economic Review,* September 1947, pp. 535–51.

R. C. Geary, ed., Future in Figures, Amsterdam, 1962.

Giscard d'Estaing, Valery, Minister of Finance, address at Harvard University Graduate School of Business Administration, June 8, 1863, Ambassade de France, *French Affairs,* June 8, 1963.

Hacket, John, and Hackett, Anne-Marie, *Economic Planning in France,* Cambridge, Mass., 1963.

Johnson, Harry G., "Economic Growth and Economic Policy," *J. S. McLean Memorial Lecture,* Ontario Agricultural College, Guelph, February 1963.

Johnstone, Allan W., *United States Direct Investment in France: An Investigation of the French Charges,* Cambridge, Mass., 1965.

Kindleberger, Charles P., "The Postwar Resurgence of the French Economy," *In Search of France,* eds. Stanley Hoffman *et al.,* Cambridge, Mass., 1963.

Maddison, Angus, *Economic Growth in the West,* New York, 1964.

Malmgren, H. B., "Information, Expectations and the Theory of the Firm," *Quarterly Journal of Economics,* August 1961.

Marczewski, J., "The Fourth French Plan (1962–1965)—'Conjuncture' and Planned Development," *Economie Appliquée,* June 1962.

Marjolin, Robert, "Do We Need a Plan for Europe?" *E. E. Bulletin,* July 1962.

Massé, Pierre, "French Economic Planning," address given in London, April 22, 1961, at symposium organized by National Institute of Economic and Social Research, Ambassade de France, *French Affairs,* December 1961.

———— in Preface to François Perroux, *Le IVe Plan Français,* 1st ed., Paris, 1962.

————, speech to the Superior Council of the Plan, July 3, 1963, reported in "La Vie Economique," *Le Monde,* July 4, 1963.

McKinnon, R. I., "Optimum Currency Areas," *American Economic Review,* September 1963.

McLaughlin, W. Earle, "Plan or No Plan—or Un-Plan," mimeographed speech before Canadian Manufacturers Association, Toronto, Ontario, June 3, 1963.

Mundell, Robert, "A Theory of Optimum Currency Areas," *American Economic Review,* September 1961.

Nossiter, Bernard, *The Mythmakers, An Essay on Power and Wealth,* Boston, 1964.

OECD (Organization for Economic Cooperation and Development), *Government Incentives to Encourage Private Investment,* Paris, 1962.

Perroux, François, *Le IVe Plan Français,* Paris, 1962.

PEP (Political and Economic Planning), "Economic Planning in France," *Planning,* August 14, 1961.

Private Planning Association of Canada: L. A. Skeoch and David C. Smith, *Economic Planning: The Relevance of West European Experience for Canada,* Montreal, 1963.

Reuss, Frederic, *Fiscal Policy for Growth Without Inflation: the German Experiment,* Baltimore, 1963.

Royal Institute for International Affairs, *New Directions for World Trade,* London, 1964 (offset edition).

Sheahan, John, *Promotion and Control of Industry in Postwar France,* Cambridge, Mass., 1963.

Sohmen, Egon, "Competition and Growth: The Lesson of West Germany," *American Economic Review,* December 1959.

Streeten, Paul, in review of John Sheahan, "Promotion and Control of Industry in Postwar France," *American Economic Review,* December 1963.

Swann, D., and McLachlan, D. L., "Programming and Competition in the European Communities," *Economic Journal,* March 1964.

United Nations, Economic Commission for Europe, *Some Factors in Economic Growth in Europe During the 1950s,* Geneva, 1964.

Wallich, Henry C., *Mainsprings of German Revival,* New Haven, Conn., 1955.

Wellisz, S., "Economic Planning in the Netherlands, France and Italy," *Journal of Political Economy,* June 1960.

Wickham, S., "French Planning: Retrospect and Prospect," *Review of Economics and Statistics,* November 1963.

COMMENT

Stanislaw Wellisz, *Columbia University*

My task is to discuss Professor Kindleberger's "catalogue raisoné" of writings and opinions on French planning. The catalogue is comprehensive and well balanced; so a critical review (suggesting, perhaps, some additional entries or correcting minor distortions) would be rather dull. At the end I would have to agree with Professor Kindleberger that after a careful weighing of experts' opinions on French planning, it is not possible to decide what effects planning had on the French economy. The catalogue is excellent, but the task of cataloguing proved to be futile.

Why is it that experts cannot agree on what French planning does? The main reason is, I think, that it is virtually impossible to make meaningful comparisons between the planned French economy and an unplanned "control group." A comparison between the preplan and the planned French economy is meaningless because too many other changes have occurred in the intervening period. Comparisons between planned French development and the development of other West European countries is also unlikely to bring to light the effects of planning. Although France's "planned development" is frequently contrasted with West Germany's "free market growth," the differences between the two systems are much less striking than the similarities. As Angus Maddison said, all the West European countries "in their various ways are free enterprise or neo-capitalist economies, with most production activities in private hands. . . . The state modifies rather than determines the flow of income. The economy [of Western Europe] is a managed market economy." [1] France, West Germany, and the other West European countries are closely connected by trade; they share a common technology and have comparable factor endowments. As a consequence it does not come as too much of a surprise that the French "economic miracle" looks so much like the German or the Italian "economic miracle." [2] These "miracles" provide useful ammunition to the advocates of the various systems, but they are of little help to the scholar who tries to make an appraisal of the comparative virtues of the institutional frameworks. [3]

The alternate approach, that of asking "How well do the French plans come out?" does not seem much more promising at first sight. The difficulties of arriving at a conclusion on the basis of internal evidence are well summed up by Massé:

. . . the Plan is in principle normative, the projection [on which the plan is based] is partly normative and partly predictional. Plan and projection not being identical, the invalidation of the projection does not necessarily mean failure for the plan. This is why the question "To what extent are the French plans implemented" is *ambiguous*. This ambiguity cannot be removed simply by comparing projection with reality. Falling short in relation to the projection is not in itself significant. In measuring the success or failure of the Plan, one must assess, to a certain extent subjectively, the underlying significance of falling short in any particular way. [4]

Taken at its face value, such a statement made by a man who heads the French Planning Commissariat and who combines high technical skills with excellent policy judgment should be enough to discourage any inquiries into the virtues of French planning. Since we cannot make valid international comparisons and since we cannot judge plans by their results, how are we to know (short of accepting the efficacy of French

[1] Angus Maddison, *Economic Growth in the West,* New York, 1964, p. 15.

[2] See Josselyn Hennessy, Vera Lutz, and Giuseppe Scimone, *Economic "Miracles,"* London, 1964.

[3] Of course there exist differences among the institutions of West European countries, as well as differences in economic performance, but if one takes all the important factors under consideration the difference between "planning" and "no planning" is swamped by differences in capital endowment, skills, rates in population growth, external burdens, etc.

[4] Pierre Massé, "The French Plan and Economic Theory," *Econometrica,* April 1965, p. 267.

planning as an article of faith) what French planning does to the economy?

Actually by telling us how not to judge French plans Massé points to a possible method of analysis, which is largely yet to be undertaken.

The first question which may be asked is how well the French planners foresee the development of the economy. For purposes of this inquiry it is irrelevant whether the goodness of the "fit" results from correct forecasting or from plan enforcement. The results of an inquiry which used Theil's inequality coefficients as a measure of fit showed that the "forecast for 1963" implicit in the Fourth French Plan [5] gave a substantially better fit than a GNP blowup, a multiple-regression forecast, and a projection of the 1959 input-output table.[6] The evidence is as yet limited, but further evidence should throw light on the performance of French planners as "forecasters."

Assume for the moment that we have succeeded in establishing the degree of success and of failure of French planners as forecasters. To what extent is the correctness of the forecasts due to the exact nature of the previsions, and to what extent is it ascribable to plan enforcement? To answer this question one must seek to determine the degree of control which the government exercises over plan fulfillment in the different sectors of the economy. If different sectors are equally easy to forecast, then a correlation between the closeness of adherence to the plan and the degree of planners' control gives a measure of plan enforcement.

The primary tool of control over plan enforcement in France consists of controls over financial means, including the granting of preferential credit terms in exchange for cooperation with the planners. In the inquiry referred to above a rank correlation of sixteen sectors of the French economy in terms of (1) plan fulfillment as compared with (2) the degree of reliance on government funds for investment purposes, and (1) plan fulfillment as against (3) the degree of self-financing has yielded rank correlation coefficients of 0.64 and −0.59 respectively, both of which were significant on the 5 per cent level.[7] These results

[5] The Fourth Plan takes 1959 as its starting point and contains a projection for 1965, the plan's final year. At the time of the analysis, the 1965 results were not available; hence, a forecast for 1963 was prepared by interpolating between the initial year of the plan and the final figures. The alternate forecasts were prepared on the basis of the same data as the plan.

[6] Armand Van Nimmen, "French Planning: An Essay in Evaluation," paper presented at International Economics Workshop, Columbia University, Spring 1965 (mimeographed).

[7] The "predictability" of the various sectors was checked by comparing forecasts and forecast outcomes for the corresponding sectors in various European countries; no significant correlation was obtained between "predictability" and plan fulfillment in France.

do not constitute a proof positive of plan enforcement, but they point to a method for the elimination of the mystery surrounding French planning.

A third question, perhaps the most important of all, concerns the effects of the plans on the economy. If planning influences resource allocation, we should be able to compare the results of the sectors which closely fulfill the plans with those which deviate from the plans—and to observe differences. We may assume, for instance, that the plan strives to achieve a Pareto-optimal resource distribution at the end of the planning period. If the plan were correctly formulated, and if all branches of industry conformed to the plan, there would be equal marginal rates of return in all the industrial branches. Upward deviations from the plan would result in a lower, and downward deviations in a higher, marginal rate of return. The theoretical conclusions can be translated into a testable hypothesis, all the more easily since France has a well-developed stock market. Alternate formulations of the goals of planning can also be made, and they can be translated into empirically testable propositions. Unfortunately, the data available to the public are so highly aggregated that they do not lend themselves to this sort of analysis. The answer-seeker will have to fight his way into the commissariat's archives where (rumor has it) there is a vast treasure of detailed information.

The results of any quantitative investigation will have to be tempered by good judgment. The commissariat does valuable work "in opposing state intervention that distorts the normal price fixing mechanism without due reason" [8] and in fighting against irrational meddling by policymakers. On the other hand, the commissariat does a substantial amount of meddling on its own. Moreover, while the widespread participation in the work of specialized commissions contributes to the diffusion of important economic information, it also gives an opportunity to business to form exclusive arrangements and to monopolize the economy. Such factors cannot readily be quantified, but they must be taken into account in an over-all appraisal of French planning. Yet the core of an appraisal must consist of quantitative analysis. An inquiry which limits itself to literary weighing of possible advantages and of possible disadvantages of planning cannot yield fruitful conclusions, no matter how well informed the inquirer. Professor Kindleberger has most skillfully weighed all the literary economists' opinions, yet all that he (and we) have learned is that opinions differ.

[8] Massé, *Econometrica*, April 1965, p. 273.

Planning in India

RICHARD S. ECKAUS

MASSACHUSETTS INSTITUTE OF TECHNOLOGY

Introduction

Indian planning is an open process. Much of the controversy and the debates that accompany the preparation of the plans are public. The initial aggregate calculations and assumptions are either explicitly stated or readily deducible, and the makers of the plans are not only sensitive but responsive to criticism and suggestions from a wide variety of national and international sources. From original formulation through successive modifications to parliamentary presentation, plan making in India has evolved as a responsive democratic political process.

NOTE: An unusually large group of people have made major contributions to the research on which this paper is based, so much so, in fact, that the author feels he should be regarded as the *rapporteur* of a joint effort, especially with respect to the formulation of the model described. Yet, each individual might present and evaluate the results differently; so no one but the author is responsible for the opinions of this paper and any errors which it might contain. Credit for whatever merit there may be is shared with Professor S. Chakravarty of the Delhi School of Economics, Professor Louis Lefeber of Brandeis University, who participated in the original version of this paper, and Dr. Kirit Parikh, research associate of the Center for International Studies, M.I.T. The author is also indebted to Professors Max Millikan and P. N. Rosenstein-Rodan of M.I.T. Assistance has been provided by Mrinal Datta-Chaudhuri, Dr. T. Krishnam, Dr. Jayant Shah, and T. Weisskopf which has gone far beyond doing calculations to order, and the author regards them as having been close associates. Professor Nino Andreatta of the University of Bologna; Dr. Ashish Chakravarti, Indian Statistical Institute; James A. Mirrlees, Cambridge University; and Dr. Per Sevaldson of the Central Bureau of Statistics, Oslo, Norway, were instrumental in starting the original project; and their early advice has continued to be useful. The research has been financed by the India Project of the Center for International Studies, M.I.T., and the U.S. Agency for International Development, neither of which is responsible for the analysis and opinions expressed here. The M.I.T. Computation Center has been generous and cooperative in making its facilities available.

In revising the paper after the conference, the comments of Professors A. Manne and T. Koopmans were particularly helpful.

The wide political participation in the preparation of the plan is understandable if one realizes that the plan is not only intended as a set of prescriptions for economic behavior but represents the diverse aspirations of a nation for social advancement. Yet, the nation is not a homogeneous political entity; it is composed of a variety of regional, linguistic, economic, cultural, and political groups. The many particular and frequently contradictory interests of each of these groups have to be recognized and to the degree it is possible, accommodated within the framework of the plans. The political process which leads to the formulation of the final document is undoubtedly an impressive manifestation of the workings of an open society. By its very nature it generates many problems from the point of view of mapping an optimal strategy for economic development. Though there has been a considerable amount of debate over the plans, there has been relatively little explicit attention given to alternative strategies or paths of economic growth and development. In fact the political discussions have been only tangentially concerned with questions of alternative compositions of national targets and much more with the capacity for saving and taxation, problems of direct controls and price stability. The latter are, of course, directly related to the setting of social-economic goals and to the mapping of the paths leading toward them. However, the relationships have not been spelled out, and the significance of the plan targets for current and future welfare has been left implicit.

Although participation in the debates which accompany the preparation of the plans is widespread, unfortunately it has not been well informed either on the welfare implications of the plan goals or on many other plan implications. Planning efforts have been absorbed in attempting to make a single plan whose goals, resource requirements, and resource availabilities were consistent. Alternative policies have received only limited consideration in part because the alternatives remain relatively unknown. Plausible and consistent alternative plans are difficult to prepare, and the enormous amount of information needed for their formulation is not readily available to individuals and organizations outside the central government. Hence, in order for a range of alternatives to be available for consideration, the Planning Commission and the concerned ministries would have had to prepare them, and this has not been done. The preparation of alternative plans and the comparison of their implications is not advocated as a service to potential critics. It is an essential part of the planning process, for only in this way can the full implications of any single plan be appreciated.

This criticism of Indian planning must be seen in proper perspective.

No conceptually satisfactory techniques of planning or more generally of making economic policy for development were readily at hand when the Indian plans were first being made. Even now, in spite of considerable progress the operational techniques are relatively crude. Among the less-developed countries the Indian approach to planning is one of the most sophisticated. It may be just because of this fact that higher standards are set in judging Indian performance than would be appropriate elsewhere.

There are many important aspects of Indian planning which will not be dealt with in this paper. In particular, issues related to implementation of the plans will not be discussed. However, this omission should not be taken as implying that the issues of plan implementation are unimportant. After a brief discussion of the techniques and functions of planning in India the focus will turn to a method of analyzing the implications for development of alternative targets and the significance of such alternatives. This is, I believe, one area in which more intensive economic analysis can help improve planning procedures.

The Techniques of Indian Planning

The First Five-year Plan, though prepared in haste, embodied a projection of an aggregate growth path generated by capital accumulation and financed largely by domestic saving described by a linear savings function. The aggregate growth model was of a Harrod-Domar type; however, the linearity of the savings function implied a marginal savings rate higher than the average. This in turn indicated a decreasing reliance on foreign assistance in spite of the higher levels of investment projected. This simple model, it should be noted, was a projection, not a plan which could be implemented, although it did have implications for policy with respect to foreign exchange availability and government saving. Sectoral investment allocations were determined in the public sector by the particular projects which were proposed. A glance at the First Plan will dispel, however, any notion that there was a lack of concern for the distant future. This plan had in fact the most explicit set of aggregate calculations. Yet it is not surprising that at this early stage detailed analyses were not made of the significance of alternative future compositions of output.

In the formulation of the Second Plan a simple aggregative Harrod-Domar growth model was again used for over-all projections with parameters that were based on an optimistic extrapolation of the First Plan experience. For the purpose of answering questions about the strategy of resource allocation to such broadly defined sectors as agriculture and industry, Professor P. C. Mahalanobis, director of the Indian Statistical Institute and member of the Planning Commission, prepared two- and four-sector models which may have been influential in drawing up the Plan.[1] The two-sector model, reminiscent of the Foldman model,[2] was used to demonstrate the relations between the allocation of investment between the sectors and the over-all growth rate. It distinguishes consumer goods and investment goods, the latter usable to create capacity in either sector. A linear structure of production is assumed and a constant marginal utility of consumption, so that future and present consumption would provide the same benefits. The model ignores foreign trade and consumption maintenance requirements for labor. Given these conditions it follows that the long-run rate of growth depends on the relative allocation of investment to the capital goods producing sector. While the conclusion will not necessarily be maintained if the assumptions are modified the model did serve the purpose of emphasizing the significance of the choice of planning horizon.

Mahalanobis's four-sector model was intended to indicate the investment allocations which would achieve prescribed growth rates and employment levels. Here, again, foreign trade was ignored, and demand conditions for investment and consumption were taken into account only insofar as the investment allocation suggested by the two-sector model could be assumed to be relevant. Both models were too limited in scope to indicate the most desirable allocation of resources among interdependent sectors. No attempt was made to find optimal allocations; dynamic interrelations were not taken into account; and the targets were defined in highly aggregative terms. The models were not employed to examine the significance of alternative long-term programs and in fact could have been used for that purpose only with substantial modification.

The detailed program of the Second Plan consisted of a collection of particular projects including both unfinished First Plan undertakings and proposals for new ones. Though the sum total of the

---

[1] "The Approach of Operational Research to Planning in India," and "Draft Plan Frame for the Second Five Year Plan," *Sankhya,* December 1955, pp. 3–89. These models have been the subject of a number of critical analyses which will not, therefore, be repeated here. See S. Tsuru, "Some Theoretical Doubts on India's Plan Frame," *Economic Weekly* (annual number), January 1957; S. Chakravarty, *The Logic of Investment Planning,* pp. 43–48; R. Komiya, "A Note on Professor Mahalanobis' Model of Indian Economic Planning" *Review of Economics and Statistics,* February 1959, pp. 29–35.

[2] See E. Domar, "A Soviet Model of Growth," *Essays in the Theory of Economic Growth,* 1957, pp. 223–62.

investment costs of these projects was subject to over-all constraints derived from the aggregate projections, there were nonetheless enough residual or "buffer" sectors to reduce the constraining influence of aggregate resource limitations on these projects. The exception was the limitation imposed by the scarcity of foreign exchange; however, this restriction operated primarily not as aggregate constraint but in terms of availability of foreign exchange financing for separate projects.

There was no explicit mechanism visible in the Second Plan for coordinating the development of the various sectors so as to avoid either bottlenecks or surpluses. To the extent that coordination and scheduling was achieved it was through the screening procedures of the interministerial committees and working groups that met with Planning Commission representatives. These committees were responsible for the setting of the detailed targets in the plans, as well as for the approval and phasing of projects. As one of their working tools these committees apparently did prepare commodity balances for the entire plan period, at least for particular items and sectors.

However, one must not conclude with the impression that the setting of the targets and the design of projects was or is now left entirely to the deliberations of expert working committees of the central government. The economic influence of the Indian states makes itself felt both at the highest political levels and through negotiations with the Planning Commission and the other union ministries. The state governments come to the center not only as petitioners but as powerful advocates backed by substantial resources. They are determined to have a voice not only in matters affecting their regional economies, such as the location of new plants, but on over-all economic policy as well.

The approach to the Third Plan was similar to that taken in the preparation of the Second Plan. Again there were macroeconomic projections which, though less explicit, were accompanied this time by a clearer recognition of the alternative possible values of parameters which in turn made some of the parameters themselves a matter of policy. One of the initial and continuing debates over the formulation of the Third Plan concerned the over-all magnitude of the plan in relation to aggregate resource availabilities.[3] This time, however, there was no apparent attempt to use models such as those prepared by Professor Mahalanobis for the formulation of the Second Plan for determining sectoral priorities. Instead, the consultation and review procedures appear to have

[3] As an aspect of this discussion see I. M. D. Little, "Tax Policy and the Third Plan," *Pricing and Fiscal Policies, A Study in Method,* ed. P. N. Rosenstein-Rodan, Cambridge, Mass., 1964, pp. 30–76.

operated more intensively and the calculations of commodity balances were done more extensively, in more detail and with greater attention given to improving the basic data. It is impossible for an outsider to reconstruct the procedures by which relative priorities and scheduling were established. The interplay of ministerial and state and local ambitions appear in some cases to have had as much influence as any over-all direction from the Planning Commission itself. Indeed as John Lewis pointed out, a framework was not provided by the Planning Commission or by any of the ministries in which these various interests could be reconciled in a drive toward coordinated objectives.[4]

The detailed supervision of target setting, project choice, and resource allocation by groups of experienced persons can go quite far in taking into account the most significant economic interactions. This is particularly true when there are only limited feedback effects of one committee's decisions on the work of other committees. However, India is too large a country and its economy is too complex for such a condition to hold completely. Of course, where interactions exist, overlapping committee membership and pyramided committee organization can at least partially recognize and account for feedback effects. More than that, no mechanical model of planning could ever substitute for the judgment which such a system of committees could bring to bear on the formulation of policy. At the same time the system is necessarily a cumbersome one, and its operation could be significantly improved by providing these committees better analytical tools than are currently available.

Though Indian planning is an open process with broad political participation, it is also true that the latter has, for the most part, made itself felt on the marginal rather than on the central issues. This is in part because the central issues which relate to questions of welfare, income distribution, time preference, and the social control of economic activities have not always been adequately identified.

In addition to the Planning Commission and economic ministries there are other groups formally charged with economic planning responsibilities: the National Development Council, the advisory committees

---

[4] See John P. Lewis, "India," *Planning Economic Development,* ed. Everett B. Hagen, 1963, pp. 98–104 and also his *Quiet Crisis in India,* Washington, 1962, especially Chaps. 4 and 5. Lewis's description of a "planning backward" approach in which a set of final demands are broken down by steps into specific phased projects would have provided a clearer conceptual framework than that which appears to have dominated the Planning Commission. However, the detailed means of its implementation are by no means clear in Lewis's description, nor does this approach provide adequate recognition of the issues involved in setting the final demand goals, the constraints of initial conditions, and the importance of generating alternative plans.

on problems of individual sectors, and a consultative committee of members of Parliament. There are also informal groupings such as the consultative committee of the Prime Minister.[5] For various reasons including inadequate staff, limited time, and, in some cases, with limited significance given to their roles, these groups have not provided guidance for informed political participation in the process of planning. As a consequence, in the procedures for formulation of the plans there has been relatively little consideration of the specific composition of economic targets in the light of social preferences concerning present and future consumption subject to resource availabilities.[6] These issues have tended to become prime subjects of political debate only under the pressure of a new budget embodying substantial tax increases or under the impact of price inflation.

The Functions of Indian Planning

The function of economic planning is to provide guidelines for the use of scarce resources and to indicate the methods of implementation. But what is the practical content of this function in the mixed government–private enterprise system of India? The aggregative growth models implicit in the plans have not provided particulars of economic policy but rough guidelines to total resource requirements. They have had only general implications for the government's current and capital budget, over-all investment licensing, foreign exchange use, as well as fiscal and monetary policy. Although the Indian plans encompass the entire economy, the decisions of the private sector can be only partially controlled by the government. Hence, the Indian plans as for most mixed economies naturally speak with greater authority about the government than the private sectors. The five-year plans are sometimes represented as a set of detailed blueprints of a development program. It is nearer to the truth to characterize the plans as a general statement of government intentions as to its own programs as well as with respect to those sec-

[5] An informative description of the administrative and organizational structure of the Indian planning process is given in S. R. Sen, *Planning Machinery in India*, Economic Commission for Asia and the Far East, Conference of Asian Economic Planners, New Delhi, 1961.

[6] However, this does not mean that Indian planning is particularly backward in this respect. The same criticism would be valid for most planning activities. Fundamental criticisms of the planning process have been raised in India by Professor Shenoy of Ahmedabad University among others. Professor Shenoy's objections are so basic, however, that they would appear to be more easily avoided than would the criticisms of persons committed in a general way to the prevailing brand of Indian socialism but skeptical of its implementation.

toral programs open to private initiative. As far as implementation is concerned, public sector projects can be carried out subject only to government financial and organizational constraints. For example, the plans contain extensive chapters on such specific topics as community organization and development, conservation, education and training, family and health planning, and scientific and technological research. All of these are important and proper concerns of development policy. At the same time, these are the programs whose precise effects on economic development are difficult to assess. Furthermore, many of these programs are carried out by the state governments which in the Indian federal system have major responsibility for agricultural policy, education, and welfare programs. Although the state governments are fully involved in the planning process, their effectiveness in implementing the plans is often lower than that of the union government. This is due partly to the generally lesser administrative capacity of the local governments. In addition, and perhaps more importantly, the inevitable political differences among the states, which cannot be fully resolved, manifest themselves in varying degrees of commitment to particular plan objectives.

As mentioned above, the plans cannot be detailed blueprints for those sectors which are predominantly reserved for private initiative. In these areas the plans indicate the types and levels of activity which are considered to be consistent with the over-all targets. Control of expansion is exercised by means of investment licensing and foreign exchange quotas and other controls on resource allocation. Furthermore, guidance to private investors is provided through the publication of sectoral targets and access to the "industries officers" of the various ministries as well as by the agricultural extension members. In certain instances extension of private investment over and above the targeted levels has been permitted. This was, for instance, notably the case during the Second Plan, when the rate of expansion of coal mining scheduled for the government sector was not achieved and private mining companies made up the deficiency.

The public sector can be directed toward plan targets by administrative fiat and with the financial resources of the central and state governments. The private sector cannot be so directed. Its response to economic incentives is regulated by the extensive system of direct controls. The incentives themselves are modified by monetary and fiscal policy. However, the goals of free market forces and of plan targets do not necessarily coincide, and the operations of the private sector have not always been well coordinated with those of the public sector and with plan targets. Shortfalls in production, investment licenses which are allowed to lapse, and unforeseen price increases are all signs of inadequacies in carrying out this intrinsically difficult task.[7]

The function of the plans in setting the context and climate for private activity can hardly be overemphasized. More than what can be accomplished with general statements of intent and speeches, the plans give quantitative indications of the rate and direction in which the government intends to move the economy. The quantitative specifications of the plans attempt to project precise relationships between activities in the government and the private sectors. Given the natural sensitivity of private enterprise to India's avowedly socialist goals, it is particularly important to have concrete and explicit statements of government policy toward private business. The plans play an even larger role, however. To dismiss as window dressing the ringing phrases contained in the introductory chapters of the plans would be a mistaken reaction, and more than that, it would indicate a lack of understanding of the catalytic effect of planning on Indian society. The plans provide symbolic leadership and orientation to a developing society.

Description of a Planning Model [8]

Indian planning will be analyzed in this paper by means of a linear programing model in which the intertemporal relations involved in planning are treated explicitly. It is a programing model because optimization with respect to constraints is presumably what planners try to do. Linearity is an unfortunate restriction which for the present is imposed by analytical, computational, and information constraints. Compared to the real world and to certain aspects of planning procedures actually

[7] It has been a continuing complaint about Indian planning by Indian businessmen, and many foreign observers as well, that the private sector has suffered from excessive controls and inadequate incentives. This may reflect, however, a set of goals different from the plan targets as well as mistakes in calculation of what is necessary to achieve the targets. These issues will not be followed up here though they are far-reaching in their significance.

[8] The model used in this study is a generalization of the model presented in R. S. Eckaus and L. Lefeber, "Capital Formation: A Theoretical and Empirical Analysis," *Review of Economics and Statistics,* May 1962, pp. 113–22 and L. Lefeber, "A Simple Optimizing Planning Model," *Capital Formation and Economic Development,* ed. P. N. Rosenstein-Rodan, Cambridge, Mass., 1964, pp. 83–109. It has been further developed by the contributions of Lefeber, Chakravarty, Parikh, and the author. It has a clear heritage from the programing models of Chapters 11 and 12 of *Linear Programming and Economic Analysis,* New York, 1956, by R. Dorfman, P. A. Samuelson, and R. Solow. P. Sevaldson and Professor N. Andreatta were instrumental in recommending the approach.

in use the model is a gross simplification in a number of respects. In other aspects it is more sophisticated than methods currently used. It should be emphasized at the outset that the model is not intended nor able to produce the "best" possible plan for India. It is a device for checking consistency and exploring alternatives. After presenting the model and some of the results obtained by it the strengths and weaknesses of the approach will be evaluated.

The maximand of the model is the weighted sum of annual aggregate consumption for the entire planning period, T, which at five years is that of the Indian plans. This is a linear objective function:

$$(1) \qquad U = \sum_{t=1}^{T} w(t)C(t)$$

In Equation (1) $w(t)$ represents the relative weight placed on consumption in period t. The ratio between pairs of adjacent weights reflects a social discount factor. Thus, setting the weight corresponding to the first time period equal to 1, the value of the objective function corresponds to the present discounted value of the stream of aggregate consumption over the entire plan period. The discount rate is assumed to remain constant over the plan horizon.[9]

Though the model is multisectoral, consumption is treated in the objective function as a single, composite commodity since it is stipulated that sectoral outputs enter consumption in fixed proportions. In Equation (2), $F(t)$ represents the column vector of sectoral outputs designated for consumption, and c is a diagonal matrix whose elements indicate the composition of $C(t)$:

$$(2) \qquad cC(t) \leq F(t); \; c = |c_i|; \sum_i c_i = 1, \text{ for } t = 1, \ldots, T$$

Although the use of a composite good as the consumption variable is undoubtedly a major abstraction it has computational merit in that it avoids the nonlinearities which may be associated with explicit demand elasticities and also circumvents the problem of separately weighting each good that enters consumption. This undoubted advantage has to be balanced against the damage done to reality by the imposition of a constraint which forbids substitution among types of consumption. In interpreting the significance of the assumption with respect to the computations to be presented, it should be kept in mind,

---

[9] The assumption of constant discount rate is necessary to avoid the "regret" problem of R. Strotz, analyzed in "Myopia and Inconsistency in Dynamic Utility Maximization," *Review of Economic Studies,* 1956, pp. 165–80.

however, that the level of aggregation is quite high. It is unlikely that in a country like India the composition of consumption would change very much among grossly defined sectors over such a short period as five years. In any case, this is only a convenient formulation, and the consumption proportions will be varied by exogenous specification, taking income levels into account, in order to explore the implications of alternative composition.[10]

Annual consumption levels provided by a plan cannot be set without taking into account socially desired levels and growth rates of consumption, such as satisfaction of "minimum requirements" and either a stable or monotonically increasing pattern. Substantial fluctuations in consumption are not likely to be politically acceptable. Yet, in this model's solutions, satisfactory levels and growth rates of consumption cannot be assured if they are not explicitly imposed as constraints. The behavior of consumption over time will otherwise depend on the inter-relationships between the productivity of the system, the discount rate, initial endowments, and terminal requirements. Depending on the relative magnitudes of these quantities consumption behavior could be monotonic but concentrated at the beginning or end of the planning period or fluctuate over time.

To ensure a rising pattern of consumption over time a set of "monotonicity" constraints are added as shown in (3).

$$(3) \qquad C(t+1) \geqq C(t)(1+\rho), \text{ for } t = 1, \ldots, T-1$$

These inequalities require that consumption in any one period must be at least as great as consumption in the previous period augmented by a growth factor $(1+\rho)$ where ρ is a politically determined parameter, which will presumably take into account the population growth rate. A lower bound is also placed on $C(1)$ to ensure that at least a minimum level of consumption is attained in the first period. This is shown by relationship (4).[11]

$$(4) \qquad\qquad C(1) \geqq \overline{C(1)}$$

There are other relations which explain the availability and other uses of resources and output: the products of the different sectors may

---

[10] Pseudovariable proportions can be introduced into the market basket by stipulating overlapping upper and lower limits within which the proportions themselves can change. T. Weisskopf has experimented with consumption goods composed on this principle. The disadvantage is computational, and is due to the inevitable increase in the number of inequalities.

[11] In the computations actually carried out for this paper the constraint in (4) was frequently not imposed for reasons explained below.

be used as inputs into current production, for capital formation, and for the satisfaction of government and export demand. Furthermore, these products may originate from domestic output or imports or—in some suitable combination—from both. This is described by the distribution relationships shown in (5), of which there is a set for each time period.

$$(5) \quad aX(t) + F(t) + N(t) + Q(t) + H(t) + G(t) +$$

$$E(t) - M(t) - X(t) \leqq 0, \text{ for } t = 1, \ldots, T$$

All terms of this sum are to be read as column vectors, the elements of which represent the different uses of the outputs of each sector. a is the Leontief matrix of input coefficients and $X(t)$ is the column vector of the domestic outputs corresponding to all sectors. Hence, the product, a column vector, shows the sum of the intermediate demands by all sectors for the goods of each sector.[12] Other uses, i.e., consumption, new capital formation, capital replacement, inventory accumulation, government consumption, and exports are represented by the column vectors $F(t), N(t), Q(t), H(t), G(t)$, and $E(t)$, respectively, of which the last two will be stipulated exogenously. The negative term $M(t)$ is a column vector of supplies from imported sources.

Domestic production requires only capital capacity. The production functions are described in (6).

$$(6) \quad bX(t) - K(t) \leqq 0; \text{ where } b = |b_{ij}|, \text{ for } t = 1, \ldots, T$$

b is a diagonal matrix composed of capital-output ratios. Capacity, $K(t)$, is a composite capital which is committed to a particular sector, but which may change from period to period depending on the rate of depreciation and the investment which is carried out in that sector.

The formation of capacity in each sector is shown in (7), where $Z(t + 1)$ denotes new capacity which first becomes available for use in period $(t + 1)$. $D(t + 1)$ is the amount of capital stock which is disabled by the depreciation of some part of it. $R(t + 1)$ is the amount of the disabled capital stock which is made productive again by the replacement of the depreciated component.

$$(7) \quad K(t + 1) - K(t) - Z(t + 1) + D(t + 1) - R(t + 1) \leqq 0,$$

$$\text{for } t = 1, \ldots, T + 2$$

New additions to capacity are formed by blending different sectoral outputs in fixed proportions and with specified gestation periods. Thus,

[12] The a matrix itself, of course, is a summary of many production relationships.

in order to have the desired capacity increase in a particular sector available at period t, designated parts of it must be completed in periods $t - 1$, $t - 2$, and $t - 3$.[13] p_1, p_2, and p_3 are matrices which indicate the proportions in which each sector must deliver output to form capacity which is to become effective one, two, and three periods later. Thus,

$$(8) \quad p_1 Z(t + 1) + p_2 Z(t + 2) + p_3 Z(t + 3) - N(t) \leqq 0,$$

$$\text{for } t + 1, \ldots, T$$

To account for depreciation a "one-horse-shay" model of capital is assumed, so that productive services flow from capital at a constant rate after its creation until the end of its lifetime, at which point it loses all productivity. Capital lifetimes of twenty years for equipment and thirty-three years for construction are assumed, so that within a five-year planning model depreciation is exogenous. Given the different lifetimes for different components, productive capacity is lost by the depreciation of only a part of a unit of capital and, likewise, may be restored by the replacement of only the depreciated part. The depreciation in each period is

$$(9) \qquad D(t) = \overline{D(t)}, \text{ for } t = 1, \ldots, T + 3$$

The proportions of depreciation of each type in each sector are indicated by a square matrix r whose terms are D_{ij}/D_j. The terms r_{ij}/p_{ij} are the ratios of depreciation proportions to the proportions in which the component parts are required for capacity. Thus, multiplying $D_j(t)$ by r_{ij}/p_{ij} will indicate the productive capacity lost through depreciation of each component. The actual capacity lost in each sector is the maximum of $D_j(t)$ $(r_{1j}/p_{1j}, r_{2j}/p_{2j}, \ldots, r_{nj}/p_{nj})$. The diagonal matrix d is formed from the matrix each of whose terms is the maximum of r_{ij}/p_{ij} for each i and j. The capacity lost through depreciation is then

$$(10) \qquad V(t) = D(t)[d], \text{ for } t = 1, \ldots, T + 3$$

The optimizing mechanism can now decide to restore all or part of the depreciated capacity by replacing the worn-out components. Thus,

$$(11) \qquad\qquad R(t) \leqq V(t)$$

[13] Alternatively, it would have been possible to provide for deliveries of investment goods with variable gestation periods on which lower bounds would be set. This would provide additional flexibility which might in some circumstances be of particular utility as it would permit uncompleted investment to be carried over without penalty. This latter formulation was not chosen for several reasons. It would, first of all, increase the computational burden. Secondly, on the basis of admittedly casual observation, this additional flexibility does not appear to be practically an important phenomenon.

Like new investment, replacement requires a gestation period depending on the type of component. So deliveries for replacement must look three periods ahead to the actual replacement which the model decides to undertake, i.e.,

$$(12) \quad Q(t) = r^1[d]^{-1}R(t+1) + r^2[d]^{-1}R(t+2) +$$
$$r^3[d]^{-1}R(t+3), \text{ for } t = 1, \ldots, T$$

In addition to capacity formation, capital formation takes place also in the form of inventory accumulation. Assuming that the latter is proportionate to changes in the levels of sectoral outputs, the demand for inventory increases, $H(t)$, is described by relationship (13).

$$(13) \quad s[X(t+1) - X(t)] = H(t); \; s = |s_i|, \text{ for } t = 1, \ldots, T$$

In order to provide a basis for computing inventories in the first period an "anticipated" level of output is specified equal to $(1 + \alpha)[\overline{X(0)}]$. Thus,

$$(14) \qquad H(1) = s\{X(2) - (1 + \alpha)[\overline{X(0)}]\}$$

s is a diagonal matrix of coefficients for inventory change.

Government demands for goods and services are exogenously stipulated for each sector.

$$(15) \qquad G(t) = \overline{G(t)}, \text{ for } t = 1, \ldots, T$$

Exports are also specified exogenously:

$$(16) \qquad E(t) = \overline{E(t)}, \text{ for } t = 1, \ldots, T$$

Foreign aid and long-term capital movements, i.e., foreign transfers, are also exogenously determined. The sum of the two, $FA(t)$, expressed in constant domestic currency, plus exports, $FA(t) + \sum_i E_i(t)$, defines the availability of foreign exchange at any time period. The sum of imports by all sectors must, of course, not exceed the availability of foreign exchange. This is shown by relationship (17).

$$(17) \quad \sum_i M_i(t) \leqq FA(t) + \sum_i E_i(t), \text{ for } t = 1, \ldots, T$$

In a linear model such as that presented here the solution would necessarily involve a movement toward specialization of imports. In this case unconstrained specialization would manifest itself by allocating all foreign exchange resources so as totally to replace domestic production by imports in one or a few sectors.[14] This kind of specialization in a highly aggregated system would inject an extreme lack of realism into the solution. At the same time the model should be given some freedom to allocate foreign exchange to the sectors where it is most useful. This is done by imposing both import ceilings in all importing sectors and import floors where such should be necessary. The latter consists of sectoral minimum import requirements that are "noncompetitive" in the special sense that they must be satisfied before other imports are allowed. If foreign exchange is left over after these minimums are satisfied, it is allocated according to cost advantage, i.e., competitively, to other sectors.[15] But now the import ceilings become operational; so imports cannot completely displace domestic production in any one sector.

Relationship (18) describes the division of total imports into noncompetitive imports, $\left[\sum_i M_i{}^1(t)\right]$ and competitive imports $\left[\sum_i M_i{}^2(t)\right]$.

These are obtained for each time period by summing over the sectoral amounts.

$$(18) \quad \sum_i M_i(t) = \sum_i M_i{}^1(t) + \sum_i M_i{}^2(t), \text{ for } t = 1, \ldots, T$$

Import floors, i.e., the minimum levels of noncompetitive imports, are determined for each sector in terms of given proportions $m_i{}^1$ of the sectoral domestic outputs. This is shown by (19).

$$(19) \quad M_i{}^1(t) = m_i{}^1 X_i(t), \text{ for } t = 1, \ldots, T$$

Whatever foreign exchange is left over after satisfying noncompetitive input requirements can be distributed for competitive imports with the

[14] If some foreign exchange were left over after the total displacement of domestic production in one or more sectors, it would be allocated to another sector where, as a consequence, domestic production and imports would take place simultaneously. This, of course, would not contradict the contention that the system moves toward specialization; it means only that the system, quite sensibly, would not throw away good foreign exchange resources.

[15] Cost advantage depends on the initial distribution of capital capacities as well as the structure of production coefficients. Therefore, the allocation of the foreign exchange resources may be dominated by the initial conditions rather than a more comprehensive interpretation of cost advantage. Furthermore, changes in foreign prices are also neglected, and exports are exogenously stipulated. Hence the concept of cost advantages is different in a number of respects from a dynamic interpretation of Ricardian comparative advantage.

limitation that not more than a given proportion m_i^2 of the remaining foreign exchange can be spent for imports in that sector. This is described under (20).

$$(20) \quad M_i^2(t) \leqq m_i^2(t)[FA(t) + \sum_i E_i(t) - \sum_i M_i^1(t)],$$

$$\text{for } t = 1, \ldots, T$$

$\sum_i m_i^2$ must be chosen so as to exceed unity; otherwise the maximizing

mechanism has no freedom to allocate competitive imports according to cost advantage.

Up to this point constraints have been described which relate to the intraplan periods. The determination of the initial and terminal conditions must now be described. The initial conditions summarize the productive capacity of the economy in existence at the start of the planning period, i.e., the initial capital stocks $K(1)$. Furthermore, since capacity increases follow a lagged gestation pattern, the incomplete projects from the preplan period which are available for completion during the first years of the plan must also be specified. Their completion may or may not be efficient—the decision on this is left to the optimizing mechanism. The initial conditions in the form of column vectors are shown in (21). Capacity increases maturing in the first period are not listed since they are already included in $K(1)$ as potentially active productive capacity at the beginning of the plan.

$$(21) \quad K(1) = \overline{K(1)}; I^3(0) = \overline{I^3(0)}; I^2(0) = \overline{I^2(0)}; I^2(-1) = $$
$$\overline{I^2(-1)}$$

$I^2(0)$, for example, is the investment carried out in period 0 for completion in period 2.

While the initial conditions reflect the state of the economy when the planning period begins, the terminal conditions summarize the state of the economy to be attained by the end of the planning period. For a variety of reasons plans must be truncated at some point, and it is the function of the terminal conditions to reflect the postplan future into the planning period. Barring terminal capital requirements set so high as to be infeasible, the planner has considerable scope for choice with respect to these terminal conditions. The issues related to this choice have received so little explicit attention in Indian planning that it is hard to avoid the belief that their significance has not been adequately appreciated. Although there are good reasons for making short plans, the choice of a planning period is essentially arbitrary. Yet short plans should be consistent with both the long-run and continuing goals of society as well as more immediate needs. The former objectives will include raising the standard of living of the nation; the latter, for example, may reflect urgently felt military requirements. There are a variety of techniques which can be employed to bring these postplan considerations within the purview of a truncated planning period.

The terminal conditions will be set in two ways in the solutions which follow. First the targets of the Third Plan will be used. They will be extrapolated by means of the sectoral intraplan growth rates as a basis for determining the investment necessary within the plan period for postplan period growth. With such terminal conditions the model will be called the Target Model and its solutions, Target solutions. The next analysis will use a method of setting targets which makes them endogenously determined as part of the solution. The technique is a variation of that presented by Chakravarty and Eckaus [16] and by R. Stone and Alan Brown.[17] The level of composite consumption attained in the last period of planning is taken as the basis for the future growth path of consumption. Even in this case, government purchases, exports, and foreign exchange reserves (exports plus foreign aid) continue to be specified exogenously. Thus, because the last period's consumption is an endogenously determined variable of the optimizing system, the post-terminal sectoral output levels required to sustain a given rate of post-terminal consumption growth also become endogenously determined variables. Since in this case the model solution provides an optimal transition to exogenously specified post-terminal growth rates it will be called the Transit Model; and its solutions, Transit solutions.[18]

The determination of the post-terminal sectoral output levels required to sustain a given rate of consumption growth is shown by relationships (22) and (23). Equation (22) is the distribution relationship (5) into which the appropriate growth terms have been substituted, and (23) is the sum of the particular solutions corresponding to the nonhomogeneous elements of the post-terminal growth: consumption, government, exports and imports. The homogeneous elements in (22) relate to interindustry flows and to gross capital formation as well as inventory requirements.

[16] S. Chakravarty and R. S. Eckaus, "An Approach to a Multisectoral Planning Model," *Capital Formation and Economic Development,* especially pp. 112–15. General considerations involved in setting terminal conditions are discussed in S. Chakravarty and R. S. Eckaus, "Choice Elements in Intertemporal Planning," *Capital Formation . . . ,* pp. 68–83.

[17] *A Computable Model of Economic Growth,* London, 1962.

[18] The nomenclature in the first version of this paper was not so specific. Originally what is now called the Transit Model was called the Basic Model and the Target Model was not given a name.

They are the terms multiplied by the b, d, and s coefficients. The non-homogeneous elements are the terms indicating the growth of C, G, E, and M, based on the levels which they attain in the last plan period and the exogenously stipulated growth rates.

$$(22) \quad X(t) = aX(t) + b^1[X(t + 1) - X(t)] + b^2[X(t + 2)] +$$
$$b^3[X(t + 3) - X(t + 2)] + s[X(t + 1) - X(t)] +$$
$$(1 + \phi)^{t-T}F(T) + (1 + \delta)^{t-T}R(T) + (1 +$$
$$\gamma)^{t-T}G(T) + (1 + \epsilon)^{t-T}E(T) + (1 + \mu)^{t-T}M(T),$$
$$\text{for } t = T + 1, T + 2, T + 3$$

$$(23) \quad X(t) = [I - a - (b^1 + s)\phi - b^2(1 + \phi)\phi - b^3(1 +$$
$$\phi)^2\phi]F(T)(1 + \phi)^{t-T} + [I - a - (b^1 + s)\delta -$$
$$b^2(1 + \delta)\delta - b^3(1 + \delta)^2\delta]R(T)(1 + \delta)^{t-T} +$$
$$[I - a - (b^1 + s)\gamma - b^2(1 + \gamma)\gamma - b^3(1 +$$
$$\gamma)^2\gamma]G(T)(1 + \gamma)^{t-T} + [I - a - (b^1 + s)\epsilon -$$
$$b^2(1 + \epsilon)\epsilon - b^3(1 + \epsilon)^2\epsilon]E(T)(1 + \epsilon)^{t-T} +$$
$$[I - a - (b^1 + s)\mu - b^2(1 + \mu)\mu - b^3(1 +$$
$$\mu)^2\mu]M(T)(1 + \mu)^{t-T}, \text{for } t = T + 1, T + 2, T + 3$$

The b coefficients are defined by

$$(24) \quad b^1 = p^1b; b^2 = p^2b; b^3 = p^3b$$

where $p^i = \sum_j p_{ij}$

The coefficients ϕ, δ, γ, ϵ, and μ are the specified post-terminal growth rates for private consumption, replacement, government consumption, exports, and imports.

In the initial computations reported below the consumption composition has been maintained unchanged throughout the postterminal period by projecting the sectoral components of consumption of the last plan period with identical rates. This, of course, is not necessary; a more general framework could project the components of the last plan period's consumption with different growth rates. Thus, as post-terminal consumption levels increase, a faster growth could be registered for more income-elastic components. The particular approach taken was chosen for its computational simplicity in the early stages of the research.

The extrapolation of imports is also based on a distribution that is endogenously determined in the last planning period. This is convenient because the post-terminal path itself has no built-in optimizing mechanism for the determination of choice variables, and the alternative procedure would be an arbitrary allocation of foreign exchange. Since imports as well as exports are projected at given growth rates over the entire post-terminal path, the post-terminal levels of foreign aid (or long-term capital flows) must be residually determined if a balance-of-payments relationship is to be satisfied. Whether the need for aid increases or decreases in the post-terminal period depends on the absolute amount of the deficit in the terminal year as well as on the growth rates at which exports and imports are projected post-terminally. Since exports and foreign aid are exogenously stated for the planning period itself, a stipulation of the post-terminal growth rates of exports and imports is sufficient to know whether the requirement for aid will increase or fall post-terminally.

The other nonhomogeneous elements, i.e., government demand and depreciation, do not require explanation. Both of these are exogenously stipulated already for the plan period. The projection of government demand is exogenous for the post-terminal period also. Since the model cannot decide for the post-terminal period what proportion of actual depreciation to replace, the terminal period's level of replacement is projected.

As mentioned earlier, (23) provides the sum of the particular solutions corresponding to the nonhomogeneous elements discussed above. Equation (23) expresses the post-terminal sectoral output levels required to sustain the stipulated rates of growth as a function of the nonhomogeneous components from which the required terminal capacities can readily be calculated with the help of the sectoral capital-output ratios. Again, because of the investment lag structure, the post-terminal output levels and capacity requirements must be determined for the first three post-terminal time periods.

The statement of the terminal conditions completes the system. The solution is obtained by maximizing the objective function, i.e., the present discounted value of the consumption stream over the plan period, subject to all the constraints. Given the parameters of the constraints, there will be a different solution for each specified rate of discount or corresponding set of $W(t)$. These solutions will be at vertices of the feasible region in the consumption space defined by the intersection of the given sets of constraints. Of course, there may be different feasible regions corresponding to different selections of the parameters of the constraints. By varying the discount rate in combination with the parameters of the constraints it is possible to derive all portions of the social production feasibility surfaces which are relevant for economic planning. Of course, of the multifold infinity of possibilities, only the consequences of those changes in parameters which can be controlled by economic policymakers and which are likely to be descriptive of changes in the real economy will be interesting.

The solution is accompanied or sustained by a set of shadow prices which are the choice variables of the dual-minimum problem. Since the sectoral capacities and the supply of foreign exchange are the only scarce resources in the system, the dual problem consists of imputing those rents to the use of capacities and for the use of foreign exchange which exhaust the value of the total product as well as minimize the cost of production. The shadow price of foreign exchange must always be positive, since imports can always be used to increase the value of the maximand at some time. The shadow prices or rents of capacities will be positive or zero depending on whether the capacities of particular sectors are fully or only partially utilized. Because of arbitrary initial conditions as well as other rigidities such as the fixed composition of the consumption good, it is not surprising that excess capacity should exist in some time periods. Though the rents corresponding to these capacities will be zero on such occasions, the respective outputs will still be positively priced as long as their production requires inputs of scarce commodities. If all sectors deliver intermediate goods to all other sectors it follows that none of the outputs can have a zero shadow price even if all capacities but one are redundant.

The shadow price of a given sectoral output in any one time period cannot be greater than the cost of producing a unit. Neither can the arbitrarily stipulated weight or market price of the composite consumption good exceed the cost of those current outputs which are required to make up a market basket. In other words, $\sum_i c_i u_i(t) \geqq W(t)$, where c_i is the proportion of the output of sector i needed to make up a unit of composite consumption good, and u_i is the shadow price of the good. When the inequality holds, the cost of putting together a market basket will exceed its current worth, and production for consumption will not take place. When, on the other hand, the equality holds, part of the sectoral outputs will be used for providing consumer goods. Since the relationship between the W's of adjacent time periods embodies the social discount factor, the shadow prices of the commodities are correspondingly also discounted over time. Though the shadow prices are the analogues of competitive market prices, they cannot be adopted for the actual market implementation of a plan. They refer to broad aggregates rather than specific commodities; hence they can serve only as indicators of the relative scarcities of a composite output of each sector.

Moreover they reflect the particular constraints of the model. For example, the shadow price that corresponds to the balance-of-payments constraints is a shadow rate of foreign exchange but one which reflects the import constraints. If the balance-of-payments constraint is expressed in domestic currency then it will indicate what the current domestic value of a unit worth of foreign exchange converted at some constant exchange rate should be in any one time period. The foreign exchange shadow price will not, however, reflect its value to sectors whose demand for foreign exchange is arbitrarily limited by the constraints on specialization of use of foreign exchange. In these sectors the value of foreign exchange will be greater than the dual price associated with the over-all foreign exchange constraint.

Each solution generates a complete specification period by period of the uses of resources for various types of production and the flows of goods to various uses all of which are consistent with the constraints and optimize the objective function. In this paper the time paths of outputs and inputs generated by the model will not be emphasized. Attention will be concentrated on the terminal-year output levels and certain over-all characteristics of the solution, recognizing that they are supported by a feasible and consistent set of resource allocations in each period.

Description of the Data

One of the crucial problems in implementing planning models is that of matching the information requirements of the theoretical frameworks with the limited data which are practically available. Many of the compromises which have been made between a more sophisticated theoretical structure and the practical formulation of the planning model have been due to limitations in data. In a number of cases the compromises have been necessary because the work has been carried out in a context removed from original sources of data and actual planning activities.

The Indian Third Five-year Plan period provides the basic setting for the numerical implementation of the model. The structure of the economy reflected in most of the calculations is intended to be that of India at the beginning of the Third Plan period. The magnitudes chosen for the exogenous elements in the models are based on Indian conditions expected to prevail during the plan.[19]

[19] The alternative computations which will subsequently be compared are all based on the same set of data and statistical assumptions. Hence, whatever the weaknesses of the data, I do not believe they detract from the strength of the qualitative comparisons.

The numerical solutions remain hypothetical exercises. Though a strenuous attempt has been made to provide realistic data, assumptions of convenience have been made in estimating parameters which would not be tolerable if the purpose of calculations were to make specific plans for India rather than to gain general, order-of-magnitude insights. In particular, I should like to emphasize that I do not presume to be laying down guidelines for Indian policymakers. The empirical results are intended to be illustrative rather than definitive.

It should also be emphasized that the numerical estimates presented are all based on secondary and public sources. No special data collection activities have been undertaken for the purpose of the computations described below, although officials of the government of India, especially in the Planning Commission, and members of the Indian Statistical Institute have cooperated most generously.[20] Thus, all the information used for the empirical implementation of the model is an adaptation of data originally designed to serve other purposes, but it does appear to conform to those on which Indian planning was based.

PRODUCTION DATA

As indicated in the description of the models the Leontief input-output assumptions of "fixed coefficients" of production have been adopted to describe production conditions. The production data with which the model is provided are a set of ratios for each sector. These ratios indicate for each type of use of a sector's outputs the inputs which are required. The ratios can be changed exogenously from period to period and from one solution to the next. However, the models are not provided with technological alternatives from which to make a choice. The general structure and logic of input-output tables have been discussed in detail elsewhere [21] so that only a brief description will be given here of the tables used and of the adjustments which have been made in them. For complete and detailed descriptions of the tables it is necessary to apply to the original sources.

THE CURRENT-FLOW MATRICES

The first input-output flow tables for India were prepared for the middle 1950s in the Indian Statistical Institute in Calcutta. Some original numerical experiments were made using an expanded version of

---

[20] I am particularly indebted to Professor Alan Manne for his explanations of the background of the data in whose preparation he was a major collaborator.

[21] W. Leontief *et al.*, *Studies in the Structure of the American Economy*, New York, 1953.

these original tables prepared by Ashish Chakravarti, now of the Indian Statistical Institute, Delhi. However, in early 1964, two new input-output tables became available for 1959–60. One, issued by the Indian Statistical Institute, Delhi, and referred to here as the I.S.I. table, was prepared under the direction of Dr. A. Rudhra and with the cooperation of Professor A. S. Manne of Stanford University, who was then a member of the India Project of the Center for International Studies, M.I.T. The second table was estimated in the Inter-Industry Study Group of the Planning Commission under the direction of Dr. K. S. Khrisnaswamy, chief, Economic Growth Section, and will be referred to here as the I.S.G. table. Inasmuch as somewhat more information as well as other supporting data was currently available for the I.S.I. table as compared to the I.S.G. table, the former has been used in the computational trials.

The 1959–60 I.S.I. table which has been used is basically that presented in *Notes on Perspective of Development, India: 1960–61 to 1975–76.*[22] It is a thirty-sector table with inputs valued at producers' prices. The final uses of output are for the household, government, and export sectors, for stock (inventory), gross fixed capital formation, and others, a miscellaneous sector. In addition to the inputs of the intermediate producing sectors, wages and salaries, gross profit, and margins are distinguished. The latter includes wholesale and retail trade margins and indirect taxes and subsidies. In this table only five sectors produce fixed capital: the urban and rural construction sectors and the electrical, transport, and nonelectrical equipment sectors. Such industries as cement, iron and steel, and nonferrous metals, rather than supplying outputs directly for fixed capital formation deliver to the construction sector which in this table is a processing rather than service industry. It receives such inputs, processes them, and delivers fixed capital.

Many of the special features of the I.S.I. table have been suppressed, and it has been modified in several ways consistent with the objective of developing a technique of general applicability and to reduce computational requirements.[23] Although the thirty-one sectors of the I.S.I.

[22] Perspective Planning Division, Planning Commission, April 1964, pp. 183–87.
[23] In several sectors there was a negative input entered in the miscellaneous "others" sector as an aggregative correction to overestimation of inputs to other sectors. These negative inputs were eliminated by allocating them among the other inputs of the sector using the proportions of the positive inputs as a guide. The undistributed inputs of the rail and motor transport sections were allocated using the proportions from the I.S.G. table.
Another major change in the I.S.I. table was the creation of a residential housing sector, which provides rental services. This sector constitutes approximately 7 per cent of the consumer budget; it is also the sector with the largest capital-output ratio. The original experiments with the 1955–56 I.S.I. table rein-

table already represent a high degree of aggregation, preliminary trials indicated that further aggregation was necessary in order to accommodate the model to the available computational capacity. Unfortunately, this aggregation could not be done in a way which would both satisfy theoretical criteria and avoid bias and misrepresentation.[24] This is due to the lack of empirical knowledge which the criteria require and the previous aggregation which has already been done on a theoretically unsatisfactory basis. Further aggregation to eleven sectors was carried out, and Table 1 presents the revised 1959–60 I.S.I. table on an eleven-sector basis as used in the empirical experiments.

THE FIXED CAPITAL FORMATION RELATIONSHIPS

Capital is one of the two scarce factors, and its formation is the major source of growth in the planning models described above. This does not represent a refusal to grant the importance of natural resources or labor inputs or changes in technology. The obstacles to an explicit treatment of factors other than capital are partly analytical, partly computational and partly owing to the lack of adequate empirical information. It would, for example, require only a slight elaboration of the theoretical structures of the model in order to treat labor as if it were a capital factor formed by education, health services, and similar inputs. That, however, would not be completely satisfactory from a theoretical viewpoint, nor are there corresponding empirical relationships which are reasonably well established.

The capital formation relationships are a kind of modified acceleration principle with a detailed breakdown of sectoral inputs. There is a rich literature on the theoretical issues raised by such coefficients, and there is no point in summarizing it here. The use of the related aggregate

forced the view suggested by these characteristics that over-all results would be sensitive to the size and growth rate for this sector. It was, therefore, decided to isolate residential housing from the miscellaneous "others" sector. In order to construct a residential property row, it was assumed that this sector delivers only to private consumption, and the amount of the delivery was the 520 crores of rupees estimated as the output of the sector in the official national income accounts. This amount was subtracted from the delivery of the "others" sector to private consumption. The residential housing column was formed by allocating the row total among the input sectors, using the relevant coefficients of the 1955–56 I.S.I. input-output table.

The "others" sector was made into a producing sector receiving inputs as indicated by its column vector. For the corresponding row vector the margin row was consolidated with the others row. This treatment of margins was done to conform to the usual practice for wholesale and retail trade.

[24] See for example, A. A. Waters, "Production and Cost Functions: An Econometric Survey," *Econometrica,* January–April 1963, pp. 5–11.

TABLE 1

Revised I.S.I. Input-Output Coefficient Matrix

	1	2	3	4	5	6	7	8	9	10	11
1. Agriculture and plantations	.080	.000	.017	.051	.131	.505	.000	.000	.043	.000	.035
2. Mining and metals	.000	.208	.231	.025	.052	.004	.131	.041	.146	.005	.001
3. Equipment	.000	.020	.037	.016	.003	.003	.000	.000	.016	.000	.001
4. Chemicals and fertilizers	.010	.020	.037	.199	.081	.028	.028	.185	.008	.000	.000
5. Cement, glass, and wood	.000	.011	.005	.011	.025	.003	.000	.000	.221	.015	.003
6. Food and clothing manufactures	.008	.002	.002	.034	.018	.057	.000	.000	.000	.000	.000
7. Electrical generation	.001	.023	.013	.016	.022	.013	.000	.004	.000	.000	.001
8. Transportation	.007	.145	.073	.098	.070	.049	.118	.042	.026	.007	.021
9. Construction	.000	.000	.000	.000	.000	.000	.000	.000	.000	.000	.026
10. Housing	.000	.000	.000	.000	.000	.000	.000	.000	.000	.000	.000
11. Other and margin	.005	.028	.135	.032	.089	.055	.068	.017	.107	.045	.000
Total	.111	.458	.550	.480	.491	.718	.346	.288	.567	.071	.087

capital-output ratios for projections is well known and also much discussed. As with so many aspects of computable multisectoral models, credit should be given to W. Leontief and his associates for their pioneering work on the structure of capital.[25]

Although the empirical information necessary to fill in the capital coefficients matrix is far from satisfactory, a substantial amount of data is available. With some major exceptions the quality of information of this type for less developed countries such as India may be superior to that for more developed economies. The relatively small size of many of the modern sectors, as well as the extent and variety of reporting required for the implementation of various government regulations, should facilitate the estimation of sectoral marginal capital coefficients. The major exceptions are in agriculture and the traditional services and handicrafts which bulk large in the economy. In these sectors there is no simple and reliable relation of capital accumulation to capacity changes. These sectors could have been treated exogenously in our models and in a real planning application might be handled best in that way. Consistent with the experimental approach adopted here, these sectors have been put on the same basis as other sectors, with calculations being made for alternative estimates of their capital-output ratios.

In order to carry out the first trial computations on the alternative models with a plausible set of numbers a complete matrix of capital coefficients for India was first estimated in the Center for International Studies, M.I.T. This had to be done in an extremely rough way, but all the various sources of information publicly available were used. The Indian Third Five-year Plan and various studies of the Indian Planning Commission were the most important of these. In 1964 a new matrix of capital coefficients was estimated in the Indian Statistical Institute, New Delhi, by Vinod Prakash. These estimates appear to have been based on many of the same sources as well as other information not publicly available. A comparison of the two capital-coefficient matrices showed considerable agreement. The Prakash matrix was used as the basis of most of the computations as the most recently available authoritative estimates. The original capital-coefficient matrix was used to obtain additional detail beyond that available in the Prakash capital coefficients and as a source of the alternative estimates of capital requirements used in our sensitivity analyses. Since the Prakash estimates were presented in the thirty-one-sector detail of the 1959–60 I.S.I. matrix,

[25] *Studies in the Structure of the American Economy.*

they were also aggregated using the 1959 output levels as weights. Table 2 indicates the aggregate capital-output ratios for each sector.

In the model described there is scope for presenting some detail of the capital gestation process. The next step in data preparation, therefore, was the disaggregation of the capital matrix by periods. The existence of gestation periods of varying lengths is a major source of the problems of coordinating the growth of different sectors in development programs. In addition, since in the less-developed regions delays

TABLE 2

Aggregate Capital-Coefficient Matrix

Adapted from I.S.I. Estimates

Agriculture and plantations	1.51
Mining and metals	2.42
Equipment	0.91
Chemicals and fertilizers	0.88
Cement, glass, and wood	0.89
Food and clothing manufactures	0.55
Electrical generation	6.26
Transportation	2.22
Construction	0.15
Housing	10.00
Other and margin	0.15

in making capital effective have a particularly high cost, it is important to be able to analyze such delays. In India there has been particular concern expressed over this problem of planning. On the other hand, published empirical information about the gestation periods of capital projects is relatively scarce both for developed and less-developed regions. There is a substantial body of informed comment, moreover, which holds that gestation periods in the more-developed countries are quite different from practices prevailing in the less-developed areas, but there is relatively little organized information. Although the existence of several studies of the time patterns of capital creation indicates the feasibility of such investigations, the secondary sources now available are completely inadequate for this purpose, and no independent estimation was attempted. In these circumstances a simple arbitrary pattern which could easily be modified as more information became available was adopted to represent the gestation process. It was assumed that in order to achieve an increment of capacity in period t one-third of the total eventual contribution of the construction sector had to be forthcoming in each of three preceding periods. For the contribution of the equipment-producing sectors it was assumed that one-half of the total requirements had to be provided in each of two periods preceding the period in which capacity was to become effective. With these assumptions the matrices showing proportions of total requirements supplied by each sector at period t for investment in every other sector which will mature in periods $t + 1$, $t + 2$, and $t + 3$ were estimated for India for the 1960s, as shown in Tables 3, 4, and 5, respectively.

THE INVENTORY INVESTMENT RELATIONSHIPS

Although in some cases there may be technical requirements which put close limits on inventories, in most sectors the stock-holding decisions are subject to a variety of influences whose net effect, in developed countries at least, is a particularly volatile type of behavior. The patterns of inventory-holding in the less-developed areas have not been studied intensively, however, and relatively little empirical information is available. Such information is notoriously difficult to collect, and the statistical reporting systems of these areas have not been able to cover this aspect of investment in a thorough and continuous manner. Some data which do exist suggest that inventory accumulation may be a relatively more significant part of total investment in less-developed areas than in advanced countries, however. The limitations of transport and communications and other uncertainties associated with deliveries would contribute to such a pattern.

The assumptions behind the inventory investment relations which have been used are that a certain ratio of inventories to output is maintained in each sector and that the proportions in which the individual sectors contribute to these inventories are fixed. These lead to the inventory accelerator relationships and for implementation require the projection of inventory-output ratios. An initial source of information used to implement these assumptions was the matrix of coefficients estimated for India by Mr. Chakravarti. The aggregate ratios in this table were compared with separate estimates prepared by Professor A. K. Sen.[26] These sources of information were complemented with scattered data more recently available. The matrix of inventory coeffi-

[26] "Working Capital in the Indian Economy: A Conceptual Framework and Some Estimates," *Pricing and Fiscal Policies*, pp. 125–46.

TABLE 3

Proportions of Total Requirements for Investment in Each Sector Supplied by Each Sector

at Period t to Mature in Period t + 1

	1	2	3	4	5	6	7	8	9	10	11
3. Equipment	.069	.248	.258	.245	.222	.314	.202	.442	.327	.000	.160
9. Construction	.282	.147	.139	.149	.166	.097	.181	.000	.087	.333	.213
11. Other and margin	.009	.032	.034	.032	.029	.041	.026	.057	.042	.000	.021
Total	.359	.427	.431	.425	.417	.452	.409	.500	.456	.333	.393

TABLE 4

Proportions of Total Requirements for Investment in Each Sector Supplied by Each Sector

at Period t to Mature in Period t + 2

	1	2	3	4	5	6	7	8	9	10	11
3. Equipment	.069	.248	.258	.245	.222	.314	.202	.442	.327	.000	.160
9. Construction	.282	.147	.139	.149	.166	.097	.181	.000	.087	.333	.213
11. Other and margin	.009	.032	.034	.032	.029	.041	.026	.057	.042	.000	.021
Total	.359	.427	.431	.425	.417	.452	.409	.500	.456	.333	.393

TABLE 5

Proportions of Total Requirements for Investment in Each Sector Supplied by Each Sector

at Period t to Mature in Period t + 3

	1	2	3	4	5	6	7	8	9	10	11
3. Equipment	.000	.000	.000	.000	.000	.000	.000	.000	.000	.000	.000
9. Construction	.282	.147	.139	.149	.166	.097	.181	.000	.087	.333	.213
11. Other and margin	.000	.000	.000	.000	.000	.000	.000	.000	.000	.000	.000
Total	.282	.147	.139	.149	.166	.097	.181	.000	.087	.333	.213

cients finally used, however, was based on the I.S.I. input-output table and is presented in Table 6.

DEPRECIATION

The manner in which the productive capacity of capital stock diminishes with time and use undoubtedly varies both with the type of capital and the purposes for which it is employed. These differences could not be taken into account at the level of detail at which these models are cast. Instead, as in other cases, a convention was adopted which would not unduly complicate the models while providing a first approximation to the effects of depreciation. The time pattern of decay was assumed to be that in which each unit of capital maintains its original productivity over its complete lifetime.

The operating life of many types of capital is twenty to twenty-five years or more, which is substantially longer than the planning horizon of the short-term models. The pattern of capital decay chosen for the model means, therefore, that depreciation is exogenous to the plan period, being determined by the investment which took place in years previous to the start of the plan. With this approach it became necessary to estimate investment during the early postwar years for which relatively little statistical information existed. The actual amounts of depreciation specified exogenously for the five-year model starting in 1960–61 are shown in Table 7.[27] Since there was relatively little investment in the 1940s, the assumption of a constant amount of replacement requirements in each period was considered not unrealistic. The replacement requirements to restore the depreciated capacity are shown in Table 8; and the proportions for restoring depreciated capacity, in Tables 9, 10, and 11.

IMPORTS

It is desirable to provide empirical information on the basis of which the planning models can assist in decisions on the type and quantity of goods to import rather than produce domestically. For this purpose, it is important to distinguish noncompetitive imports from competitive imports. The former are imports for which no domestic capacity exists or can be created, while the latter represent sectors for which a "make or buy" decision is relevant. Strictly speaking, noncompetitive imports

[27] These estimates are different from those used in the initial version of this paper. Re-examination indicated those initial estimates were likely to be substantially too low and it appeared to be preferable to accept the I.S.I. estimates. As will be pointed out below, this change has had significant effects on the Third Plan Target solutions in particular.

TABLE 6

Matrix of Inventory Coefficients

	1	2	3	4	5	6	7	8	9	10	11
1. Agriculture and plantations	.315	.000	.022	.029	.094	.292	.000	.000	.007	.000	.007
2. Mining and metals	.001	.140	.248	.018	.036	.002	.106	.011	.023	.000	.000
3. Equipment	.000	.038	.044	.052	.002	.002	.000	.000	.003	.000	.000
4. Chemicals and fertilizer	.040	.012	.045	.377	.058	.017	.023	.008	.001	.000	.001
5. Cement, glass, and wood	.002	.012	.007	.007	.018	.002	.000	.000	.035	.000	.000
6. Food and clothing manufactures	.031	.004	.003	.022	.012	.039	.000	.000	.000	.000	.000
7. Electrical generation	.004	.033	.015	.024	.016	.008	.000	.001	.000	.000	.000
8. Transportation	.000	.000	.000	.000	.000	.000	.000	.000	.000	.000	.000
9. Construction	.000	.000	.000	.000	.000	.000	.000	.000	.000	.000	.000
10. Housing	.000	.000	.000	.000	.000	.000	.000	.000	.000	.000	.000
11. Other and margin	.000	.000	.000	.000	.000	.000	.000	.000	.000	.000	.000
Total	.393	.240	.384	.528	.237	.361	.129	.020	.068	.000	.008

TABLE 7

Depreciated Capacity by Sectors

(rupees crores)

	1962-63	1963-64	1964-65	1965-66	1966-67	1967-68	1968-69
Agriculture and plantations	277.4009	281.6406	285.8804	290.1202	294.3599	298.9025	303.4451
Mining and metals	71.4057	72.4970	73.5884	74.6798	75.7711	76.9404	78.1097
Equipment	16.0887	16.3346	16.5804	16.8263	17.0722	17.3357	17.5992
Chemicals	50.7788	51.5549	52.3310	53.1071	53.8832	54.7147	55.5462
Cement, glass, and wood	16.1588	16.4058	16.6527	16.8997	17.1467	17.4113	17.6759
Food and clothing manufactures	32.7314	33.2316	33.7319	34.2322	34.7324	35.2684	35.8044
Electricity	48.3195	49.0581	49.7966	50.5351	51.2736	52.0648	52.8561
Transportation	84.5926	85.8855	87.1784	88.4713	89.7642	91.1494	92.5347
Construction	1.5697	1.5936	1.6176	1.6416	1.6656	1.6913	1.7170
Housing	186.8442	189.6999	192.5556	195.4113	198.2670	201.3266	204.3863
Other and margins	136.8277	138.9189	141.0102	143.1015	145.1927	147.4333	149.6740

TABLE 8

Replacement Requirements by Sectors

(rupees crores)

	1962–63	1963–64	1964–65	1965–66	1966–67	1967–68	1968–69
Agriculture and plantations	143.6563	145.8519	148.0475	150.2431	152.4388	154.7912	157.1437
Mining and metals	65.8512	66.8577	67.8642	68.8706	69.8771	70.9554	72.0338
Equipment	14.6194	14.8428	15.0662	15.2897	15.5131	15.7525	15.9919
Chemicals	47.9160	48.6483	49.3806	50.1130	50.8453	51.6300	52.4146
Cement, glass, and wood	13.0896	13.2897	13.4898	13.6898	13.8899	14.1042	14.3186
Food and clothing manufactures	30.2738	30.7365	31.1992	31.6619	32.1246	32.6203	33.1161
Electricity	40.5330	41.1525	41.7720	42.3915	43.0110	43.6747	44.3385
Transportation	84.5926	85.8855	87.1784	88.4713	89.7642	91.1494	92.5347
Construction	1.2641	1.2834	1.3027	1.3220	1.3414	1.3621	1.3828
Housing	186.8274	189.6828	192.5382	195.3937	198.2491	201.3085	204.3679
Other and margins	134.1757	136.2264	138.2771	140.3278	142.3786	144.5758	146.7730
Total	916.0000	930.0000	944.0000	958.0000	972.0000	967.0000	1,002.0000

TABLE 9

Proportions for Restoring Depreciated Capital in Period t + 1

	1	2	3	4	5	6	7	8	9	10	11
3. Equipment	.000	.000	.000	.000	.000	.000	.000	.000	.000	.000	.000
9. Construction	.233	.130	.119	.138	.126	.077	.216	.000	.027	.333	.217
11. Other and margins	.000	.000	.000	.000	.000	.000	.000	.000	.000	.000	.000
Total	.233	.130	.119	.138	.126	.077	.216	.000	.027	.333	.217

TABLE 10

Proportions for Restoring Depreciated Capital in Period t + 2

	1	2	3	4	5	6	7	8	9	10	11
3. Equipment	.133	.269	.284	.259	.275	.339	.156	.442	.406	.000	.154
9. Construction	.233	.130	.119	.138	.126	.077	.216	.000	.027	.333	.217
11. Other and margins	.017	.035	.038	.034	.036	.045	.021	.057	.054	.000	.020
Total	.383	.435	.441	.431	.437	.461	.392	.500	.487	.333	.391

TABLE 11

Proportions for Restoring Depreciated Capital in Period t + 3

	1	2	3	4	5	6	7	8	9	10	11
3. Equipment	.133	.269	.284	.259	.275	.339	.156	.442	.406	.000	.154
9. Construction	.233	.130	.119	.138	.126	.077	.216	.000	.027	.333	.217
11. Other and margins	.017	.035	.038	.034	.036	.045	.021	.057	.054	.000	.020
Total	.383	.435	.441	.431	.437	.461	.392	.500	.487	.333	.391

cannot be fitted within the classification scheme for the domestic economy, and recognition of each type would require creation of a separate sector. Likewise, the requirements for each type of noncompetitive import should be related separately to its uses in the producing or final demand sectors. The treatment of competitive imports should provide for the decision between domestic production or import and take into account the changing basis for such decisions as domestic capacity changes.

A rigorous distinction of competitive and noncompetitive imports and the adjustment of import requirements with the development of domestic capacity was not possible within the limitations of the model structure, computational capacity, and data availability. Noncompetitive imports were treated as fixed fractions of the total output of the sectors in which they were assigned. The ratios of noncompetitive imports to output were calculated from the I.S.G. matrix mentioned above and used as noncompetitive import coefficients. Table 12 lists these coefficients by sector.

As noted previously, in order to handle competitive imports within the model structure, ceilings were set on the use in each sector of the foreign exchange left over after the satisfaction of noncompetitive import needs. These ceilings were in the form of ratios to sectoral output of uncommitted foreign exchange. The ratios were based on the import information in the I.S.I. and I.S.G. tables, with some adjustments based

TABLE 12

Import Coefficients by Sector

	Noncompetitive	Competitive
Agriculture and plantations	.01600	.301
Mining and metals	.14500	.199
Equipment	.23500	.348
Chemicals and fertilizer	.26100	.162
Cement, glass, and wood	.00400	.020
Food and clothing manufactures	.00008	.027
Electrical generation	.00000	.000
Transportation	.00000	.000
Construction	.00000	.000
Housing	.00000	.000
Other and margin	.00000	.020

on judgment as to the sectors in which government policy would be more or less restrictive in permitting import substitution for domestic production. These ratios are shown in Table 12.

EXPORTS

The exogenous treatment of this use of output is justified on the argument that the satisfaction of foreign demands is not affected by domestic policy. This is only partly true, of course. Export duties or subsidies and exchange rate policy can certainly change relative prices, but these influences are not within the structure of the model in any case. Although for most of the major export sectors the domestic use of output is not a major alternative, the choice between exporting and using output domestically is significant for a number of sectors. No attempt was made to bring this choice within the framework of the model either, although it might be possible to do so in some cases.

The practical problem is the choice of methods for extrapolation of exports in each sector. The technique used here is a simple one. The initial level of exports was estimated from preplan years, and an average growth rate was projected for all exports. This is an arrangement of convenience which could be refined. The export levels projected are listed for each sector in Table 13.

TABLE 13

Export Levels Projected for the Third Plan Period

(rupees crores)

	1960-61	1962-63	1963-64	1964-65	1965-66
Agriculture and plantations	198.188	206.370	214.552	223.037	231.826
Mining and metals	40.090	41.745	43.400	45.117	46.894
Equipment	4.336	4.515	4.694	4.880	5.072
Chemicals and fertilizer	15.088	15.711	16.334	16.980	17.649
Cement, glass, and wood	2.793	2.908	3.023	3.143	3.267
Food and clothing manufactures	215.656	224.560	233.463	242.696	252.259
Electrical generation	0.0	0.0	0.0	0.0	0.0
Transportation	0.0	0.0	0.0	0.0	0.0
Construction	0.0	0.0	0.0	0.0	0.0
Housing	0.0	0.0	0.0	0.0	0.0
Other and margin	177.836	185.178	192.519	200.133	208.019
Total	645.000	681.000	708.000	736.000	765.000

TABLE 14

Government Expenditures by Sector

(rupees crores)

	1961-62	1962-63	1963-64	1964-65	1965-66
Agriculture and plantations	0.0	0.0	0.0	0.0	0.0
Mining and metals	0.0	0.0	0.0	0.0	0.0
Equipment	97.596	101.204	104.993	108.601	112.209
Chemicals and fertilizer	28.402	29.452	30.555	31.605	32.655
Cement, glass, and wood	0.0	0.0	0.0	0.0	0.0
Food and clothing manufactures	109.120	113.154	117.389	121.423	125.457
Electrical generation	4.923	5.105	5.296	5.478	5.660
Transportation	0.0	0.0	0.0	0.0	0.0
Construction	108.200	112.200	116.400	120.400	124.400
Housing	0.0	0.0	0.0	0.0	0.0
Other and margin	192.758	199.884	207.367	214.493	221.619
Total	541.000	561.000	582.000	602.000	622.000

GOVERNMENT

The government sector in the planning models is assumed to consist entirely of "public consumption," so resources delivered for this purpose do not contribute to productive capacity nor act as intermediate inputs to producing sectors. Again there is a substantial literature on the extent to which these assumptions are justified for various types of expenditure, and so the issues will not be reviewed here. The problem becomes one of finding a reasonable basis on which to project an exogenous sector.

Considerable detail is available on the uses of funds in the budgets of the union government and less detail for the state government budgets. For neither type of budget was it possible to find the detail on function reclassified according to types of inputs used. The I.S.I. table provides such a breakdown in the year for which it was estimated. With this information and the Third Plan projections to aid in establishing growth rates, future deliveries to the government sector were estimated exogenously. Table 14 presents these estimates.

FOREIGN AID

This is truly an exogenous element. For the purpose of the basic model net annual foreign aid was set at $500 million. As noted above, the allotment of foreign aid on an annual basis will lead to different results than specification of a total amount to be available over the entire plan in whatever annual pattern is desired.

CONSUMPTION

The models require specification of the proportions in which the total consumer budget is allocated among the outputs of the producing sectors. These proportions in actuality depend on the incomes achieved and the patterns of relative prices and the price and income elasticities associated with the products of the various sectors. In this case the constraints of the analytic framework are more severe than the data constraints. Estimates of price and income elasticities are available for many of the sectors, especially the more significant ones, though there are high levels of variance associated with the estimates, and for some sectors there is almost no information. On the assumption that, for sectors defined as grossly as those in this paper, consumption proportions would not change markedly in a short period, the distribution of consumption was specified in advance.

For the purposes of the models computed here initial consumption proportions were calculated from the I.S.I. transactions tables for 1959–60. These are shown in Table 15.

INITIAL CAPACITY AND UNCOMPLETED CAPITAL

The endowments of capital stocks with which the plan period starts are initially the only productive resources available. These endowments

TABLE 15

Consumption Proportions Based on 1959 I.S.I. Table

Agriculture and plantations	.42941
Mining and metals	.00048
Equipment	.01471
Chemicals and fertilizer	.02384
Cement, glass, and wood	.00501
Food and clothing manufactures	.14101
Electrical generation	.00087
Transportation	.01476
Construction	.00000
Housing	.04516
Other and margin	.32475

are the result of events in the preplan period and exogenous to the plan itself. Likewise, the amounts of uncompleted capital whose construction had started prior to the plan period with a view to completion during the plan period are exogenous. A rational planning procedure would coordinate the end of one plan with the beginning of another. In actuality, however, the Indian five-year plans have suffered somewhat from a lack of coordination between the plans. The Third Five-year Plan, though referring to projects started during the Second Plan and to be completed during the Fourth Plan, does not provide a detailed description of the degree of completion of such projects at the beginning of the Third Plan nor a detailed sectoral classification. There were no other sources of public data from which such information could be extracted. It was assumed, therefore, for the purposes of our trial computations that the Indian Planning Commission had attempted to schedule investment activity to provide a smooth transition between the plans. The growth of capital estimated for each sector in the Third Plan was extrapolated backward in order to estimate the amounts of investment which would have taken place in the preplan period under this assumption to achieve the desired capital formation. The capital coefficient matrices described previously were used for this latter purpose. In order to establish the initial capital stocks the sectoral output levels in the year immediately prior to the plan are multiplied by the aggregate capital-output ratios. These totals were then adjusted for depreciation. The capital in process at the beginning of the plan is described in terms of the maximum amount of capital which could be formed in each sector in the first and second plan periods, as this is determined by preplan investment activity. The major source of information for these calculations was a report prepared by M. R. Saluja as part of a joint project of the Indian Statistical Institute and the Center for International Studies.[28] It was also assumed that all sectors were operating at full capacity in the initial period.[29] Table 16 presents the initial conditions as computed above. The annual availability of foreign aid was set at five hundred crores of rupees. This, with the projected exports, determines the total availability of foreign exchange.

[28] "Methods and Sources for Output Levels, 1960–61 and 1965–66," Delhi, August 3, 1964.

[29] An attempt was made to adjust for the extent of initial idle capacity in the various sectors, but the data were not available in a form which would make this possible. The adjustment for less than full use of capacity in order to determine initial effective capital endowment is a significant one since even small errors here may correspond to a substantial portion of the annual amounts of investment. The well-known problems of defining capacity occur in an aggravated form in such sectors as traditional agriculture.

TABLE 16

Preplan Output Levels and Capital in Process

(rupees crores)

	Preplan Outputs	Maximum Capital Formation in Period 1	Maximum Capital Formation in Period 2
Agriculture and plantations	7577.0	798.75	825.73
Mining and metals	462.0	293.24	332.02
Equipment	670.5	158.49	186.67
Chemicals and fertilizer	612.5	147.68	163.60
Cement, glass, and wood	450.6	58.21	62.46
Food and clothing manufactures	2442.0	99.83	103.53
Electrical generation	108.0	162.29	180.50
Transportation	779.0	245.51	260.58
Construction	1617.0	30.76	33.89
Housing	579.8	399.98	410.40
Other and margin	5854.6	191.78	196.99

Analysis of the Indian Third Five-year Plan Period

The analytic framework for planning presented above is certainly an oversimplification of the real world and the problems of economic development. Likewise, the brief description of the data inputs cannot do full justice to their inadequacies. Yet the framework is more sophisticated than that of other formal models currently employed, and the data are not substantially different from those actually in use. Formal sophistication, however, is not itself an adequate criterion for judging planning methods. Less sophisticated techniques may be more realistic and more flexible, for example, in not being constrained to linearity in production relations and other constraints and in balancing a variety of objectives. Fortunately a choice need not be made, and a variety of approaches to economic policy can be used simultaneously and consistently. The scope and comparative advantage of the approach described here may be appreciated better after an application to the Indian Third Five-year Plan is described. In using the model to judge the consistency, feasibility, and optimality of the Third Plan, criteria and constraints are applied which are believed to be reasonable. However, the caveat must be registered that these are not necessarily the criteria and constraints implicit in the Third Plan itself. The issues involved in this point will be discussed in greater detail below.

The application is in two stages. The first application is that of the Target Model to the exogenously specified Third Five-year Plan targets, and the results are examined for a number of alternative specifications of parameters and constraints. Secondly, the Transit Model is solved with terminal conditions endogenously determined, using equations 22 and 23, also for alternative parameters and constraints. The results of the two types of solutions are compared, and finally an appraisal is attempted of the model and its results.

The full solution of the model indicates not only the value of the maximand but all the allocations necessary to achieve it: the capital formation in each sector in each period, the intensity of use of capital and foreign exchange, and the distribution of output for its various uses. The solutions will not be presented here in their full detail, but the values of the maximands and some of their other major features will be compared, especially the general nature of the resource uses and scarcities in each solution.

THE THIRD PLAN TARGET SOLUTIONS

The over-all growth rate implied in the Indian Third Five-year Plan was about 5 per cent. As one would expect, the growth rates projected for specific sectors varied quite substantially from this average figure. Table 17 indicates the 1960 gross output levels, the projected 1965 levels, and the implied average annual growth rates for the thirty-sector detail of the I.S.I. input-output table.[30] In inspecting the table it is useful to recall that only the construction and equipment sectors in this classification are capital-creating sectors.

Growth rates can be misleading as to the relative emphasis of the plan, since the initial output levels in some cases are so low. This is the case to some extent in both the crude oil and fertilizer sectors. In addition, these are levels and growth rates of gross output and do not in themselves indicate the planned growth of the Indian economy as measured by final output or capital accumulation. Yet the over-all picture is

---

[30] It is difficult from the Third Five-year Plan itself to construct a detailed yet comprehensive breakdown of sectoral targets. W. B. Reddaway in his book, *The Development of the Indian Economy*, London, 1962, provides a substantial amount of detail as does the publication of the Planning Commission, *Selected Plan Statistics*. A recent study by Saluja, "Methods and Sources for Output Levels, 1960–61 and 1965–66," is the source of the data reproduced here. The others sector is omitted, as are margins; so the total is not equivalent to gross output of the economy.

TABLE 17

Third-Plan Targets Compared to Preplan Output Levels

(rupees crores)

Sector	1960-61	1965-66	Growth Rate (average annual)
Construction, urban and industrial	1201.0	1980.0	10.5
Construction, rural	416.0	436.0	0.8
Electrical equipment	126.0	362.0	23.5
Transport equipment	201.0	417.0	15.7
Nonelectrical equipment	343.5	888.0	20.7
Iron and steel	269.0	909.0	27.6
Iron ore	7.8	22.0	23.1
Cement	52.6	88.0	10.8
Other metals	32.0	80.0	20.0
Other minerals	45.4	77.0	11.1
Plantations	196.0	250.0	5.0
Leather and leather products	189.0	220.0	3.1
Animal husbandry	1130.0	1323.0	3.2
Food industries	1323.0	1733.0	5.5
Food grains	3751.0	4767.0	4.9
Grain milled	223.3	279.0	4.5
Cotton and other textiles	800.0	1093.0	6.5
Jute textiles	130.0	165.0	4.9
Other agriculture	2097.0	2571.0	4.1
Chemical fertilizers	20.7	166.0	51.7
Glass, wooden, and nonmetallic mineral products	398.0	620.0	9.3
Forestry products	180.0	262.0	7.9
Motor transport	325.0	580.0	12.3
Petroleum products	237.1	659.0	22.6
Crude oil	3.2	46.0	70.3
Rubber products	67.5	127.0	13.5
Rubber, synthetic		17.0	
Chemicals	284.0	742.0	21.2
Railways	454.0	640.0	7.1
Electricity	103.4	286.0	22.6
Coal	109.0	206.0	13.6

relatively straightforward. With the exception of fertilizers the highest growth rates in the table are in the capital-producing sectors, their most important suppliers, and in several import-substituting sectors. The sectors supplying consumer goods, which in India include relatively small amounts of consumer durables, on the whole had lower growth rates projected for them. The rationalization of this relative emphasis would presumably be based on two related arguments. First, capital is needed to provide the means by which to increase output in the consumer goods sector, and the well-known "accelerator effect" accounts for the more rapid growth of the capital goods sector itself. Secondly, capital is also needed to provide import substitutes to reduce the reliance on foreign aid and, again, the capital equipment sectors must grow more rapidly than the sectors which they are supplying. Of course, the relative emphasis as between capital and consumer goods production, the planned import substitution, and, therefore, the requirements of foreign exchange reflect decisions as to the growth rate of the economy and the distribution of the benefits of the growth both in the intraplan and postplan periods.

Although aggregate projections were made in the plan itself for the post-Third Plan period no set of detailed sectoral postplan growth rates was presented. Since short-term planning requires this specification it was assumed for the purpose of the Target Model calculations that the intraplan sectoral growth rates would be carried into the future. This amounts to saying that no substantial changes in the composition of output would be expected in the early postplan years.[31] Otherwise the Target Model was solved with the data inputs given in the previous section.

For the purposes of the solution, condition (4), which specified a minimum initial level for consumption, was omitted in order to reduce the possibility of finding that all the requirements could not be met. This change now permits the optimization procedure to reduce the consumption levels in the initial plan year as low as necessary in order to meet the consumption growth constraint of later years. The feasibility issue in this respect thus becomes one of political acceptability of the solution unless, even with zero consumption, no economically feasible solution can be found.

In fact, with the specified parameters and constraints no feasible

---

[31] It should be recalled at this point that the amounts of unfinished capital carried into the first years of the plan are set in the calculations by assuming that the last years of the Second Five-year Plan were phased to provide smooth growth of capital and output to the Third Plan targets.

solution could be found which was consistent with the Third Plan targets. Even with the maximand reduced to zero, that is, with no consumption at all permitted in the plan period, there was no allocation of available resources which would meet the constraints and achieve the targets. The point made above about the absolute inflexibility of the constraints must be constantly kept in mind, however. It is possible that these constraints create some small bottleneck which if relieved ever so slightly would permit the achievement of the targets with a substantial and generally satisfactory level of consumption for the maximand. To investigate this possibility the constraints limiting the use of foreign exchange for competitive imports were, first of all, removed completely. It had been found from previous experience that this would often result in a substantially improved performance.[32] In this case it was still not possible to achieve a feasible solution. At this point, rather than to continue to search blindly for some way of obtaining a feasible solution, the targets were reduced across the board, one percentage point at a time, until a feasible solution was achieved. With a feasible solution there are shadow prices and other indicators of relative scarcities which help indicate the reasons for the infeasibility of the full targets.[33]

A feasible solution was found when the targets were reduced by 4 per cent. If an average annual rate of growth of 5 per cent had been postulated for the Third Plan, a reduction in target year outputs and

[32] The parameters of the noncompetitive import constraints were based on data from the I.S.G. table. The significance of this result will be discussed below.

[33] Since, in the version of this paper originally presented, a feasible solution was presented with the Third Plan targets, it appears desirable to explain this new result. Subsequent to those calculations a number of minor changes have been made in the coefficients. The major change, however, and that responsible for this new result, was in the method of treating depreciation and the magnitude of the depreciation estimates. The total and sectoral depreciation estimates used originally were revised using the methods described briefly above. The new annual total of depreciation is about 500 crores above the original estimate. It is interesting to quote the Third Plan on meeting depreciation requirements: "The estimate of investment on replacement shown (150 crores for industry only) falls short of the minimum requirements of the cotton textile, jute textile and woolen textile industries in regard to which special studies have been made recently. The backlog of replacements in these three industries alone has been estimated at about Rs. 169 crores. The estimate that investment on replacement account in the Third Plan will be of the order of Rs. 150 crores is more or less a projection of the actual performance during the Second Plan. Even so it is on the optimistic side in view of (a) the pressure on available resources of private enterprise and institutional agencies for new investment and (b) the fact that mills with large backlogs of replacement are in no position to provide resources for renovation commensurate with needs and (c) the small allocation made in the Plan to enable the N.I.D.C. to assist these programs financially" (*Third Five Year Plan*, p. 460).

capital stocks of 4 per cent corresponds to a reduction in the average annual growth rate to 4.15 per cent. It is this 96 per cent level of the Third Plan targets which will now be the subject of further analysis here and which will, hereafter, be referred to as the Target solutions.

The value of the maximand or discounted value of consumption over the Third Plan period, with a social rate of discount of 10 per cent and at the 96 per cent level of targets, was Rs. 24,710 crores. The corresponding undiscounted value of consumption was Rs. 32,712 crores. While this is feasible in the sense of being consistent with a solution to the linear programing problem, certainly no plan for which this was a true implication would be regarded as politically acceptable. The average annual level of consumption in this solution of only Rs. 6,542 crores with the 96 per cent level of targets compares with the level of consumption in 1959–60, prior to the beginning of the Third Plan, of approximately Rs. 12,600 crores. In the solution the 1961–62 level of consumption was only Rs. 2,347 crores, and it grew at the minimum permissible rate until the fourth and fifth year, when a total of Rs. 25,300 crores of consumption was permitted.

In spite of the low level of the maximand in this target solution there were substantial amounts of idle capital throughout the plan period. Examination of the sectors in which this occurred, of the relative amount of investment in the various sectors, and of the shadow prices will help in appreciating the kind of strain which the targets impose on the system. The largest amounts of idle capital relative to availabilities occur in the consumers goods sectors and their major suppliers. In the first period only construction capital is used to its fullest extent, and after that full capacity is reached in only the equipment and the mining and metals sectors until the last and post-terminal periods, when there is virtually full-capacity operation in all sectors. This idle capacity is the result, again, of all the constraints, but in this case it is probably the fixed input proportions and fixed consumption proportions which are mainly responsible. Since only the construction sector in the first period is a bottleneck and that sector is, in reality, relatively easily expanded, a slight relaxation of input proportions or an increase in the productive capacity of that sector might substantially improve the maximand. For example, housing requires little in the way of current inputs; yet its capacity is kept idle in the early periods because its proportion of consumption is fixed and capacity is a limitation in other sectors. Similar adjustments to improve the maximand for the second, third, and fourth periods in the equipment and mining and metals sectors, where capacity is formed less easily, would be more difficult to justify. While a reduction in the consumption proportions of these sectors might increase the maximand, these consumption proportions are already small. A further reduction would probably imply price increases in these sectors or the use of price controls to avoid such an eventuality.[34]

An additional calculation was made on the Target Model solution in order to test the significance of the rigidities in input proportions and in consumption proportions. For this purpose it was assumed that output in the major consumer goods sectors could be produced in these sectors without any current inputs whatsoever beyond those provided in the solution and by the sector itself. Using the idle capacities generated in a Target Model solution the additional potential output was computed and allocated to various uses on the basis of the model's allocations in the fifth period, when capacity was being utilized almost fully. The addition to consumption under these generous assumptions was roughly Rs. 32,500 crores and, with the amount produced otherwise, the total consumption would be roughly Rs. 65,000 crores during the five years. That would not be enough to maintain a constant per capita level of consumption given a population growth rate of at least 2 per cent, even if the total could be distributed at will over the five-year period.

The real limitation on the level of consumption in the Target Model solutions is the size and composition of the Third Plan targets. These do not allow enough of current inputs and new capital to be diverted into the consumption goods sectors and their major suppliers to produce acceptable levels and rates of growth of consumption.

Anything which increases resource requirements for growth when resources are scarce will obviously reduce the level of performance as measured by the maximand. Anything which reduces resource requirements when resources are scarce or loosens a binding constraint will improve the maximand. A number of such changes and other modifications have been tested in alternative solutions. The results are summarized in Table 18.

Column 1 of Table 18 lists the value of the maximand, i.e., discounted consumption, for each of the alternative solutions. Undiscounted consumption over the five years is presented in column 2. The third and fourth columns list the net investment and replacement investment required by the targets. Since in some sectors where only one type of capital input is required the model is indifferent between carrying out net new investment and replacement, some small amounts can be shifted between these two categories without affecting the results in any

---

[34] There were, in fact, substantial price increases in coal in the early years of the Third Plan.

TABLE 18

A Summary of Target Model Solutions with Third Plan Targets[a]

(rupees crores except column 8)

	Maximand (discounted consumption) (1)	Undiscounted Consumption (2)	Total Net Investment over the Plan (3)	Total Replacement over the Plan (4)	Total Net Domestic Savings over the Plan (5)	GNP in Last Year (6)	Gross Domestic Product in Last Year (7)	Net Domestic Savings/NNP in Last Year (8)
1. Third Plan Targets				infeasible				
2. Third Plan Targets, net foreign capital inflow increased by 100%				infeasible				
3. Third Plan Targets, net foreign capital inflow increased by 100%, no competitive import ceilings				infeasible				
Solutions with 96% level of Third Plan targets:								
4. 96% of Third Plan Targets, Reference Solution	24,710	32,712	16,076.8	3,253.5	13,576.8	21,320.2	28,591.3	.191360
5. Social discount rate, $W(t)/W(t+1)-1, = 0.0\%$	32,713	32,713	16,076.8	3,253.5	13,576.8	21,325.3	28,601.3	.191125
6. Social discount rate, $W(t)/W(t+1)-1, = 20.0\%$	19,387	32,712	16,076.8	3,253.5	13,576.8	21,320.2	28,591.3	.191360
7. $C(t+1) \geq 1.025C(t)$	24,851	32,849	16,077.0	3,253.3	13,577.0	21,320.6	28,592.0	.191377
8. $C(t+1) \geq C(t)$	25,002	32,996	16,077.1	3,253.3	13,577.1	21,320.9	28,592.7	.191394

(continued)

TABLE 18 *(continued)*

	Maximand (discounted consumption) (1)	Undiscounted Consumption (2)	Total Net Investment over the Plan (3)	Total Replacement over the Plan (4)	Total Net Domestic Savings over the Plan (5)	GNP in Last Year (6)	Gross Domestic Product in Last Year (7)	Net Domestic Savings/NNP in Last Year (8)
9. Initial construction capacity increased by 5%	31,490	39,547	16,064.7	3,225.4	13,564.7	21,158.5	28,286.4	.183393
10. All initial capacities increased by 10%	64,996	78,732	13,243.1	2,722.9	10,743.1	22,203.5	29,113.1	.115798
11. All initial capacities reduced by 10%				infeasible				
12. Capital output ratio in agriculture increased to 2.5 from 1.5				infeasible				
13. Capital output ratio in housing reduced from 10 to 7.5	32,612	40,841	16,143.0	3,163.1	15,643.0	21,164.0	28,295.3	.183646
14. No competitive import ceilings	31,177	40,482	16,399.3	2,878.4	13,899.3	21,344.0	28,642.5	.191706
15. Net capital inflow increased by 25%	28,068	37,178	16,197.6	3,115.5	15,573.6	21,339.9	28,601.8	.186896
16. Net capital inflow increased by 50%	28,378	37,563	16,189.6	3,125.6	15,438.6	21,347.0	28,595.6	.182694
17. Net capital inflow increased by 100%	28,948	38,264	16,176.3	3,139.1	15,176.3	21,354.9	28,569.2	.174373

(continued)

TABLE 18 (concluded)

	Maximand (discounted consumption) (1)	Undiscounted Consumption (2)	Total Net Investment over the Plan (3)	Total Replacement over the Plan (4)	Total Net Domestic Savings over the Plan (5)	GNP in Last Year (6)	Gross Domestic Product in Last Year (7)	Net Domestic Savings/NNP in Last Year (8)
18. Net capital inflow increased by 100%, no import ceilings	36,291	46,253	16,204.4	3,106.5	11,204.4	21,427.4	28,710.6	.173393
19. Net capital inflow reduced by 25%	19,750	26,107	15,657.6	3,744.6	13,782.6	21,352.8	28,645.6	.188254
20. No net capital inflow				infeasible				
21. Intraplan export growth rate at 3%	24,445	32,355	15,797.8	3,579.1	13,297.8	21,349.8	28,621.7	.184108
22. Intraplan export growth rate at 5%	25,194	33,360	15,655.3	3,746.8	13,155.3	21,349.7	28,620.0	.184773

[a]Since replacement in some sectors requires the same type of capital inputs as new net investment the model is indifferent in these cases as to the classification of the investment. This accounts for most of the small variations in the totals of net investment and replacement.

way. Column 5 contains the net domestic savings estimate obtained by subtracting the net foreign capital inflow from the calculated net investment requirements. Terminal-year gross domestic product and gross domestic output are listed in columns 6 and 7, and the ratio of net domestic savings to net national product in the last year of the plan is in column 8.[35]

The Target solutions can be envisaged as taking place in three steps. First, the investment requirements of the targets are calculated from the stipulated initial and terminal conditions, using the specified capital-output ratios. Secondly, the model decides whether or not those requirements can be met, given all the other constraints. Finally, it utilizes whatever freedom it has to distribute the investment over the plan period in order to maximize consumption. Only in the last step is the optimization feature called upon.[36] The first step is really a straightforward calculation with capital-output ratios, but it is a comprehensive calculation. The calculated initial conditions are the capital capacities at the beginning of the plan period. These are greater than the capacities which produced the output of the preplan year by the amount of capital which matures in the preplan year. The targets are not the outputs of the last plan year but the capacities with which the plan ends for the capacity maturing in the last plan year, though it does not contribute to output, requires investment and saving. Moreover, in order to insure post-terminal growth some investment and saving is required within the plan period for investment which will mature after the plan. The investment assumed to have taken prior to the plan period for the plan period can be subtracted, however. Inventory investment for all sectors must be added. All these calculations are performed as part of the target solutions.

The estimate of investment requirements in run 4, shown in column 3 of Table 18, provides additional insight as to the reasons for the character of the Target solutions. It indicates that for the 96 per cent level of Third Plan targets adjusted as explained above, over Rs. 16,000 crores of net investment would be required as compared to the Rs. 10,000 crores estimated in the Third Plan itself. While some part of the discrepancy may be due to differences in capital-output ratios and other parameters, I do not believe such differences would account for the very

[35] This table contains more information than was originally presented at the conference. Perhaps if it had been included originally it might have prevented some misunderstandings.

[36] In some situations the model might as a result of optimization provide more capacity than called for by targets. This is not the case in the present circumstances, however.

sizable discrepancy. Rather it seems likely that some part of the necessary components of investment were omitted or underestimated in the Third Plan preparations.

In runs 5 and 6 the discount rate applied to consumption in each period in the maximand was changed with negligible results for the value of consumption and the allocation of resources. This is due in part to the shortness of the planning period and the constraints on output which operate from both ends of the period. All subsequent trials were made with a discount rate of 10.0 per cent in the maximand.

In runs 7 and 8 the growth constraints on consumption were successively reduced and each time only a modest change resulted. This suggests that any tendency in the solutions to shift consumption toward the beginning or end of the plan period was not important, probably because of all the other constraints imposed.

In solution 9, the initial capacity in construction, the bottleneck sector at the outset of the plan period, was increased by 5 per cent, resulting in a substantial increase in the maximand. A 10 per cent across-the-board increase in initial capacities in run 10 breaks many bottlenecks, and the value of consumption rises beyond that which a 5 per cent growth rate would produce, as is confirmed by the fact that the consumption growth constraints are not binding. A 10 per cent increase in capacities has the effect of putting the system almost half-way toward achievement of the 96 per cent level of targets. Presumably with a somewhat lower value of maximand the degree of achievement of the targets could be raised. Of course, while all the additional capacity is eventually useful, the most important effect of such a change is to break the bottlenecks. If initially available capacities were reduced by 10 per cent, as in trial 11, the 96 per cent level of Third Plan targets becomes infeasible.

The agricultural sector bulks large in the Indian economy, and the expansion of its output has posed especially difficult problems. The sensitivity of the solutions to success in this field is only indirectly and very partially tested by changing the capital-output ratio in this sector. This was tried, however, in solution 12, in which the capital-output ratio was raised to 2.5 from 1.5 with the result that the 96 per cent level of targets became infeasible again.

The housing sector, though not so large in terms of output, has the largest capital-output ratio of any sector. This was reduced in run 13 from 10 to 7.5 with substantial effects on the maximand as compared to solution 4, as it reduced the requirements for inputs from the construction sector in particular.

In solutions 14 through 22, various conditions relating to imports, exports, and foreign assistance were modified. In run 14 the constraints were eliminated on the use of the foreign exchange left over after satisfying the noncompetitive imports. This resulted in a substantial increase in the value of the maximand. The implication is that a relative use of foreign exchange by the various sectors which was different from that which had prevailed at the end of the Second Plan at least would improve the performance of the system. In runs 15 through 22, the availability of foreign aid is varied. When foreign aid is increased, in run 15, by 25 per cent, a total of Rs. 625 crores, the value of consumption rises by more than seven times that amount as compared to solution 4. The successive increases in runs 16 and 17 have a much smaller effect, as the bottleneck of domestic resources remains intractable. When a doubling of foreign aid is combined with greater freedom in the use of foreign exchange, in solution 18, another substantial increase in the maximand takes place. In run 19, the reduction of foreign aid by Rs. 625 crores over five years reduces the available consumption almost ten times. With no foreign aid, as shown in Target solution 20, the 96 per cent targets become infeasible.

It is interesting to note that reducing the growth rate of exports during the plan period actually reduces the value of the consumption available in spite of exports being a drain on domestic resources. As shown in runs 21 and 22, at the level at which the system operates in the Target Model solutions the domestic resource requirements for increasing exports do not clash directly with the resource requirements for reaching the targets, and the increased exports do provide additional foreign exchange.

During the Third Plan period there have been general shortfalls with respect to the plan targets. The reasons for these are certainly more complex than can be explained by a linear programing model. Yet it is worth noting that the Target solutions can be interpreted as being consistent with the shortfalls and with the manner in which they occurred. The model produces a "feasible" solution only by scaling down the Third Plan targets and by reducing per capita consumption levels. Since in actuality consumption could not be so constrained, resources would be pulled into agriculture and the other consumer goods sectors to such a degree that targets could not be achieved elsewhere. Yet the government's commitment to the targets was sufficiently strong that resources were not shifted wholesale to the consumption-supplying sectors, and per capita consumption has risen only slightly. A set of alternative—or aggravating—explanatory factors for the Third Plan period are the bad monsoons and the increase in the military budget in reaction to the Chinese border invasion. Further study would be necessary to put each of these influences and explanations in proper perspective.

THE TRANSIT MODEL SOLUTIONS AND COMPARISONS WITH THE TARGET
SOLUTIONS

The second stage in applying the model to the data was the computation of a number of alternative solutions with terminal conditions set endogenously by means of equations 22 and 23. These will be called the Transit Model solutions. In these solutions the targets reflect the conditions that consumption, government expenditures, exports, and imports grow at rates which are specified exogenously in this set of solutions at 5 per cent, 2½ per cent, 4 per cent, and 3 per cent respectively. The plan targets are now determined as part of an optimal solution and are only one aspect of the solution. There are a number of reasons why none of the Transit Model solutions may represent the best possible "plan" for India. These will be described in detail in the last section of the paper and at this point the caveat will only be registered.

Table 19 summarizes some features of the solutions for alternative specifications of the parameters and constraints. The differences between the Target solutions and the Transit Model solutions are striking. The values of the maximand of the Transit Model solutions are higher in every case. On reflection, however, it is not completely surprising that it should be so. The Transit Model is optimizing the weighted sum of aggregate consumption and also ensuring a capability for post-terminal growth of which consumption is the largest component. The composition of consumption is not allowed to change within or after the plan period nor is the composition of the government and export demands. Thus, the Transit Model maintains a substantial degree of consistency between the orientation of the economy during and after the plan. Investment is provided in the Transit Model solution in proportions and amounts completely consistent with the exogenous specifications on the pattern of consumption, etc., and with the intraplan optimization of the consumption maximand. It is interesting to note that the total amount of net investment in the Transit Model solutions is usually close to the Rs. 10,000 crores originally estimated for the Third Plan. The Third Plan targets are apparently not in the same way compatible with the maximand, and the Third Plan Target Solutions reflect this fact. The shadow prices of output and capital and the distribution of idle capacities in the Transit Model solutions also reflect the different orientation. In the Transit Model solutions there is less idle capacity over-all, and it is con-

TABLE 19

Transit Model Solutions for Third Plan Period

(rupees crores)

	Maximand (discounted consumption) (1)	Undiscounted Consumption (2)	Total Net Investment over the Plan (3)	Total Replacement over the Plan (4)	Total Net Domestic Savings over the Plan (5)	GNP in Last Year (6)	Gross Domestic Product in Last Year (7)	Net Domestic Savings/NNP in Last Year (8)
1. Reference solution; social discount rate = 10%	59,435	72,034	9,822.4	2,963.6	7,322.4	20,210.1	26,054.8	.079201
2. Social discount rate, $W(t)/W(t+1)-1=0\%$	72,034	72,034	9,826.4	2,963.6	7,326.4	20,214.1	26,061.0	.079300
3. Social discount rate, $W(t)/W(t+1)-1=20\%$	50,674	72,007	9,304.2	2,979.0	6,804.2	19,975.5	25,744.3	.079005
4. $C(t+1) \geq 1.025C(t)$	60,009	72,641	9,863.7	2,894.3	7,363.7	20,184.1	26,030.9	.079924
5. $C(t+1) \geq C(t)$	60,009	72,641	9,863.7	2,894.3	7,363.7	20,184.1	26,030.9	.079924
6. All initial capacities increased by 10%	65,009	79,402	10,900.1	2,787.2	8,400.1	22,022.3	28,425.9	.078865
7. Postterminal consumption growth rate reduced to 2.5%	59,997	72,820	7,861.0	2,419.4	5,361.0	19,579.1	25,563.3	.029871
8. Postterminal consumption growth rate increased to 7.5%	58,258	70,507	12,096.4	2,852.3	9,596.4	20,448.4	26,852.8	.130031

(continued)

TABLE 19 *(concluded)*

	Maximand (discounted consumption) (1)	Undiscounted Consumption (2)	Total Net Investment over the Plan (3)	Total Replacement over the Plan (4)	Total Net Domestic Savings over the Plan (5)	GNP in Last Year (6)	Gross Domestic Product in Last Year (7)	Net Domestic Savings/NNP in Last Year (8)
9. $C(1) \geq 1.05\overline{C}(0)$				infeasible				
10. No competitive import ceilings	59,949	72,724	10,135.3	2,912.1	7,635.3	20,221.0	25,888.7	.077516
11. Net capital inflow increased by 25%	59,785	72,496	9,834.7	2,951.9	7,334.7	20,239.6	26,059.1	.073079
12. Net capital inflow increased by 50%	60,034	72,832	9,839.3	2,956.4	7,339.3	20,099.3	25,816.1	.063780
13. Net capital inflow reduced by 25%	59,118	71,547	8,848.4	2,931.5	6,348.4	19,647.3	25,317.4	.081237
14. Net capital inflow eliminated	57,684	69,811	8,887.6	3,291.9	6,387.6	19,794.2	25,672.6	.107955
15. Intraplan export growth rate at 3%	59,475	72,066	9,658.2	2,942.9	7,158.2	20,112.5	25,911.1	.077773
16. Intraplan export growth rate at 5%	59,445	72,021	9,671.3	2,898.1	7,171.3	20,082.1	25,871.6	.079556

centrated in the capital-goods-producing sectors and their major suppliers. The shadow prices also reflect the emphasis on capital formation in the consumer goods sectors.

The growth rate for consumption associated with solutions 1 and 2, with a 10.0 per cent and 0.0 per cent rate of discount in the maximand, respectively, is 10.2 per cent. The monotonicity constraint is binding only between the second and third and the third and fourth periods. It is not binding at all when the constraint is reduced to 2.5 per cent in solution 4; so its complete elimination in solution 5 does not further affect the maximand.

The 10 per cent increase in capacities substantially improved the consumption goods output in Transit Model solution 6 but by no means as radically as in the Target solution. This corresponds to a result achieved when the Target model was solved for 80 per cent level of the Third Plan targets. In both the former and the latter case the targets become relatively easy to achieve, and the model can concentrate on producing as much consumption as possible during the plan periods so that the Target solution comes to resemble the Transit Model solution.

A reduction in the desired post-terminal growth rate of consumption by 2.5 per cent, in solution 7, amounts to about Rs. 400 crores in the first post-terminal year, for example. This change increases the value of consumption available in the plan period by about twice that amount. But an increase in the post-terminal consumption growth rate to 7.5 per cent, in solution 8, reduces the availability of consumption by Rs. 1,500 crores. The terminal-year capital stock goes up by 500 crores. The increase is relatively small because the model is still free to set the initial level of consumption and tries to "cheat" on the constraints of meeting terminal requirements by reducing initial levels of consumption by 169 crores. The rate of growth of consumption in this latter case is still 4.2 per cent. If the level of consumption in the initial period were fixed at 5 per cent above that of the preplan period, a Transit Model solution became infeasible, as shown in 9 in Table 19.

Elimination of the import ceilings for competitive imports in solution 10 increases the amount of consumption available by about Rs. 500 crores and the terminal capital stocks by about Rs. 200 crores. The improvement in the corresponding Target solution when this change was made was much more dramatic. This was partly because in that solution there was more idle capacity which could be used if the various constraints permitted it and partly because there was more imbalance between capacities and targets which increased the significance of foreign exchange and the ability to use it freely. On the other hand, the difference between the solutions also suggests for further research the possibility that the Indian foreign exchange controls were not so compatible with their targets as they would be in achieving a different set of targets.

As could be expected from the above discussion, a 25 per cent increase in the availability of foreign exchange, in solution 11 in Table 19, makes less difference than in the case of the Target solution, permitting only Rs. 489 crores of additional consumption. The next 25 per cent increase in foreign aid, in solution 12, has a slightly bigger payoff in terms of additional consumption in the plan period for the Transit Model solution than the Target solution. Likewise, reducing foreign aid had a smaller impact on the Transit Model solution as shown in its runs 13 and 14. The reduction in the capital stocks at the end of the fifth period from Rs. 31,863 crores to Rs. 31,077 crores was much less than the reduction in consumption during the plan period as a result of the complete elimination of foreign aid.

When the stipulated rate of growth of exports is reduced by 1 per cent, in solution 15, increased resources become available for domestic use, but foreign exchange available is also reduced. The net effect of such a change or a 1 per cent increase in the rate of growth of exports, in solution 16 is relatively unimportant.

It is instructive to compare typical national income accounts associated with the Target and Transit Model solutions. This is done in Table 20 for solution 4 in Table 18 and solution 1 in Table 19. In the first year the Target solution puts a great deal of effort into breaking the bottlenecks and keeps all other activities at a low level, partly because of the fixed consumption and input proportions. It also does this in part because a higher first-year consumption would, because of the consumption growth constraints, only increase the consumption requirements in future years. The domestic savings rates in all years after the first are in the Target Model solution at levels which would generally be regarded as infeasible.[37]

The national income accounts associated with the Transit Model solution look more conventional. On the other hand the domestic savings

[37] This is, by no means, a new criticism of the Third Plan, although it has taken different forms depending on the analytical framework used and individual judgment as to the parameters which are within government control. Thus, P. N. Rosenstein-Rodan thought the over-all capital-output ratio implicit in the plan was too low ("Alternative Numerical Models of the Third Five Year Plan of India," *Capital Formation and Economic Development,* pp. 23–33). Other commentators, while accepting the implicit capital-output ratio, have considered the implicit domestic savings rates as too high.

TABLE 20

National Income Accounts: Target and Transit Model Solutions with Third Plan Targets

(rupees crores; targets reduced to 96.0 per cent)

	1961-62	1962-63	1963-64	1964-65	1965-66
Target Model Solution 4:					
Consumption	2,346.95	2,464.31	2,587.52	10,181.89	15,131.30
Inventory change	-2,965.95	788.60	2,284.87	1,536.94	723.98
Fixed investment, net	1,952.21	2,403.09	2,572.89	3,031.39	3,748.74
Total investment	-473.55	3,804.52	5,433.57	5,147.25	4,952.25
Government expenditure	540.99	560.99	581.99	601.99	621.99
Value added by government	899.75	933.01	967.94	1,001.20	1,034.46
Exports	653.98	680.98	707.98	735.98	764.98
Imports	1,153.98	1,180.98	1,207.98	1,235.98	1,264.98
Gross national product	2,814.15	7,262.85	9,071.04	16,432.34	21,240.02
Replacement	540.19	612.83	575.80	578.90	479.52
Net national product	2,273.96	6,650.02	8,495.24	15,853.44	20,760.50
Savings	-973.55	3,304.52	4,933.57	4,647.25	4,452.25
Gross national output	5,476.27	9,956.23	12,406.36	22,046.08	28,511.14
Intermediate product	2,206.80	3,470.85	4,145.37	6,454.70	8,143.01
Consumption/gross national product	0.83	0.33	0.28	0.61	0.71
Total investment/gross national product	-0.16	0.52	0.59	0.31	0.23
Savings/gross national product	-0.34	0.45	0.54	0.28	0.20

(continued)

TABLE 20 *(concluded)*

	1961-62	1962-63	1963-64	1964-65	1965-66
Transit Model Solution 1:					
Consumption	12,929.92	13,576.41	14,255.23	14,978.98	16,293.47
Inventory change	4.30	189.84	318.65	464.44	341.18
Fixed investment, net	1,803.86	1,776.32	1,637.95	1,583.04	1,702.76
Total investment	2,232.81	2,426.79	2,411.39	2,632.82	2,657.56
Government expenditure	540.99	560.99	581.99	601.99	621.99
Value added by government	899.75	933.01	967.94	1,001.20	1,034.46
Exports	653.98	680.98	707.98	735.98	764.98
Imports	1,153.98	1,180.98	1,207.98	1,235.98	1,264.98
Gross national product	16,103.48	16,997.22	17,716.57	18,715.01	20,107.50
Replacement	424.63	460.62	454.77	585.33	613.62
Net national product	15,678.85	16,536.60	17,261.79	18,129.68	19,493.88
Savings	1,732.81	1,926.79	1,911.39	2,132.82	2,157.56
Gross national output	20,786.62	21,959.49	22,844.25	24,160.85	25,952.13
Intermediate product	5,429.68	5,739.74	5,937.73	6,286.81	6,716.52
Consumption/gross national product	0.80	0.79	0.80	0.80	0.81
Total investment/gross national product	0.13	0.14	0.13	0.14	0.13
Savings/gross national product	0.10	0.11	0.10	0.11	0.10

rate is substantially lower than that which has been actually achieved. This suggests, as indicated earlier, that the economy could achieve a higher growth rate in capital stock if it so desired. The savings rates associated with Transit Model solution 9 in fact run up to 15.6 per cent in the last period. The differences in savings rates result in a greater accumulation of total capital stock in the Target solutions, as would be expected. The total stock is 7.5 per cent higher in Target solution 4 than in Transit Model solution 1 in the fifth year of the plan period. In the post-terminal years the differences are even larger. As would be expected, the Target solution provides for a larger accumulation in the capital goods sectors and their major suppliers and for a smaller accumulation in the consumer goods sectors.

AN APPRAISAL OF THE MODEL AND ITS APPLICATION

The lack of realism in the assumptions of the model was obvious when they were made. The consequences of those abstractions in the solutions are less obvious, and the final task is to try to assess these consequences and, therefore, the usefulness of the method. The application of the model to the Indian Third Five-year Plan period provides a concrete context for the discussion. To summarize the results of that application: There are no economically feasible solutions to the Target model with the Third Five-year Plan targets inserted. Economically feasible solutions were obtained when the targets were reduced by 4 per cent. Even these would not be politically feasible, however, as they require a reduction in per capita consumption during the plan period. To put the results another way, these solutions are not consistent with other plan goals of increasing per capita consumption. The solutions of the Transit Model with endogenously determined terminal conditions provide uniformly larger levels and growth rates of consumption. The differences between the solutions are due to the size and composition of the investment and output targets. The Third Plan targets require much more investment and place relatively greater stress on investment and output of the capital goods sectors and their major suppliers as compared to the Transit Model solutions.

In actual planning situations the objective function and the constraints are never so simple as those stipulated in the model. Increased employment and improved income distribution are examples of the many goals which have had an important place in development debates but which are not explicit in the model. If additional constraints or multiple objectives could be taken into account, what would be the effect on the solutions? The answer cannot be given in detail, of course, without solving the broader problems, but the general nature of the consequences are clear. If the additional constraints are binding, i.e., make any difference at all in the solutions, the maximand in both the Target solutions and the Transit Model solutions would be reduced and, in other than exceptional circumstances, by different amounts. Thus, adding realism by adding employment constraints, for example, might or might not diminish the difference between the Target and Transit Model solutions, but it would certainly not help with respect to the question of feasibility of the Third Plan targets. Moreover, the fact that employment and other goals have not been treated explicitly in the model does not mean that the results are without implications for these goals. The usual way of computing the employment implications of a plan is to divide output by some productivity coefficients, and that could easily be done for both the Target and Transit Model solutions if data were available on productivity. Likewise, if it is possible to associate changes in income distribution with relative sectoral changes, these implications could also be worked out.

The planning horizon for the model is short, the five years corresponding to the Indian plans. No detailed plans have been prepared by the Planning Commission which cover a longer period, but long-run strategies of development have been enunciated such as "import substitution," "balanced development of agriculture and industry," and so on. Unfortunately, even the most fully elaborated strategies do not provide the concreteness of quantitative projections; so it is impossible to determine the consistency of any particular set of plan targets with longer-run goals. In any case, having a longer horizon for the model would again not make any difference as far as the Third Plan Target solutions are concerned. Resources cannot be transferred from the future to the present, and a longer planning period would not help in achieving the Third Plan targets. The implications of the Transit Model solutions for the future are fully revealed in the post-terminal conditions maintained and thus provide an explicit basis for judgment. However, it cannot be presumed that the Transit Model solutions for the Third Plan period would be identical to optimum solutions obtained for a longer planning horizon. In fact, that is almost certainly not the case. Having a longer horizon provides added flexibility in a number of respects, and general considerations suggest that the solutions will be sensitive to the length of the planning horizon.[38] It is impossible to predict in this short-term model the effects of lengthening the planning

[38] See S. Chakravarty, "Optimal Savings with a Finite Planning Horizon," *International Economic Review*, September 1962, pp. 338–55.

horizon. In models such as that used here the solutions are of the "flip-flop" type, meaning, in this case, that consumption if unconstrained would tend to be concentrated at either the beginning or end of the plan. Due to the three-year gestation periods, the initial and terminal conditions create direct constraints on each period's outputs. In addition, the growth constraints on consumption help prevent the flip-flop tendency. Further work is in progress to explore the significance of extending the planning horizon. Meanwhile, one can only say that the Transit Model solutions are optimal with respect to the objective function, all the constraints, and the time period. They help indicate in a rough way the type of changes which would have been necessary to create a set of feasible Third Plan targets. It is not suggested, however, that these solutions provide the best of all alternative paths. For example, some of the Third Plan objectives, such as creating the capacity to produce import substitutes, transcend the plan period itself. The Transit Model solutions for five years cannot give an answer to the question of optimal import substitution policy, though the performance of any particular solution in this respect can be gauged through the post-terminal conditions which are stipulated for export and import growth.

The models are unsatisfactory in their production technology, omitting any possibility of diminishing returns or externalities or the contribution of any other factor but capital and foreign exchange. Less sophisticated formal analyses can take such influences into account in detailed sectoral studies. Unfortunately, the integration into over-all plans of sectoral studies which embody increasing returns, has not yet been accomplished, though work is proceeding in that direction.

Technical coefficients can be changed exogenously in the models when such changes are known to be happening. In a practical application further disaggregation would help in dealing with some of the problems associated with changing coefficients. It is particularly important to extend the model structure to embody such changes since the creation of new sectors and the transformation of traditional sectors is of essential importance in the growth of less-developed areas.[39]

Agriculture provides, perhaps, the prime example of a sector whose technology is being transformed with the absorption of increasing

---

[39] Technical coefficients were not changed in the model solutions presented above due to the relative shortness of the time span covered and lack of knowledge of what could be expected. Since in the Transit Model solutions the shadow prices tend to be lower than in the Target solutions changes in technical coefficients are likely to be of less importance in the former.

amounts of inputs from the industrial sectors. If such changes had been taken into account the values of the maximand would have been reduced in both the Target and Transit Model solutions and, probably, by greater amounts in the former due to the greater strain imposed there on industrial capacity.

Other qualifications have been mentioned earlier and, with additional time and space, still more could be described. It is important to have them always in mind as they condition all the interpretations of the results. Finally, however, in judging the model the real issue is not whether it is a perfect and completely comprehensive approach, for no one would argue that, but whether it can do its particular job better than other approaches which are available.

COMMENT

Edward S. Mason

The paper under discussion consists of two parts; the first, a relatively short account of planning procedures in India and how they have developed; the second, a presentation in preliminary and tentative form of a linear programing model for India. The connection between the two parts is established by the author's conviction that the principal deficiency in Indian planning is the lack of a technique that would permit the planners rapidly to map out the implications of alternative sets of social preferences and the merits of alternative paths to development.

The author has shown that a model of fairly complicated structure can be adapted to computation and has derived output values for alternative sets of inputs. The critical question is whether one "development path" can be shown by this exercise to be "better" than alternative paths within any meaning of "better" that is significant for current planning operations. A judgment on this question rests on the validity of the statistical underpinning, the reasonableness of the very numerous constraints introduced to facilitate computation and the relationship of the assumptions—the implied social preferences—to the social preferences that do and must underlie any realistic planning effort. In my opinion such a model is not yet ready for use as a practical planning instrument. This is not to deny that it represents an important methodological step toward what may in time become such an instrument.

Before turning to a consideration of the model, a few observations on the planning process in India are in order. I conceive of planning in the broad as consisting of technical advice on the totality of governmental decisions affecting the use of economic resources. Since, in a country like India, well over three-quarters of economic activity, however measured, are in the private sector, with agriculture, commerce and small-scale industry predominant, the governmental decisions that are of particular importance in affecting resource use have to do with taxation and subsidies, price controls, licensing, import duties, foreign exchange rates and allocations, and the like. In this area, an examination of alternatives is important and very much needed in India, but the Planning Commission here stands on the periphery of decision-making.

The field of capital formation is another matter, and here the public sector accounts for well over half of new investment. What role does the Planning Commission play in the allocation of these funds? Whatever the part played by its technical personnel, the Planning Commission of an earlier era, led by a strong prime minister, was centrally involved in the fundamental decisions to emphasize the heavy industry and import substitution that have shaped the Indian development program since the beginning of the Second Plan. But these decisions, once made, have inevitably had the effect of changing the relations between the commission and the ministries in the further expansion of public sector industrialization.

The heavy industrial complex which began to take shape some ten years ago provides its own justification for investment funds and grows in an enclave with little connection with the rest of the Indian economy. The steel mills supply material to the heavy engineering installations at Ranchi and, in turn, receive equipment from them. Both the mills and Ranchi require electric power, and thermal plants are built to supply these needs. The thermal plants need equipment, and the heavy electrical equipment plant at Bhopal is established and, in turn, secures its supplies from the steel mills. All these enterprises require coal, and the government opens new mines, thus creating a demand for heavy mining equipment from Ranchi. This enclave touches the rest of the economy as a demander of food stuffs and other consumer goods for its growing labor force, and these demands for food have, perhaps, received inadequate attention in Indian planning. It also demonstrates an insatiable demand for transportation; and in the seven years following 1955–56, coal, iron and other ores, limestone and dolomite, iron and steel products, petroleum, and cement accounted for more than 80 per cent of the increase in railway ton-miles. But to date this industrial complex has affected very little the rest of Indian economic activity. As in the Soviet economy, on whose development process this complex was indeed modeled, investment goods have been devoted to the production of other investment goods. Whether this has represented an optimal allocation of development expenditures in India, I do not know, and I doubt very much whether any techniques of economic analysis, including linear programing, would give us the answer. The point I am making is that these fundamental decisions on the development of heavy industry having once been taken establish the flows of a large segment of public investment for a long time to come.

By the same token, they shift somewhat the center of gravity of the planning operation away from the Planning Commission toward the ministries and other government agencies that are concerned with implementation. The author, while recognizing the importance of implementation, puts these problems to one side in order to focus attention on planning decisions. But the dividing line between planning and implementation is not so clear-cut. In the process of carrying out decisions, the ministries become the repositories of the information essential to the making of further planning decisions. The ministries become increasingly the planners within the areas of their responsibilities, looking only to the Ministry of Finance for financial authorization and allocations of foreign exchange. The Planning Commission comes increasingly to play the role of mediator and compromiser among claimant states and ministries, attempting mainly to insure consistency among these competing claims.

As I read the story, the power and prestige of the Planning Commission was at a high point some years ago when Prime Minister Jawaharlal Nehru took his position as chairman seriously and when the membership consisted of powerful officials and influential nonofficials. Since that time, successive appointments to the commission itself have not maintained the earlier standards, and the initiative of the commission has been progressively transferred to other ministries and, particularly, the Ministry of Finance. The commission plays an important role in negotiations with the state governments, leading to the preparation of annual development plans; but central government development expenditures are largely a matter of negotiation between Finance and the development ministries; and the Planning Commission has little or nothing to do with the preparation of the foreign exchange budget. The five-year plans still help shape the course of development, but the role of the Planning Commission is increasingly that of a negotiator and compromiser rather than an initiator of development strategy.

The author, of course, recognizes—in fact, emphasizes—the fact that the Planning Commission is not the sole planning agency. He describes

Indian planning as an open process with broad political participation, and calls attention to the activities of the economic ministries, the National Development Council, the advisory committees on problems of individual sectors, the consultative committee of members of Parliament, and the various state governments. He goes on to say, however, that, ". . . these groups have not provided guidance for informed political participation in the process of planning. As a consequence, in the procedures for formulation of the plans there has been relatively little consideration of the specific composition of economic targets in the light of social preferences concerning present and future consumption subject to resource availabilities."

One question that concerns us is whether the position of the Planning Commission in the present power structure is such as to make it possible to initiate effectively the "consideration of the specific composition of economic targets in the light of social preferences"? A second question is whether the availability of techniques of analysis capable of establishing the relation of alternative types of resource use to economic growth and other social objectives would put the Planning Commission in this position? A third question, to which we now turn, is whether a linear programing model, of the sort developed here, will do the trick?

It seems somewhat out of place, to say the least, to assign the task of appraising a linear programing model for India to one who is, in Kindleberger's phrase, quoting Frisch, merely a "conversational economist." But I shall do the best I can. Let me say, at the outset, that I find it difficult to judge how seriously the author takes this model as an actual planning instrument. The results are described as preliminary and tentative. A number of defects are pointed out which may be correctible by exogenous specifications or by changing coefficients as more information becomes available. As a first effort toward what, in the course of time, may well become an effective planning instrument, the model deserves high marks. But I doubt whether such a technique, even considering possibilities of improvement, is likely to have much applicability for the Fourth, Fifth, and possibly the Sixth Plan. And I wonder, in the meantime, whether a type of analysis specifying capital as the sole factor limiting growth is quite what India needs at this juncture.

As I understand it, the primary purposes of the model are to answer the questions: How much of current output should be saved and invested? What types of investment will yield the largest present value of consumption over a five-year period while providing terminal capital installations capable of supporting a specified pattern and rate of growth of output into the indefinite future? The answer is found, mainly, by comparing the effects of alternative plan targets on the productivity of investment. The greater the productivity, the larger should be the preference of future over present consumption. There are, of course, other social choices, and the model may or may not be useful in providing information relevant to these choices. But here we are concerned with the choice between present and future consumption as it may be affected by prospective yields in alternative combinations of resource use.

For this purpose the paper specifies capital investment as the only productive input. Foreign exchange is also recognized as a scarce input, but its quantity is exogenously specified. The volume of savings and investment in a plan period in conformity with social preference is the difference between the capital capacities at the beginning of the period and the terminal capacity requirements needed to make possible stipulated post-terminal rates of growth for consumption, government expenditures, and exports. The problem of the planner is so to use the flow of investment funds as to maximize the present value of consumption during the period while at the same time preserving terminal capital capacities needed for post-terminal rates of growth. The optimizing mechanism depends on the discount rate used to determine the present value of consumption and the yields to capital and foreign exchange inputs in alternative sectoral combinations.

A good deal could be said about the difficulties of establishing initial capital capacities on the basis of information now available in India. And more could be said about the propriety of establishing terminal capital requirements on the basis of stipulated post-terminal growth rates—an invariant composition of post-terminal output for consumption, government use, and exports—through the use of highly aggregated capital-output ratios, input-output coefficients, and linear relationships. But I should like to focus attention on certain other difficulties.

It would appear to me that, considering the very large scope of economic activity that is exogenously stipulated or governed by constraints, the optimizing mechanism has a relatively small space in which to operate. The commodity composition of consumption is assumed to be fixed, and a minimum rate of growth of consumption is stipulated. Consumption accounts for 75–80 per cent of Indian output. As the author admits, a good deal of information exists on price and income elasticities of various consumer goods, but this information cannot be fitted into a linear model. Government consumption is assumed to grow at 2.5 per cent a year and exports at 4 per cent, and the composition of government consumption and exports is given. Since the growth of export earnings is fixed and total capital inflows are stipulated, foreign exchange availability is exogenously determined. Public developmental expenditure on education, social welfare, research and development, and community development lie outside the optimizing procedure because it is difficult to assess the relationship of these expenditures to growth. What appears to lie within the model is the allocation of construction and equipment outputs to the nine other sectors of the eleven-sector model after the construction and equipment requirements of private consumption, government consumption, exports, and governmental developmental expenditures on various services have been excluded. It would seem that a large part of planning decisions for which alternatives are worth considering have been left outside the optimizing procedures.

Within the model the relationships between investment and output are stated in terms of fixed composite capital coefficients per unit of highly diverse combinations of outputs. There are no diminishing returns to capital investment and no economies of scale. Spatial relationships lie outside the compass of the model. The large steel–heavy industry–coal–electric power–chemical complex developing in northeast India is having a substantial impact on transport requirements. The average length of haul on the Indian railways, which increased steadily to 1963, has now started to decline. Changes in the structure of Indian industry may be producing significant alterations in other input coefficients.

According to the author, "the relatively small size of many of the modern sectors as well as the extent and variety of reporting required for implementation of various government regulations facilitate the estimation of sectoral, marginal capital coefficients." Modern sectors usually include both public and private enterprises and there may be, as for example in steel, considerable difference between capital inputs per unit of output in public as against private enterprises. The capital requirements for a given expansion of output may depend on whether the expansion is in the public or private sector. If such difficulties are encountered in the estimation of marginal capital coefficients in the case of steel, the difficulties are presumably much larger in estimating marginal coefficients for the mining and metals sector as a whole, which embraces a wide range of diverse activities.

The determination of such coefficients from historical data for such relatively new enterprises as Bhopal and Ranchi would seem to be grossly misleading as to what one might properly expect in the future. Rates of return for twelve public enterprises in 1960–61 varied all the way from 0.2 per cent for Hindustan Shipyards to 20 per cent for Hindustan Antibiotics. These returns were in part determined by output prices, and these prices in turn were to a considerable extent under government control. Hindustan Antibiotics, for example, operates largely by packaging imported ingredients for sale on a monopoly market. Implicit to the model is the notion that historically derived capital-output ratios can be used as a basis for determining requirements for new investment. This could only be so if the historically determined coefficients are typical of what can be expected in the future, which, in an economy in the process of rapid structural change, is unlikely to be true.

The allocation of capital and foreign exchange is supposed to be influenced in the model by the imputed returns to inputs of capital and foreign exchange in the various sectors. Apart from the fact that these imputed returns would be initially influenced by India's heavily distorted price structure, I have great difficulty in understanding what relation these imputed returns have to the earnings of investment as ordinarily understood. According to the author, "Since the sectoral capacities and the supply of foreign exchange are the only scarce resources in the system, the dual problem must consist of imputing those rents to the use of capacities and for the use of foreign exchange which exhaust the value of the total product as well as minimize the cost of production. The shadow price of foreign exchange must always be positive, since imports can always be used to increase the value of the maximand at some time. The shadow prices or rents of capacities are positive or zero depending on whether the capacities of particular sectors are fully or only partially utilized."

Marginal rents then are either zero or positive depending on whether there is excess capacity. In any particular sector there are likely to be industries with and without excess capacities. Presumably the optimizing mechanism refrains from allocating new investment to areas according to the specifications of the aggregate capital coefficients matrix. Different combinations of output targets yield different statements of capital requirements. "Barring terminal capital requirements set so high as to be infeasible," says the author, "the planner has considerable opportunity for exercising choice. . . ." In fact, the political forces in India as in many other less developed countries almost invariably set targets that do establish infeasible capital requirements. They may well be in process of doing it again in the Indian Fourth Plan, and there is nothing in a linear programing analysis that can prevent this from happening. But even if this were not so, the choices which the model maps out for the planner are, in my judgment, technocratic rather than economic choices. There are any number of combinations of outputs that can fulfill consistency conditions for current and capital inputs, and a model such as this can suggest some of them. One of these combinations is "better" than others, however, only within so limiting a set of assumptions and constraints as to be of doubtful utility as a guide to policy decisions.

Whether any model in which it is assumed that income elasticities of demand remain constant, price elasticities of all inputs and outputs are assumed to be zero, there are no diminishing returns to investment short of the point at which excess capacity is reached, no economies of scale, no substitution of factors, and no technological change can pretend to offer guidance to optimal investment decisions is certainly open to doubt. As the author says, within any five-year period, changes in the composition of consumer demand and various substitutions that are possible within the productive process may be small, but a specification of terminal conditions on the assumption that subsequent growth will leave these relationships unchanged would seem to perpetuate the rigidities in the system over a longer period.

As I have said earlier, it is somewhat unclear to me whether the author sees the model as a planning instrument that can be put to effective use in the near future. If it is to be envisaged as a tentative first step toward the creation of a much more complex model capable of taking account of considerations now neglected and awaiting for its application a very substantial accretion and refinement of data, much of the criticism I have offered is irrelevant. I would be inclined to be impressed and depressed by the thought that models of this type are just the sort of thing that planners love to play with were it not for the fact that initial reactions in India seem to indicate doubts as to policy applicability at least as great as those suggested above. Still, in its present form, it may well support what seem to me two unfortunate tendencies in Indian planning: a tendency to think of capital and foreign exchange as the only necessary inputs and a penchant for controlled rather than market solutions.

There are many alternatives that need to be examined by Indian planners, but they do not seem to fit very well into a linear programing model. Among these are alternative forms of management in public-sector corporations; alternative price policies in electric power, coal mining, transportation, and some other areas; alternative ways of handling the serious overvaluation of the rupee; alternative ways of distributing fertilizers, etc. Changes in these and other policies and practices will, of course, have repercussions throughout the economy, and it would be highly desirable to have available some technique of general interdependence analysis that would help to trace through these repercussions. The input-output relations *can,* at least roughly, be traced through. But economics at this juncture is not quite capable of providing an effective optimizing instrument, I think—at least not in India. I see no alternative, under present circumstances, to the slow iterative procedures now being followed in most effective planning operations.

Alan S. Manne, *Stanford University*

The Eckaus model of India's Third Plan is a welcome addition to the literature on planning methodology. Unlike most other numerical models with interindustry detail, attention is focused on the time path of adjustment. Rather than assume a *smooth* transition from the initial to the terminal conditions, the intertemporal choices are examined explicitly. However, before taking the numerical conclusions of this model too seriously for policy purposes, the following technical points should be borne in mind:

1. In principle, the model could make allowance for technological change, but, in fact, this has not been done. Without having allowed for upward changes in input coefficients of certain consuming industries, it is clear that the resulting output targets have a downward bias. This would lead to significant errors in a number of rapidly growing and capital intensive sectors: chemical fertilizers, electric power, petroleum, and steel. E.g., without allowing for an increase in the input coefficient of chemical fertilizers into agriculture, the fertilizer output target will be grossly underestimated.

2. It is not a safe gamble to suppose that output in the agricultural sector will respond within a three-year period with the capital investment coefficients assumed here. True, better organization and education within this sector (plus fertilizers and improved seeds) could by themselves do the job. Nevertheless, it seems to many observers that this sector is going to require massive injections of fixed capital: irrigation work of all types, soil improvement, tractors, and implements. These major investments constitute an alternative route—albeit an expensive one—for increasing agricultural output. It appears unwise to recommend that India's planners ought to gamble exclusively on the low-cost route via organization and education.

If these things are so, it follows that the most significant computer runs are those based on a pessimistic capital-output ratio for agriculture —perhaps 2.0:1 or even higher.

3. From the written presentation, it is not clear how much optimism

has entered into the assessment of possibilities for import substitution. Informally, the author commented that the shadow price on foreign exchange occasionally turned out to be less than unity, and so it appears that foreign exchange did not constitute a serious bottleneck for the model.

To most Indian planners, the foreign exchange bottleneck appears critical. This is what motivates the emphasis upon the heavy engineering industries. It would be desirable if the author were to present a more detailed tabulation of the model's allocations of foreign exchange.

4. With a time horizon as short as five years, together with the initial conditions applicable during the first three of these years, it is little wonder that the model is insensitive to alternate forms of the payoff function. An investment allocation model of this type probably needs to be studied in the context of a time horizon of at least ten years. The longer time horizon is particularly important since it is known that aggregative models of this type (maximum discounted instantaneous consumption) have a curious tendency toward flip-flop behavior. Whenever the discount rate lies below a certain critical level, nothing is consumed and everything is invested during the initial phase. Above this critical rate, everything is consumed and nothing is invested. The author has not yet established that flip-flop behavior will fail to occur in a disaggregated model with a ten- or twenty-year time horizon.

Economic Planning in Yugoslavia

JAROSLAV VANEK

CORNELL UNIVERSITY

The Economic Setting

Since the end of the 1940s—that is, since the break from Soviet hegemony—Yugoslavia has entered upon a path of profound political and economic transformation. While it is impossible to say that today, fifteen years later, this process of transformation has been completed, fundamental political, institutional, and economic forms have emerged that can be deemed lasting, and thus lending themselves to, and calling for, systematic analysis. Among these forms, economic planning is one of the most characteristic and perhaps the most important for understanding the operation of the Yugoslav economy.

However, planning in Yugoslavia cannot be treated in isolation. It can be studied and understood only as an integral part of the economic system. Now because the economic system of present-day Yugoslavia is *sui generis* as much as Yugoslav planning itself, I consider it necessary to discuss briefly in this section that system in general terms, and to place the narrower subject of economic planning in its proper perspective. Only in this way will it be possible to devote the later sections to the principal technical aspects of the planning procedure without being forced to go over questions that really do not belong to the topic of this analysis.

The salient characteristics of the economic system of Yugoslavia can most conveniently be explained by considering the function of each of the three fundamental decision-making units, that is, the firms (producers' associations), the public sector, and the households. With respect to firms, two sets of principles must be discussed: (1) those governing the behavior of individual firms and (2) those governing relations among firms and between firms and other economic agents.

The rights and obligations of Yugoslav firms all derive from one basic principle of ownership peculiar to the Yugoslav system: While the means of production belong to the society (social ownership), the direct *usufructus* from property, after payment of some basic charges to, and compliance with some legal provisions established by, the society (the public sector), belongs to all those who work in the enterprise. The basic operating principle of Yugoslav firms consistent with such a form of ownership is maximization of profit (return) per worker. Current business decisions of a Yugoslav firm, as much as those of an American firm, will be affected by the public sector only through indirect policy tools, such as various forms of taxation, rules of depreciation, etc. The difference between a U.S. and a Yugoslav firm in this respect is only one of degree and not one of substance: The legal "rules of the game" in Yugoslavia are much more numerous and subject to change more frequently. The important point to be made is that no provision of the economic plan (itself a law adopted by the National Assembly) is binding for any particular firm.

Yugoslav firms will conform with provisions of the National Plan only to the extent that tools of economic policy are shaped in such a way as to generate the planned targets, and not because they would be forced to do so by direct order of the authorities. It is this basic principle that distinguishes the Yugoslav economic system from the so-called centrally planned economies, and which, as we will see presently, gives the Yugoslav planning mechanism a character entirely its own.

The rule governing economic relations between individual firms and the rest of the economy—excepting relations with actual or potential employees—is the law of markets. Each firm is entitled to sell at the highest price it can and buy at the lowest price it can. As a general rule prices are established through free market forces, but in some instances, and at various times, prices may be regulated by the authorities in order to prevent extreme inefficiencies of resource allocation and/or income distribution.

While workers themselves are in very much the same position as Western workers regarding choice of employment, Yugoslav firms do not hire at a contractual fixed wage, but rather in exchange for a given share in the net income of the enterprise. Of course, to each job description corresponds a certain minimum income guaranteed to the worker, and it is possible to think of that minimum as a wage. The Yugoslav worker thus carries part of the risks of the Western entrepreneur, and in turn benefits from good performance of his enterprise. He also participates in a significant manner in the running of the enterprise.

We may now turn to the role of the authorities. Clearly, we are concerned here only with their economic functions. Among these, preparation and implementation of economic plans is probably the most important. The second important function of public authorities—central, regional, and especially local—is that of initiation or entry of new enterprises. Indeed, this is the one significant instance where the general principle of the transfer of entrepreneurship onto the workers is vitiated. Bodies of workers who, once the enterprise is established, work in and manage the enterprise, generally are not in a position to form an enterprise. Thus, by and large, the function of entry of new firms is fulfilled by the public sector. However, as soon as the operation of the enterprise begins, the usual duties and prerogatives are assumed by workers.

Finally, the authorities, generally local, participate with the workers' representative bodies in the selection of the director of the enterprise. However, once the director is chosen, he is bound only by law and is responsible only to the workers of his enterprise.

The planning function of the public authorities is the main subject of this paper, and consequently we do not have to elaborate on it here. Only a few introductory observations are in place at this point.

First, we may ask the very general question, What is the role of economic planning in Yugoslavia? Besides its psychological (or moral) impact—that is, creation of a certain plan-consciousness—three real roles can be identified.

1. The plans and the measures designed to implement them tend to minimize misallocations of resources and disequilibriums of all types, especially in the intermediate and the long run.

2. The plan has the function of transferring decisions concerning the rate of capital formation and savings from the sphere of consumers' to the sphere of social (or political) sovereignty. And there is no doubt that the implicit social rate of interest (or time preference) is far below the private.

3. The third broad function of Yugoslav planning is regional, and in some cases sectoral, equalization of income distribution, especially in the long run.

The extraordinary performance of the Yugoslav economy in the past ten years can be attributed only in part to Yugoslav planning. Decentralization of economic decision-making, a virtually complete autonomy of individual producing units, and distribution of net profits among workers are other factors certainly not less important in Yugoslavia's rapid growth.

Another subject ought to be discussed briefly before we turn to the technicalities of the planning procedure. In an economic system endowed with so high a degree of individual producers' autonomy and decentralization, clearly the plan cannot assume any other than an extremely general form. The final (five-year) plan document—fifty pages or so—contains only very general, sectoral targets. The latter, although the plan in Yugoslavia is a law, are binding for no one in the productive sector. It has to be followed—often with additional inter-pretation—only by official or semi-official bodies whose express task it is to implement the plan.[1]

Plan Preparation

The entire process of plan design and elaboration, as it evolves from its initial stages through the presentation to and enactment by the National Assembly, is an intricate interaction between various political bodies, professional institutions, producers' associations, regional organs, and others. It is not the purpose of this paper to elaborate on this subject. Let it only be said that the focal role in the process is played by the National Planning Institute; it is this body's comparatively tech-nical task of economic analysis entering the planning process that we will be primarily concerned with in this section.

The subject to be treated in this section naturally falls into two distinct parts, corresponding to two distinct stages of Yugoslav plan-ning method, namely, (1) analysis of initial conditions (of most recent data) and historical trends and (2) preparation of plan projections (estimates) for the future, using information derived under (1) and some externally given parameters. Detailed discussion of the subject will be organized according to these two headings.

Compared with many other countries, and probably with all others at a similar stage of development, Yugoslavia enjoys an important ad-vantage in the availability of statistical data suitable for stage (1).[2] This is in part the consequence of a deliberate effort, in part a natural result of the operation of the economic system. In fact, the major—if not the only—control that a decentralized socialist economy has over the operation of independent forces is control via detailed accounts and

[1] We will return to these questions in greater detail in the last section. Also, some of the answers that the reader may want to seek at this point are implicit in the next section.

[2] My principal source for the information in this section is Jakov Sirotkovic, *Problemi Privrednog Planiranja u Jugoslaviji,* Zagreb, 1961.

other reporting by these firms. For example, statistics are published annually by the National Bank of Yugoslavia, giving for each of the approximately 2,500 firms employing more than twenty workers about 150 figures describing just about every aspect of the operation of these firms. Several input-output tables are available for various years, giving various degrees of detail, and 80-sector tables are to be constructed every two years.

In spite of the abundance and quality of statistics, Yugoslav planners do not use—or at least have not reached the stage of using—a single, all-inclusive planning procedure. In other words, the plan is not based on a closed general equilibrium system where all targets and policies would be derived simultaneously. Rather, a number of partial plan elements and procedures are employed, and fitted together, when necessary, through a process of successive approximations.

By no means is it implied, however, that the planning methods employed in Yugoslavia are rudimentary or inadequate. It is just the opposite, judging from my rather incomplete knowledge of other planning procedures; Yugoslav planning compares quite favorably.

Several distinctive characteristics of the planning procedure ought to be mentioned from the outset. Following the Marxian concept of "enlarged reproduction," the Yugoslav planners most scrupulously and at all stages make the distinction between means of production (i.e., capital goods and intermediate products), on the one hand, and consumers goods, on the other. Thus, unconsolidated gross national product becomes the key planning magnitude, rather than the Western (consolidated) GNP; this approach both provides a first step toward a more comprehensive input-output technique, and permits an analysis of structural and parametric changes which otherwise would go unobserved.

Yugoslavia's attempt to study from historical data changes in key parameters, such as the capital output coefficients for various branches of industry, and to project such trends into the future, is another aspect of the planning method deserving mention. Still another characteristic, related to that just stated, is the comparatively limited use of simultaneous econometric methods. Use of that tool presupposes a certain stationary condition of the economic universe; and indeed, such stability cannot be counted on in countries that, like Yugoslavia, find themselves in a comparatively early stage of development and grow at a rapid pace.

Now let us turn to what has been termed earlier in this section Stage 1 of the procedure, namely, study of initial conditions and historical trends. Several key tables (or economic balances) are used for that purpose. The most important among these is the basic economic balance, reproduced as Table 1 for 1956.

In that balance we find a set of key economic data for three different production sectors—capital goods, intermediate products, and consumer goods—as well as for two aggregates—the total economy and total means of production. The top part of the table reflects the principal stock data, while all the rest of the information presented are flow variables.

The basic economic balance is, so to speak, the cornerstone of the Yugoslav planning procedure. As we will see presently, a set of basic relationships can be derived from it and used for global plan projections. Moreover, as the basic economic balance is available for every year starting with 1952, it is possible to study the changes in the basic relationships over time.

From the basic economic balance a simple input-output table is derived (Table 2), relating principal supply and final demand sectors. Together with information on capital stocks in the three principal sectors (top of Table 2), it constitutes the key tool of the planning procedure.

A brief scrutiny of Table 2 brings out the fact that only the most aggregative structural phenomena can be analyzed by using the seven sectors listed. As we have noted in the preceding section, the customary form of Yugoslav plans calls for a greater degree of disaggregation. Hence the basic economic balance is supplemented by four supply-demand balances, providing necessary detail consistent with Yugoslav plans.

The first of the four (Table 3), and the most comprehensive, reflects the balance of available resources and purchasing power for the whole economy. It will be noted that the total supply and demand of 3,374 billion dinars equals the sum of the first three elements of column or row 8 of the input-output table (Table 2) diminished by the net foreign trade balance.

Total supply and demand for capital goods can be disaggregated in a similar fashion, by producing sectors on the one hand and type of assets on the other. This is shown in Table 4. The sum of 401 billion dinars again is consistent with total output of domestic capital goods and the net trade balance as given in the input-output table.

Finally, in Tables 5 and 6 we recognize the supply and demand balances for intermediate products and consumer goods respectively. They again represent a disaggregation of totals to be found in the basic economic balance.

TABLE 1

Yugoslavia: The Basic Economic Balance for 1956

(billion dinars, current prices)

	Total Economy (1)	Means of Production			Consumer Goods (5)
		Total (2)	Capital Goods (3)	Intermediate Products (4)	
Capital stock	4,628.8	2,817.5	283.0	2,534.5	1,811.3
Fixed capital	3,747.0	2,246.4	229.6	2,016.8	1,500.6
Working capital, total	881.8	571.1	53.4	517.7	310.7
In output, total	675.0	497.7	26.3	471.4	177.3
Raw materials	386.8	290.7	17.5	273.2	96.1
Work in progress	106.7	79.2	4.5	74.7	27.5
Finished products	181.5	127.8	4.3	123.5	53.7
In turnover, total	206.8	73.4	27.1	46.3	133.4
Employment (thousands)	7,278.0	3,733.6	349.3	3,384.3	3,544.4
Depreciation	188.0	125.0	16.0	109.0	63.0
Current material input	1,677.0	1,112.0	221.0	891.0	565.0
All material costs	1,865.0	1,237.0	237.0	1,000.0	628.0
Wage bill	577.0	312.0	53.0	259.0	265.0
Surplus value	896.0	584.0	85.0	499.0	312.0
National income	1,473.0	896.0	138.0	758.0	577.0
Global value of output	3,338.0	2,133.0	375.0	1,758.0	1,205.0
Foreign trade					
Exports	366.0	243.0	52.0	191.0	123.0
Imports	369.0	235.0	26.0	209.0	134.0
Balance	–3.0	+8.0	26.0	–18.0	–11.0
Gross available resources	3,374.0	2,141.0	401.0	1,740.0	1,233.0
Net available resources	1,509.0				
Commodity turnover	1,248.0	424.3	167.2	257.1	823.7
Net available resources	1,509.0				
Personal consumption	848.0				848.0
Collective consumption	47.0	(131.0)			47.0
State and national defense	183.0	(196.0)			183.0
Total	230.0	(327.0)			230.0
Nonproductive investment	97.0				97.0
Accumulation, total	295.6	268.9	34.5	234.4	26.7
In fixed capital	191.9	144.7	12.1	132.6	47.2
In working capital, total	103.7	124.2	22.4	101.8	–20.5
All production	66.5	114.6	16.8	97.8	–48.1
Raw materials	11.6	42.6	9.2	33.4	–31.0
Work in progress	37.4	38.0	2.3	35.7	–0.6
Finished products	17.5	34.0	5.3	28.7	–16.5
In turnover	37.2	9.6	5.6	4.0	27.6
Reserves and undistributed					

Source: Jakov Sirotkovic, *Problemi Privrednog Planiranja u Jugoslaviji,* Zagreb, 1961, p. 184.

TABLE 2

Yugoslav Input-Output Relations, 1956

(billion dinars, current prices)

	Capital Goods (1)	Intermediate Products (2)	Consumer Goods (3)	Investments		Consumption (6)	Exports (7)	Total (8)
				In Working Capital (4)	In Fixed Capital (5)			
Fixed assets	229.6	2,016.8	1,500.6					3,747.0
Working assets	53.4	517.7	310.7					881.8
1. Capital goods				21.0	327.9		26.0	375.0
2. Intermediate goods	192.0	771.8	522.2	63.0			209.0	1,758.0
3. Consumer goods				58.3	52.0	1,052.0	134.0	1,244.0
4. Imports	29.0	119.2	42.8			123.0		366.0
5. Depreciation	16.0	109.0	63.0					188.0
6. Wage bill	53.0	259.0	265.0					577.0
7. Surplus value	85.0	499.0	351.0					935.0
8. Total	375.0	1,758.0	1,244.0	142.3	379.9	1,175.0	369.0	5,443.0

Source: Sirotkovic, *Problemi Privrednog Planiranja u Jugoslaviji*, pp. 293, 347.

As we have noted previously, the central tool of the Yugoslav planning procedure is the information contained in Table 2. The results obtained using that tool can be termed Stage 1 of the planning procedure. The final outcome of Stage 1 is an estimate of all the basic aggregates entering Table 2 for the target period of the plan. In other words, Stage 1 can be visualized as a transformation of Table 2, for a basic period 0 (say, the most recent year recorded prior to the beginning of a new five-year plan) into another such table for the target plan period T. Schematically,

$$(\text{Table 2})_0 = \begin{bmatrix} \alpha \\ \beta \end{bmatrix} = (\text{Table 2})_T$$

where α and β are two sets of factors performing that transformation. The set α contains exogenously given (preassigned) elements, such as the planned over-all rate of growth of certain aggregates. The set β, on the other hand, contains the rates of change over time $\delta^x m / \delta t$ of coefficients x_m reflecting certain basic proportions contained in Table 2.

Call each of the 49 elements of the bottom part of Table 2 a_{ij} ($i,j = 1, \ldots, 7$) and a_{ia} and a_{sj} the row and column sums respectively. Further, call the six elements of the top part of Table 2 b_{km} ($k = 1,2$; $m = 1,2,3$) and b_1 and b_2 the two row sums. Then there are 17 coefficients ($m = 1, \ldots, 17$) whose rates of change over time enter β, defined as follows:

Fixed capital coefficients:

$$x_1 = \frac{b_{11}}{a_{1s}}, \; x_2 = \frac{b_{12}}{a_{2s}}, \; x_3 = \frac{b_{13}}{a_{3s}}$$

Working capital coefficients (also referred to as turnover coefficients):

$$x_4 = \frac{a_{1s}}{b_{21}}, \; x_5 = \frac{a_{2s}}{b_{22}}, \; x_6 = \frac{a_{3s}}{b_{23}}$$

Technological coefficients:

$$x_7 = \frac{a_{21} + a_{41}}{a_{s1}}, \; x_8 = \frac{a_{22} + a_{42}}{a_{s2}}, \; x_9 = \frac{a_{23} + a_{43}}{a_{s3}}$$

Coefficients of imports:

$$x_{10} = \frac{a_{41}}{a_{21} + a_{41}}, \; x_{11} = \frac{a_{42}}{a_{22} + a_{42}}, \; x_{12} = \frac{a_{43}}{a_{23} + a_{43}}, \; x_{13} = \frac{a_{45}}{a_{s5}}, \; x_{14} = \frac{a_{46}}{a_{s6}}$$

Coefficients of exports:

$$x_{15} = \frac{a_{17}}{a_{s1}}, \; x_{16} = \frac{a_{27}}{a_{s2}}, \; x_{17} = \frac{a_{37}}{a_{s3}}$$

The rates of change of the x_m's over time are estimated from past trends (recall that Table 2 is available for a number of years preceding the base period) and after considering a variety of predictable factors affecting these rates. Consequently, the x_m's can be taken as (at least approximately) known for a future period—specifically, for the target year of the plan.

Let us now turn to factor α of the transformation. It contains the rates of growth of a_{1s} and a_{3s}, that is, of gross output of capital goods and of consumer goods. The two rates, r_1 and r_3, are obtained independently of the procedure here discussed, using a model of the Harrod-Domar variety, together with postulates about the future rate of accumulation and future balance-of-payments conditions and an estimate of the capital output coefficients.

The levels of a_{1s} and a_{3s} in the target period thus are exogenously given. From these two and the projected values of coefficients x_7, x_8, and x_9, a_{2s} then is calculated from

$$a_{2s} = a_{1s}x_7 (1 - x_{10}) + a_{2s}x_8 (1 - x_{11}) + a_{3s}x_9 (1 - x_{12}) \\ + a_{2s}x_{16} + a_{24}$$

where a_{24} is an estimate of intermediate goods investment in working capital.[3] The three terms on the right-hand side of the relation, it will be observed, give the estimates of a_{21}, a_{22}, a_{23}, and a_{27}.

Using the expected values of the fixed and working capital coefficients, the entire upper part of Table 2 can be evaluated for the target date of the plan. The three export coefficients x_{15}, x_{16}, and x_{17} are sufficient to determine terms a_{17}, a_{27}, and a_{37}. The first three import coefficients x_{10}, x_{11}, and x_{12} lead to the planned values of a_{41}, a_{42}, and a_{43}.

Assuming that in the target period investments of capital goods in working capital will be zero, a_{15} can be computed as a residual. Total investments in working capital, a_{s4}, must be consistent with the rate of growth of b_2, and thus a_{s4} is obtained. The term a_{24} being known already, accumulation of inventories of consumer goods, a_{34}, is obtained. Consumption of domestically produced consumer goods, a_{36}, can also be obtained as a residual.

The sums over columns 5 and 6 together with the two remaining import coefficients, x_{13} and x_{14}, suffice to evaluate a_{45}, a_{46}, a_{s5}, and a_{s6}. Thus all the column sums of the input-output table and all elements of the first four rows are determined for the planning target date.

---

[3] Professor Sirotkovic's exposition referring to this stage of the argument is unclear, and appears erroneous. The equation presented here is my reconstruction of the relationship. It is impossible to ascertain from Sirotkovic how the term a_{24} is estimated.

What remains to be determined are only the terms representing amortization, the wage bill, and the surplus value for each of the three output sectors. The three amortization terms a_{51}, a_{52}, and a_{53} are determined by the Yugoslav planners from postulated amortization rates and the implied capital structure in the three sectors.

Because the total gross outputs a_{s1}, a_{s2}, and a_{s3} are known, only one of the two remaining rows has to be determined to obtain the other. It is this distribution between the wage bill and the rest of net value added that plays an important role in matching supply with demand for products of various types, such as private consumption, collective consumption, and investment. This distribution, an important tool of short-run economic policy, is influenced by an intricate system of fiscal and other obligations on the part of Yugoslav enterprises. We will return in greater detail to this subject in the following section.

At present let us come back to the main stream of the argument for this section. Knowledge of the principal aggregates entering Table 2, for the terminal year of the planning period, does not provide all the detail called for by the final plan document, nor would it be sufficient to guide those who implement the plan. However, the key data whose derivation we have explained thus far are the indispensable basis for further sectoral projections.

It will be recalled that among the principal statistics underlying the planning procedure, use was made thus far in our exposition only of the basic economic balance (Table 1) and its derivative Table 2. The other information—the sectoral economic balances (Tables 3 through 6) together with available input-output estimates (primarily the *a*-matrix) and a host of other statistical data—becomes relevant at this point. We have observed already the consistency of the totals of the sector economic balance with certain entries, or subaggregates, appearing in Table 2. This set of relations must be valid for the target plan period as much as it was in the base period. Consequently, the totals of projected sectoral balances are given, at least as a first approximation, by the estimate of Table 2 for the target period.

The distribution of total supply and demand aggregates (such as capital goods, intermediate products, and consumer goods) appearing in Table 2 then is estimated from historical data. The principal element in this estimation procedure is—as with the transformation factor β explained already—the analysis of the behavior of relative shares of the various supply and demand sectors over a number of past periods. For example, the target share of industry in total supply of consumer products certainly is not statistically independent of that share in the base period. Neither, if that share has revealed a certain trend in the past, can it be doubted that the expected value of that share in a future year would be dependent on that trend. Moreover, a great deal of subsidiary evidence, such as the study of consumer behavior, or detailed input-output relationships, can be used in arriving at detailed projections of future demands and supplies.

Once such disaggregated estimates are obtained, their impact on the basic structure (Table 2) can be studied. And if the two are found inconsistent, the latter can be recomputed on the basis of new evidence. This iterative process can be repeated at will.

However, the process does not have to be overly exhaustive, nor do the Yugoslav planners have to be overly worried about possible minor inconsistencies. Indeed, the great advantage of Yugoslav planning is the very fact that the plan is not the absolute *conditio sine qua non* of the economy, as it is in centrally planned nonmarket economies. It can be counted on that the final iteration—necessarily convergent— will always in Yugoslavia be performed by market forces. Possible imperfections of the plan will then only be reflected in an imperfect attainment of the social optimum. But there can hardly be any doubt that such imperfections are far less important than those that would, or could, arise in the absence of a plan.

Plan Implementation

We have already noted in the preceding two sections the considerable degree of decentralization and reliance on the market mechanism enjoyed by the Yugoslav economy. These attributes are also apparent in the context of plan implementation. There is not much in the technique of implementing the plan that can be labeled as direct intervention. Yugoslav policy measures are generally as indirect as are those in an average Western economy. There is little difference in substance between Yugoslav techniques of influencing the course of the economy and our own. Both, at least to an economist, will appear as the policy tools or instruments of the type known to us from Professor Tinbergen's writings.

There are differences, but of degree rather than substance. The Yugoslav policymaker has at his disposal a far greater number of tools than we generally find in Western economies. This, while desirable in theory because a larger number of targets becomes attainable, can in practice become a hindrance, at least for a time. The Yugoslavs themselves often recognize that certain policies were misused or used to an inappropriate extent.

Yugoslav policy tools, while not different in basic quality, are often directed toward long-run rather than short-run targets. Indeed the principal purpose of the plan is long-run equilibrium growth, and short-run adjustment either is secured (or is hoped to be secured) as a by-product, or is relegated to the market mechanism.

There are five categories of policy instruments at the disposal of Yugoslav planners: (1) fiscal instruments, (2) credit instruments, (3) price instruments, (4) wage instruments, and (5) foreign trade instruments. The fiscal tools form a whole spectrum. Almost without exception, they are applied at the level of the firm, and can most conveniently be explained in connection with the distribution of income of the enterprise. A schematic representation of such a distribution is presented in Figure 1.

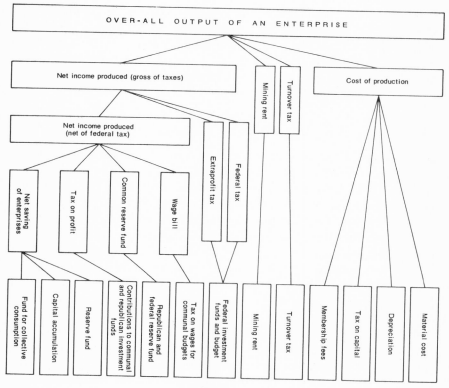

Figure 1

As the schema is to a large extent self-explanatory, only a few general comments are in order. On the side of production costs, only the so-called tax on capital calls for comment. In fact, it is an interest liability—generally of 6 per cent—levied on all fixed and working capital. Its impact on efficiency of resource allocation is obvious. What the Yugoslavs call the turnover tax is actually a value-added tax (in some respects more efficient than a turnover tax). It is levied selectively, either as a tool for discouraging consumption or to counteract monopolistic advantages. Similar advantages in mineral industries are coped with through a mine rent liability.

Federal taxes are levied on the residual. What remains after federal taxes is the net income of the enterprise, allocated more or less freely [4] between the wage (plus bonus) bill and net profit. Each part is subject to further taxes and reserve fund contributions.

Some of the tools can be adjusted, if necessary, to fit comparatively short-run targets, even though their principal function is a long-run balance consistent with the plan. In this sense, they can be understood as an insurance against more important miscalculations on the part of the planners, or as a last-resort forced iteration of the process outlined in the preceding section.

Two types of credit policy must be distinguished, one directed toward short-run credit—primarily financing of working capital—the other regulating long-run credit. The former, besides influencing formation of working capital, is also the most important regulator of monetary expansion and hence of the over-all price level. In this respect it resembles the operations of our own Federal Reserve Board. In recent years, as part of an over-all effort to increase the share of capital formation by producers, enterprises have been called on to finance most of their working capital themselves.

But by far the more important of the two credit policies is regulation of long-term credit for "productive" capital formation. This is done by federal, national, and local banks. The most important among these is the National Investment Bank, which manages central investment funds. These funds, while deliberately being reduced as a share of total investment resources, still are about one-third of those resources.

Because as a general rule federal resources are employed to supplement other official, or firm funds (especially in major projects), the leverage of the instrument is considerably greater than what would correspond to one-third of national investment resources. Thus, influencing

---

[4] More will be said on this point in connection with wage policy.

the allocation of, say, one-half of total investment funds, the National Investment Bank is in ample possession of the means to attain the sectoral and regional targets of the plan. Actually, it is the principal, if not the only, obligation of the bank to bring about the over-all structural results called for by the plan.

This, of course, leaves the bank with a good deal of freedom to decide on how its funds will be allocated. By and large, criteria of economic efficiency are being followed. Private-type profitability is perhaps the most important one; if social marginal returns become the dominant consideration (e.g., allocation of funds to a poor region in spite of low returns), this will be stated by the legislators explicitly as an instruction to the bank. But the profitability index is not the only one used in deciding who among the applicants for loans will receive the limited resources of the central funds. Foreign exchange (net) requirements of a given project will also play a role, as will the repayment period, degree of participation of other funds in a project, and the rate of interest to be paid by the recipient on debt outstanding.

We may now turn briefly to the wage and price policies. The Yugoslavs, during the years of their "economic independence," have moved a long way in the direction of free determination of labor income by individual enterprises. Most recently, it can be said that wage rates are largely determined by enterprises. The authorities pursue wage policies through general and quite flexible instructions about wage determination in relation to productivity, industry, and/or branch averages, and other general indicators. Local and state commissions are attentive that excessive wage distributions should not arise in situations of monopoly and/or windfall advantage.

It can safely be postulated that the basic philosophy of (relative) price formation in Yugoslavia is that of the market price mechanism. This is not to say that all prices are free of control; most of the controls, however, can be designated as temporary. The only ones of more lasting character (as, undoubtedly, in most Western economies) are those directed toward situations of monopoly. Indeed, greater social efficiency can be attained using such controls.

To the extent that the plan reflects adequately its premises, and is correctly elaborated, relative prices *among* sectors reflect relative scarcities intended by the planners. Once the distribution of national income between investment and consumption is decided on (according to social or other criteria) it is only rational to try to maximize consumers' satisfaction. If the objective function is social rather than private utility, that is, if consumers' sovereignty is not recognized in some respects, then taxes of various forms can be employed to set prices and outputs *within* sectors at desired levels and to prevent maldistributions of (producers') income.

Now, turning to the actual practice in Yugoslavia, let it be said that at present about one-fourth of the output of intermediate goods is subject to price ceilings. The ratio for consumer goods is about one-third; however, in this case the controls are not price ceilings but rather an obligation on the part of sellers to report an intended price increase in advance. The authorities then have the right to question or even refuse the price rise. In practice this happens only very seldom. With the exception of the case of monopoly, mentioned already, the existing price controls can be largely explained as a device to prevent major maladjustments in a period of transition from administrative pricing to a full-fledged market mechanism.

In the sphere of foreign transactions, Yugoslavia has had since 1961 a single rate of exchange. At that time a provisional system of tariffs was adopted, to cushion disruptions that would otherwise have arisen from an abolition of multiple rates.

Even though there is a single rate, various import categories receive a different treatment. Certain products, primarily essential materials and intermediate products, can be imported perfectly freely at the given rate of exchange. A special treatment is given to imports of capital goods; these are imported either subject to licensing within an over-all capital goods quota, or subject to certain specifications relative to the use of depreciation (replacement) funds. Also, the National Investment Bank provides foreign exchange for capital goods necessary for projects it finances. Foreign exchange for other purposes is subject to various forms of licensing, and clearly, because of the secondary importance of such imports for the economy, is quite scarce.

On the export side, a combination of export subsidies and tax refunds is temporarily applied to exports that previously (before introduction of a single rate) were exported at preferential rates.

The general purpose of these various arrangements, as in many other developing economies, is to provide infant industry stimulation, whether to import-competing or exporting industries. Also, these measures have the purpose of making smooth and gradual the alignment of previously highly distorted internal prices with world prices.

The relation between external and internal prices in conjunction with import policies is also an important tool of farm price policy. Actually, prices of imported foodstuffs together with price ceilings and/or stimulation for major farm inputs are the principal regulators of income and tools of economic policy in the predominantly nonsocialized agricultural sector.

COMMENT

John M. Montias, *Economic Growth Center, Yale University*

It is symptomatic of the underdeveloped state of Yugoslav studies that radically divergent views can coexist on the economic system of Yugoslavia. Some scholars—Professor Vanek foremost among them—take it to be what Belgrade's ideologues say it is: A socialist market system guided by macroeconomic instruments in the framework of long-term plans. Others are rather inclined to see in it "an ambivalent system, partly governed by the laws of imperfect competiton and partly administratively controlled." [1]

In 1958 I came away from a cursory study of Serbian and Croatian economic periodicals and from a number of interviews with directors of Yugoslav enterprises with the impression that the second of these views was essentially correct.[2] Vanek's paper gave me an occasion to follow up on later developments. I found that in 1960 and 1961 moderate progress had been made toward making the decentralized scheme work, but that the administrative controls imposed to combat the inflation in more recent years have brought back a degree of centralization that, at least at the beginning of 1964, seemed greater than six years ago.

Since long-term planning, on which Vanek's paper is concentrated, is least bound up with the way the economy is run, I may start my discussion at this point and thence go on to the more controversial aspects of the study.

Although I have read with care the book by the Croatian economist Sirotković on which Vanek relies for his analysis of Yugoslav planning,[3] I still cannot tell whether Sirotkovic meant to describe Yugoslav planning practice in the late 1950s or to prescribe for its improvement. He seems to have melted together what is with what should be—a practice that will be familiar to readers of Soviet economic literature.

But even the idealized version of Yugoslav planning that Sirotković

---

[1] Professor Bicanic of Zagreb University, cited by Ljubor Sirc in "Control and Competition in Yugoslavia" in M. Miller *et al., Communist Economy Under Change,* London, 1963, p. 149.

[2] Cf. my article "Reform and Retreat in the Yugoslav Economy," *Foreign Affairs,* January 1959.

[3] J. Sirotković, *Problemi Privrednog Planiranja u Jugoslaviji,* Zagreb, 1961.

lays out before us is short on theoretical sophistication. If the Yugoslavs follow his scheme, I can hardly go along with Vanek's claim that Yugoslav planning procedures compare "quite favorably" with those employed in other countries or with his denial that their methods are "rudimentary or inadequate." Sirotković's normative prescriptions hardly go beyond the projection of past trends in coefficients, a doubtful practice when one considers the favorable circumstances under which the Yugoslavs stepped up their output from 1953 on—fuller utilization of capacity, relative abundance of the labor force, tail-ends of investment projects started in the late 1940s, foreign credits, etc. Moreover, the fixed and working capital coefficients he focuses on (X_1 to X_6 in Vanek's paper) are so aggregated and made up of such heterogenous elements that they are most unlikely to behave as constants. I should expect these coefficients to be sensitive to changes in the magnitude of all the variables in the system. They cannot therefore be used for the purpose of relating variables at a future point in time with any degree of reliability.

In general, it would appear that even the crudest linear programing techniques based on aggregated data would be an improvement over the mechanical scheme advocated by Sirotkovic. As Professor Ragnar Frisch has pointed out, if one attempts to map out a large investment program without the aid of some form of linear programing, "one is practically certain to be taken by surprise afterwards in unexpected balance of payments difficulties and other troubles." [4] One of these "other troubles" in a partially decentralized economy such as Yugoslavia's is the occurrence of inflationary pressures—a problem to which I shall return at a later point of this Comment.

It may not be entirely fair to test the pudding of Yugoslav planning by its eating, since changing circumstances have a way of upsetting the initial hypotheses on which long-term plans are based, but it should at least be noticed that the execution of the 1961–65 plan ran so far off course that the plan had to be abandoned less than two years after its inception. The Fourth Plenum of the League of Communists resolved that henceforth less ambitious plans would be drawn up, which would be sure to keep the economy moving in a balanced and stable way.[5] The deviations from plan in 1961 and 1962 that prompted this reappraisal included rates of growth of gross national product and industrial output that came to only about half the rates planned for those years. Exports which were supposed to rise by 8.4 per cent in 1961 fell by

---

[4] Quoted in Hollis Chenery, "Comparative Advantage and Development Policy," *American Economic Review,* March 1961, p. 33.

[5] As reported by Wolfgang Eggers in *Osteuropa Wirtschaft,* 1964, p. 43.

1.8 per cent. In 1962 they rose by 21.5 per cent as compared to a plan of 18 per cent, while imports fell by 2.2 per cent when they were scheduled to rise by 6 per cent. Nonagricultural employment and gross fixed investments also lagged appreciably behind plan.[6]

The discrepancy between plans and realizations, incidentally, is not necessarily an indication of the high degree of decentralization of the Yugoslav economy. The Soviet Union and the East European nations are rarely, if ever, able to stick to their long-term plans, even though the planners keep nearly all the reins of economic power in hand. Miscalculations and the inability to predict future trends in labor, capital, and material productivity are usually more to blame than the devolution of responsibilities to lower organs (although, exceptionally, the failure of the Czechoslovak plan for 1961–65, which was also abandoned in 1962, had much to do with a poorly conceived attempt at a partial decentralization).

This brings me back to the thorny problem of the nature of the Yugoslav economic system and of the role that planning plays in it.

It is obvious that the necessity of planning and the impact of errors in predicting future trends will be less if the government confines its role to maintaining an appropriate level of effective demand, while allocations among alternative uses are made by the market. The first question to be asked then is the extent to which the allocation of resources in Yugoslavia is governed by prices shaped under the influence of supply and demand. According to Vanek, restrictions on the price mechanism are minor and temporary and designed mainly to curb monopoly situations. He claims, without citing any source, that only about a quarter of the output of intermediate goods is subject to price ceilings, while one-third of the output of consumer goods consists of items whose prices cannot be increased without prior notification to the Federal Price Office. I have doubts about both these figures. In 1956, according to a well-known Yugoslav economist, price ceilings were imposed on 52 per cent of the domestic output of intermediate goods. These amounted to 27 per cent of the gross output of industry.[7] As far as I know, there has been no tendency to decontrol prices since then, nor have the relative proportions of controlled and uncontrolled materials changed radically.

[6] United Nations, Economic Commission for Europe, *Economic Survey of Europe in 1961,* Part I, Geneva, 1962, Chap. I, p. 43; *Economic Survey of Europe in 1962,* Part I, New York, 1963, Chap. II, pp. 47–48.

[7] Nikola Ćobelić, *Politika i metodi privrednog razvoja Jugoslavije (1947–1956),* Belgrade, 1959, p. 309.

On the other hand, about 40 per cent of total retail trade is subject to maximum markups, which effectively rule out "speculations" in the trade network on these items, while "virtually all the other goods," according to a 1964 source, fall under the price-control law.[8] While it is true that controlled prices may be raised one month after authorization has been requested from the Price Office if this authorization has not been formally denied, it must also be taken into account that these requests are in practice only made when they are "justified" by cost increases. Enterprises do not normally raise prices to take advantage of an especially favorable market situation, whether this advantage is of a monopolistic character or simply due to an excess of effective demand. The Communist Party, often working through the enterprises' workers' councils, brings its influence to bear on management to act according to the norms of "social conscience." The role of prices as a device to ration off demand, to call forth marginal amounts of supply, or to attract resources in the short run—which might justify extraordinary profits in certain situations—is not officially sanctioned or even recognized. Where the dominant market position is exploited is not so much in overt price gouging but in quality deterioration and in cost padding—typical phenomena associated with controls everywhere.

It is symptomatic of the official attitude toward price formation that the government in 1964 raised prices of electric power, coal, and a number of agricultural products on the assumption that these price increases would have no effects on other prices of the industrial consumers of these products because in effect no such repercussions would be tolerated.[9]

Vanek writes that "once the distribution of national income between investment and consumption is decided on . . . , it is only rational to try to maximize consumers' satisfaction." If I understand him correctly, he implies that with the exception of special taxes designed to correct prices for disparities between social and private utility, Yugoslav markets achieve this aim. To do so, consumers must express their tastes through their consumption decisions in retail trade. We have already seen that prices of consumer goods were fairly tightly regulated. But there is another, perhaps even more serious reason, why consumers' preferences were not transmitted with any degree of precision to producing enterprises: The personnel of socialized retail establish-

[8] *Ekonomska politika,* September 26, 1964, p. 1343.
[9] *Ibid.,* September 19, 1964, p. 1319. Actually the cost increases due to higher prices of primary materials eventually forced up the prices of many processed products, despite this injunction.

ments had little or no incentive to do so. At least up to 1961, the date of the source of my information, the wage fund of these enterprises depended on their turnover rather than on their profits.[10] This regulation had the effect of discouraging trade in slow-moving items, of reducing the range of products traded (thus restricting choice), and of limiting personal service to customers to a bare minimum.[11] The shortcomings of Yugoslav retail shops, as far as I could observe in 1958, were similar to those in Poland or Czechoslovakia, where incentives were also based mainly on the volume of sales rather than on profits or on value added.

As to industrial enterprises, it is not so clear either that they are profit-maximizers, whether at the imposed ceiling prices or at the prices they choose to set. Benjamin Ward suggested some years ago that in enterprises where the workers' council was strong, profits per employed worker might be maximized rather than total profits. This behavior, systematically pursued, would lead to quite different decisions on the scale of operations and the choice of inputs from those we should expect in a profit-maximizing situation.[12] While I doubt that the councils are normally powerful enough to impose such a course on the management board, there may be enterprises where these distortions occur. Another problem, which is perhaps unavoidable in the socialist framework in which enterprises operate—where directors of enterprises have little security of tenure and can be turned out at the request of the workers' council with the concordance of the local peoples' committee [13]—is that enterprises may be managed with a view to making the largest possible profits in the short run, at the expense of their long-run interests or those of society as a whole. This characteristic helped to undermine the investment-auction system tried out for a brief period in the mid-1950s. Managers who tendered the highest bids for credits—that is, who offered to pay the highest interest rates—were those in the most difficult financial situation and/or those who knew that they would not be around when the time came to repay the loans.[14] This system soon had to be abandoned

[10] Velimir Vasic, *Ekonomska Politika Jugoslavije,* Belgrade, 1961, p. 242.

[11] It will of course also have undesirable effects on the cost side, but these are unrelated to the failure to cater to consumers' taste.

[12] Benjamin Ward, "The Firm in Illyria," *American Economic Review,* September 1958.

[13] On the conditions under which directors may be dismissed, see G. W. Hoffman and F. W. Neal, *Yugoslavia and the New Communism,* New York, 1962, pp. 241–42.

[14] Source cited in Sirc, "Control and Competition," p. 152.

and replaced by the administrative rationing of funds by the Investment Bank (at least for projects financed neither from the enterprises' own funds nor from those at the disposal of the republics, districts, and communes).

Where the market fails as an allocating device—for the distribution of most intermediate goods and for the bulk of investment funds [15] —it is evident that some sort of central coordination and direction is needed to avoid the waste that would be caused by decentralized decisions governed by false indicators of relative scarcities. In the realm of investments, I have mentioned that the Investment Bank fulfills this function. (It is commonly asserted in Yugoslavia that the chief leverages of centralized bureaucratic controls over the economy were transferred in the process of revamping the economic system in 1952 from the Planning Commission, where these controls had been vested prior to that date, to the Investment Bank.) Vanek in his paper asserts that in so doing it follows "by and large criteria of economic efficiency." This I find hard to interpret. He cannot mean that funds are dispensed chiefly according to monetary rates of return: Heavy industry, which received 69 per cent of the total investment credits allotted to industry from centralized investment funds in 1961,[16] exhibited appreciably lower rates of return than industries producing for the consumer market.[17] (This was in part due to the fact that their prices were more rigidly controlled.) But if he has in mind some nonmonetary standard of "social profitability," then I wonder what quantitative criteria the bank can apply: Since current prices do not reflect relative scarcities, and shadow prices, as far as I know, are not calculated from economy-wide programs, then where are these "criteria of economic efficiency" to be found? The best the bank can do is to conform to the plan, whatever might be its shortcomings.

The Investment Bank of Yugoslavia controls another key input in

[15] Vanek asserts that the Investment Bank accounts for a third of "investment resources" and "influences" perhaps 20 per cent more. According to the statistical yearbook of Yugoslavia for 1963, the decentralized funds at the disposal of investors made up less than 20 per cent of total investments in 1960, 23 per cent in 1961, and 38 per cent in 1962. In industry alone they came to only 17.7 per cent in 1961 (Savezni Zavod za Statistiku SFRJ, *Statisticki Godišnjak SFRJ 1963*, pp. 264–65). All other investment outlays were from centralized investment funds, local and republican budgets, and blocked amortization funds.

[16] *Ibid.*, p. 265. In this calculation I included in "heavy industry" the following sectors: electric power, coal mining, petroleum, ferrous metals, nonferrous metals, minerals, metal processing, shipbuilding, electrical, chemical, and building materials.

[17] Cf. the approximate calculations made by Sirc, "Control and Competition," p. 153.

the production process, namely, foreign exchange. As Vanek points out, the system of variable "coefficients," which amounted to a highly differentiated schedule of exchange rates designed to protect inefficient domestic industries from foreign competition and to encourage the exports of high-cost goods, was abolished in 1961. But the Investment Bank continued to exercise administrative controls over the allocation of foreign exchange; in particular, it went on channeling scarce exchange to purchase foreign equipment for heavy industry, while agriculture, transportation, trade, tourism, and catering had to do with declining allotments for this type of imports.[18] There are no more "private-type profitability" criteria in this type of allocation than in the case of investments.

So far I have said nothing about the nonmarket allocation of materials subject to price ceilings. It is apparent that intermediate goods, such as steel, whose prices have remained virtually constant since 1954, while the inflation spread to other sectors,[19] cannot be obtained by consumers in any desired quantities and that some formal or informal rationing must take place to distribute available supplies. In practice the most important institution that effected this distribution prior to June 1960 was the branch association of producers (*udruzenje*). Since that date the branch councils (*saveti grana*) in the framework of Federal Industrial Chambers have been supervising the procurement of materials for their associated enterprises.[20] Under the old associations, the member-enterprises distributed available supplies among themselves. Although I was informed in 1958 that there were frequent differences of views as to how this distribution should proceed, the fear of direct government intervention kept these conflicts "within the family." My guess is that the reorganization of 1960 increased the government's role in supervising industry *via* the industrial chambers. But it will take a good deal of research—of the type David Granick and Josef Berliner once conducted on informal decision-making processes in the Soviet economy—before we shall have any firm understanding of the nature and the degree of centralization of allocation channels bypassing the market in the Yugoslav economy.

To conclude this Comment I should like to speculate on the reason

[18] See the *Annual Report* of the Yugoslav Investment Bank for 1961, Novi Sad, 1962, pp. 14 and 15.

[19] The price of steel rails of commercial quality remained fixed at 80,000 dinars from 1954 to at least September 1961. In the meantime the cost of living had risen by 55 per cent (Savezni Zavod za Statistika, *CENA,* July–September 1961, Belgrade, 1962, pp. 24–25).

[20] Vasic, *Ekonomska politika,* pp. 54–55.

why the Yugoslav government found it necessary to superimpose so many direct and indirect controls on what was originally meant to have been a real market mechanism.

If we leave aside the possible political reasons why the state may have wished to retain centralized controls over the economy, we can say that these interventions were essentially due to a conflict between the strategy of economic development the Yugoslavs pursued and the institutional model they adopted to implement it. Between 1950 and 1952 Yugoslavia started to veer away from the Soviet model without ever giving up on the Soviet strategy of development, consisting in high ratios of investments to national income and the concentration of investments on heavy industry. Furthermore, the government was committed to a policy of evening out the enormous disparities in the level of development of the six different republics making up the federation. (As late as 1955 the national income per head of Slovenia was two and a half times greater than that of Macedonia.[21]) This meant that a part of the profits earned in the more developed republics—Slovenia and Croatia—were earmarked for investment in more backward areas —Montenegro, Macedonia, and Bosnia-Herzegovina. The government wished to grant economic powers to the republics and particularly to the communes (*opstine*) to allow them to found new enterprises and to carry on their own development. The established industries in the more industrialized parts of the country had to meet heavy demands on their gross profits from the federal government for investment elsewhere, from their republic, from their commune, and finally from their own workers and staff, through the latter's association in the workers' councils. The resolution of these conflicting demands was to some degree determined by the so-called financial instruments described in Vanek's paper, but there was necessarily considerable uncertainty, *ex ante*, both as to the magnitude of the value added by each firm and its final distribution each year. This uncertainty was compounded by the greater freedom given to the workers' councils in 1961 to determine workers' wages from these margins and by the decision taken in 1964 to allow the communes to take a larger part of enterprises' net proceeds.

It was well-nigh impossible to calculate with any accuracy the sums that would be distributed in the form of wages and those earmarked for decentralized investments by enterprises, communes, and other recipients of funds from producers. This uncertainty in the application of the instruments, along with a fairly liberal short-term crediting policy on the part of the National Bank and increasingly favorable terms for

[21] Computed from data in *Statisticki Godisnjak 1963*, p. 356.

the farm sector, gave rise to a perennial inflationary problem.[22] Since the financial instruments were too blunt to keep the inflation in check, direct controls on prices were resorted to. As these controls distorted the price structure, they made market criteria increasingly inadequate to guide allocation decisions. To cope with these market failures, more direct controls had to be instituted. This institutional disequilibrium eventually led to the present "ambivalent system."

Interestingly enough, a strong opposition has grown in recent years, especially among Croatian and Slovenian economists and politicians, to what Vladimir Bakaric, the Secretary of the Communist League of Croatia, calls the present "administrative-centralist system." Many Yugoslav economists would agree with Bakaric that "the difficulties which are in essence the product of the old [centralist] system cannot be overcome by using methods stemming from that system." The economy must break out of this vicious circle. What is needed, in other words, is not more controls to patch up the system but "more freedom in the economy." [23] There is also increased understanding among influential Yugoslav officials of the point made by Dr. Branko Horvath, in his article in the *Economic Journal* of December 1958, that excessively high investments, carried out at the expense of consumption, may so destroy workers' incentives as to be self-defeating for the purpose of maximizing the rate of expansion of the economy. Bakaric hints that excessive capital transfers from the more advanced to the less advanced republics may also have the effect of retarding over-all growth.[24]

If these and other liberal-minded economists and politicians could have their way, the Yugoslav economic system would be transformed into something more closely resembling the market economy described in Professor Vanek's paper.

[22] Between January and August of 1964, for instance, investments, which were slated to rise by 10 per cent according to the plan for the entire year, actually went up by 40 per cent compared to the same period of 1963 (investments by communes and districts rose by 51 per cent and investments from bank credits by 213 per cent). According to one source, there was an increase of 540 billion dinars in effective demand since last year "which was not matched by a comparable increase in the volume of goods available for consumption and fixed investment." Bricks, one of the few building materials whose prices are not controlled, were 23 per cent more expensive in the summer of 1964 than in 1963 (*Ekonomska Politika*, September 5, 1964, p. 1219; *ibid.*, September 19, 1964, p. 1307). Other details on the inflation are contained in *ibid.*, September 12, 1964, p. 1285.

[23] Speech by Bakaric in *Vjesnik* (Zagreb), September 21, 1964 and his interview with *Ekonomska Politika,* published on October 10, 1964.

[24] In his speech reported in *Vjesnik,* September 21, 1964. He also argues in the same speech that the necessity of these transfers is the "greatest cause or pseudo-cause of the retention of the administrative-centralist system."

Index